Officer Candidate Tests
FOR DUMMIES®

**by Jane R. Burstein and Carolyn C. Wheater
with LTC Richard Dahoney, U.S. Army, Ret.**

WILEY

Wiley Publishing, Inc.

Officer Candidate Tests For Dummies®

Published by
Wiley Publishing, Inc.
111 River St.
Hoboken, NJ 07030-5774
www.wiley.com

WILEY

About the Authors

Jane R. Burstein, MA, has taught high school English for 36 years and has been a tutor and writing consultant for 25 years. She is the coauthor of several CliffsNotes test prep books, and she and Wheater are coauthors of *CliffsNotes ASVAB AFQT Cram Plan*.

Carolyn C. Wheater teaches middle school and upper school mathematics at the Nightingale-Bamford School in New York City. Educated at Marymount Manhattan College and the University of Massachusetts, Amherst, she has taught math and computer technology for more than 30 years to students from preschool through college.

Richard Dahoney is a retired Army Lieutenant Colonel, having served in Korea, Japan, Viet Nam, and numerous locations in the United States. He is now the principal author of disbursing policy guidance for the U.S. Department of Defense, with over 47 years of experience in military financial management. He holds a BA in Business Administration from Rutgers University and an MBA in Comptrollership and Finance from Indiana University's Kelley School of Business. He is also a graduate of the U.S. Army Command and General Staff College and the Industrial College of the Armed Forces.

Authors' Acknowledgments

Thanks to acquisitions editor Erin Calligan Mooney, who chose us to author this book and ironed out all the preliminary details to make this book possible.

Tim Gallan, our project editor, deserves a loud cheer for serving as a gifted and patient collaborator and editor — shuffling chapters back and forth, shepherding the text and graphics through production, making sure any technical issues were properly resolved, and serving as the unofficial quality control manager. Christine Pingleton and Jessica Smith, copy editors, earn editors of the year awards for ferreting out our typos, misspellings, grammatical errors, and other language foe paws (or is it faux pas?), in addition to assisting Tim as reader advocates. We also tip our collective hat to the production crew for doing such an outstanding job of transforming an enormous hodgepodge of text, equations, and images into such an attractive bound book.

Thanks also to Joe Kraynak who pitched in with his expertise in coordinating our efforts and making everything a little easier for the editorial crew.

And a big thanks to Kent Butcher for contribution to the chapters covering mechanics and electronics. They wouldn't exist without his work. Kent currently serves as a lieutenant in the Navy at Norfolk Naval Shipyard, where he is a project manager for submarine maintenance and modernization.

Publisher's Acknowledgments

We're proud of this book; please send us your comments through our Dummies online registration form located at http://dummies.custhelp.com. For other comments, please contact our Customer Care Department within the U.S. at 877-762-2974, outside the U.S. at 317-572-3993, or fax 317-572-4002.

Some of the people who helped bring this book to market include the following:

Acquisitions, Editorial, and Media Development

Senior Project Editor: Tim Gallan

Acquisitions Editor: Erin Calligan Mooney

Copy Editors: Christine Pingleton, Jessica Smith

Technical Editors: Amy Nicklin, LeAna Richards

Assistant Editor: David Lutton

Editorial Manager: Michelle Hacker

Editorial Assistants: Jennette ElNaggar, Rachelle S. Amick

Art Coordinator: Alicia B. South

Cover Photo: © iStockphoto.com/bwilking

Cartoons: Rich Tennant (www.the5thwave.com)

Composition Services

Project Coordinator: Nikki Gee

Layout and Graphics: Carl Byers, Carrie A. Cesavice, Mark Pinto, Corrie Socolovitch, Laura Westhuis, Erin Zeltner

Proofreader: Betty Kish

Indexer: Sharon Shock

Publishing and Editorial for Consumer Dummies

> **Diane Graves Steele,** Vice President and Publisher, Consumer Dummies

> **Kristin Ferguson-Wagstaffe,** Product Development Director, Consumer Dummies

> **Ensley Eikenburg,** Associate Publisher, Travel

> **Kelly Regan,** Editorial Director, Travel

Publishing for Technology Dummies

> **Andy Cummings,** Vice President and Publisher, Dummies Technology/General User

Composition Services

> **Debbie Stailey,** Director of Composition Services

Contents at a Glance

Table of Contents

Introduction

••

You've set your sites on becoming an officer in the armed forces. Congratulations! Your fellow citizens extend a big thank you as well. Not everyone has the fortitude and confidence to step into a leadership position. To become an officer, however, you need to prove yourself, and one of the first hurdles you must clear is one of the Officer Candidate Tests (OCT) — any of several tests required for admission into Officer Candidate School or Officer Candidate Training.

To do well on the test, you need the knowledge and skills you acquired (or should have acquired) in high school. You must be able to make sense of what you read and pick out key details and ideas from reading passages; prove that you have a solid vocabulary and know how to use it, both in speaking and in writing; be a whiz at basic math, including geometry and algebra; have a firm grasp of general science, including the life sciences, chemistry, and earth sciences; and, depending on the test, have the ability to solve problems related to mechanics and electronics.

Don't worry. You probably knew a lot of what you need to know on the test at some point in your life. So a refresher course and some practice should be sufficient to tone your brain cells and hone your skills. We're here to help. This book provides you with everything you need to know along with test-taking strategies and tips for doing your very best when test day rolls around.

About This Book

Officer Candidate Tests For Dummies is for smart, highly motivated individuals like yourself who need to get up to speed in a hurry in a few key subject areas and need to sharpen your skills for test day. We carefully constructed this book to cover the fundamentals you're most likely to encounter on the test in easily digestible chapters and sections. You don't even need to read the book from cover to cover. Just flip, skip, and dip into the chapters and sections you need most. Throughout the book, we provide

- ✔ Lots of how-to guidance explaining how to read effectively, build vocabulary, solve mathematical problems (even word problems), and think logically.

- ✔ Sample questions that test you along the way so you can develop confidence through practice.

- ✔ Insight into what's covered on each OCT subtest.

- ✔ Strategies and tips for reading and understanding questions and choosing the correct answers most efficiently.

- ✔ Guidance on how to prepare for test day so you feel less anxious and more confident knowing what to expect.

- ✔ Several complete, timed practice tests so you gain experience taking tests when the clock's ticking.

- ✔ Answers and explanations to identify your weaknesses and learn from your mistakes.

Conventions Used in This Book

Although we don't like to think of our book as conventional, we follow several conventions throughout to make the information more accessible:

- ✔ We use *italics* both to stress important words and to highlight words we define. Spot an unfamiliar word in italics, and you're almost guaranteed to find its meaning in the next sentence or the one after that.

- ✔ We use **bold** text to highlight keywords in bulleted lists, the action parts of numbered steps, and the correct answers in our answer keys.

- ✔ We use `monofont` for Web addresses. Keep in mind that some Web addresses may extend to two lines of text. If you use one of these addresses, just type the address exactly as you see it, pretending that the line break isn't there.

What You're Not to Read

You may notice some text stuffed into gray boxes. These boxes, which are called sidebars, contain bonus information on topics we thought you might find educational or entertaining (hopefully both). While these sidebars are interesting, you don't have to read them to do well on the test. So, if you're short on time, feel free to skip them.

Foolish Assumptions

We assume you're using this book in preparation for taking one of the OCT: the Armed Services Vocational Aptitude Battery (ASVAB), the Air Force Officer Qualifying Test (AFOQT), or the Aviation Selection Test Battery Officer Aptitude Rating (ATSB OAR). If that's a false assumption, you're in the wrong class. We also assume that you're a highly motivated student. You want to learn, you want to do well on the test, and you're willing to invest the time and effort in gathering information and building the requisite skills. You may have just graduated from high school or college, or you may have been out of school for some time. That doesn't matter. What matters is that you want to learn and succeed.

How This Book Is Organized

This book is divided into five parts to make the information more manageable. For example, if you typically do better in math and science than in English, you probably want to spend more time in Part II brushing up on vocabulary and practicing your reading skills. The following sections function as a road map, briefly describing the contents of each part so you have a clear idea of where you need to go first.

Part I: An Officer and a Test

Part I is basic training. Chapter 1 traces the various paths you may follow from point A to point B — from where you are right now to where you want to be as an officer in the military. Chapter 2 answers the all-important question: What's on the test? It describes the different OCT, the subtests that comprise the OCT, and the number of questions and amount of time you have to complete each subtest. Finally, in Chapter 3, we reveal numerous test-taking strategies and tips to improve your performance on any standardized test.

Part II: Getting Schooled in English

The chapters in Part II provide guidance on how to strengthen your word skills and tips on how to assess the meaning of words from common roots, prefixes, and suffixes. We also show you how to identify the main idea in a reading passage, pick key facts and figures out of paragraphs, and infer the meaning of what you read from clues within paragraphs. These chapters provide plenty of practice questions so you know exactly what to expect on test day and how to approach the different English sections of the tests.

Part III: Back to School with Math and Science

Part III is what most people consider the geeky part of the book. Here you refresh your memory and sharpen your skills in basic mathematics, geometry, algebra, general sciences, mechanics, and electronics. Basic mathematics covers a lot of ground — everything from whole numbers, fractions, and decimals to roots, radicals, quadratic equations, and geometry. We even help you figure out how to solve those pesky word problems that nobody likes.

This part also covers the general sciences, including biology, chemistry, geology, astronomy, human anatomy, and more. We also bring you up to speed in a hurry on the mechanics and electronics portions of the OCT so you have a clear idea of what to expect on the test. We can't possibly cover everything you may encounter, but we can give you a solid foundation for fielding the most common questions and figuring out the answers to less common ones.

Part IV: Practice Tests

This part features four practice tests:

- ✔ The Air Force Officers Qualifying Test (AFOQT)
- ✔ The Aviation Selection Test Battery Officer Aptitude Rating (ASTB OAR)
- ✔ The Armed Services Vocational Aptitude Battery General Technical (ASVAB GT)
- ✔ The Armed Services Vocational Aptitude Battery Marine Officer Candidate School (ASVAB Marine OCS)

By taking these tests, you discover your strengths and weaknesses, learn how to pace yourself, get a better feel for what's on the test so you're better equipped to answer different types of questions, and sharpen your problem-solving skills for test day. Practice is essential in improving memory recall and critical thinking skills, and this part provides plenty of problems to run through.

Part V: The Part of Tens

No *For Dummies* book would be complete without a Part of Tens. In this quick and easy part, we give you tips for studying well and strategies for dealing with multiple-choice questions. By improving memory retention and knowing how to answer multiple-choice questions more accurately and efficiently, you have the tools you need to achieve peak performance.

Icons Used in This Book

Throughout this book, you'll notice icons in the margins. These icons flag important information to take note of. Here's what they mean:

This icon highlights the most important information and insights in the book. In short, this material should be read and applied often.

Strategy is no substitute for knowledge and skills, but it certainly can help you answer questions faster and with greater accuracy. So when you see this icon, you know you're staring at one of our tips to improve your performance.

The test is peppered with pitfalls, and we're here to point them out and steer you clear of them. Look for the Warning icon to spot trouble before it sinks you on the test.

We believe that the best two ways to learn anything is by viewing and doing — seeing how it's done and doing it yourself. We use the Example icon to flag these opportunities for you to practice what you've learned.

Where to Go from Here

Where to go from here really depends on you. To get the most out of this book, we recommend reading it from cover to cover. However, you may take a different approach, and this book is structured in a way that makes it conducive to a variety of study methods.

For example, you may want to take one of the practice tests in Part IV first, sort of as a diagnostic tool to identify your weak and strong subject areas. You may then focus more of your efforts on chapters related to your weakest subjects. If you choose to take a test as a way to get a baseline of your skills, consider reading Chapter 3 first to improve your performance without having to spend time exploring specific subject areas.

Another option is to warm up with material you already firmly grasp and then work up to more challenging subjects. For example, if you're confident in your vocabulary and reading skills, start with the chapters in Part II and then work on your weaker areas. Also, if you're familiar with a given subject area and don't want to spend a great deal of time reviewing what you already know, consider skimming the chapter for tips and warnings. And be sure to check out the examples to improve your performance without acquiring new knowledge or skills.

Part I
An Officer and a Test

The 5th Wave · By Rich Tennant

"It's an Armed Services aptitude test taken on a computer, and you're telling me my hours of experience playing World of Warcraft count for <u>nothing</u>?!"

In this part . . .

Consider Part I to be your basic training for the Officer Candidate Tests. Here, we show you how to go from Point A to Point B: from where you are right now to the point at which you become a bona fide officer. We bring you up to speed on the tests you'll be taking so you know what to expect. And we reveal valuable test-taking tips and strategies that'll pay handsome dividends when test time rolls around.

Don't get us wrong. You still have a lot of preparation ahead of you before you're ready to ace the test, but this part sets a solid foundation on which to build your knowledge, skills, and confidence.

By the way, Chapter 1 presents some general information that you're unlikely to encounter on any of the tests. It does, however, give you an idea of some of the basics you'll run into in the military environment relating to structure, pay and benefits, and occupational specialties as well as links to more information.

Chapter 1

The Path to Becoming an Officer

So you want to be an officer? Good for you!

Military service — the "Profession of Arms" — is an honorable, enjoyable, and rewarding pursuit, but it's not without challenges. When the time comes, you'll take an oath to

> *Support and defend the Constitution of the United States against all enemies, foreign and domestic, to bear true faith and allegiance to the same, to obey the orders of the President of the United States and the orders of the officers appointed over me, in accordance with regulations and the Uniform Code of Military Justice.*

Taking this oath is a significant commitment to yourself as well as to your country and to your subordinates, peers, and superiors. To fulfill your duty, you must be true to yourself and committed to serving others through leadership. Significant responsibilities and expectations accompany the position, and achieving officer status requires considerable effort and training. But don't let the challenge stop you. If you're dedicated to becoming an officer, this book is here to help. This chapter reveals what you can expect as an officer in the United States armed forces and shows you how to pursue your goals toward becoming one.

Officer as leader

Wanting to be an officer presumes that you also want to be a leader. Not all leaders are officers, but all officers are called on and expected to be leaders. Prerequisites for being an officer include integrity, honesty, and ethics. Most importantly, you must be more concerned about others and fulfilling your mission than you are about yourself.

The concept of leadership focuses on two things: your mission (or job) and your people. Most of the time, you can balance the two, but if you encounter a situation that requires you to make a choice, the mission *must* come first. Making this choice is almost always difficult, but that's why you get paid the big bucks!

The old quote "You are an officer and a gentleman, by Act of Congress only," isn't quite 100 percent accurate. First, the quote needs a gender update. The military in recent decades — to its great credit — has substantially expanded opportunities for women. And second, you do indeed become an officer by Act of Congress, but whether you act as a lady or gentleman is entirely up to you!

As a final note on leadership, consider what General Colin L. Powell, former Secretary of State and former Chairman of the Joint Chiefs of Staff, said: "Leadership is the art of accomplishing more than the science of management says is possible."

Exploring Military Officer Occupations and Opportunities

Opportunities abound in the military, especially when you achieve officer status. Start thinking now about your areas of interest and where you feel your strengths lie. The military can help place you on a career path that leads you to success and satisfaction. The following sections provide details about various specialties in the armed forces.

Not all of the specialties in the following sections are available in all branches of the military, but most are.

Combat specialty officers

When people hear the term "military officer," they often think of combat specialty officers. These folks plan and direct military operations, supervise missions, and lead forces in combat. They typically specialize by type of unit (for example, infantry, artillery, armor, or special operations). They may further specialize based on mission type or weapon system.

Engineering, science, and technical officers

Engineering, science, and technical officers focus on several different areas. Here's a brief rundown:

- **Army engineer officers** may plan and supervise everything from the design and building of bridges, dams, and living quarters to the establishment of minefields in a combat environment.

- **Environmental science officers** may oversee the testing of air, water, and soil quality as well as direct environmental cleanup efforts.

- **Officers in technical fields** may design and oversee development of aircraft, ships, and weapons systems within the research and development programs of each of the services. Computer engineers, many of whom are in the communications field, often develop and implement large, complex computer systems.

Executive, administrative, and managerial officers

The military is a large, mostly self-sustaining community that must maintain a group of executives, administrators, and managers to carry out the daily business of serving the community's needs. These officers must plan, implement, and manage departments large and small in areas including finance, health administration, personnel management, purchasing and contracting, and international relations. Senior executives and administrators coordinate the activities and budgets of the various departments, including giving testimony at Congressional hearings, so the entire military organization runs like a well-oiled machine.

Healthcare officers

The military has its own healthcare system that's fully staffed with officers who serve as doctors, nurses, dentists, veterinarians, occupational and physical therapists, speech and hearing specialists, dieticians, pharmacists, psychiatrists and psychologists, optometrists, and any other healthcare specialist imaginable. These officers perform the same services as their civilian counterparts (and thus need the same credentials). The only difference between the two is that the officers serve in the armed forces and may find themselves treating patients in combat situations.

Human resources officers

If you count all the people of all the armed forces who are involved in human resources (HR), the armed forces probably have the largest HR department in the country. The armed forces employ officers who serve as recruiting specialists, career counselors, personnel managers, and education and training directors. Human resource development officers must ensure that all service members have the resources they need to achieve their full potential.

Legal services officers

Legal issues aren't limited to the civilian population. The military deals with all sorts of legal issues as well; these issues pertain to both the military itself and to military personnel and their families. Attorneys and paralegals in the Judge Advocate General's (JAG) Corps often advise their commanders on issues related to government contracting, international relations, administrative and environmental law, and civilian and military personnel law.

The various JAG Corps officers also provide legal counsel to commanders and individual service members in formal legal proceedings of courts martial and in the more informal nonjudicial proceedings. And they provide legal assistance with such things as wills and powers of attorney, both of which are critical to members who may be deployed anywhere in the world on short notice.

Lawyers often become officers through direct commission, as explained in the section "By appointment only: Receiving a direct commission," later in this chapter.

Media and public affairs officers

Media and public affairs officers serve as liaisons between the military and civilian populations. They develop and produce radio and television commercials and Web content for recruiting purposes, videos for training, and press releases and news reports for informing the public. Some officers even coordinate the activities of military bands and various public displays and demonstrations, including flyovers at major sporting events and holiday celebrations.

Protective service officers

The responsibilities of protective service officers extend far beyond the oversight of military police to deal with all aspects of protecting the safety of people and property on military bases and vessels. While military police focus primarily on law enforcement, emergency management officers plan and prepare for emergencies and respond when disaster strikes.

Support services officers

Support service officers attend to the basic physical, emotional, and social needs and well-being of military personnel and their families. They oversee food service, conduct worship services and address spiritual needs (as chaplains), and strive toward establishing an environment (as social workers) that's less conducive to common social ills, including substance abuse and racism.

Transportation officers

Transportation officers play a key role in every military operation by ensuring that personnel, equipment, and supplies arrive where they need to and when they need to. Officers typically specialize by mode of transportation — air, sea, or land — according to their training and experience. Some officers specialize as navigators. Engineers may oversee operations aboard ships and other large vessels, including the vessel's maintenance, repair, electrical system, and power generation. Transportation officers also may oversee the efforts and activities of various departments in meeting their collective transportation needs and goals.

Grasping the Basics of Military Rank

Every organization has a structure that enables individuals to work together to achieve organizational goals. Knowing the military's structure provides you with an organizational chart that enables you to see where you fit in, what opportunities you have to advance, and what you can expect in terms of responsibility and compensation.

The following sections feature charts to help you envision the overall rank and structure of the military along with pay grades for each group: enlisted personnel, warrant officers, and commissioned officers.

Enlisted personnel

Figure 1-1a and Figure 1-1b show the various ranks and associated pay grades (E-1 to E-9) for enlisted personnel.

Pay Grade	Army	Navy / Coast Guard	Marines	Air Force	
E-1	No Insignia — Private	Seaman Recruit	No Insignia — Private	No Insignia — Airman Basic	
E-2	Private First Class	Seaman Apprentice	Private First Class	Airman	
E-3	Lance Corporal	Seaman	Lance Corporal	Airman First Class	
E-4	Corporal / Specialist Four	Petty Officer Third Class	Corporal	Senior Airman	
E-5	Sergeant	Petty Officer Second Class	Sergeant	Staff Sergeant	
E-6	Staff Sergeant	Petty Officer First Class	Staff Sergeant	Technical Sergeant	
E-7[1]	Sergeant First Class	Chief Petty Officer	Gunnery Sergeant	Master Sergeant	First Sergeant

Figure 1-1a: Enlisted personnel ranks and pay grades.

E-8[2]	Master Sergeant	First Sergeant	Senior Chief Petty Officer	Master Sergeant	First Sergeant	Senior Master Sergeant	First Sergeant	
E-9[3]	Sergeant Major	Command Sergeant Major	Master Chief Petty Officer	Fleet/ Command Master Chief Petty Officer	Master Gunnery Sergeant	Sergeant Major	Chief Master Sergeant	First Sergeant	Command Chief Master Sergeant
E-9[4]	Sergeant Major of the Army		Master Chief Petty Officer of the Navy		Sergeant Major of the Marine Corps		Chief Master Sergeant of the Air Force		

[1]When the senior enlisted person in an Air Force unit is an E-7, he or she wears the First Sergeant rank insignia.

Figure 1-1b: Enlisted personnel ranks and pay grades.

[2]The Army, Marines, and Air Force have two positions at pay grade E-8. Whether one is a First Sergeant or Master Sergeant/Senior Master Sergeant depends on the person's job assignment. The First Sergeant is the senior enlisted member of the unit.

[3]The Command Sergeant Major (Army), Fleet/Command Master Chief Petty Officer (Navy and Coast Guard), Sergeant Major (Marines), and Command Chief Master Sergeant (Air Force) are the senior enlisted members of their respective units.

[4]This insignia represents the senior enlisted person of each Service. The incumbent in each position is the spokesperson for the enlisted force at the highest level of each of the Services.

Commissioned and warrant officers

Figure 1-2 shows the various rank insignia and associated pay grades for both commissioned (O-1 to O-10) and warrant (W-1 to W-5) officers.

Pay scales and benefits

As with a career in any field, pay and benefits in the military correspond with each individual's level of responsibility, expertise, experience, and years of service. The compensation package consists of several components, which are covered in the following sections.

Base pay (salary)

The military determines base pay (or salary) by pay grade and years of service. The higher the pay grade and the longer you serve, the more money you earn. The following list provides some ballpark figures applicable in 2010 for enlisted personnel, warrant officers, and commissioned officers:

- ✔ **Enlisted personnel:** Base pay ranges from $1,447 per month (E-1 with less than 2 years of service) up to $5,113 (E-9 with more than 18 years of service).

- ✔ **Warrant officers:** Base pay ranges from $2,682 per month (W-1 with less than 2 years of service) up to $5,905 (W-4 with more than 18 years service).

- ✔ **Commissioned officers:** Base pay ranges from $2,745 per month (O-1 with less than 2 years service) up to $12,121 (O-8 with more than 18 years service).

Military pay and allowances usually change annually. For up-to-date, detailed information about military pay and other forms of compensation, visit www.dfas.mil/militarypay.html.

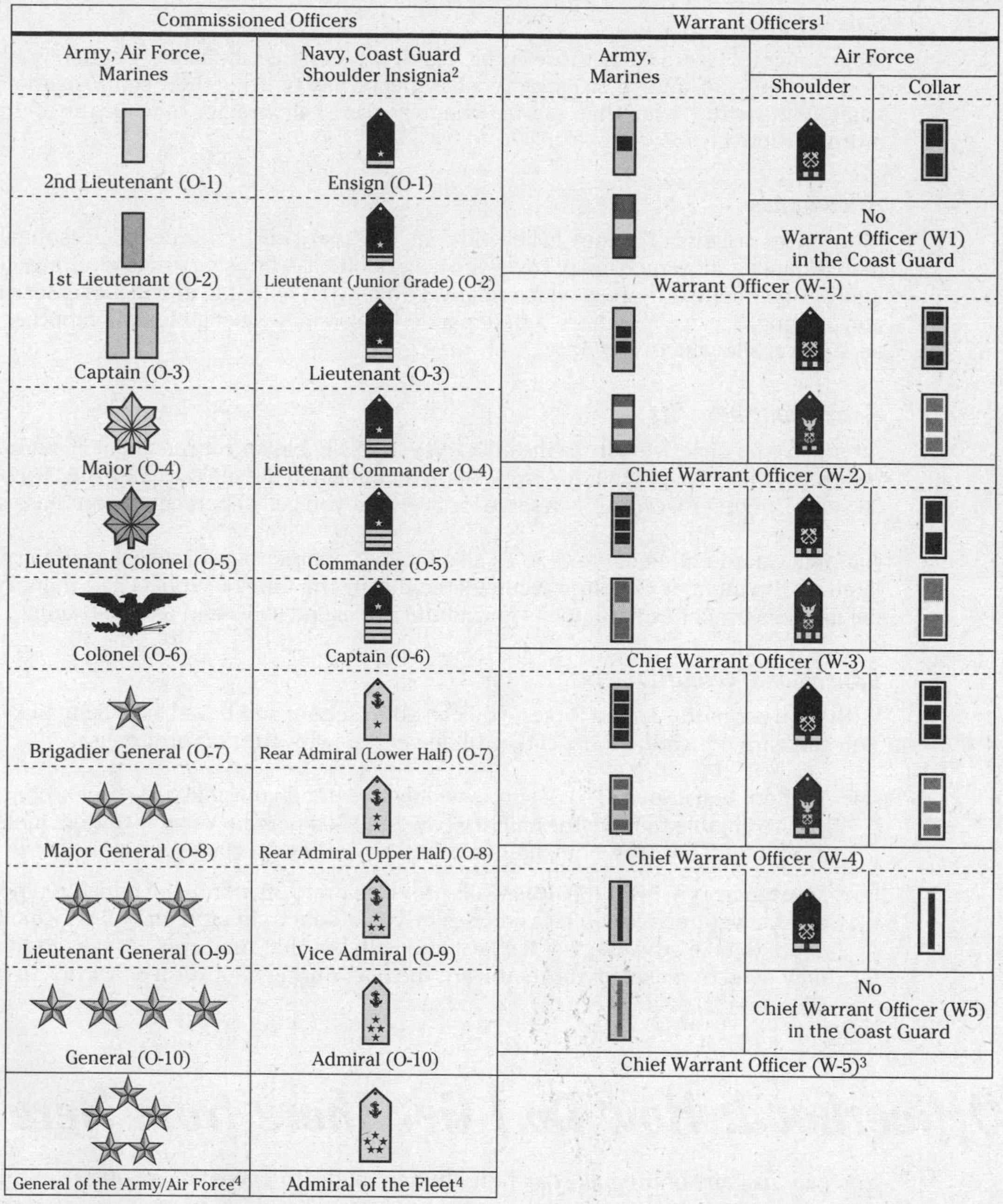

Commissioned Officers		Warrant Officers[1]		
Army, Air Force, Marines	Navy, Coast Guard Shoulder Insignia[2]	Army, Marines	Air Force	
			Shoulder	Collar
2nd Lieutenant (O-1)	Ensign (O-1)			
1st Lieutenant (O-2)	Lieutenant (Junior Grade) (O-2)		No Warrant Officer (W1) in the Coast Guard	
		Warrant Officer (W-1)		
Captain (O-3)	Lieutenant (O-3)			
Major (O-4)	Lieutenant Commander (O-4)	Chief Warrant Officer (W-2)		
Lieutenant Colonel (O-5)	Commander (O-5)			
Colonel (O-6)	Captain (O-6)	Chief Warrant Officer (W-3)		
Brigadier General (O-7)	Rear Admiral (Lower Half) (O-7)			
Major General (O-8)	Rear Admiral (Upper Half) (O-8)	Chief Warrant Officer (W-4)		
Lieutenant General (O-9)	Vice Admiral (O-9)			
General (O-10)	Admiral (O-10)		No Chief Warrant Officer (W5) in the Coast Guard	
		Chief Warrant Officer (W-5)[3]		
General of the Army/Air Force[4]	Admiral of the Fleet[4]			

Figure 1-2: Commissioned and warrant officer ranks and pay grades.

[1]There are no warrant officers in the Air Force.

[2]Collar insignia is the same as Army, Air Force, and Marines at comparable levels.

[3]Also referred to as "Master Warrant Officer."

[4]Also O-10. No equivalent rank in the Marine Corps or Coast Guard. This rank is generally reserved for wartime use only.

Incentive pay

Military personnel, including officers, may receive additional compensation in the form of *incentive pay,* including flight pay for pilots, submarine pay, diving-duty pay, career sea pay, parachute pay for paratroopers, and extra pay for foreign language proficiency.

Special pay

Some officers, particularly those in the health professions (medicine, dentistry, nursing, veterinary medicine, and so on), may receive special pay to bring their compensation somewhat in line with that of their civilian counterparts in an attempt to make the military option more attractive.

Allowances

Allowances consist of money in lieu of room and board and, for enlisted personnel, clothing maintenance. Allowances may cover the cost of off-base housing, food, clothing, cost of living adjustments for areas with a relatively high cost of living, moving, overseas expenses, and lodging. Service members with dependents also may be eligible for a monthly family separation allowance.

Retirement benefits

After 20 years of active duty in the military, you're eligible for retirement at 50 percent of your base salary plus 2.5 percent for every year you remain in the military past the 20 years (up to 30 years). In other words, if you serve for 30 years, you get 75 percent of your base salary.

National Guard and Reserve retirees also receive a percentage of their base salary calculated on the number of points accumulated during the time of service. The military personnel in these branches earn points for monthly weekend drills and annual training.

Educational benefits

With a career in the armed forces, you can go to school and have Uncle Sam pick up the tab. You can earn educational benefits with one of the following two programs:

- **Tuition Assistance (TA):** If you're willing to extend your military service contract, you're eligible to have the military pay up to 100 percent of your tuition, including enrollment, lab fees, computer fees, and any other special fees.
- **Montgomery GI Bill (MGIB):** MGIB provides up to 36 months of education benefits to eligible veterans for college courses or vocational training. You typically have ten years to take advantage of the MGIB benefit, but that time may vary. In addition, you may need to make payments toward the plan during your term of service to be eligible. (For details, visit www.gibill.va.gov.)

Officerhood: How Do I Get There from Here?

You can take any of the following four different paths to becoming an officer in the military:

- Complete training in Officer Candidate School (OCS) or Officer Training School (OTS)
- Enroll in and complete the Reserve Officers' Training Corps (ROTC) program while in college
- Graduate from a military academy
- Receive a direct commission

The following sections describe each of these paths in detail.

No matter which path you take, each branch of the armed forces has its own requirements for becoming a commissioned officer, so check with recruiters or admissions counselors for specifics. The following are the basic requirements that pertain to all branches of the military:

- **Age:** 19 to 29 years for OCS/OTS; 17 to 21 for ROTC; and 17 to 22 for military academies
- **Aptitude:** As proven by score on officer qualification test
- **Citizenship:** U.S. citizen
- **Education:** Four-year college degree from accredited educational institution
- **Marital status and dependents:** May be single or married; maximum number of dependents varies according to branch; must be single to enter and graduate from one of the military academies
- **Moral character:** No criminal record
- **Physical condition:** Good overall health and vision; height 5 feet to 6 feet 5 inches for men and 4 feet 10 inches to 6 feet 5 inches for women; healthy weight for age and height
- **Waivers:** Some qualifications may be waived depending on individual circumstances

Taking the fast track with OCS or OTS

OCS and OTS provide a fast track to becoming an officer for those who have a bachelor's degree and didn't benefit from attending a military academy or participating in ROTC. Competition for entrance into one of these programs is stiff, but if you're accepted, you're on track to becoming an officer in 16 to 17 weeks.

Training focuses primarily on leadership, but physical training, military history, and basic drill (marching) also are part of the program. Entrance requirements and program curriculum (and length) vary among the different branches of the military. For details, check out the Web site for the branch that interests you:

- **Air Force:** www.au.af.mil/au/holmcenter/OTS
- **Army:** www.goarmy.com/ocs
- **Coast Guard:** www.gocoastguard.com/find-your-career/officer-opportunities/programs/officer-candidate-school
- **Marines:** officer.marines.com/marine/making_marine_officers/officer_candidates_school
- **Navy:** www1.netc.navy.mil/nstc/otc/ocs.asp

Hopping on the college track with the ROTC

The ROTC is the path to becoming an officer that's specifically intended for college students. If you earn your undergraduate college degree while completing the ROTC program, you obtain a commission in one of the United States' armed forces. This type of commission isn't the same as a direct commission as discussed later in this chapter.

Can you enjoy the "college life" if you're involved in an ROTC program? Absolutely! Hundreds of colleges or universities in the United States offer ROTC programs, and participating in one of the many programs requires a modest commitment of time and effort. You must do the following to participate:

- Take ROTC as an elective course
- Participate in additional activities, including physical fitness training
- Wear your ROTC uniform for special events and weekly meetings

You can participate for two or four years to earn a partial or full scholarship. In exchange for your participation in the program, ROTC offers the following benefits:

- **Tuition assistance:** All ROTC participants receive some form of tuition assistance. Students who qualify also can apply for ROTC scholarships to cover room, board, and books.
- **Leadership skills:** ROTC-learned skills benefit you in any walk of life because leadership is a valuable asset in the business world and in any community in which you choose to live or become a member. You learn at an early stage the basics of being in charge.
- **Career guidance:** If you're interested in a particular career, military service can help you pursue your interests and acquire the knowledge, skills, and experience you need to be successful in the field you choose.
- **Training and experience:** Aside from an advanced education, you gain job experience at the same time.

Start with a leg up! If you enter the service on active duty following graduation and completion of ROTC, you start at a management level as an officer. As a result, you start using what you've learned right out of school. You won't find many other employers who hire you in as a manager upon graduation.

For the most up-to-date information on the ROTC program, visit `www.rotc.com`.

Attending and graduating from a military academy

The most thorough and rigorous officer training occurs at four-year military academies, including West Point. In these academies, officer training is an integral part of each student's college education. The learning environment is highly structured and disciplined. Students must not only complete their course work, but they must also participate in leadership courses, physical fitness training, and drill (marching).

Competition and entrance requirements are stiff. You must

- Be a U.S. citizen
- Obtain a congressional nomination (not required for the Coast Guard Academy)
- Be between 17 and 22 years of age
- Have solid SAT/ACT scores
- Be physically fit and pass a physical fitness exam
- Meet high school GPA requirements
- Be single and remain single until after graduation

Chapter 1: The Path to Becoming an Officer

Applicants with a stellar high school record, including participation in team sports, student government, and community service have an edge. Being a team captain or president of an organization or serving in a comparable leadership position is an added plus, because it demonstrates leadership experience.

The United States has five military academies. Each provides a first-class education. Upon graduation, you receive a bachelor's degree and a commission in the armed forces. For the most detailed, accurate, and timely information about the available military academies, go to the following sources:

United States Air Force Academy
ATTN: Public Affairs Officer
2304 Cadet Drive, Suite 320
Colorado Springs, CO 80840-5016
(719) 472-2990
www.usafa.af.mil

United States Coast Guard Academy
ATTN: Public Affairs Officer
15 Mohegan Avenue
New London, CT 06320-4195
(203) 444-8270
www.cga.edu

The Coast Guard reports directly to the Department of the Navy only in wartime; in peacetime it falls under the jurisdiction of the Department of Homeland Security.

United States Merchant Marine Academy
ATTN: Public Affairs Officer
300 Steamboat Road
Kings Point, NY 11024
(516) 773-5000
www.usmma.edu

The Merchant Marine Academy has a close relationship with the United States armed forces, as noted on its Web site, but it isn't part of the Defense Department.

United States Military Academy
ATTN: Public Affairs Office
Taylor Hall, Building 600
West Point, NY 10996-1788
(845) 938-2006
www.usma.edu

United States Naval Academy
ATTN: Public Affairs Officer
121 Blake Road
Annapolis, MD 21402-5000
(410) 267-2291
www.usna.edu/Admissions

Valuable perks accompany a military academy education. Every student is, in a sense, on scholarship, because his or her education is paid for by American taxpayers. Not only that, each student also gets paid while in school!

If you're already enlisted, you may still have the opportunity to take this path toward becoming a commissioned officer. Contact your base/post education office for details.

By appointment only: Receiving a direct commission

Not all commissioned officers have had to participate in the grueling officer candidate training. A little more than 10 percent of officers receive their commissions via direct appointment. These are usually professionals with advanced degrees or training, including doctors, attorneys, and clergy, but there are other possibilities.

Investigating Reserve and Guard Opportunities

You may be able to earn a commission in the National Guard or Reserve, primarily through state-run schools and training programs. Some ROTC programs also permit you to accept a commission directly into one of the Reserve Components. For details, contact a local recruiter for the desired branch of the armed forces:

Air Force
www.afreserve.com
(800) 257-1212

Army
www.goarmy.com
(888) 550-2769

Coast Guard
www.uscg.mil/reserve
(800) 883-8724

Marine Corps
www.marines.com/main/index/making_marines/eligibility/officer
(800) 627-4637

Navy
www.navalreserve.com
(800) 872-8767

Army National Guard
www.nationalguard.com
(800) 464-8273

Checking Out Warrant Officer Opportunities

Warrant officers serve as specialized officers within the Army, Navy, Coast Guard, and Marines. (The Air Force discontinued its warrant officer program in 1959.) Unlike commissioned officers, warrant officers ordinarily do not serve in typical officer command roles, and their careers emphasize depth rather than breadth of experience. While commissioned officers focus on expanding their horizons through higher levels of command, warrant officers concentrate on enhancing their expertise and leadership within the career field of their choice.

Here's the typical path to becoming a warrant officer: First you apply to Warrant Officer Candidate School (WOCS). Assuming you're accepted, you attend a Basic Combat Training (BCT) course, which typically lasts nine weeks. You then must complete WOCS.

If you already serve in the military and maintain a superior level of technical or tactical expertise, you also may be encouraged to enter the warrant officer program. Warrant officers in the aviation track attend the Warrant Officer Flight Training (WOFT) program after completion of WOCS.

Warrant officers account for a small percentage of active-duty military personnel — approximately 1.1 percent. They currently serve as senior technical experts and managers in a wide variety of occupational specialties and, in the Army, as pilots of various types of aircraft, including both helicopters and fixed-wing crafts. Most, even in the army, aren't pilots. Some warrant officers enter military service directly from civilian life, but most have served in the senior enlisted ranks.

In rank, warrant officers fall between enlisted personnel and commissioned officers.

To qualify to become a warrant officer, you must

- Be 18 years old at the time of enlistment
- Be a United States citizen
- Have a high school diploma
- Earn a minimum score of 110 on the ASVAB GT (Armed Forces Vocational Aptitude Battery General Technical)
- Pass all events on the Army physical fitness test
- Be less than age 33 (if you're on the aviation track)

Chapter 2

The Tests at a Glance

In This Chapter

▶ Getting a feel for the types of questions on the OCT

▶ Knowing what to expect on the ASVAB, AFOQT, and ASTB

At one point or another, almost everyone has asked, "What's going to be on the test?" Even if we knew all the test questions and answers, the military understandably prohibits the disclosure of actual questions or answers that appear on the test. We can, however, describe the knowledge and skills that the questions target and can provide some sample questions for you to study and work through.

In this chapter, we provide a glimpse of what to expect along with a breakdown of each of the Officer Candidate Tests (OCT) — the ASVAB, AFOQT, and ASTB — into their corresponding subtests. This review can help you more effectively tailor your expectations and preparation.

Recognizing the Different Question Types

Although the Armed Services Vocational Aptitude Battery (ASVAB), Air Force Officer Qualifying Test (AFOQT), and Aviation Selection Test Battery (ASTB) are different tests, they have a few similarities. All the tests, for example, include Verbal and Math subtests. Some tests include a General Science subtest, but others don't. Later in this chapter, the section "Knowing What to Expect on the Different Tests" reveals the subtests included on each test. For now, take a look through the following sections, which introduce you to the types of questions you can expect to encounter on each of the subtests.

Studying the verbal ability questions

Any organization as large as the armed forces is swamped with paperwork. Everything must be documented — and most likely in triplicate! Orders, requisitions, regulations, technical material, directions . . . the list is endless. To be accurate and efficient (qualities highly prized by the military), you must have verbal aptitude. In other words, you must be able to understand and communicate clearly in written and spoken English. (And don't forget about understanding the 10,000 acronyms in military jargon!) These skills are essential to effective leadership.

Although the format of the questions varies on the different OCT, most verbal ability questions test your vocabulary knowledge and reading comprehension skills. In addition, the AFOQT tests your understanding of word relationships in analogies, which are designed to measure your vocabulary and reasoning skills. The following sections provide a rundown of the three types of verbal ability questions you'll encounter.

Word Knowledge questions

The Word Knowledge subtests assess your mastery of English vocabulary. The more words you know, the better you'll do on these questions. All these questions ask you to find a word that most nearly means the same as the word in the question; in other words, you're looking for *synonyms*. Some questions present the word alone; others give the word in a sentence. If you feel that you may be weak on vocabulary, don't worry. Chapter 4 has you covered, and Chapter 5 puts your word knowledge to the test. The following is a sample Word Knowledge question. For this question, you must choose the word that most nearly means the same as the word provided.

TREPIDATION

(A) escalation

(B) fear

(C) conflagration

(D) harmony

(E) hatred

The correct answer is Choice (B). *Trepidation* is a noun that means *fear*. If you didn't know that, fear not. In Chapter 4, you can discover a host of ways to develop an extensive vocabulary; deduce meanings from a word's prefix, suffix, and root; and identify *synonymous* words (words with the same or similar meanings).

Verbal Analogies questions

Verbal analogies are reasoning questions that test both your vocabulary and your ability to reason and perceive relationships between words and their meanings. After you understand the relationship between the two words in the question, you have to find an answer that presents the same relationship. Some questions give you the first word in the second analogy; others don't. Here's an example of the type of questions you'll encounter on the Verbal Analogies subtest.

AGGRESSIVE is to TIMID as

(A) SLY is to UNDERRATED

(B) OPEN-MINDED is to FOOLISH

(C) ARGUMENTATIVE is to QUARRELSOME

(D) ASTUTE is to DULL-WITTED

(E) ROBUST is to HEALTHY

The correct answer is Choice (D). Aggressive and timid are opposites.

These analogy questions may be kind of tricky, especially if you're not 100 percent certain of each word's meaning. But don't worry, because Chapter 4 is ready to assist you in answering questions like these and in pointing out the common pitfalls to avoid. In addition, Chapter 5 presents you with 25 analogy questions to hone your skills.

Reading Comprehension questions

Because most officers read forms, orders, regulations, and even the post newspaper every day, most of the OCT include a Reading Comprehension subtest (also called the Paragraph Comprehension or Reading Skills subtest, depending on which test you're taking). Reading Comprehension questions test your ability to understand the main idea and purpose of a paragraph, recognize supporting details, and draw inferences from what's implied in the paragraph. You need to apply your vocabulary skills and your critical thinking ability to comprehend the paragraphs and successfully answer the questions on the tests. The following is a sample Reading Comprehension question.

An eerie radiance emanates from the edges of the pond, an isolated watering hole deep in the Amazon jungle. A closer look reveals that the small dots of glowing light are the larvae of the *Lampyridae*. In its adult form, this insect, most commonly called the firefly, emits intermittent light. Bioluminescence, the production and emission of light by a living organism, is the source of the ghostly glow.

According to the passage, which of the following statements is true?

(A) Only the adult firefly has bioluminescence.

(B) All insects that are capable of emitting light are classified as *Lampyridae*.

(C) The only location in which bioluminescent creatures are found is deep in the Amazon jungle.

(D) At least two stages in the development of the *Lampyridae* are bioluminescent.

The correct answer is Choice (D) because the passage specifically mentions larvae and adult. If you picked the wrong answer choice, you probably did so because you were reading without focus or didn't go back to the passage to find support for your answer. But don't worry; Chapter 6 reveals techniques to prevent future mistakes like these.

Becoming acquainted with the math subtests

Although the math subtests are challenging, the challenge is reasonable. You're not expected to know calculus and trigonometry. A refresher course in high-school math along with some practice is sufficient preparation for the math that's covered on the tests. Coverage is fairly broad, but the types of questions you'll encounter can be broken down into two types: basic math and arithmetic reasoning (word problems). The following sections briefly describe each type.

Basic math

Basic math covers a lot of ground — everything from whole numbers, fractions, and decimals up to solving quadratic equations. Unlike arithmetic reasoning problems, which tend to require logic in addition to math skills, basic math problems are fairly straightforward. Answering correctly is simply a matter of knowing the concepts and doing the math accurately. If you need some help, head to Chapter 8. It brings you up to speed on basic math, including whole numbers, fractions, and decimals; the order of operations; percentages and proportions; algebra; and geometry.

Arithmetic Reasoning (word problems)

Arithmetic Reasoning problems are a little like brainteasers. You need to think a bit before solving them — you must formulate a strategy, translate the word problem into math, and then do the math. Following is an example of an arithmetic reasoning problem.

If a ferry carries 10 cars across a river at a time, how many times does the ferry need to cross the river to transport 50 cars from one side to the other?

Before you can do the math, you need to think a little, because the ferry must make a round trip, crossing the river twice for each of the 10 cars. The math itself is a snap: $50 \div 10 \times 2 = 10$.

If you struggled with this question, that's okay. Chapter 10 provides guidance and strategies for translating English into math and solving word problems faster and with greater accuracy.

Understanding what general science covers

General science is so broad that we can't possibly cover all the subject matter you're likely to come across on the OCT. However you can be sure that you need a firm foundation in the following scientific fields to be prepared for the General Science subtest:

- **Applied sciences:** These are the "practical" sciences, including genetics, nutrition, and agriculture.

- **Astronomy:** Astronomy questions demand a fundamental understanding of the solar system and of certain phenomena related to the movement of planets and moons (such as eclipses and tides). You also may encounter questions about meteors, stars, black holes, and other cosmic stuff.

- **Biology:** Biology is the study of living organisms — plants, animals, fungi, molds, single-celled critters, and so forth. Expect to encounter questions about classifications of life (for example, determining which kingdom or species a particular animal comes from), photosynthesis, the parts of a cell and the function of those parts, the reproductive organs of a plant, and so on.

- **Chemistry:** Chemistry questions are likely to cover topics like these: the structure of an atom, the difference between an atom and a molecule, the concept of chemical states (solid, liquid, or gas), the different types of reactions, and the periodic table (a list of elements, including hydrogen, oxygen, and gold).

- **Earth sciences:** The earth sciences cover our home planet from core to crust and beyond — from the edge of the exosphere to the depths of the ocean floor. You need to know a great deal of earth trivia, including the following: the three types of rock, the earth's five geological layers and five atmospheric layers, details about the five oceans and the seven seas, the forces that make the weather, and the all-important water cycle.

- **Human anatomy and physiology:** Human anatomy covers the various parts that make up the human body and discusses how the various systems, such as the digestive, circulatory, and respiratory systems, function.

- **Metric system:** Although the rest of the United States has yet to adopt the metric system of measurement, scientists adopted it long ago. So being able to think, measure, and perform calculations in metrics is essential. You must know the different metric measures for length, volume, mass, and temperature; the metric abbreviations and prefixes; the common conversion factors (for example, to convert inches into centimeters); and the temperature scales and conversions.

- **Scientific method:** The word *science* often conjures up images of scientists in white coats performing experiments in a laboratory. While this image of scientists is true, they aren't out there just randomly experimenting. When performing experiments, scientists are expected to follow a strict protocol called the *scientific method*. This method is a step-by-step procedure to help ensure that the results and conclusions drawn from the experiments are valid.

Head to Chapter 12 to begin beefing up your science knowledge in the preceding fields.

Science questions are essentially trivia questions to test your knowledge of the world, solar system, and universe in which you live. Check out the following example.

Which planet in our solar system has the longest day?

(A) Mercury

(B) Earth

(C) Venus

(D) Jupiter

(E) Neptune

Venus's day is approximately 247 Earth days. Mercury has the second longest day, which lasts approximately 59 Earth days. Jupiter and Neptune have the shortest days, being only about 10 and 16 hours, respectively. Earth, of course, has a day of about 24 hours. So the correct answer is Choice (C).

As you can see from this one example, with science questions you either know the answer or you don't. If you don't know it, reason may help eliminate one or two choices and improve your chances of answering correctly. However, no amount of reasoning or figuring is going to help you pick the right answer. On the bright side, this book covers several of the subject areas that are frequently tested to help you do better on these types of general knowledge questions.

Developing a feel for what's on the Mechanical Comprehension subtest

As you may guess, the Mechanical Comprehension subtest is all about machines, including work-saving devices like levers, wedges, pulleys, gears, and jacks. Much of mechanics is about gaining leverage. As a result, it involves a great deal of *physics* — the study of matter and energy and the forces that put objects in motion. To do well on the Mechanical Comprehension subtest, you must have a solid grasp of basic math and a clear understanding of fundamental concepts in physics, including mass, energy, the types of forces that act on objects, Newton's laws of motion, and the different types of machines and rotational motion and forces.

The questions on the Mechanical Comprehension subtest are like science or math questions; that is, you're either going to be asked a fact question, such as the type of mechanical device a crowbar is, or you will be asked a math/reasoning question, such as the one in the following example.

A round swimming pool is 8 feet across and 4 feet deep. When filled with water, what is the pressure exerted on the bottom of the pool?

(A) 0.87 psi

(B) 2.4 psi

(C) 1.74 psi

(D) 1.23 psi

For this question, you use the unit weight of water, 62.5 lbm/ft³, and assume that the pressure being calculated is due to the water alone (you don't need to take into account pressure due to the atmosphere). Now all you need to know is the amount of pressure the water column exerts on the bottom of the pool. Use the formula $P = \rho g h$ or $P = \gamma h$, where P is pressure, ρ is density, g is gravity, h is the height of the water column, and γ is the unit weight. Because you know the unit weight of water, you just need to take into account the height of the water column. Therefore, the correct answer is Choice (C). Chapter 14 brings you up to speed on more physics and mechanics problems like this one.

Tailoring your expectations for the Electronics subtest

The Electronics subtest covers everything from the very nature of electricity to modern electronic circuitry. You can expect to encounter questions dealing with the following: the flow of electrons through a circuit, voltage, current, resistance, magnetism and its relationship to electricity, and simple and complex circuits.

As with the Mechanical Comprehension subtest, you may encounter two types of questions: pure fact questions (you know it or you don't) and math/reasoning questions. The following is a sample electronics question that falls into the second category.

Twelve volts is applied across a 6-ohm resistor, what is the current?

(A) 2 watts

(B) 6 amperes

(C) 2 amperes

(D) 3 watts

To answer this, you first need to know that current is measured in amperes (amps). You also need to know the formula for current based on Ohm's Law: $I = V/R$. If you plug the numbers into the formula, here's your answer: $I = 12/6$, or 2 amperes. So the correct answer is Choice (C). Chapter 16 reveals what you need to know to tackle these electronics questions.

Knowing What to Expect on the Different Tests

Your preparation for taking the OCT largely depends on which OCT you're planning to take. All branches of the U.S. military use the ASVAB for enlistment, but applicants for officer training take different tests for different branches of the military. Here's a rundown of the tests that each branch uses:

- **Army:** If you don't have a bachelor's degree, the Army uses ASVAB, SAT, or ACT scores to assess your qualifications for Officer Candidate School (OCS).

- **Air Force:** The Air Force uses the AFOQT.

- **Navy:** The Navy, like the Air Force, has its own test for aspiring officers: the ASTB. Many of the subtests assess overall aptitude, including ability in math, reading, and word knowledge. Some subtests are used only for those who are interested in becoming aviators.

- **Marines:** If you're striving to become an officer in the Marine Corps, you have the option of qualifying with SAT or ACT scores or with scores from portions of the ASVAB. If you're interested in becoming an aviator in the Marines, you also need to take the ASTB.

- **Coast Guard:** To join the Coast Guard, you must have a minimum qualifying score on portions of the ASVAB and on the SAT and ACT. If you want to be an aviator, you also must take the ASTB. The Coast Guard currently uses the ASTB score to select pilot candidates for training and uses a subcomponent score for its nonaviation officer commissioning program. Each service and program requires a different minimum score.

The following sections provide a brief description of each test and a list of subtests on each test so you have a better idea of what to expect.

Armed Services Vocational Aptitude Battery General Technical (ASVAB GT)

The ASVAB is a placement test that allows the military to place enlistees on career paths that they're best suited for based on their knowledge and skills in eight distinct areas.

Table 2-1 presents the subtests for these eight areas. General Technical (GT) refers to a composite score of Verbal Expression (Word Knowledge + Paragraph Comprehension) + Arithmetic Reasoning. The Army requires a minimum GT score of 110 for entrance into Army Officer Candidate School.

Table 2-1	ASVAB Subtests		
Subtest	*# of Questions*	*Minutes Allotted*	*Seconds for Each Question*
General Science	25	11	26
Arithmetic Reasoning	30	36	50
Word Knowledge	35	11	19
Paragraph Comprehension	15	13	52
Auto and Shop Information	25	11	26
Mathematics Knowledge	25	24	58
Mechanical Comprehension	25	19	46
Electronics Information	20	9	27

The ASVAB is offered in two versions: Pencil and Paper (P&P) or Computer Adaptive Test (CAT). Approximately 90 percent of examinees take the CAT version, which allows you to move from one subtest to the next at your own pace rather than having to wait for time to expire for each section. Flip to Chapter 3 for more details on the two versions of the ASVAB.

For each ASVAB subtest, you receive a score that reflects your percentile ranking compared to other test-takers in the same grade or level. Your ASVAB summary results present your subtest percentile rankings along with the following three Career Exploration Scores:

- Verbal
- Math
- Science and technical

The Career Exploration Scores are designed to help the military identify positions you may be best suited for and to guide you in making career choices.

Air Force Officer Qualifying Aptitude Test (AFOQT)

The AFOQT consists of 12 subtests, including a Self-Description Inventory that doesn't really qualify as a bona fide test. Table 2-2 lists the 12 subtests including the number of questions and time allotted for each. All examinees must complete all subtests regardless of the program they want to pursue.

We cover the first four subtests throughout this book and provide coverage of general science in Chapters 12 and 13.

Table 2-2	AFOQT Subtests		
Subtest	# of Questions	Minutes Allotted	Seconds for Each Question
1. Verbal Analogies	25	8	19
2. Arithmetic Reasoning	25	29	70
3. Word Knowledge	25	5	12
4. Mathematics Knowledge	25	22	53
5. Instrument Comprehension	20	6	18
6. Block Counting	20	3	9
7. Table Reading	40	7	10
8. Aviation Information	20	8	24
9. General Science	20	10	30
10. Rotated Blocks	15	13	52
11. Hidden Figures	15	8	32
12. Self-Description Inventory	220	40	11

The AFOQT assesses aptitudes of student pilots, navigators, technical trainees, and officers in general. Subtests are scored separately, and your scores represent your ranking compared to other examinees. Test results present the following five composite scores (the numbers that follow the name of each composite represent scores from subtests in Table 2-2 that are included in the composite):

- **Pilot (2, 4, 5, 7, 8):** Includes results of subtests that measure verbal ability, math knowledge, ability to read and understand flight instruments and tables, and an understanding of fundamental aviation concepts. Spatial abilities also are tested. Here are the minimum score requirements: 25 for Pilot, 50 for combined Pilot and Navigator, and 10 for Quantitative.

- **Navigator (1, 2, 4, 6, 7, 9):** Navigator and Pilot composites overlap in 2, 4, and 7 — math, arithmetic reasoning, and table reading. Instrument Comprehension and Aviation Information scores aren't included in the Navigator composite, but tests that measure verbal and spatial abilities and general science knowledge are included. Here are the minimum score requirements: 10 for Pilot, 50 for combined Pilot and Navigator, and 10 for Quantitative.

- **Verbal (1, 3):** Reflects verbal knowledge and skills, including the ability to reason, read and understand paragraphs on various topics, recognize synonyms, and identify relationships between words. A minimum Verbal composite of 15 is required of all candidates.

- **Quantitative (2, 4):** Reflects math knowledge and skills along with the ability to decipher and solve word problems. A minimum Quantitative composite of 10 is required of all candidates.

- **Academic Aptitude (1, 2, 3, 4):** Reflects verbal and math knowledge and skills and the ability to read and understand written English. No minimum score is required for this composite.

Aviation Selection Test Battery Officer Aptitude Rating (ASTB OAR)

The Navy, Marine Corps, and Coast Guard all use the ASTB as one measure of readiness for applicants to the officer aviation program. These branches of the military use the battery to predict performance and attrition. The ASTB measures math knowledge and skills, the ability to understand written material, mechanical knowledge, spatial perception, and knowledge of fundamental aviation and nautical concepts. The entire battery consists of the six subtests listed in Table 2-3. This book focuses on the first three subtests.

Table 2-3	ASTB Subtests		
Subtest	*# of Questions*	*Minutes Allotted*	*Seconds for Each Question*
1. Math Skills	30	25	50
2. Reading Skills	27	25	55
3. Mechanical Comprehension	30	15	30
4. Spatial Apperception	25	10	24
5. Aviation and Nautical Information	30	15	30
6. Aviation Supplemental	34	25	44

The first three subtests comprise the Officer Aptitude Rating (OAR) of the ASTB. The Navy uses this composite to predict academic performance in Navy Officer Candidate School. If you take only this portion of the test, you receive only one score that reflects your aptitude in math, reading, and mechanical comprehension. Scores range from 20 to 80 with a mean score of 50.

If you take all the subtests, you receive the OAR along with the following three composites:

- ✔ **Academic Qualifications Rating (AQR):** Predicts the academic performance in aviation preflight instruction (API) and primary-phase ground school. A score of 3 is the minimum required to become a Navy pilot or flight officer.

- ✔ **Pilot Flight Aptitude Rating (PFAR):** Predicts primary flight performance for Student Naval Aviators (SNAs). A minimum score of 4 is required to qualify as a Navy pilot.

- ✔ **Flight Officer Flight Aptitude Rating (FOFAR):** Predicts primary flight performance for Student Naval Flight Officers (SNFOs). A minimum score of 4 is required to qualify as a Navy flight officer.

Chapter 3

Test-Taking Tips and Techniques

Many people describe themselves as poor test-takers, as if test-taking is an innate talent that can be traced back to their gene pool. The fact is that test-taking is a learned skill. First and foremost, you need to know your stuff — hitting the books and exercising your brain cells have no substitutes. Couple your knowledge with some test-taking strategies and plenty of practice, and you have all the skills and confidence you need to perform well.

This chapter is designed to make you a better test-taker. We explain how to plan and prepare for test day, present field-proven strategies for answering multiple-choice questions, and reveal effective tactics for scoring higher on computer tests (if you're required or choose to take your test on a computer). We begin with guidance that applies to all tests and then address specifics related to each type of test: the Armed Services Vocational Aptitude Battery (ASVAB), the Air Force Officer Qualifying Test (AFOQT), and the Aviation Selection Test Battery (ASTB).

The ASVAB is an entire battery of eight or nine subtests (depending on the version). Four of the subtests comprise the Armed Forces Qualification Test (AFQT), which determines whether examinees are qualified to serve in the Unites States' armed forces. The remaining four or five subtests are used for career placement within the military.

Prepping Prior to Test Day

In any endeavor, planning and preparation are the keys to success. Through careful planning and preparation, you know what to expect and have the resources to deal with both expected situations and unexpected circumstances.

Taking the Officer Candidate Tests (OCT) is no different. You need to study to get your mind in tip-top condition, practice taking tests so you can effectively set your pace and answer questions quickly and confidently, and show up on test day feeling your best and remembering everything you're required to bring with you to the testing center. The following sections help you get ready for test day.

Focus on your weakest skills

You will likely do well in the fields of study that interest you most. Because of this, you may gravitate toward spending more time studying and practicing in subject areas you already know well. Obviously, doing so isn't the best approach when preparing for a test that covers diverse subject matter. You'll do better by focusing your efforts on gaining knowledge and skills in your weakest subject areas. To identify subject areas on which you need to focus most, take the following approach:

1. **Identify the subject areas covered on the test you plan to take.**

   If a subject isn't on the test, don't waste precious time focusing on it. Chapter 2 lays out exactly what's covered on the various OCT.

2. **Work through the subject areas in this book that are covered on the test, noting the subject areas in which you excel and those in which you struggle.**

   Be fairly detailed in your assessment, and be honest with yourself. While you may be a math whiz, for example, geometry may be easier for you than, say, algebra or word problems.

3. **Prioritize subject areas from those in which you struggle most to those in which you struggle least.**

This book doesn't include actual test questions, so acing the tests in this book may not result in acing the actual tests. Use this book to identify subject areas you need to work on most, and then use other educational resources, possibly including textbooks, for more in-depth study. Visit www.dummies.com, where you can find other books in the *For Dummies* series to help you master a variety of subjects.

Study regularly and productively

Training your mind for a standardized test is like training to run a 10K. You need to establish a regular routine and spend at least 30 minutes, preferably more, per day "working out." This mental workout should be a focused one without distractions — no TV, radio, cellphone, or chatter from cohabitants.

Match the amount of time you spend studying each day to your needs. Study time really depends on your existing knowledge and ability and how much time you have between now and test day. If you have a solid understanding in all subject areas and have several weeks before the test, 30 minutes per day refreshing what you already know and practicing should do the trick. On the other hand, if you're weak in several areas, you may need to start studying a month or two before the test and may need to spend more time per day studying.

Quality is as important as quantity when it comes to study time. A 30-minute block of focused study is better than two hours during which you're constantly distracted and interrupted. Don't overdo it, either. Give your brain a break every so often. Shelve the books for one day a week, so your mind has time to rest and absorb the subject matter. A day of rest often clears a muddled mind and makes it more receptive to grasping new material.

Practice taking tests

Test-taking is sort of like golf: You can read all about how to do it and know everything required to do it well, but until you actually do it, you really don't have a feel for it. To succeed at any endeavor, you need to combine what you know with plenty of practice. Read through the chapters in this book that pertain to the subject matter you'll be tested on, and then work through each subsequent chapter to test your skills. When you feel ready for the total test-taking experience, head to Part IV, where you can find several types of sample tests (and their answers), including the AFOQT, ASTB OAR, and ASVAB-AFQT.

As you practice, try to re-create the experience of taking the test. Most importantly, time yourself to get a better feel for the pace you need to establish in order to complete each subtest on time. Don't use a calculator. And sit still for the duration of the test.

By working through exercises and practice problems and challenging your skills, you benefit in several ways, including the following:

- ✔ **Reduce potential test anxiety:** Nothing cures test anxiety better than practice. Knowing what to expect is always reassuring and improves results.

- ✔ **Learn how to pace yourself:** Taking a test while racing against the clock adds a new dimension to the test-taking experience. By practicing with timed tests, you know whether you need to work faster or whether you have extra time to slow down and really think through each question.

- ✔ **Get hands-on experience with test-taking strategies and tips:** Applying the strategies you discover in this chapter and other chapters in this book makes them second nature to you. When you encounter a specific type of question, you can quickly size it up and choose the best strategy for answering it.

- ✔ **Know which questions give you the most trouble:** As you score the practice tests, you quickly see which questions are the most challenging for you, so you know what you need to work on.

- ✔ **Reinforce the knowledge and skills you've acquired:** Whenever you put any knowledge into practice or try teaching it to others, you improve your understanding and retention and your ability to recall what you know.

- ✔ **Boost confidence:** As you gain experience answering tough questions correctly, you begin to become more confident and less likely to talk yourself out of a correct answer, which is a common pitfall.

Take care of yourself and arrive on time

As a member of the military, you don't need to be reminded to get a good night's sleep the night before a big day and to eat a light breakfast the morning of, but we'd be remiss if we failed to mention a few things that *are* easy to overlook. In the following sections, we provide some important reminders for test morning.

Rescheduling, if necessary

You want to take the test when you're feeling great or at least fine. If you don't feel well the morning of the test, consider rescheduling it. You didn't invest all this time and effort preparing for the test to actually take it when you're functioning at less than 100 percent.

Dressing in layers

Test sites may be too hot or too cold for your liking. Dress in layers so you can adjust to the temperature and remain comfortable for the duration of the test. In other words, bring a sweater or jacket.

Avoiding too much caffeine and other fluids

Caffeine is great for perking you up in the morning, but too much of a good thing can give you the jitters, cause you to lose focus, and send you running to the restroom every 20 minutes. You may want to hold off on drinking too much coffee, caffeinated soda, or anything else for that matter about an hour before test time.

Arriving early

If you show up late on test day, you're likely to be turned away, in which case you'll need to reschedule. Give yourself plenty of time — plus an extra 15 minutes — to get to the testing center. If you're unsure of its location, use an online mapping site like www.mapquest.com or www.googlemaps.com to get directions. Consider driving out to the center a day or two before test day so you're not frantically searching for the center (and a place to park!) the morning of the test. Test sites vary by test type, as explained in the later sections "Taking the ASVAB-AFQT," "Taking the AFOQT," and "Taking the ASTB."

You want to be as calm as possible on the morning of the test. The best way to remain calm is to be prepared. Know where you're going, when you need to be there, and what you need to bring with you.

Pack the right items

Packing for test day means packing light. All you need is valid identification, usually with your picture, which usually means a driver's license (although a passport is acceptable, too). Just make sure your driver's license isn't expired. The test site provides scratch paper and typically requires that you use their #2 pencils, but you may want to bring your own pencils just in case. Even if you're taking a computerized test, you need something with which to write on your scratch paper.

Calculators and cellphones are prohibited, so leave yours at home.

Mastering Multiple-Choice Questions

All questions on the OCT are in the multiple-choice format. Each question begins with a *question stem* followed by several *answer choices* (usually four or five). Your job is to pick the correct answer or the answer that's *most* correct. Here's an example:

What is the boiling point of water in Celsius?

(A) 212°

(B) 350°

(C) 100°

(D) 451°

The question stem is "What is the boiling point of water in Celsius?" and it's followed by four answer choices, one or more of which are carefully crafted to trip you up. For this question, Choice (A) is the trip wire. Water does boil at 212 degrees, but in Fahrenheit, not Celsius. Choice (C) is correct.

The only thing simpler than answering a multiple-choice question is answering a True/False question. However, beware of the "always" or "never" trap. Unless you're dealing with a finite arithmetical expression, such as $2 + 2$ is always 4 (assuming base 10), "always" or "never" choices are usually (but not always) false.

You can pick up some strategies to improve your odds of choosing the correct answer to multiple-choice questions. The following sections reveal several effective strategies.

Read and understand the directions

Before you even think about tackling the first question in a section, read the directions for the section carefully but quickly, and make a mental note of the following three key pieces of information:

- ✓ The number of questions
- ✓ The time limit
- ✓ What's being tested

Using the number of questions and the time limit, quickly gauge the time allotted for answering each question. If you have 29 minutes to answer 25 questions, for example, you have a little more than one minute per question — 69.6 seconds, to be precise (29 minutes × 60 seconds per minute = 1,740; 1,740 ÷ 25 = 69.6). Knowing the amount of time you have per question helps you set a pace that gives you sufficient time to consider all the answers and still complete the section on time.

Knowing what's being tested gives you a basic understanding of the context of a particular section. By knowing, for example, that a section of the test is focusing on synonyms, you can kick your mind into synonym identification mode. As a result, you'll be on high alert to look for words with similar meanings.

Taking the practice tests in this book familiarizes you with the directions you can expect to encounter on the actual tests. Here's an example of the instructions you may see on a Word Knowledge subtest:

> **Time:** 11 minutes for 35 questions
>
> **Directions:** Each question consists of an underlined word alone or in a sentence. You must find the word in the answer choices that most nearly means the same as the underlined word in the question.

From these directions, you know the test has 35 questions, you have 11 minutes to complete the test (about 19 seconds per question), and you're looking for words with similar meanings.

Read and understand the question

Before choosing your final answer, take the following steps to ensure that you understand the question and have given all answer choices due consideration:

1. **Carefully read the question so you clearly understand what it's asking.**

2. **Read through *all* the answer choices and identify the answer you think is correct.**

3. **Compare the answer you think is correct with the other answer choices to confirm your choice.**

Following these steps is a general approach to answering multiple-choice questions. In some cases, you may want to formulate your own answer before reading through the choices. In later chapters, we address variations to this standard operating procedure.

Read the entire question before beginning to solve or answer. The requested information is typically at the very end of a question, so, in military lingo, "Don't anticipate the command!" This advice is especially important when answering math questions that deal with percentages of interest, depreciation, or tax. Here's an example of two similar questions with very different answers:

You invest $10,000 at a rate of 7% interest, compounded annually. How much interest will you have earned at the end of the first year? **Answer:** $700.

You invest $10,000 at a rate of 7% interest, compounded annually. What is the total value of your investment at the end of the first year? **Answer:** $10,700.

You can bet that both of the preceding amounts will appear in the answer choices. If you fail to read the last part of the question carefully enough, you're much more vulnerable to being led astray by a tempting — but wrong — answer.

Don't spend too much time on one question

Diligence and determination are admirable qualities, but if you're not careful, they can work against you on a standardized test. If you get hung up on a challenging question, determined to arrive at the correct answer, you can lose all sense of time and fail to complete the test.

If you're taking a pencil and paper (P&P) version of a test (versus a computerized version, which we discuss later), skip the questions you can't answer in a reasonable amount of time and come back to them later if you complete the section with time to spare. If you're taking a computerized test, you don't have the luxury to skip around the section. So for each question, eliminate as many of the wrong answers as possible, as suggested in the following section, and take your best guess from the remaining choices.

Leverage the power of the process of elimination

If you can't tell which answer choice is correct, try identifying all the answer choices that are *incorrect.* If you're very lucky, you can eliminate all but one of the answer choices and pick the correct one. If you're sort of lucky, you can eliminate one or two incorrect choices and significantly improve your odds of guessing correctly.

If you don't know, guess

The OCT doesn't penalize for wrong answers as some standardized tests do, so take your best shot when you don't know the answer. To make an educated guess, use the process of elimination as explained in the preceding section. Then pick from the remaining answer choices.

Random guessing, which probably won't do you much good, is generally best avoided. Try to identify at least a couple answer choices that seem most wrong. However, if you're running out of time at the end, random guessing is acceptable.

Be careful marking answers (paper test only)

The P&P directions explain the correct way to mark your answer choices, so follow those directions carefully. If you change your answer choice, fully erase your original choice. Also, be sure the number next to the answer choices matches the number of the question you're answering. Marking an answer for the wrong question number (answering Question 6 when you meant to answer Question 5, for example) is an easy and fairly common mistake that can throw off your answers for all subsequent questions.

Double-check to be sure the question number matches the number next to the answer choice you're about to mark.

Review answers if time allows (paper test only)

On a computerized test, you don't have the luxury of going back to check your answers, but on the P&P you do, assuming you have some time left at the end. First, quickly scan your answer sheet for any possible problems, including the following:

- ✔ Unanswered questions — questions you skipped
- ✔ Improperly marked answers, such as ovals that aren't fully filled in or dark enough
- ✔ Two answer choices marked for the same question
- ✔ Errant marks anywhere on the answer sheet

After scanning for problems on your answer sheet, focus your review on any questions you skipped over and those you found most challenging. If you have additional time, you can review the easier questions and your answers to them.

You're not allowed to check answers on a previous subtest. On the P&P, you're also not allowed to proceed to the next subtest until time expires and you're instructed to proceed. (On a computerized test, you can proceed to the next subtest whenever you've completed the current subtest.)

Taking the ASVAB-AFQT

When taking the ASVAB-AFQT, you have some special considerations to make sure you're well prepared and know what to expect. The following sections bring you up to speed.

For additional details about the ASVAB-AFQT, along with some sample questions for each section of the test, visit www.official-asvab.com.

Test version

The big question you face when taking your ASVAB-AFQT is whether to take the paper-and-pencil (P&P) version of the test or the computer adaptive test (CAT). About 90 percent of test-takers currently take the CAT. You may not have a choice of which version to take, but if you do, you need to make a well-informed decision. The following sections explain the pros and cons of each.

P&P ASVAB-AFQT testing

The P&P version of the test carries the following benefits and drawbacks:

- ✔ Questions range from easy to difficult. This range enables the P&P to be used for test-takers ranging from low to high in terms of ability. Depending on your ability level, you may encounter questions that are way too easy or far too difficult for you.

✔ You mark your answers on paper, which requires more time and introduces additional opportunities for error. You need to be careful to mark your answer choices as directed and to mark the answer that corresponds to the correct question number.

✔ You can skip questions and come back to them later, which you can't do on the CAT.

✔ You can review and change answers, which you can't do on the CAT. This can be a pro or a con. Usually, when test-takers change an answer, they change a correct answer to an incorrect one.

✔ You must wait longer to receive your P&P test results, because the paper test must be scanned and scored. This process typically takes several days.

CAT ASVAB-AFOT testing

Most test-takers prefer the CAT, which has its own pros and cons (mostly pros):

✔ Scheduling to take the test is much more flexible.

✔ Tests are *adaptive,* meaning two people taking the tests may get different questions based on their ability levels. If you answer a question correctly, the next question is likely to be more difficult. If you answer a question incorrectly, the next question should be easier. This adaptability enables the CAT to assess ability level with fewer, more targeted questions.

✔ You answer fewer questions and spend less time taking the test — 1.5 hours for the CAT versus about 3 to 4 hours for the P&P.

✔ Test results are available the same day or the next day.

✔ You can't skip questions or go back and review or change previous answers.

✔ Little room for error exists, because you can't possibly mix up the question and answer numbers or fail to appropriately mark an answer choice. Of course, you do face the possibility of clicking and entering an answer unintentionally.

✔ You have more freedom to work at your own pace. When you've completed a subtest, you can immediately proceed to the next subtest.

✔ Answers are weighted according to difficulty, so if you encounter more difficult questions near the end that you answer incorrectly, you may still score well.

Although the P&P and CAT are intended to be equal in evaluating each test-taker's ability, test-takers generally score slightly higher on the CAT.

Strategies and tips for taking the CAT

Taking the CAT is a different experience altogether from taking the P&P. Knowing the differences and what to anticipate may be most valuable in improving your score. Here's what you can expect on the CAT:

✔ Prior to the test, you'll receive training on using the keyboard and mouse, answering questions, and obtaining help.

✔ As on the P&P, each CAT subtest includes directions specifically for that subtest.

✔ You're probably not going to run out of time before completing a CAT subtest. Almost all test-takers complete each subtest with time to spare.

✔ You can check the lower right corner of the screen to see the time and number of questions remaining so you can more effectively pace yourself.

✔ You can proceed to the next subtest whenever you're ready. You don't need to wait for a proctor's permission.

✔ You may leave the test center immediately after you've completed all subtests that comprise the battery.

The following sections provide some additional guidance on taking the CAT version.

Use the process of elimination

You can't skip questions on the CAT. If you don't know an answer, use the process of elimination, take your best guess, and then proceed to the next question.

Don't get hung up on a single question, but don't give up too quickly either. Spend a sufficient amount of time on a question before deciding to give up and guess.

Confirm your answers

When taking the CAT, confirming your answer upfront against the other choices is even more important than on the P&P version, because you can't go back and change your answer later. Whichever answer you choose is your final answer, so make sure it's your best answer.

Be ready for increasing difficulty

Don't be surprised or discouraged if the questions seem to get more difficult. This increased difficulty is most likely a sign that you're doing quite well on the exam. Embrace the challenge and step up your game to score even higher.

Now, if the questions seem to be getting easier, you may not be doing so well. The decreased difficulty may mean that you're unable to answer more difficult questions. Or it may indicate that you're not being careful enough in reading questions or evaluating answer choices. Try taking a little more time to fully understand each question, choose an answer, and confirm your choice before making a selection.

Locations

To find out where to take the ASVAB-AFQT, contact your recruiter or check with your base education office. Assuming you're qualified to take the test, you'll be scheduled for a testing time.

The CAT ASVAB-AFQT is administered at the nearest Military Entrance Processing Station (MEPS) or an affiliated Military Entrance Test (MET) site, typically located in a Federal government office building, National Guard armory, or Reserve center.

The P&P ASVAB-AFQT is typically administered at MET sites or by traveling MEPS teams at National Guard barracks for test-takers not located near a MEPS. However, an Internet version of the CAT ASVAB-AFQT, called iCAT, has recently been developed. This version allows traveling MEPS teams to administer the computerized version.

Scores

If you take the CAT ASVAB-AFQT, your scores should be available the same day or the next day. Check with your recruiter or base education office. If you take the P&P, you may need to wait several days for the answer sheets to be scanned and scored.

Your scores are presented as national percentiles ranging from 1 to 99 and indicate the percentage of test-takers in a specific group (for example, 18- to 23-year-olds) that you outscored. A score of 78, for example, means you scored higher than 78 percent of the test-takers in your group.

You can use your scores for up to two years from the date of testing to enlist in the armed forces.

Retaking the test

If you're not satisfied with your scores, you can retake the ASVAB-AFQT, but the following stipulations apply:

- ✔ **First retake:** You must wait one calendar month to retake the test.
- ✔ **Second retake:** You must wait one calendar month from the date of your retake to take the test again.
- ✔ **Third retake:** Before you can retake the test a third time, you must wait six calendar months from the date of your second retake.

Your most recent score is the one that counts. If you score lower on a retake, that score replaces your previous score.

Taking the AFOQT

If you're taking the AFOQT, you probably have all sorts of questions, including whether you'll take the test on paper or on a computer, where the test is administered, and whether you can retake the test. The following sections answer these questions and more.

For more about the AFOQT, visit www.afrotc.com/admissions/qualifying-test.

Test version

The question as to which version of the test you have to take is easy with the AFOQT. As of the writing of this book, the AFOQT is available only as a P&P version. It takes about three and a half hours to administer.

Locations

To find out where to take the AFOQT, contact your recruiter or check with your base education office. Assuming you're qualified to take the test, you'll be scheduled for a time to take the test at the nearest Military Entrance Processing Station (MEPS) or another approved testing site. Many locations offer the test, including active duty, guard, and reserve bases.

Scores

Answer sheets must be mailed within one duty day of the date on which the test was administered. They typically take 7 to 10 days to reach the Air Force Personnel Center (AFPC), where they are scored. The AFPC scores tests once or twice per week, so your scores should be available in 10 to 14 days.

Your scores are presented as national percentiles ranging from 1 to 99 and indicate the percentage of test-takers in a specific group (for example, 18- to 23-year-olds) that you outscored. A score of 78, for example, means you scored higher than 78 percent of the test-takers in your group. AFOQT scores never expire.

Retaking the test

You can take the AFOQT only twice unless you're granted a waiver, and a waiver isn't likely. So you get only one retake, and you have to wait 180 days from your first test date to take the test again. The most recent score is the one that counts. So if you score lower the second time around, that's still your official score.

Taking the ASTB

If you're taking the ASTB, you probably want to know which versions of the test are available (paper or computerized), where you can expect to take the test, how it's scored, and whether you can retake it. The following sections provide the information you need.

For more about the ASTB, visit www.med.navy.mil/sites/navmedmpte/nomi/nami/pages/astbinformation.aspx.

Test version

The ASTB comes in both the P&P and computerized versions, but the computer version isn't an adaptive test. It's identical to the paper version, but instead of selecting answers with a pencil, you use a mouse. The computerized version is administered through a Web-based system called APEX.NET.

Three different versions of the test are available. Each version has different questions but follows the same format and tests the same subject matter. You can expect to spend about two and a half hours taking the test.

Studies reveal no difference in pass rates between the paper and computerized versions of the ASTB.

Locations

You can take an ASTB at most Navy and Marine Corps recruiting centers. Coast Guard Education Services Officers (ESO) also may obtain the test for 30 days at a time from the Naval Occupational Medicine Institute in Pensacola, Florida, or administer the online version. Check with your recruiter or base education center for details.

Scores

If you take the computerized version of the ASTB, your scores should be available immediately. Ask your recruiter, or have him or her contact Naval Operation Medicine Institute (NOMI) at 850-452-2257, extension 1060.

The P&P version of the ASTB must be sent to NOMI for scoring, so you're looking at a 10- to 14-day waiting period before your test results are available. Test-takers and recruiters may call for test scores by dialing 850-452-2257. Listen to the message, and then press option 3 followed by option 5 for test scores.

If you take only the Officer Aptitude Rating (OAR) portion of the test, you receive a single score that's used to predict your academic performance in the Navy Officer Candidate School. If you take the entire ASTB, you receive four scores derived from various combinations of subtest results. Each of the four scores is used to predict your success in various areas you may pursue. See Table 3-1 for details.

Table 3-1	Score Components and Ranges	
ASTB Score Component	Score Predicts	Score Range
Academic Qualifications Rating (AQR)	Academic performance in Aviation Preflight Indoctrination (API) and primary phase ground school	1 to 9
Pilot Flight Aptitude Rating (PFAR)	Primary flight performance for Student Naval Aviators (SNAs)	1 to 9
Flight Officer Flight Aptitude Rating (FOFAR)	Primary flight performance for Student Naval Officers (SNFOs)	1 to 9
Officer Aptitude Rating (OAR)	Academic performance in Navy Officer Candidate School (OCS)	20 to 80

Retaking the test

If you're not satisfied with your test score, you can retake the test up to two times (a three-test lifetime limit is in place). Each time you take the test, you must take a different version of it. Also, you must wait until the 31st day from the original test date to retake the test. If you decide to retake it again, you must wait until the 91st day following the previous retake date.

Retaking the test prior to the 30- or 90-day waiting period or retaking the same version of the test results in an illegal test, which is counted against your three-test lifetime limit even though the score isn't counted as valid.

Part II
Getting Schooled in English

The 5th Wave   By Rich Tennant

In this part . . .

Regardless of whether English was your favorite subject in school, you need to brush up on some basics to perform well on the Officer Candidate Tests. Fortunately, you're not going to be asked to diagram sentences and label parts of speech or identify the past participle of the verb "to be." The English portions of the tests deal more with your ability to understand the language and make sense of what you read.

In this part, we provide guidance on how to strengthen your word skills and tips on how to assess the meaning of words from common roots, prefixes, and suffixes. We also show you how to identify the main idea in a reading passage, pick key facts and figures out of paragraphs, and infer the meaning of what you read from clues within paragraphs.

Of course, you'll encounter plenty of practice questions to give you a clear sense of what to expect and how to approach the different English sections of the tests and the various types of questions.

Chapter 4

Building Word Skills

So, you plan to be an officer. Well, the military wants to know whether you have what it takes to be an effective leader, and one of the most important qualities of a good leader is effective communication skills. To express yourself clearly in spoken and written English and better understand what others express to you, you need all the tools at your disposal — and the tools for communication are words.

Because words are the most valuable tools human beings have for spoken and written communication, all the Officer Candidate Tests (OCT) have at least one section that tests your command of the English language.

This chapter provides guidance on how to build an extensive vocabulary; more accurately guess the meanings of words by examining their roots, prefixes, and suffixes; and understand the relationships between word sets so you can answer more of those brain-boggling analogy questions correctly.

You're probably not going to use many of the words you're likely to encounter on the test on a daily basis, but you still need to be able to accurately assess their meanings to clear this particular hurdle.

Reading Your Way to an Extensive Vocabulary

One of the best ways to build vocabulary is to read — novels, how-to books, magazines, newspapers, Web-based content, you name it. Reading introduces you to the most commonly used words in the English language and presents them in a context that helps you understand the connotations and nuances of how they're used.

Reading in itself, however, isn't always enough. Like anything else, you get better results by doing it right, and that means reading the right way. The following sections explain how.

Read what interests you

If you're not already a big reader, motivating yourself to start reading may be a huge obstacle, so start by exploring topics that interest you — topics you want to know more about.

You can find an enormous amount of information in print and on the Internet covering every conceivable topic — and plenty of inconceivable topics, too. If you're interested in fishing, for example, read a fishing magazine, take a book out of the library, purchase a book about fishing (may I recommend *Fly Fishing For Dummies* by Peter Kaminsky [Wiley]?), or go online to one of the thousands of Web sites dedicated to fishing enthusiasts. Interested in iguanas? Great battles of World War II? Same routine. If you're reading about a topic that fascinates you, you won't find reading painful or time-consuming.

Choose a wide range of subjects

Here comes the challenge: Don't limit yourself to just one or two subjects. Doing so exposes you to the risk of becoming *provincial* — a word that means limited, unsophisticated, or as though you never left your hometown.

Try to expand your interests. Let your fascination with deep sea angling lead to exploration of books about all deep sea creatures, about the people who study them, and about the modern machinery that facilitates deep sea exploration.

After you've grasped the basics, challenge yourself with more advanced material on the same topic. Doing so exposes you to more difficult vocabulary and concepts.

Hunt for contextual clues

A sentence or paragraph typically provides clues to meanings of words within that sentence or paragraph. As you read, try to figure out the meaning of unfamiliar words from contextual clues. This skill is an important one to develop so you're better able to deduce the meaning of unfamiliar words on a test. For example, even if you don't know the formal definition of *deduce,* you can tell from the context of the preceding sentence that it means to figure out.

In some cases, you may need to read quite a bit of an article to discover a word's meaning through its context. Say you come across the following headline in a fishing magazine: "Anglers Aiming for the Ubiquitous Bass." You may never have seen the word *ubiquitous.* Fortunately, the article provides all the contextual clues you need to figure it out. It discusses the popularity of bass as a game fish and its abundant presence in all 48 contiguous states. Using contextual clues, you can figure out that *ubiquitous* probably means something like present everywhere.

Look up new words

If you can't comprehend a word's meaning from its context, grab a dictionary and look it up. If no dictionary is handy, look it up on the Web. Google has a nifty feature that enables you to check a word's meaning. Just type "define: [word]" (replacing "[word]" with the word you want defined) and click the Search button. If you don't like that idea, head to `dictionary.reference.com`, where you can look up the word.

Never skip over a word you're unsure of assuming that because you get the gist of the article, one particular word doesn't matter. When you're reading in preparation for an Officer Candidate Test, you're reading to build vocabulary, too, so look up the meanings of unfamiliar words.

If you have one of those new-fangled cellphones, you probably can find a dictionary app for it.

Feed your curiosity

Curiosity may have killed the cat, but that same curiosity makes your word power stronger! Question and wonder while you read. If a writer makes a point you don't understand or you believe is incorrect, don't just skip over it. Try to figure it out. Go to another source and read more information about the topic or search the Web. Don't just automatically accept everything you read as the absolute truth. Questioning and wondering exercise the mind and often add to your growing vocabulary.

Jot down unfamiliar words

Jot down (or type up) unfamiliar words and their meanings as you encounter them. Why? Consider these three reasons:

- The act of writing is a tactile learning activity proven to help most people, especially tactile learners, retain what they've learned.
- Writing gives you an additional encounter with the word and its definition. Your first encounter is reading the word and looking up its definition. Your third encounter may be to actually use the word.
- The result is a log of previously unfamiliar words to review later.

Keep a separate list of interesting topics or ideas you'd like to explore later. One article often leads to another, expanding your knowledge of a topic and exposing you to additional topics — and their accompanying vocabulary.

Enlist the assistance of vocabulary builders

Vocabulary building tools are ubiquitous. One of the best known is the *Reader's Digest* Word Power feature, which is almost guaranteed to expose you to a few words you've never heard of. Here are a few additional suggestions:

- **Use a word-a-day calendar.**
- **Check out word-of-the-day Web sites.** On most of these sites, such as `www.merriam-webster.com`, you can sign up to receive your word of the day via e-mail.
- **Take online vocabulary tests.** If you use your favorite search engine to search for "vocabulary test," you'll find plenty of links to print and online tests.

Play word games

Playing word games is a great way to expand your vocabulary and reinforce the words and definitions you already know. Consider playing the following word games regularly:

- Crossword puzzles
- Scrabble
- Boggle

Word games are readily available on smartphones such as the iPhone and Android phones. You're more likely to play these games if you merely have to reach into your pocket to access them.

Discovering vocabulary in unexpected places

You're likely to encounter complex words in some of the most unexpected places. Sports writers and announcers, for example, often season their commentary with challenging vocabulary. Many magazines, including *Vanity Fair* and *GQ,* use skilled writers who have a mastery of English vocabulary and aren't afraid to use big words for more precise expression.

If you're lucky, you may pick up several vocabulary words that appear on the test. As well-known college basketball broadcaster Dick Vitale would say, "Serendipity, baby!"

Listen for unfamiliar words, too

You can pick up loads of new vocabulary on the street, so get your nose out of that book and perk up your ears to listen for unfamiliar words while talking to friends, listening to the radio, or even watching TV.

Suppose someone mentions a movie with a *convoluted* plot. Don't just smile and nod. Ask what the word means or try to figure it out from the context. (Or, smile and nod and then look it up later.) If the speaker goes on to talk about all the twists and turns in the plot, you may be able to figure out from the context that *convoluted* means very twisted or complex.

Study! Study! Study!

Looking up the definition of a word or even jotting it down is rarely enough to brand that word and definition onto your brain cells. You need to study those words to reinforce your learning. The following sections offer techniques to improve retention.

Make and use flashcards

Grab your list of unfamiliar words and their definitions, along with any vocabulary lists you downloaded from the Web, and create your own flashcards. Write the words on the front of the index cards and their respective definitions on the back. Flip through the cards front-side up and try to define each word. Flip through the stack back-side-up and try to guess the word from its definition.

Carry your flashcards everywhere. They're a great way to fill idle time with a valuable learning activity. You can review vocabulary on your commute to work or school, while waiting at the doctor's or dentist's office, or even before you doze off to sleep at night.

Follow the 15-minutes-a-day plan

Commit to spending at least 15 minutes every day looking over the words you've collected, and then follow through on your commitment. As you memorize words, consider removing them from your stack and adding new words in their places.

Use it or lose it

Just as your muscles get stronger with use and *atrophy* (wither away) with disuse so will your new and improved vocabulary. Try to use a few new words each day in your speaking and writing. Dazzle your family, friends, and colleagues with your *erudition* (deep knowledge and scholarliness)!

Stick with the program

Working a little on vocabulary building every day can improve results significantly, so stick with it. Just think: If you add only one word a day to your working vocabulary, by the end of the year you'll have added 365 words to your verbal arsenal. Give up after the first month, and you're down to 30.

Most people who fall short of their goals do so due to a lack of persistence or stick-to-itiveness. They express their desire to learn Spanish or play the guitar, but they don't take lessons, read books, watch videos, use interactive programs, or do anything else that remotely resembles putting an effort into it. Thirty years later, they're still wishing they could speak Spanish or play the guitar.

Inferring Meaning from Roots, Prefixes, and Suffixes

Most words in the English language come from other languages — usually Latin or Greek. By knowing the common origins, or *roots,* of these words along with the meaning of any prefix and/or suffix appended to the word, you usually can figure out the meanings of unfamiliar words. Consider the definitions for the following words:

- **Root:** A word or part of a word that conveys the core meaning in the absence of a prefix or suffix.
- **Prefix:** An add-on to the beginning of the root that alters the root meaning in some way.
- **Suffix:** An add-on to the end of the root that alters the root meaning in some way.

Using this system of roots, prefixes, and suffixes is a highly efficient technique for acquiring new vocabulary, because words become modular, sort of like the alphabet. With the alphabet, you learn 26 letters and can create all the words in the English language with various combinations of those letters. In a similar way, many words are formed through various combinations of roots, prefixes, and suffixes. By learning a handful of these vocabulary components, you can deduce the meanings of numerous words.

Consider the word *incredible:*

- **Root:** *cred,* meaning belief
- **Prefix:** *in,* meaning not
- **Suffix:** *ible* (variation of *able*), meaning capable

Put the parts together and you get *not-belief-able,* which is a sorry excuse for a word, but it enables you to readily see that *incredible* means unable to be believed or very surprising.

So far, so good. Now consider a slightly more complicated word, *irrevocable,* and examine its parts:

- **Root:** *voc,* meaning to call
- **Prefix:** *ir,* meaning not
- **Prefix:** *re,* meaning again or back
- **Suffix:** *able,* meaning capable

Follow the same process: Assemble the parts, and you get *not-back-call-able* or, better yet, *not-call-back-able,* and you can figure out that *irrevocable* means permanent or irreversible.

TIP

Focus first on the roots, because they convey the core meaning. Unless you know the core meaning, common prefixes and suffixes are of little use. Table 4-1 lists common roots along with their meaning and examples of how they may be used in specific words. Tables 4-2 and 4-3 list and define numerous prefixes and suffixes commonly used to alter root meanings.

Table 4-1		Common Roots
Root	*Meaning*	*Example*
ami, amic	friend	*amiable* (friendly), *amicable* (friendly)
anthro	mankind	*anthropology* (the study of humans and their works), *misanthrope* (one who dislikes people)
aud	sound	*audible* (able to be heard)
bell or belli	war	*belligerence* (warlike or aggressive behavior), *bellicose* (eager to fight)
bio	life	*biography* (the story of someone's life), *antibiotic* (a chemical substance that takes life from bacteria)
brev	briefness	*abbreviation* (a shortened version), *brevity* (briefness)
cap	take or seize	*capture* (to take prisoner or to seize), *captivate* (to hold the attention of)
ced	to go, yield	*accede* (to give consent), *secede* (to withdraw from)
chron	time	*chronological* (in time order), *anachronism* (something out of place in time)
cogn	know	*cognition* (the process of knowing)
corp	body	*corpse* (a dead body), *corporeal* (having material substance)
crac, crat	rule, ruler	*autocrat* (an absolute ruler)
cred	believe	*incredulous* (disbelieving), *credulous* (gullible)
culp	guilty	*culprit* (a guilty person), *exculpate* (free from guilt)
cur, curs	to run	*concurrent* (running at the same time)
dem(o),	people	*democracy* (rule by the people), *epidemic* (a disease that affects many people)
dic	speak, say	*dictate* (a command), *dictum* (an authoritative pronouncement)
equ	equal	*equable* (steady, even, not varying)
fac, fact, fect, fic	to make or do	*effective* (to make useful), *malefactor* (one who makes evil)
gen	birth	*generate* (to create or breed), *progeny* (offspring)
graph	writing	*autobiography* (the life story of the writer)
greg	group	*gregarious* (sociable, likes to be in a group), *aggregate* (to cluster together)
gress	to step or move	*regress* (to move backward)
laud	praise	*applaud* (to clap hands in an expression of praise)
luc	light	*elucidate* (to clarify or shed light on)
min	small	*minute* (very small)
mor	death	*moratorium* (an official halt in an activity), *moribund* (dying)
mut	change	*mutation* (a change in form), *transmute* (to change from one form to another)

Root	Meaning	Example
nov	new	*novice* (a beginner), *novelty* (something new)
nym	name	*pseudonym* (false name)
pac	peace	*pacifist* (one who is peace-loving)
path	feeling	*sympathy* (compassion, understanding)
phon	sound	*euphony* (pleasant sounds), *cacophony* (unpleasant sounds)
pug	fight	*pugnacious* (tending to fight), *pugilist* (a fighter or a boxer)
quer, quis, quir	ask	*query* (question), *inquire* (to ask), *inquisition* (harsh or prolonged questioning)
sci	to know	*science* (knowledge of the material or physical world)
scrib, scrip	to write	*prescription* (a written direction)
sens, sent	to feel	*sensitive* (having feelings for others), *sentient* (having sensation or consciousness)
simil	same	*similitude* (similarity)
son	sound	*sonar* (a method of locating objects using sound waves)
soph	wisdom	*philosopher* (one who investigates profound questions of life)
spec	to look	*circumspect* (cautious, looking around carefully)
sta, stat	to stay in position	*stagnant* (lacking movement or development), *stationary* (unmoving)
temp	time	*temporary* (lasting only for a specific time period, not permanent), *temporal* (pertaining to time)
terra	earth	*terrain* (a tract of land)
the, theo	god	*theocracy* (government in which God is supreme ruler), *atheist* (one who denies the existence of God)
vac	empty	*vacuum* (a space empty of matter), *vacuity* (absence of thought or intelligence)
ver	truth	*verify* (to prove true), *verity* (truth)
vert	to turn	*convert* (to change in form or purpose), *invert* (to turn upside down)
vit, viv	life	*vital* (essential to life), *vivacity* (liveliness)
voc, vok	call	*vocal* (spoken aloud), revoke (to call back)

Table 4-2		Prefixes
Prefix	**Meaning**	**Example**
a-	not, without	*atypical* (not typical), *amoral* (without morals)
ab-	away from	*abnormal* (not normal), *abstain* (to refrain from)
ambi-	both	*ambidextrous* (skillful with both hands), *ambivalent* (seeing both sides)
anti-	against	*antiviolence* (against violence)
auto-	self	*autonomy* (self-rule), *automobile* (self-propelled)

continued

Table 4-2 *(continued)*

Prefix	Meaning	Example
bene-	good	*benefit* (something that promotes well-being), *beneficent* (performing acts of kindness)
circum-	around	*circumnavigate* (travel around), *circumscribe* (to draw a circle around or to restrict within bounds)
con-, com-	with, together	*congregate* (gather together), *congruent* (in agreement), *community* (a group of people living together)
contra-	against	*contradict* (to speak against), *contrary* (opposed to)
de-	down, away	*descend* (to go down), *decelerate* (to decrease speed)
dys-	bad, ill	*dysfunction* (impaired function), *dyslectic* (impairment of the ability to read)
eu-	good	*euphoria* (a feeling of happiness), *euphony* (pleasant sounds)
ex-	away from, out of	*expatriate* (one who lives away from his/her native land), *exonerate* (take away blame)
hetero-	different	*heterogeneous* (different)
homo-	same	*homogeneous* (the same)
hyper-	over	*hyperactive* (overly active)
hypo-	under	*hypothyroidism* (underactive thyroid gland)
il-, im-, in-	not	*illogical* (not logical), *improbable* (not likely), *insincere* (not sincere)
inter-	between	*intervene* (to come between)
intra-	within	*intrastate* (within the state)
ir-	not	*irreducible* (not able to be reduced), *irresponsible* (not responsible)
mal-	bad	*malign* (to speak badly of), *malignant* (evil, harmful)
micro-	small	*microcosm* (miniature world)
mis-	bad, wrong	*misconduct* (bad conduct), *misaligned* (wrongly aligned)
mono-	one	*monopoly* (exclusive control by one group), *monotheism* (belief in one god)
multi-	many	*multifaceted* (many sided), *multifarious* (varied, diverse)
neo-	new	*neologism* (new word), *neophyte* (beginner)
ob-	against	*object* (to express opposition), *obdurate* (hardened against feeling)
phil- (prefix or suffix)	lover	*bibliophile* (lover of books), *philanthropist* (lover of mankind)
poly-	many	*polygon* (a many-sided figure), *polyglot* (composed of several languages)
post-	after	*postscript* (something added after the closing in a piece of correspondence)
pre-	before	*presage* (to know beforehand), *precedent* (that which has previously occurred and may be used as an example)

Prefix	Meaning	Example
pro-	forward, in favor of	*proponent* (one who is in favor of), *progress* (to go forward)
pseudo-	false	*pseudonym* (a false name)
re-	again	*recede* (to go back again), recapitulate (to repeat in brief form)
retro-	back	*retrospect* (to look at the past)
sub-	below, under	*subordinate* (belonging to a lower class), *submission* (under the power of another)
super-	above, beyond	*superfluous* (beyond what is needed, extra), *superlative* (of the highest order)
sym-, syn-	with, together	*symmetry* (an even relationship of parts), *synchronize* (to occur at the same time)
trans-	across	*transmit* (to send from one person or place to another), *transplant* (to move from one place to another)
un-	not	*uneventful* (without incident), *unfruitful* (not productive)

Table 4-3		Suffixes
Suffix	**Meaning**	**Example**
-able, -ible	able, can do	*portable* (able to be carried)
-agogue	leader	*demagogue* (one who gains power by false promises)
-cide	to kill	*patricide* (the killing of the father)
-er or -eur	one who	*saboteur* (one who sabotages)
-ish	resembling	*foolish* (resembling a fool)
-ism	belief in	*socialism* (a system of government based on community ownership)
-ly	like	*innocuously* (in an innocent manner)
-ness	state of	*credulousness* (in a state of believing everything)
-ology	study of	*psychology* (the study of the human mind)
-phobia	fear of	*arachnophobia* (fear of spiders)
-tude	state of	*certitude* (certainty), *rectitude* (rightness)

Stockpiling Synonyms

When actually using words in written or spoken communication, *diction* (choosing the most precise word) matters. On the Officer Candidate Tests, shades of meaning are less important. Many of the Word Knowledge sections of the OCT challenge your ability to identify a *synonym* — a word that has pretty much the same meaning as the word in the question. Grouping words with similar meanings in your own mind helps you answer these questions correctly.

Many of the Word Knowledge sections of the OCT simply present a word and ask you to find the choice that is closest in meaning to the word in the question. Here's a sample synonym question:

The word <u>bolster</u> most nearly means

(A) seek.

(B) reject.

(C) contradict.

(D) support.

(E) encompass.

In this example, *bolster* is used as a verb, which you can figure out because all the words in the choices are verbs. (*Bolster* also can be used as a noun.) Your knowledge of Greek and Latin roots won't help because *bolster* is a word with Anglo-Saxon origins. In the best-case scenario, you know the meaning because you've encountered the word, either in your reading, conversations, or word study.

If the definition of *bolster* doesn't immediately pop into your mind, try to think of a situation in which you have heard or seen the word. It may occur to you that the pillows on your bed or couch at home are called *bolsters*. That thought may trigger an image of a bolster supporting your body, which would lead you to select Choice (D), *support*. When used as a verb, *bolster* means to support or to add to as in "to bolster public confidence in our elected officials."

On the AFQT (Armed Forces Qualifying Test) some of the synonym questions present the word in a sentence that may give you contextual clues. These clues allow you to use logical deduction to eliminate some (or sometimes all) of the incorrect choices. Here's a sample synonym question with the word used in a sentence:

By slipping through the forest, the troops <u>eluded</u> the enemy.

(A) relocated

(B) assembled

(C) invoked

(D) escaped

Avoid the distracters — words like *relocate* or *assemble* that are associated with troops — and apply logic and word knowledge to eliminate Choices (A), (B), and (C). The words *relocate* (to move to a new location), *assemble* (to gather together), and *invoke* (to call for or appeal to) don't make sense in light of the context clue in the sentence — "by slipping through the woods." It's logical, however, that slipping through the woods is an effective strategy for escaping enemy troops. The correct answer is Choice (D), *escaped*. *Elude* means *to avoid* or *escape*.

Try using index cards to help you study. Begin by writing a heading on the top of the card with the meaning of the words in the synonym cluster. Then list all the words that are similar in meaning to the word in the heading, grouping them by part of speech (adjectives, nouns, verbs, and so on). The following words and synonym clusters give you a head start on creating your first batch of cards.

Afraid

Adjectives: aghast, alarmed, apprehensive, cowardly, cowed, craven, distressed, frightened, horrified, petrified, shocked, terrified, timid

Arrogant

Adjectives: bombastic, conceited, egotistical, haughty, imperious, overbearing, peremptory, presumptuous, pretentious, pompous, proud, snobbish, supercilious, vainglorious

Bold or Courageous

Adjectives: adventurous, audacious, courageous, daring, dauntless, fearless, forceful, intrepid, resolute, valiant, valorous

Changeable

Adjectives: arbitrary, capricious, erratic, fickle, fluctuating, inconsistent, irresolute, mercurial, mutable, vacillating, variable, volatile, whimsical

Criticism/Criticize

Nouns: censure, disapprobation, disapproval, disparagement, obloquy, opprobrium, shame

Verbs: abuse, assail, bash, belittle, berate, blame, carp, castigate, censure, chastise, chide, condemn, denounce, disparage, excoriate, fulminate, impugn, malign, reprehend, reprimand, reprobate, revile, scathe, vilify

Hard-Working

Adjectives: assiduous, diligent, indefatigable, industrious, persistent, sedulous, unflagging, unrelenting

Harmful

Adjectives: baleful, baneful, deleterious, detrimental, inimical, injurious, lethal, malicious, nocuous, noxious, pernicious, sinister, virulent

Hatred/Hate

Nouns: anathema, animosity, animus, antipathy, aversion, malevolence, odium, repugnance, repulsion

Verbs: abhor, abominate, deprecate, despise, detest, execrate, loathe

Noisy

Adjectives: blatant, boisterous, clamorous, deafening, obstreperous, raucous, rowdy, strident, vociferous

Praise

Nouns: accolade, acclaim, adulation, approbation, commendation, encomium, eulogy, kudos, laudation, panegyric, reverence

Verbs: celebrate, commemorate, exalt, extol, laud, revere, worship

Quiet or Reserved

Adjectives: brief, brusque, concise, curt, laconic, pithy, reticent, succinct, taciturn, terse, uncommunicative

Short-Lived

Adjectives: ephemeral, evanescent, fleeting, fugitive, impermanent, transient, transitory

Stubborn

Adjectives: adamant, inflexible, intractable, intransigent, obdurate, obstinate, recalcitrant

Wordy or Talkative

Adjectives: effusive, garrulous, loquacious, prolix, redundant, voluble

Although slight differences in meaning among synonyms may not matter so much on the test, understanding the nuances of meaning helps improve your communication skills. For example, *obstinate, obdurate,* and *intractable* all mean *stubborn,* but the word that's best depends on the context or situation. At home, you may call a child or even your better half *stubborn,* but in a professional setting, *obstinate* may be the better choice. When describing a disease or symptom that's difficult to cure, neither *obstinate* nor *stubborn* really sounds right — *intractable* is the better choice.

Developing Meaningful Relationships with Analogies

If you're taking the AFOQT (Air Force Officer Qualifying Test), you need to brush up on not only definitions and synonyms but also the relationships between words. The AFOQT is the only Officer Candidate Test that contains *analogy questions* — questions that challenge you to determine the relationship between two words and then identify a word pair that has a similar relationship. Here's a sample:

GERANIUM is to PLANT as RACOON is to

(A) FUNGI

(B) MAMMAL

(C) RODENT

(D) ANIMAL

(E) CARTOON

In case you're curious, the correct answer is Choice (D). But relatively speaking, this example is pretty easy. The creators of the test are skilled at providing two or more answer choices that seem correct. The following sections provide valuable guidance in choosing the correct answer and ruling out the wrong ones.

If you're not taking the AFOQT, you can safely skip the following sections.

Fielding the two types of analogy questions

The AFOQT contains two types of analogy questions:

- ✔ **Three words given, you choose the fourth:** The question presents a pair of related words followed by the first word of the second pair, and you must choose the correct word to complete the second pair.

- ✔ **Two words given, you choose the correct pair:** The question presents a pair of related words, and you must identify the word pair with the most closely matching relationship.

The following sections provide examples and details of each type of analogy question, along with a technique for answering either type of question correctly.

Three words given, you choose the fourth

Here's an example of the first type of analogy question you'll encounter on the test:

COW is to CALF as CAT is to

(A) MEOW

(B) LITTER

(C) BABY

(D) KITTEN

(E) CUB

For this example, consider the relationship between cow and calf. You'd most likely describe the relationship like this: *A young cow is called a calf.* And, of course, you'd be right. Coming up with the sentence that identifies the relationship — your *relationship statement* — is the key to successfully answering analogy questions. As soon as you have that sentence, all you have to do is plug the third word into the sentence and then pick the fourth word (from the available choices) that completes the sentence best. Here's the process in a nutshell:

1. **Start with your relationship statement.**

   A young cow is called a calf.

2. **Remove the first word pair from the sentence.**

   A young _____ is called a _____.

3. **Plug the third word in the question into the first blank.**

   A young cat is called a _____.

4. **Choose the best word from the available choices to complete the sentence.**

   As you know, a young cat is not called a meow, litter, baby, or cub. The only choice that fits is kitten.

   A young cat is called a kitten.

Two words given, you choose the correct pair

Here's an example of the second type of analogy question:

CAPTAIN is to SHIP as

(A) AUTHOR is to BIOGRAPHY

(B) COUNSELOR is to ADVISOR

(C) PRINCIPAL is to SCHOOL

(D) CLIENT is to LAWYER

(E) MECHANIC is to CARBURETOR

Use a technique similar to the one described in the previous section to identify the correct answer:

1. **Start with your relationship statement.**

   A captain is the leader of a ship.

2. **Remove the first word pair from the sentence.**

   A _____ is the leader of a _____.

3. **Choose the best word pair from the available choices to complete the sentence.**

   Only one word pair makes sense:

   A principal is the leader of a school.

You can double-check your answer by trying to shoehorn the other word pairs into the sentence:

(A) *An author is the leader of a biography.*

(B) *A counselor is the leader of an advisor.*

(D) *A client is the leader of a lawyer.*

(E) *A mechanic is the leader of a carburetor.*

You can readily see that Choices (A), (B), (D), and (E) aren't even in the ballpark. The only possible answer is Choice (C).

When creating your relationship statement, make sure it includes the words that comprise the first word pair in the same order in which they appear in the question. Otherwise, you may tempt yourself to choose the wrong answer. In the following example, word order is key:

SPARROW is to BIRD as

(A) CARBURATOR is to VEHICLE

(B) CELERY is to VEGETABLE

(C) ORCHESTRA is to MELODY

(D) DOG is to BEAGLE

If your relationship sentence is *A sparrow is a type of bird,* you should choose Choice (B), which says *celery is a type of vegetable.* But if your relationship sentence is *A type of bird is a sparrow,* you may make the relationship sentence *A type of dog is a beagle,* and incorrectly choose Choice (D). While DOG and BEAGLE have the same relationship as SPARROW and BIRD, they aren't in the same order as the words in the question.

Avoiding the dreaded distracters

Distracters are choices that may pop into your mind because they're associated with the word in the question. In the "COW is to CALF as CAT is to _____" example presented earlier, Choice (A), meow, and Choice (B), litter, are distracters, because they're words we associate with cats. However, neither choice establishes a relationship with CAT that's similar to the relationship of COW to CALF.

To avoid falling for this trap, always read all the answers and plug them into your relationship statement to determine whether they fit.

By the way, Choice (C), baby, from the earlier COW to CALF example may also be considered a distracter, because if you look solely at the relationship expressed by the first word pair, you may conclude that "A calf is a baby cow," so Choice (C) is the correct answer. Unfortunately, you'd be wrong.

Minding your nouns and verbs

Just as a single meaning may be expressed in various words (synonyms), some words have more than one meaning, and some of those meanings may be totally different. Consider the word *tire.* When used as a noun, it describes the rubber part of a wheel. But when used as a verb, it means to become weary. (Hmm, we wonder why foreigners have such a tough time learning English.)

The OCT developers often use these different meanings to try to trip you up. Here are the keys to avoiding these traps:

 ✔ Never rule out an answer choice because you think a word is the wrong part of speech.

 ✔ Use your knowledge of parts of speech to help identify how a word is being used. If the question expresses a relationship in the first word pair of noun to verb, for example, *all* answer choices will have a noun to verb relationship.

 ✔ Stick with the plan to use your relationship statement to identify the correct word or word pair, and then double-check your answer.

Take a look at the following example:

SHRINK is to SIZE as

(A) INFLATE is to EXPANSION

(B) PRODUCE is to ACCOMPLISHMENT

(C) INCLUDE is to ELABORATION

(D) ENRICH is to INTENSITY

(E) FLAG is to ENERGY

At first glance, most people would be tempted to instantly eliminate Choice (E) because flag isn't a verb like shrink. Wrong move. Although flag is most commonly used as a noun to refer to a piece of cloth attached to a stick or pole, it also can be used as a verb meaning to decline in strength or vigor (which is the case here) or to signal. In this particular instance, you know flag is being used as a verb, because the question establishes a relationship in the first word pair of verb (shrink) to noun (size). Therefore, the first word of the second word pair must also be a verb, so flag must be being used in its verb form.

To answer this question correctly, stick with the plan:

1. **Start with your relationship statement.**

   Shrink is a reduction in size.

2. **Remove the first word pair from the sentence.**

   _____ *is a reduction in* _____.

3. **Choose the best word pair from the available choices to complete the sentence.**

   Flag is a reduction in energy.

Even if you don't know the meaning of *flag* as it's being used in the answer choice, you can arrive at the correct answer through the process of elimination. Plug each of the first four answer choices into your relationship statement, and you clearly see that none of the other choices fits:

(A) *Inflate is a reduction in expansion.*

(B) *Produce is a reduction in accomplishment.*

(C) *Include is a reduction in elaboration.*

(D) *Enrich is a reduction in intensity.*

Using familiar relationships to your advantage

Often the relationship in an analogy question fits into a predictable pattern. Recognize the pattern, and you significantly improve your chances of identifying the correct answer. If the first word pair expresses a relationship of opposites, for example, you know the second word pair must also be opposites. Consider this example:

HOT is to COLD as

(A) BREAD is to BUTTER

(B) SCISSORS is to PAPER

(C) HARD is to SOFT

(D) PLANT is to ANIMAL

(E) DESERT is to FOREST

Knowing that hot and cold are opposites, you can immediately identify the only word pair in the answer choices that expresses the relationship of opposites: Choice (C).

Table 4-4 presents a list of familiar relationships you can use to your advantage in answering analogy questions correctly. You certainly don't have to memorize them; just be familiar with them so you can move quickly (and accurately) through the analogy section of the test.

Stick with the plan. Use familiar relationships to construct your relationship statement. Here's an example:

1. **Start with your relationship statement.**

   Hot is the opposite of cold.

2. **Remove the first word pair from the sentence.**

   _____ *is the opposite of* _____.

3. **Choose the best word pair from the available choices to complete the sentence.**

   Hard is the opposite of soft.

Table 4-4	Familiar Relationships Used in Analogy Questions	
Relationship	*Example*	*Relationship Statement*
Type of	football is to sport	football is a type of sport
Home of	den is to lion	a den is the home of a lion
Made of	dress is to fabric	a dress is made of fabric
Part of	leg is to table	a leg is a part of a table
Characteristic of (or known for)	cheap is to miser	being cheap is a characteristic of a miser
Located in	books is to library	books are located in a library
Causes	deluge is to flood	a deluge causes a flood
Used for	wok is to cooking	a wok is used for cooking
Lacks	serious is to levity	something serious lacks levity
Unit of	ounce is to weight	an ounce is a unit of weight
An extreme degree	angry is to furious	an extreme degree of being angry is being furious
A group of	herd is to cows	a herd is a group of cows
Offspring of	gosling is to goose	a gosling is a young goose
Larger (or smaller) than	pond is to lake	a pond is smaller than a lake
Workplace of	school is to teacher	a school is the workplace of a teacher
Opposite of	content is to unhappy	someone content is the opposite of someone unhappy
Expression of	smile is to joy	a smile is an expression of joy

Chapter 5

Putting Your Word Skills to the Test

• •

Ready to test your new and improved vocabulary and try your hand at some Word Knowledge questions similar to those that appear on the Air Force Officer Qualifying Test (AFOQT) and the Armed Services Vocational Aptitude Battery (ASVAB)? This chapter is a good opportunity to evaluate your verbal ability. Are you a vocabulary guru, or do you need to spend more quality time with your personal flashcards? Answer the practice questions we provide in this chapter to find out. (If you find that more review is in order, turn to Chapter 4 for info on using flashcards and other ways to build your word skills.)

 To fully immerse yourself in the test-taking experience, time yourself on these sample tests. If you run out of time before answering all the questions, make a note to yourself that you need to improve your pace by the time the test date rolls around, and then finish answering the remaining questions.

Squaring Off with Analogy Questions

Here's your chance to practice the techniques we describe for answering analogy questions in Chapter 4. The following questions measure your word knowledge and your ability to reason. Choose the answer that best completes each analogy.

 Don't dawdle — the analogy section of the AFOQT has 25 questions, and you have just 8 minutes to answer all the questions. That boils down to about 19 seconds per question, which means you have to work very quickly. The route to success with analogies lies in creating good relationship sentences.

1. ANGLER is to FISHING as MARKSMAN is to

   (A) HIKING

   (B) SWIMMING

   (C) SPRINTING

   (D) RIFLERY

   (E) DRAWING

2. PEPPER is to SPICE as

   (A) ONION is to TEARS

   (B) KNIFE is to CUT

   (C) BAYONET is to WEAPON

   (D) DOE is to DOVE

   (E) COFFEE is to TEA

3. PISTON is to ENGINE as

    (A) BLACKSMITH is to IRON

    (B) ORE is to GOLD

    (C) WHEEL is to ROUND

    (D) CAR is to BRAKES

    (E) ACT is to PLAY

4. TALKATIVE is to RETICENT as HUMBLE is to

    (A) SILENT

    (B) ARROGANT

    (C) STINGY

    (D) BLEAK

    (E) GENEROUS

5. GYM is to EXERCISE as

    (A) TRAIL is to DIAGNOSE

    (B) WINTER is to SKATE

    (C) ICEBERG is to MELT

    (D) STORE is to SHOP

    (E) ARMY is to DISCHARGE

6. FROWN is to UNHAPPINESS as SNEER is to

    (A) SYMPATHY

    (B) UNEASE

    (C) CONTEMPT

    (D) FRUSTRATION

    (E) BLISS

7. KNOT is to SPEED as

    (A) BOW is to SHIP

    (B) CENTIMETER is to LENGTH

    (C) GIANT is to HEIGHT

    (D) GRAM is to MEASUREMENT

    (E) FACET is to DIAMOND

8. ANOMALY is to STANDARD as DEVIATION is to

    (A) PATH

    (B) ABNORMALITY

    (C) FRACTURE

    (D) ENLARGEMENT

    (E) PROP

9. NOVICE is to EXPERIENCE as WASTREL is to
    (A) PRISON
    (B) GARBAGE
    (C) VIGOR
    (D) THRIFT
    (E) IGNORANCE

10. RETREAT is to POSITION as
    (A) RETURN is to RETRACTION
    (B) PROMOTE is to PROGRESS
    (C) REGRESS is to DEVELOPMENT
    (D) UNLEASH is to POWER
    (E) WHISPER is to LANGUAGE

11. CARPENTER is to SAW as SURGEON is to
    (A) NURSE
    (B) ANESTHESIA
    (C) CLAMP
    (D) SCALPEL
    (E) GLOVES

12. CAREFUL is to METICULOUS as
    (A) DURABLE is to FLEETING
    (B) IMPLAUSIBLE is to ABSURD
    (C) BRIEF is to ENDURING
    (D) FUSSY is to LENIENT
    (E) POMPOUS is to EARTHY

13. MUTINOUS is to OBEDIENCE as
    (A) SARCASTIC is to HUMOR
    (B) INDIRECT is to SUBTLETY
    (C) MYSTERIOUS is to ARCANE
    (D) INDELIBLE is to PERMANENCE
    (E) RIGID is to FLEXIBILITY

14. CREST is to WAVE as
    (A) TRUNK is to CAR
    (B) CLIFF is to PRECIPICE
    (C) VALLEY is to HILL
    (D) SUMMIT is to MOUNTAIN
    (E) TAIL is to AIRPLANE

15. OSTENTATIOUS is to DISPLAY as

    (A) MODEST is to TASTE

    (B) FLAMBOYANT is to DRESS

    (C) SEVERE is to PUNISHMENT

    (D) DIM is to ILLUMINATION

    (E) DECEPTIVE is to LIE

16. EXTRICATE is to TRAP as EXONERATE is to

    (A) PRIVILEGE

    (B) REGULATION

    (C) DEFENSE

    (D) ACQUITTAL

    (E) BLAME

17. CARNIVOROUS is to LION as

    (A) ITINERANT is to NOMAD

    (B) FLASHY is to PRUDE

    (C) INDEFENSIBLE is to CONVICTION

    (D) HOSTILE is to ELEPHANT

    (E) GREEDY is to CORPORATION

18. VACUITY is to INSIGHT as CREDULITY is to

    (A) PROPRIETY

    (B) CANDOR

    (C) SKEPTICISM

    (D) INDIGNATION

    (E) AWE

19. MERCILESS is to COMPASSION as INEPT is to

    (A) EMULATION

    (B) DISGUISE

    (C) OPPRESSION

    (D) PROFICIENCY

    (E) REFUGE

20. SAPLING is to TREE as

    (A) OFFICIAL is to SUPERVISOR

    (B) EXPERT is to BEGINNER

    (C) FLEDGLING is to BIRD

    (D) BEAR is to CUB

    (E) GANDER is to GOOSE

21. STABILIZE is to FLUCTUATION as RELIEVE is to

    (A) INSENSITIVITY

    (B) SIMILARITY

    (C) LONGEVITY

    (D) DISTRESS

    (E) AFFECTIVITY

22. AMELIORATE is to EXACERBATE as EXCULPATE is to

    (A) CONSUME

    (B) EMPOWER

    (C) DRAFT

    (D) DIVULGE

    (E) CONDEMN

23. AMIABLE is to HOSTILE as INTREPID is to

    (A) ADAMANT

    (B) FRIENDLY

    (C) COWARDLY

    (D) EFFUSIVE

    (E) PENITENT

24. DELETERIOUS is to HARM as DISGUSTING is to

    (A) DEFIANCE

    (B) REVERENCE

    (C) PERSISTENCE

    (D) ARROGANCE

    (E) REPUGNANCE

25. INCENTIVE is to ENCOURAGE as

    (A) RUSE is to DECEIVE

    (B) GLIMMER is to DIMINISH

    (C) DISASTER is to DELIGHT

    (D) SIGNAL is to PERPLEX

    (E) OVERTURE is to ENLIGHTEN

Playing The Match Game

The Word Knowledge sections of both the AFOQT and the ASVAB measure your vocabulary comprehension by testing your knowledge of synonyms. Think of this section as the Armed Services' version of *The Match Game.* You must match the word in the question to the answer that most nearly means the same.

Testing your synonym knowledge on the AFOQT

On the AFOQT, each question consists of a word and five choices. You must pick the answer that is closest in meaning to the capitalized word in the question. In other words, look for a synonym.

Charge! Move through this section of the test quickly! The Word Knowledge subtest of the AFOQT has 25 questions that you must answer in 5 minutes. So you have only about 12 seconds per question.

1. ACCLAIM
   (A) admit
   (B) unleash
   (C) insist
   (D) praise
   (E) require

2. DIVULGE
   (A) reveal
   (B) conceal
   (C) divide
   (D) risk
   (E) incite

3. TIMID
   (A) surly
   (B) profound
   (C) masterful
   (D) indulgent
   (E) fearful

4. HEARTEN
   (A) garner
   (B) encourage
   (C) revoke
   (D) overrun
   (E) dominate

5. APPRAISE
   (A) evaluate
   (B) inform
   (C) flatter
   (D) admonish
   (E) confirm

6. FEIGN

  (A) derive

  (B) rebuke

  (C) horrify

  (D) defend

  (E) pretend

7. PLIANT

  (A) omnipotent

  (B) patriotic

  (C) brilliant

  (D) supple

  (E) average

8. VALOROUS

  (A) courageous

  (B) self-centered

  (C) provincial

  (D) humorous

  (E) altruistic

9. LABORIOUS

  (A) uneasy

  (B) difficult

  (C) weary

  (D) confusing

  (E) endless

10. NAÏVE

  (A) chilly

  (B) misguided

  (C) unsophisticated

  (D) tricky

  (E) inconspicuous

11. ESTEEM

  (A) curiosity

  (B) respect

  (C) envy

  (D) humility

  (E) reserve

12. BREVITY

  (A) briefness

  (B) honor

  (C) vastness

  (D) panorama

  (E) conflagration

13. AMBIGUOUS

  (A) dexterous

  (B) specific

  (C) vague

  (D) primordial

  (E) experimental

14. PROFUSE

  (A) traditional

  (B) profound

  (C) reluctant

  (D) abundant

  (E) eloquent

15. QUALM

  (A) secret

  (B) confidence

  (C) speck

  (D) doubt

  (E) query

16. PUTREFY

  (A) spread

  (B) deepen

  (C) fawn

  (D) distill

  (E) rot

17. REITERATE

  (A) reconfigure

  (B) redirect

  (C) reconnoiter

  (D) repeat

  (E) rebound

18. AUDACIOUS
    - (A) bold
    - (B) lucky
    - (C) golden
    - (D) famous
    - (E) skillful

19. CRAVEN
    - (A) cowardly
    - (B) needy
    - (C) indirect
    - (D) particular
    - (E) yearning

20. PROBITY
    - (A) suction
    - (B) illusion
    - (C) retention
    - (D) activity
    - (E) integrity

21. TEMERITY
    - (A) delicacy
    - (B) notoriety
    - (C) obesity
    - (D) virtuosity
    - (E) effrontery

22. VERACITY
    - (A) intensity
    - (B) hostility
    - (C) severity
    - (D) truthfulness
    - (E) asperity

23. VOLATILE
    - (A) protective
    - (B) explosive
    - (C) weak
    - (D) spacious
    - (E) therapeutic

24. SULLY

    (A) dirty

    (B) soothe

    (C) conform

    (D) prevent

    (E) glide

25. ABERRATION

    (A) alignment

    (B) atonement

    (C) aspersion

    (D) anomaly

    (E) alliteration

Testing your Word Knowledge on the ASVAB AFQT

On the ASVAB AFQT, the Word Knowledge subtest consists of 35 questions followed by four answer choices. Each question consists of an underlined word alone or in a sentence. You must find the word in the answer choices that most nearly means the same as the underlined word in the question.

You have 11 minutes for this section, which means you have only about 19 seconds per question. So be speedy!

1. <u>Meddle</u> most nearly means

    (A) construct

    (B) interfere

    (C) refer

    (D) alter

2. <u>Dogmatic</u> most nearly means

    (A) cruel

    (B) ignorant

    (C) unconscious

    (D) opinionated

3. <u>Antithetical</u> most nearly means

    (A) genuine

    (B) damaged

    (C) opposite

    (D) secular

4. Remorse most nearly means

   (A) regret

   (B) remit

   (C) reinforce

   (D) regular

5. Rancorous most nearly means

   (A) pure

   (B) bitter

   (C) sluggish

   (D) energetic

6. Candid most nearly means

   (A) hidden

   (B) sweet

   (C) honest

   (D) terrible

7. Ferocity most nearly means

   (A) viciousness

   (B) abruptness

   (C) blindness

   (D) decisiveness

8. Nefarious most nearly means

   (A) ambitious

   (B) dependable

   (C) wicked

   (D) joyous

9. Innocuous most nearly means

   (A) sympathetic

   (B) sociable

   (C) reliable

   (D) harmless

10. Petulance most nearly means

   (A) affluence

   (B) irritability

   (C) nuisance

   (D) alliance

11. <u>Tacit</u> most nearly means

    (A) crooked

    (B) mammoth

    (C) unspoken

    (D) tasteless

12. <u>Euphonious</u> most nearly means

    (A) numerous

    (B) melodious

    (C) ingenious

    (D) infinite

13. <u>Curt</u> most nearly means

    (A) witty

    (B) odd

    (C) brief

    (D) bright

14. <u>Fallacious</u> most nearly means

    (A) unable

    (B) proud

    (C) insistent

    (D) false

15. <u>Evasive</u> most nearly means

    (A) avoiding

    (B) attacking

    (C) tempting

    (D) increasing

16. <u>Furtive</u> most nearly means

    (A) bestial

    (B) sneaky

    (C) shrill

    (D) spiritual

17. <u>Ludicrous</u> most nearly means

    (A) excellent

    (B) preposterous

    (C) venomous

    (D) rare

18. <u>Robust</u> most nearly means

    (A) hearty

    (B) supreme

    (C) quaint

    (D) wise

19. <u>Utopian</u> most nearly means

    (A) mystical

    (B) perfect

    (C) youthful

    (D) mighty

20. <u>Unilateral</u> most nearly means

    (A) undervalued

    (B) overrated

    (C) one-sided

    (D) inconclusive

21. The <u>opulence</u> of the mansion awed even the most sophisticated guests.

    (A) unattractiveness

    (B) bleakness

    (C) simplicity

    (D) lavishness

22. After investing in a <u>lucrative</u> land deal, the young man enjoyed his prosperity.

    (A) extravagant

    (B) profitable

    (C) frugal

    (D) unlawful

23. A veteran teacher, Mr. North <u>deplores</u> the substitution of technology for good teaching.

    (A) sustains

    (B) prioritizes

    (C) pursues

    (D) dislikes

24. Many reality TV stars find that fame is <u>ephemeral</u>.

    (A) transitory

    (B) desirable

    (C) impossible

    (D) objective

25. Unlike the sprightly writing of his previous novel, the new piece was downright <u>insipid</u>.

    (A) incredible

    (B) bland

    (C) enthralling

    (D) vicious

26. In his post-game commentary, the sportscaster <u>extolled</u> the skills of the new quarterback.

    (A) exorcised

    (B) reviled

    (C) celebrated

    (D) ignored

27. The senator's gruff manner and <u>acerbic</u> comments alienated his listeners.

    (A) caustic

    (B) sentimental

    (C) brazen

    (D) astute

28. Surprisingly, the <u>debacle</u> the townspeople expected when the mayor fired the entire police force never occurred.

    (A) accommodation

    (B) expansion

    (C) quarrel

    (D) disaster

29. As fog shrouded the region, the city landmarks became <u>indiscernible</u>.

    (A) decorative

    (B) historical

    (C) diminutive

    (D) unclear

30. The corporal was forced to face the dire consequences of his <u>seditious</u> acts.

    (A) courageous

    (B) treasonous

    (C) obscure

    (D) military

31. The <u>imperious</u> attitude of the judge irritated the defendant.

    (A) benevolent

    (B) arrogant

    (C) erratic

    (D) litigious

32. When both sides were unable to reach accord, the meeting became <u>contentious</u>.

    (A) happy

    (B) boring

    (C) argumentative

    (D) agreeable

33. The <u>rambunctious</u> kindergartners frolicked in the playground.

    (A) noisy

    (B) fretful

    (C) amiable

    (D) obedient

34. After her defection to a rival company, Ms. Richards found herself a <u>pariah</u> among her former colleagues.

    (A) leader

    (B) disciple

    (C) recidivist

    (D) outcast

35. Although the president's remarks were <u>terse</u>, most reporters appreciated his efforts.

    (A) humorous

    (B) brief

    (C) accurate

    (D) unwarranted

Looking at the Correct Answers

This section provides answers to the earlier sample word skills tests along with explanations of why each answer is correct, so use it to check your answers. If you came up with the wrong answer for a question, read the explanation to develop an understanding of why the correct answer is accurate. Doing so can help you develop the reasoning skills required for choosing correct answers on the test.

Checking your answers to the analogy questions

This section gives you the answers to the AFOQT practice questions in the earlier section "Squaring Off with Analogy Questions." The answer to the first question elaborates on how you arrive at the correct answer; the answers to the subsequent questions are more succinct, but always begin by showing you an accurate relationship statement.

1. **D.** Your relationship sentence may be something like this: "The sport of an *angler* is *fishing;* the sport of a *marksman* is _____." This sentence leads you very nicely to *riflery* — the sport of a marksman. None of the other choices has a relationship with *marksman*.

2. **C.** *Pepper* is a type of *spice; bayonet* is a type of *weapon.* None of the other choices fits a "type of" relationship.

3. **E.** A *piston* is part of an *engine;* an *act* is part of a *play.* Be careful to keep your relationship words in the correct order. Otherwise, you may be misled by Choice (D): A *car* is not part of *brakes,* although brakes are a part of a car.

4. **B.** A *talkative* person is not *reticent;* a *humble* person is not *arrogant.* None of the other choices fits this relationship sentence.

5. **D.** A *gym* is a place where you *exercise;* a *store* is a place where you *shop.* Don't be distracted by Choice (B): *winter* is a time (not a place). And don't be misled by Choice (E) either: *army* is not a place where you discharge.

6. **C.** A *frown* is an expression of *unhappiness;* a *sneer* is an expression of *contempt.* None of the other choices are expressions that are commonly characterized by a sneer.

7. **B.** A *knot* is a unit of *speed;* a *centimeter* is a unit of *length.* Don't be distracted by Choice (D): A *gram* is a unit, but it is a unit of mass, not measurement.

8. **A.** An *anomaly* is something irregular, so it diverges from the *standard.* A *deviation* diverges from the *path.* Don't be distracted by Choice (B): An *anomaly* is an *abnormality,* so this choice may tempt you. Just remember the relationship sentence rule, and you won't fall into traps like this one.

9. **D.** A *novice* lacks *experience;* a *wastrel* (someone who wastes) lacks *thrift.* None of the other choices fits the relationship sentence.

10. **C.** *Retreat* is to move back in *position; regress* is to move back in *development.* None of the other choices fits the relationship sentence.

11. **D.** A *carpenter* uses a *saw* to cut; a *surgeon* uses a *scalpel* to cut. This example is a good reminder of the importance of making your relationship sentences specific. If you just think "a carpenter uses a saw," you get multiple answers: A surgeon may use anesthesia, a clamp, a scalpel, or gloves. (In some cases, he may even "use" a nurse.) So, to be accurate, be specific and state what the carpenter uses the saw to do.

12. **B.** This is "an extreme degree" relationship. *Careful* taken to an extreme degree is *meticulous; implausible* to an extreme degree is *absurd.* None of the other choices fits the relationship sentence.

13. **E.** Someone *mutinous* lacks *obedience;* someone *rigid* lacks *flexibility.* None of the other choices fits the relationship sentence.

14. **D.** A *crest* is the top of a *wave;* a *summit* is the top of a *mountain.* Again, be sure to be specific: If you just think "a crest is a part of a wave," you may be tempted by Choice (A): *trunk* is to *car.* Or you may be tempted by Choice (E): *tail* is to *airplane.*

15. **B.** *Ostentatious* describes a very showy *display; flamboyant* describes very showy *dress.* None of the other choices fits the relationship sentence.

16. **E.** To *extricate* is to free from a *trap;* to *exonerate* is to free from *blame.* Don't be misled by words that are associated with the word *exonerate,* like *acquittal* and *defense.* While they're often used in the same context as exoneration, these choices don't fit the relationship sentence.

17. **A.** *Carnivorous* (meat eating) is a word that describes a *lion; itinerant* (traveling from place to place) is a word that describes a *nomad.* Now, you may know some flashy prudes or hostile elephants or even greedy corporations, but these aren't the essential adjectives commonly attributed to the nouns that follow them.

18. **C.** *Vacuity* is the lack of *insight; credulity* (gullibility) is the lack of *skepticism.* None of the other choices fits the relationship sentence.

19. **D.** Someone *merciless* lacks *compassion;* someone *inept* lacks *proficiency.* None of the other choices fits the relationship sentence.

20. **C.** A *sapling* is a young *tree;* a *fledgling* is a young *bird.* Choice (D) has the correct relationship in the wrong order. None of the other choices fits the relationship sentence.

21. **D.** To *stabilize* is to reduce *fluctuation;* to *relieve* is to reduce *distress.* None of the other choices fits the relationship sentence.

22. **E.** To *ameliorate* (to make better) is the opposite of to *exacerbate* (to make worse); to *exculpate* (to free from blame) is the opposite of to *condemn.* None of the other choices fits the relationship sentence.

23. **C.** *Amiable* is the opposite of *hostile; intrepid* (brave) is the opposite of *cowardly.* None of the other choices fits the relationship sentence.

24. **E.** Something *deleterious* causes *harm;* something *disgusting* causes *repugnance* (a synonym for disgust). None of the other choices fits the relationship sentence.

25. **A.** An *incentive* is used to *encourage;* a *ruse* (a trick) is used to *deceive.* None of the other choices fits the relationship sentence.

Checking your answers to the AFOQT Word Knowledge questions

Following are the correct answers to the practice questions presented in the earlier section "Testing your synonym knowledge on the AFOQT," along with an explanation of why each answer is correct.

1. **D.** *Acclaim* (noun or verb) means *praise.*

2. **A.** *Divulge* (verb) means *to reveal.*

3. **E.** *Timid* (adjective) means *shy* or *fearful.*

4. **B.** *Hearten* (verb) means *to encourage.*

5. **A.** *Appraise* (verb) means *to evaluate the worth.*

6. **E.** *Feign* (verb) means to *pretend* or *fake.*

7. **D.** *Pliant* (adjective) means *flexible* or *supple.*

8. **A.** *Valorous* (adjective) means *brave* or *courageous.*

9. **B.** *Laborious* (adjective) means *difficult* (*labor = work*).

10. **C.** *Naïve* (adjective) means *innocent, unworldly,* or *unsophisticated.*

11. **B.** *Esteem* (noun or verb) means *respect.*

12. **A.** *Brevity* (noun) means *briefness* (*brev* = *brief*).

13. **C.** *Ambiguous* (adjective) means *vague* or *unclear.*

14. **D.** *Profuse* (adjective) means *abundant.*

15. **D.** *Qualm* (noun) means *doubt* or *uneasiness.*

16. **E.** *Putrefy* (verb) means *to rot* (*fy* = *to make,* as in *to make putrid* or *rotten*).

17. **D.** *Reiterate* (verb) means *to repeat* (*re* = *again*).

18. **A.** *Audacious* (adjective) means *bold* or *daring.*

19. **A.** *Craven* (adjective) means *cowardly.*

20. **E.** *Probity* (noun) means *honesty* or *integrity.*

21. **E.** *Temerity* (noun) means *nerve, boldness,* or *effrontery.*

22. **D.** *Veracity* (noun) means *truthfulness* (*ver* = *truth*).

23. **B.** *Volatile* (adjective) means *unstable* or *explosive.*

24. **A.** *Sully* (verb) means *to dirty* or *discredit.*

25. **D.** *Aberration* (noun) means an *abnormality* or *anomaly.*

Checking your answers to the ASVAB AFQT Word Knowledge questions

Following are the correct answers to the practice questions for the Word Knowledge subtest of the ASVAB AFQT found in the earlier section "Testing your Word Knowledge on the ASVAB AFQT." We include an explanation for why each answer is correct.

1. **B.** *Meddle* (verb) means *to interfere.*

2. **D.** *Dogmatic* (adjective) means *doctrinaire* or *rigidly opinionated.*

3. **C.** *Antithetical* (adjective) means *opposite* (*anti* = *against*).

4. **A.** *Remorse* (noun) means *regret.*

5. **B.** *Rancorous* (adjective) means *bitter.*

6. **C.** *Candid* (adjective) means *honest* or *frank.* (If you think of the old TV show *Candid Camera,* you may be misled by the distracter *hidden,* but the point of the show was to catch people in honest, and often funny, situations.)

7. **A.** *Ferocity* (noun) means *fierceness* or *viciousness.*

8. **C.** *Nefarious* (adjective) means *evil* or *wicked.*

9. **D.** *Innocuous* (adjective) means *innocent* or *harmless.*

10. **B.** *Petulance* (noun) means *crankiness* or *childish irritability.*

11. **C.** *Tacit* (adjective) means *unspoken.* (A taciturn person is very quiet and aloof.)

12. **B.** *Euphonious* (adjective) means *melodious* or *pleasant sounding* (*eu* = *good; phon* = *sound*).

13. **C.** *Curt* (adjective) means *brief, abrupt,* or *rude* (because of briefness).

14. **D.** *Fallacious* (adjective) means *false.*

15. **A.** *Evasive* (adjective) means *avoiding* or *escaping*.

16. **B.** *Furtive* (adjective) means *sneaky* or *secretive*.

17. **B.** *Ludicrous* (adjective) means *ridiculous* or *preposterous*.

18. **A.** *Robust* (adjective) means *strong* or *hearty*.

19. **B.** *Utopian* (adjective) means *perfect*. (In 1516, Sir Thomas More described an imaginary island he called Utopia as a perfect society.)

20. **C.** *Unilateral* (adjective) means *one-sided* (*uni* = *one*).

21. **D.** *Opulence* (adjective) means *lavishness* or *wealth*.

22. **B.** *Lucrative* (adjective) means *profitable*.

23. **D.** *Deplores* (verb) means *dislikes* or *disapproves of*.

24. **A.** *Ephemeral* (adjective) means *short-lived* or *transitory*.

25. **B.** *Insipid* (adjective) means *tasteless* or *bland*.

26. **C.** *Extolled* (verb) means *praised highly* or *celebrated*.

27. **A.** *Acerbic* (adjective) means *bitter, cutting,* or *sarcastic*.

28. **D.** *Debacle* (noun) means a *disaster*.

29. **D.** *Indiscernible* (adjective) means *hard to see* or *unclear*.

30. **B.** *Seditious* (adjective) means *treasonous*.

31. **B.** *Imperious* (adjective) means *arrogant* or *commanding*.

32. **C.** *Contentious* (adjective) means *argumentative*.

33. **A.** *Rambunctious* (adjective) means *noisy* or *unruly*.

34. **D.** *Pariah* (noun) means an *outcast*.

35. **B.** *Terse* (adjective) means *brief* or *abrupt*.

Chapter 6

Building Your Reading Skills

In This Chapter

▶ Reading actively and staying A. L. E. R. T.

▶ Knowing where in a paragraph to find the answers you need

▶ Adapting your reading technique to suit varying subjects

▶ Skimming a passage for answers and confirmation

▶ Drawing conclusions from the facts you're given

The military is full of paperwork: forms, instructions, orders, regulations, and technical material for your job. As an officer, you must be able to read and process all the words and information contained in this paperwork efficiently and effectively. Careful reading gives you the knowledge you need to fulfill your duties and sharpens your mind. It can even prevent serious mistakes — after all, when you're dealing with life-or-death situations, a minor misunderstanding can lead to a major catastrophe. Effective reading also is the key to success in many other arenas, including the Officer Candidate Tests, or OCT.

This chapter helps you prepare for the reading comprehension sections (Paragraph Comprehension on the Armed Services Vocational Aptitude Battery-Air Force Qualifying Test, or ASVAB-AFQT, and Reading Skills on the Aviation Selection Test Battery, or ASTB) of the OCT as well as all the reading you'll be doing throughout and beyond your military career.

The Air Force Officer Qualifying Test (AFOQT) doesn't include a Reading Comprehension section.

Attention! Being an Active Reader

The OCT declare open season on subject matter, covering a variety of topics — science, history, politics, business, current events, the arts, and literature. And while the examinee sitting next to you may find the life cycle of the blue-footed booby fascinating, you may find yourself yawning your way through the reading passage, remembering only that "blue-footed booby" sounds funny. Because you have no choice of topics, you need to train yourself to be an active reader, especially when reading material you have absolutely no interest in.

Pay attention! Nothing is more dangerous to reading comprehension than *drifting* — reading in which your eyes move down the page, but your brain has drifted far away after the first two sentences. In addition to leaving you without the information you need to answer the questions correctly, drifting wastes precious time.

Basic training for active reading

The military loves acronyms, so we introduce one here that applies specifically to improving reading comprehension. To be an active reader, you have to be A.L.E.R.T:

A **Actively** engage in what the writer is discussing. Hook into the topic, and, for a few minutes at least, "care" about what you're reading.

L **Listen** to the "voice" of the writer and imagine engaging in a dialogue with him or her. Think of questions you'd ask the writer in person or comments you'd make.

E **Expect** that which is to come. Try to anticipate and predict where the writer is going. Whether your expectations prove right or wrong, they tend to help you remember the information in the passage that confirmed or refuted your expectations.

R **Restate** the main idea of the passage to yourself. Repetition is key to retention.

T **Think** while you read. Never allow your brain to go off duty.

Stay interested in the passage. Link the passage in your mind to a familiar topic — something you've read about or experienced in the past. This strategy helps you stay engaged and focused.

More reading comprehension tactics

Being an active reader is crucial to developing a clear understanding of reading passages, but when you're being tested on the material, you can do more. Following are some additional strategies for improving your reading efficiency and helping you spot key information:

- ✔ **If you're confused by a sentence, don't reread it.** Time is essential! The sentence may become clearer as you read, or the questions may not apply to that part of the passage. If you must reread, do so as you answer the questions.

- ✔ **Take notes on scrap paper if the passage is dense or confusing.** These notes don't have to be extensive; just jot down the main idea, plot, or a cause-and-effect relationship.

- ✔ **Watch for key words and phrases that indicate a shift or transition in the passage**. A passage may appear to present a position that the author supports and then do an about-face with "but" or "however," negating the stated position. If you miss the "but" or "however," a wrong answer is almost a certainty.

The benefits of reading

Although many Americans learn a lot from visual sources, including television, documentaries, and Web-based media, they still acquire most of their knowledge from reading. In almost any activity or job, you're confronted by printed material. Whether you're reading a book, newspaper, popular magazine, Web page, or training manual, you need to read effectively to understand the written word.

Reading not only equips you with knowledge and understanding, but it's also an excellent activity for keeping your brain in tip-top condition. You may not realize it, but active reading forces you to think, often on a subconscious level. Your thinking becomes sharper even when you're too deeply immersed in what you're reading to notice.

Strategies for answering reading comprehension questions

A crystal-clear understanding of a reading passage doesn't guarantee all correct answers. Answer choices are designed to trip up the unwary examinee, so be sure to extend your active reading to the questions. Here are some strategies for reading and choosing answers more carefully:

- **Don't allow your personal feelings or your own knowledge about the topic to influence your answers.** Always go back to what the text states or implies, even if you know more about the topic than the writer does. (This tactic is especially true on the ASTB Reading Skills subtest, because answering correctly requires finding textual evidence to support a statement.)

- **Always read *all* the choices before you select an answer.** Use the process of elimination as you read the choices. If you're sure an answer is wrong, eliminate it. After you've read all the choices, look again at only the choices you haven't eliminated, and evaluate their accuracy.

- **Don't second-guess questions that appear to be too easy.** If a question appears overly easy, especially near the beginning of a section, don't assume that the obviously correct answer is a trap. It may well be a trap, but it's more likely to be the correct answer. In other words, don't talk yourself out of a correct answer.

- **On the CAT-ASVAB (the computer adaptive version), take your time on the first few questions.** Because the CAT is adaptive, it adjusts to your level of ability. You want to be sure to get the first few questions correct so the computer increases the level of difficulty. Difficult questions are worth more than easy ones.

Don't be fooled by an answer that makes a correct statement but fails to address the question. A statement may be true based on the information in the passage, but it may still be the wrong answer because it doesn't address the question.

Using Paragraph Structure to Your Advantage

A paragraph, like a story, has a beginning, a middle, and an end:

- **Beginning:** Typically, though not always, this is a *topic sentence* (sometimes referred to as the *thesis*), which states the main point.

- **Middle:** Sandwiched in the middle are the details or facts that develop or support the topic sentence.

- **End:** The final sentence typically restates the main point, summarizes the supporting details, and/or extends and broadens the main idea.

Having a clear understanding of how most paragraphs are structured is valuable in identifying the main point and supporting details — the two things you need to answer most questions correctly. In the following sections, you discover how to use the predictability of paragraph structure to your advantage in choosing correct answers.

Getting the gist of it right from the start: Main ideas and main purposes

Nearly every well-written paragraph has one and only one main idea or purpose. Your job is to figure out what it is. Doing so not only helps you answer main-idea or main-purpose questions correctly, but it also provides a context for remembering the supporting details.

On the ASVAB-AFQT, don't confuse main-idea questions with main-purpose questions. The two are entirely different animals. On the ASTB, however, this distinction isn't an issue. All ASTB reading comprehension questions ask you to select a statement that can be inferred from the passage.

- Main-idea questions address *what* the passage is about.

- Main-purpose questions focus on the author's agenda — *why* the author wrote the passage — to inform, explain, or persuade.

The following sections distinguish main-idea and main-purpose questions, reveal techniques for approaching each type of question, and provide sample passages and questions to give you hands-on experience in fielding these types of questions.

Be sure to distinguish between the main idea and supporting detail. The supporting detail provides the evidence to support or prove the main idea or claim.

Answering main-idea questions

The ASVAB-AFQT may pose main-idea questions in any of the following several ways:

- What is the main idea of the passage?

- With which of the following statements would the author most likely agree?

- What is the best title for the passage?

- This passage is primarily concerned with. . . .

To answer a main-idea question, try to sum up the gist of the passage in one sentence of 25 words or less. You may even want to think about this question as you first read the passage. Here's a sample passage followed by a main-idea question similar to one you may encounter on the ASVAB-AFQT:

> Airline travel is far from the pleasurable adventure it was before events of the past decade made safety a priority. Now passengers wait in long security lines as they approach checkpoints where they empty their pockets and remove their shoes, jackets, scarves, and belts. Carry-on items such as liquids and electronics are limited and carefully scrutinized by TSA personnel. And, of course, all this increased security comes with a hefty price tag that is factored into increased fares. Flying to an exotic destination has become more of an annoyance than the start of an exciting journey.

Knowing that the main idea is usually expressed at the beginning and end of a paragraph, you can easily spot it. From the first sentence, you know that "Airline travel is far from the pleasurable adventure it was before events of the past decade made safety a priority." And from the last sentence, you learn that "Flying to an exotic destination has become more of an annoyance than the start of an exciting journey." You're now well-prepared to answer a main-idea question, such as the following:

Which of the following best states the main point of the paragraph?

(A) Passengers must remove their outerwear as they go through the security check.

(B) Rules regarding carry-on items have changed in the past decade.

(C) All passengers should arrive at the airport early because security lines are notoriously long.

(D) Increased security has made air travel more frustrating and costly than it has been in the past.

Choice (D) is the correct answer. Based on the question, you know you're looking for the main idea. Remember that the main idea is often stated in the topic sentence and summarized in the conclusion, so reread the first and last sentences of the passage. In this case, the main idea is that flying has become irritating and costly — Choice (D). Choice (A) is true, but it is a supporting detail in the passage. Choice (B) is also true, but it isn't the main point. Choice (C) is true as well, but it isn't directly discussed in the passage.

On the ASTB, the reading passages aren't followed by specific questions. Each passage is followed by four statements. Your task is to find the statement that can be accurately inferred from the information in the passage. For the preceding passage on airline travel, you may encounter the following choices on the ASTB:

(A) Every passenger on a commercial airline flight must show a picture ID before boarding.

(B) Airlines have passed on increased security costs to the consumers.

(C) Carry-on bags can contain no electronic equipment.

(D) Many airports have added X-ray technology to the routine screening of passengers.

The correct answer is Choice (B). On the ASTB Reading Skills test, you're not looking for the main idea or the main purpose. You're choosing the one statement from among the four choices that is supported by evidence directly stated or implied in the passage. Wrong answers are often true statements that aren't supported by the evidence in the passage. For example, Choices (A) and (D) are true statements, but neither is addressed in the passage. Choice (C) is inaccurate. Only Choice (B) can be supported. It's supported by the second to last sentence in the paragraph: "And, of course, all this increased security comes with a hefty price tag that is factored into increased fares."

As you read the following passage, think about the main point the writer makes. Then answer the example question, which is like one you may find on the ASVAB-AFQT.

> The conquest of the air has been the dream of mankind for uncounted centuries. As far back as we have historic records, we find stories of the attempts of men to fly. The earliest Greek mythology is full of aeronautical legends, especially the disaster which befell Icarus and his wings of wax when exposed to the glare of the midsummer sun in Greece. We find like traditions in the legendary lore of the Peruvians, the East Indians, the Babylonians, and the tribes of Africa.

What is the main idea of this passage?

(A) Many Greek legends express man's desire to fly.

(B) Comparative-culture studies reveal a cross-cultural similarity in lore.

(C) The history of aeronautics should begin with the ancient Peruvians who developed wings of wax.

(D) The desire to fly is both ancient and universal.

The correct answer is Choice (D). The topic sentence — in this paragraph, the first sentence — states the main idea. If you sum up the gist of the paragraph (in 25 words or less), you may come up with something like this: "Beginning in ancient times, human beings in many cultures have wanted to fly." Choice (A) may be true, but you don't know how many Greek legends deal with the desire to fly; in addition, this point is a supporting detail, not the main idea. Choice (B) also may be true, but it's a general statement that's larger in scope than the paragraph. Choice (C) is an inaccurate statement.

On the ASTB, the answer choices for the preceding passage may look a little different. You may encounter answer choices that look more like the following:

(A) The Babylonian legend of Icarus is the earliest known reference to manned flight.

(B) The history of mankind is filled with references to the desire to soar into the sky.

(C) Every ancient society had a myth about the human desire to fly.

(D) The true history of flight begins with Icarus, who flew to the sun on wings of wax.

The correct answer is Choice (B). The statement in Choice (B) is the main idea of the passage and is supported by the details. Choice (A) is inaccurate (Icarus is a Greek legend). Choice (C) can't be supported because the passage doesn't state that *every* society has a legend. Choice (D) is too vague and general to be supported by the evidence in the passage.

Answering main-purpose questions

Reading comprehension sections of the OCT may pose main-purpose questions in any of several ways, including the following:

- ✔ What is the writer's purpose in this passage?
- ✔ What is the writer trying to accomplish in this passage?
- ✔ Which of the following does the writer hope to achieve?

To answer these questions, think about the four main purposes of an essay — to inform, explain, persuade, or entertain. If the passage delivers straightforward information, the writer's purpose is most likely to explain or inform. If the writer seems to be taking a stand or trying to convince you, the purpose is to persuade. If the passage relates an amusing anecdote or story, the purpose is to entertain.

After identifying the writer's overall purpose, you must then examine the topic sentence and details to figure out what the writer is describing, explaining, or trying to persuade you to think or do.

As you read the following passage, think about what the writer is trying to accomplish, and then answer the corresponding question, which is similar to one you may see on the ASVAB-AFQT:

In this hygiene-conscious age, the public has embraced antibiotic soaps and lotions to what some professionals warn is a dangerous level. According to recent research, overuse of these products has the paradoxical effect of increasing the resistant bacteria in the home and workplace. Because the lotions don't kill 100 percent of the bacteria, those which survive reproduce and develop a tolerance to the antibacterial products. In fact, vigorous hand washing with soap and water is more effective than these new antibacterial lotions.

Which of the following best states the writer's purpose?

(A) to encourage extra hygiene in the home and the workplace

(B) to warn against unsanitary habits in public and private locations

(C) to oppose the substitution of antibacterial lotions for soap and water

(D) to prove that scientists are not always right in their predictions

The correct answer is Choice (C). The writer makes the point that using antibacterial lotions instead of soap and water is counterproductive. Choice (A) is inaccurate: Although the passage does refer to hand washing, the purpose of the passage isn't to encourage extra hygiene. Choice (B) is also inaccurate; the writer doesn't cover unsanitary habits in the passage. Choice (D) proposes a statement that may be true, but it doesn't answer the question of the writer's purpose in this passage.

On the ASTB, the answer choices may look more like the following statements:

(A) Every home should be equipped with a generous supply of antibacterial lotion.

(B) Frequent and energetic hand washing is the best method of combating bacteria in the home.

(C) Most people don't exercise good judgment when it comes to preventing bacterial infections.

(D) The rise in the number of antibacterial soaps and lotions is a direct response to the increase in bacterial infections.

The correct answer is Choice (B). The conclusion of the paragraph makes this point very clearly. Choice (A) is contradicted by the information in the passage. Choice (C) may be true, but it can't be inferred from the information in the passage. Choice (D) may also be true, but again, it can't be inferred from this passage.

Picking out supporting details brick by brick

Details are the evidence a writer uses to support the thesis (main idea) or the facts that tell how, what, when, where, why, or how much or how many. Reading comprehension questions often pinpoint specific details in a passage to test your ability to read carefully and accurately and to respond precisely to a question.

The key to successfully answering detail questions is to be careful and precise. Don't rely on your memory to answer a question. Remember, this is an open-book test. Dip back into the passage to find the specific detail and be accurate as you review the choices. Eliminate any choice that is inaccurate or represents a misreading of the details in the passage.

As you read the following paragraph, identify the details that support the main idea. Then answer the corresponding detail question, which is similar to one you may find on the ASVAB-AFQT.

> MRSA (methicillin-resistant Staphylococcus aureus), a hazardous staph infection, has alarmed scientists recently because of its tendency to develop strains that are both highly contagious and resistant to antibiotics. It spreads wherever people are in close contact, in community settings and hospitals where it threatens people with weakened immune systems and surgical wounds. It has become so virulent that in 2007 the mortality rate of MRSA surpassed that of AIDS.

Based on the information in the passage, which of the following is true?

(A) In 2009 more people contracted MRSA than AIDS.

(B) The MRSA bacteria are capable of mutating into the AIDS virus.

(C) One reason MRSA is dangerous is its ability to develop a resistance to antibiotics.

(D) AIDS is a staph infection that is easily spread in those with weakened immune systems and surgical wounds.

The correct answer is Choice (C). The passage specifically states that scientists are alarmed by MRSA's ability to develop a resistance to antibiotics. Choice (A) is inaccurate: The year 2009 is never mentioned in the passage nor is the number of people who contracted each disease. Choice (B) is illogical as well as unsupportable: Bacteria can't mutate into a virus, and nothing in the passage remotely supports this assertion. Choice (D) refers to AIDS as a type of staph infection, which is ridiculous and, more importantly, not stated in the passage.

On the ASTB, you may see choices such as the following for this passage:

(A) Public health scientists are seriously concerned about the rate at which hospital patients are contracting AIDS.

(B) Scientists would be alarmed by a college student with MRSA who lives in a campus dormitory.

(C) The rapid reproduction of the staphylococcus organism is the most troubling aspect of MRSA.

(D) MRSA is a more difficult disease to cure than AIDS.

The correct answer is Choice (B). A college dormitory would qualify as a place where people are in close contact, and MRSA is highly contagious. Choice (A) is inaccurate; the passage doesn't refer to the rate at which hospital patients contract AIDS. Choice (C) is incorrect because the passage doesn't refer to the reproductive rate of the staphylococcus organism. Choice (D) is not addressed in the passage.

Getting the gist at the end, too

Although you can usually size up the main point of a paragraph by reading and understanding its opening sentence, you need to read it all the way through to the end to fully understand the content as well as any opinion the author expresses. Why? Because reading comprehension questions often challenge you to identify the *conclusions* the author has arrived at. What you're looking for here is the take-home message.

The best way to identify the conclusion the author has drawn is to think critically and analyze what you're reading:

✔ Weigh the evidence and evaluate its appropriateness and effectiveness.

✔ Check for the writer's hidden assumptions or bias, if any.

✔ Follow the author's line of reasoning through to its logical conclusion. How does the author get from Point A to Point B?

Because most of the reading passages on the OCT are short, you don't have to follow a long and convoluted pattern of reasoning. Just be sure to stick with the writer's train of thought as he or she reaches a conclusion based on the information and evidence in the passage.

Read the following passage and follow the writer's train of thought to the conclusion. Then answer the corresponding question, which is similar to one you may see on the ASVAB-AFQT or the ASTB:

> In an attempt to improve the lives of Americans, scientists are exploring the links between diet and longevity. The results of almost all experiments indicate that lower calorie intake (1,800 to 2,200 calories per day) extends lifespan and improves disease resistance. While exercise is a contributing factor to overall health, it is not a substitute for calorie restriction. The time has come for all American to "undersize" rather than "supersize" their meals.

The writer of this passage concludes that

(A) The fewer the calories one consumes, the healthier one will be.

(B) Because we are a nation of "couch potatoes," most Americans are unable to accept the significance of the benefits of increased exercise.

(C) With adequate exercise, all Americans will be healthy if they follow a 2,000-calorie-per-day diet.

(D) Reducing the size and calorie content of meals will enable many American to live longer and healthier lives.

The correct answer is Choice (D). The writer presents information to support the conclusion that "lower calorie intake (1,800 to 2,200 calories per day) extends lifespan and improves disease resistance" for *most* (not all) Americans. Choice (A) is too extreme: A person who consumes too few calories may be quite unhealthy. Choice (B) may be a true conclusion, but the evidence in the passage is inadequate to support it. Choice (C) generalizes; it's impossible to state that *all* Americans will be healthy under any circumstances.

Adjusting to Different Content and Writing Styles

The OCT reading passages cover diverse subject areas, each of which has a unique style and vocabulary and requires different reading skills. You may need to adjust your speed and concentration level as you switch from one subject to another. Fiction reading, for example, generally goes faster than nonfiction. Highly technical material may require you to slow down to be sure you comprehend processes, relationships, and results. Good readers constantly monitor their reading speed and focus and adjust as the content demands.

The following sections introduce you to the different types of writing you're likely to experience on the OCT and recommend strategies for adjusting to different content and writing styles.

Read broadly. Reading only what interests you is too easy and limits your exposure to a specific content and style. Broaden your reading to include both fiction (short stories and novels) and nonfiction. In the nonfiction genre, read history and biographies; explore science and technology; read up on current events, health and medicine, travel, and so on. The point is, don't limit yourself: Stretch your reading ability.

Storytelling passages

Storytelling is a universal form of communication. Fiction passages, which include excerpts of narratives from short stories and novels, require you to follow the plot and understand the narrator's voice. You must keep track of the characters and their motivations, actions, and interactions with one another. In addition, you may have to determine the setting (time and place) and the mood (atmosphere) of the story.

As you read the following excerpt from a novel, think about the characters and their interactions. The passage is followed by a question similar to the type of question you may encounter on the ASVAB-AFQT and the ASTB.

> He was an old man, of heavy build, with a fair, shaven face and large eyes. There was something childish in those eyes, though it was not the childishness of senility. What exactly it was Miss Bartlett did not stop to consider, for her glance passed on to his clothes. These did not attract her. He was probably trying to become acquainted with them [Miss Bartlett and her companion] before they got involved in the social activity. So she assumed a dazed expression when he spoke to her.

With which of the following statements would the narrator of the passage agree?

(A) Miss Bartlett tries to resist the attraction she feels for the old man.

(B) Miss Bartlett senses that the old man would like to befriend her.

(C) The old man's senility immediately repels Miss Bartlett.

(D) The old man believes that he and Miss Bartlett had met previously when they were children.

The correct answer is Choice (B). The sentence "He was probably trying to become acquainted with them before they got involved in the social activity" is the clue that Choice (B) is correct. Choice (A) is wrong because no evidence in the passage suggests Miss Bartlett is attracted to the old man. Choice (C) can't be supported; the passage states that the old man wasn't senile. Choice (D) can't be supported by any evidence in the passage.

Scientific passages

Scientific passages test your skill in reading nonfiction about science-related topics. The questions may require you to understand a sequence of events, recall facts, and draw conclusions. Because these passages often are quite dense and jam-packed with information, monitor and adjust your speed and concentration accordingly. Pay particular attention to *signal words* that show relationships or sequences of events.

Commonly used signal words are words or phrases that:

- ✔ **Show a result:** *consequently, therefore, thus, so*

- ✔ **Present sequence or order:** *first, second,* and so on; *then; eventually; finally; next*

- ✔ **Highlight contrasting qualities or ideas:** *although, even though, however, nevertheless, on the other hand*

- ✔ **Reveal more information:** *also, furthermore, in addition, moreover*

This science passage is followed by a question similar to one that may appear on the ASVAB-AFQT and the ASTB.

> Binary fission is the form of asexual reproduction used by single-celled organisms. The process begins with DNA replication within the parent cell. Each strand of DNA separates and then attaches to opposite sides of the cell membrane. Next, the cell elongates and the cell wall grows inward transversely, creating a figure-eight shape. Finally, the sides of the cell wall meet in the middle, and the parent cell splits completely into two daughter cells.

According to the passage, which of the following statements is true?

(A) Binary fission, a form of sexual reproduction, results in the creation of multiple daughter cells from one parent cell.

(B) The replication of the DNA strands occurs simultaneously with the inward movement of the cell wall.

(C) The final stage of binary fission is the duplication of the nucleus, which contains the DNA material.

(D) Before the cell splits into two daughter cells, the cell elongates and becomes pinched together in the middle.

The correct answer is Choice (D). Choice (D) accurately states the sequence of events leading up to the separation into two cells. Choice (A) is incorrect because binary fission is asexual and creates two daughter cells from one parent cell. Choice (B) doesn't accurately state the sequence of events. Choice (C) misstates the information; the nucleus isn't mentioned in the passage.

What happened and how: Informative passages

History, sociology, psychology, geography, current events . . . all these topics show up in social science reading passages. These passages usually are informative presentations of material gathered through careful research. To answer the questions, you often have to follow the chronology of the events in the passage, understand the ramifications of political actions, or draw conclusions from a series of events.

The following social science passage is followed by a question similar to one you may encounter on the ASVAB-AFQT and the ASTB.

> The theory of politics, which men have expressed the best they could in their laws, considers persons and property as the two objects for whose protection government exists. People, by virtue of being identical in nature, have equal rights. While the rights of all as persons are equal, their rights in property are very unequal. One man owns his clothes, and another owns a county. This accident, depending primarily on the talents and skills of the parties, of which there is every degree, and secondarily on inheritance, falls unequally, and consequently, its rights are unequal.

Which of the following statements can be inferred from the passage?

(A) All people have equal rights in regard to their persons and their property.

(B) Inequities in property rights are unavoidable.

(C) A man who owns a county has an unfair advantage over a man with artistic ability.

(D) The government exists to protect the rights of persons, not the rights of property.

The correct answer is Choice (B). You may infer from the passage that property or wealth isn't evenly distributed among all men. Choice (A) is contradicted by the information that "rights in property are very unequal." Choice (C) is an illogical assumption; the passage mentions that property rights may be unequal because of inheritance or talent. Choice (D) is contradicted by the first sentence of the passage.

How-to passages: Techniques for technology

Military reading material often is highly technical. In addition to all the orders and regulations to read and forms to fill out, you may be inundated with instruction manuals that contain blueprints, diagrams, tables, and schematics. The reading comprehension sections of the OCT test your ability to handle paragraphs of a technical nature, including instructions, processes, and sequences of events.

When you come to a passage that is both unfamiliar and technical, one technique you can use is to draw on prior experience. Try to draw on a previous experience related to the material you're reading in order to place the passage in some sort of context. For example, if you're reading a passage about the global positioning system (GPS), consider your experience driving a car with a GPS. Have you ever wondered how it uses satellites to pinpoint precisely where you are?

The ensuing technical passage is followed by a question similar to one that may appear on the ASVAB-AFQT and the ASTB.

> The global positioning system (GPS) relies on 20 satellites that orbit the earth twice each day. To calculate position, a GPS first locates four satellites and analyzes radio signals to calculate its own distance from each one. By a process called trilateration, the GPS uses the intersection of three distances to pinpoint the location of the vehicle. Data from a single satellite first narrows position down to a large spherical area. Then, the data from a second satellite narrows position down to the region where the two spheres overlap. Adding data from a third satellite increases the accuracy by narrowing the intersecting areas. Data from a fourth satellite (or more) enhances precision and adds the ability to determine accurate elevation or altitude (in the case of aircraft).

Which of the following can be inferred from the passage?

(A) Trilateration utilizes radio signals that are emitted by satellites and received by the GPS.

(B) A GPS system works best when two satellites send data to a radio receiver.

(C) A GPS is only accurate when the orbiting satellite is directly above the location in question.

(D) The purpose of the fourth satellite is to reduce conflicting information from the first three satellites.

The correct answer is Choice (A). The passage implies that the radio signals are emitted by the satellites and received by the GPS. Choice (B) is contradicted by the information in the passage that states that three satellites are used. Choices (C) and (D) can't be supported by any evidence in the passage.

Scanning for Gold

Unlike many of the tests you may have taken in school for which you've had to memorize and recall a lot of facts and information, reading comprehension tests base questions on a given passage. Because the reading comprehension sections of the OCT are open-book exams, you don't have to rely on your memory. You can scan through the paragraph to find the correct answer. *Scanning* is a quick movement of the eyes through the text to find specific information.

Here are some useful techniques for scanning:

- ✔ **Know what you're looking for.** Read the question after the paragraph and rephrase it in your mind so you know exactly what the question asks.

- ✔ **Don't reread the entire paragraph.** Look for the key words that lead you to the pertinent information.

- ✔ **Know the organization of the passage.** If you're scanning for the main idea, look at the topic sentence. If you're looking for a detail, scan the middle. If you're trying to find the conclusion or solution, scan the end. (See "Using Paragraph Structure to Your Advantage" earlier in this chapter for details.)

Read the following passage and answer the corresponding question by scanning the paragraph and looking for key words:

> The structure of the human eye presents us with an apt illustration of the principle of the telescope. To see an object, it is necessary that the light from it should enter the eye. The portal through which the light is admitted is the pupil. In daytime, when the light is brilliant, the iris decreases the size of the pupil, and thus prevents too much light from entering. At night, or whenever the light is scarce, the eye needs all the light it can obtain. Consequently, the pupil expands; more and more light is admitted as the pupil grows larger. The illumination of the image on the retina is thus effectively controlled in accordance with the requirements of vision.

What structure in the eye controls the amount of light admitted through the opening in the eyeball?

(A) the retina

(B) the portal

(C) the iris

(D) the pupil

Scan the paragraph to locate the sentence that indentifies the structure that controls the amount of light coming into the eye. The answer choices are all nouns that refer to parts of the eye, but from the question, you know that the key word you're looking for is a noun related to the verb "controls." You must be careful to find the part that *controls* the opening. Because this detail is so minute, it's probably buried in the middle of the paragraph. As a result, you can almost certainly skip the first and last sentences.

The correct answer is Choice (C). Choice (A), the retina, is the structure that receives the image. Choices (B) and (D), the portal and the pupil, refer to the same structure — the pupil, which *is* the opening but does not *control* the opening. You can find the answer in the third and fourth lines: "The portal through which the light is admitted is the pupil. . . . when the light is brilliant, the iris decreases the size of the pupil. . . ."

Avoid the temptation to choose an answer solely because it contains the word or phrase that appears most frequently in the passage. In this example, the word "pupil" occurs four times, whereas "iris," "portal," and "retina" each appear only once. The test developers know how tempting this makes Choice (D).

Drawing Inferences from a Collection of Facts

Good readers understand more than just the obvious points that the writer makes. They recognize that many writers often present information indirectly; readers, then, must detect the subtle and complex ideas that are embedded in the passage. They must know how to "read between the lines" — an essential skill for all astute readers.

Using hints or clues — or reading between the lines — means drawing conclusions from information that's implied as well as that which is stated. The conclusion you arrive at through this process is called an *inference*.

Without even realizing it, you make inferences every day. Suppose you're driving along a highway when you hear a sudden bang and see a car slowly pull over to the curb. You may infer that some poor soul has had a tire blowout. You haven't seen it with your own eyes, but a blowout is the most likely explanation based on the evidence you have — the loud bang and the car pulling over. You may find out later that an action movie was being filmed in the area or a jet flying overhead caused a sonic boom, but you based your inference on the facts you possessed at the time — those you witnessed.

Hopefully, the inferences you draw during the test will be more accurate. The following sections should help with that. In these sections, you discover how to draw general conclusions from facts and identify the meanings of words from their context.

Drawing general conclusions

Drawing a general conclusion means taking information *stated* or *implied* by the text and making an educated, logical guess about what it means. Imagine you're Sherlock Holmes sifting through evidence related to a crime. Based on the evidence, you may not know for a fact which suspect actually committed the crime, but you can make logical *inferences* — or *deductions* — based on means, motives, opportunities, and other evidence. Here's an example:

> *While carrying the box of light bulbs, Jess tripped over the step. Jon immediately rushed over with a broom.*

What can you logically infer from this little incident? That the light bulbs broke. Does the passage directly state that they broke? No, but all the evidence and your own experiences with light bulbs point in that logical direction.

The next passage is followed by an inference question similar to one that may appear on the ASVAB-AFQT and the ASTB.

> Before the Civil War had ended, however, the transformation of the United States from a nation of farmers and small-scale manufacturers to a highly organized industrial state had begun. Those four years of bitter conflict illustrate, perhaps more graphically than any similar event in history, the power which military operations may exercise in stimulating all the productive forces of a people.

It can be inferred from the passage that the most important single influence on the 19th-century transformation of the U.S. from an agrarian society to an industrial one was

(A) the increase in raw materials.

(B) the influence of the war.

(C) the new methods of crop rotation.

(D) the implementation of the assembly line in small-scale manufacturing.

The correct answer is Choice (B). The passage states that the transformation occurred during the Civil War. In addition, the conclusion implies that military conflict (in this case, the Civil War) may stimulate "the productive forces of a people." No evidence in the passage should lead you to conclude any of the other choices.

Understanding vocabulary in context

When reading a passage, you may come across a word you can't define, but don't give up; you may be able to infer its meaning from the context.

For example, you may not know the exact definition of *penitent* in the following sentence, but you may be able to infer its meaning from the context:

> *Feeling penitent after her uncharacteristically rude outburst, Elena apologized to her friends.*

The context clue that Elena apologized after her rude outburst suggests that she felt remorseful or regretful. If you infer that *penitent* means remorseful, you are correct.

On the ASVAB-AFQT you may find a specific vocabulary-in-context question. The ASTB is unlikely to pose such a question, but you may still encounter questions that require you to determine the meanings of words in context. Consider this passage and then use it to answer the question that follows:

> The principal features of the motion of the moon have also been noticed with intelligence at an antiquity more remote than history. The attentive observer perceives the important truth that the moon does not occupy a *fixed* position in the heavens. During the course of a single night, the fact that the moon has moved from west to east across the heavens can be perceived by noting its position relative to adjacent stars.

It can be inferred from the italicized word *fixed* that the moon's position is

(A) repaired

(B) unchanging

(C) fluctuating

(D) unerring

The correct answer is Choice (B). In this context, the word *fixed* means not moving or unchanging. The sentence states "the moon does not occupy a fixed position." This point is supported by the last sentence of the passage, which describes the movement of the moon across the heavens. Choice (A), a common meaning of *fixed,* doesn't fit the context of the sentence. Choice (C) is the opposite of *fixed* in this context. Choice (D), *unerring* (unfailing accuracy), doesn't fit the context of the sentence either.

Chapter 7

Testing Your Reading Skills

• •

1 f you're taking the Armed Services Vocational Aptitude Battery Air Force Qualifying Test (ASVAB AFQT) or the Aviation Selection Test Battery (ASTB), consider this chapter your opportunity to put your newly honed reading skills to the test. (See Chapter 6 for how to improve your reading ability.) Here you encounter numerous reading comprehension passages similar to those you'll encounter on the tests, covering a wide variety of subjects and writing styles. Following each passage is one or more questions challenging your ability to pick out the correct answer from the passage. Near the end of the chapter are answer keys, so you can check your own answers and identify any areas you may need to work on a little more.

If you're taking the AFOQT, you don't need to spend time practicing the reading comprehension passages in this chapter because the AFOQT doesn't contain a Reading Comprehension subtest.

As you read the passages, remain on high A. L. E. R. T.: Actively engage, Listen, Expect, Restate, and Think. For more about the A. L. E. R. T. approach to active reading, see Chapter 6.

Deciphering Paragraphs on the ASVAB AFQT

You have 13 minutes to complete 15 Paragraph Comprehension questions (52 seconds per question). Carefully read each passage and the question or questions that follow. Based on what is stated or implied in the passage, select the best answer for each question from the four choices given.

> Question 1 is based on the following passage.

The Mason-Dixon Line is a demarcation line that forms a cultural boundary between the North and the South. It was created in the 1760s by two surveyors, Charles Mason and Jeremiah Dixon, to resolve a border dispute between the colonies of Maryland and Pennsylvania.

1. Which of the following states the main purpose of this passage?

   (A) to argue that the Mason-Dixon Line was a factor in causing a border dispute between Maryland and Pennsylvania

   (B) to explain the reason for the creation of this line of demarcation

   (C) to propose a solution to an ongoing political dispute

   (D) to contrast the goals of the northern states with those of the southern states

---

Questions 2 and 3 are based on the following passage.

When General Grant undertook the task of subduing Vicksburg, Captain Farragut assumed the herculean work of forcing his way up the Mississippi and capturing New Orleans, the greatest commercial city in the South. Knowing that such an attack was certain to be made, the Confederates had neglected no precaution in the way of defense. Ninety miles below the city were the forts of St. Philip and Jackson. The former, on the left bank, had 42 heavy guns, including two mortars and a battery of four seacoast mortars, placed below the water battery. Fort Jackson, besides its water battery, mounted 62 guns, while above the forts were 14 vessels, including the ironclad ram *Manassas,* and a partially completed floating battery, armored with railroad iron and called the *Louisiana.* New Orleans was defended by 3,000 volunteers, most of the troops formerly there having been sent to the Confederate Army in Tennessee.

2. Which of the following can be inferred from the passage?

   (A) The leaders of the Confederate forces were defeated because they were remiss in preparing for the attack on New Orleans.

   (B) The Union troops, led by Captain Farragut, faced a considerable defensive force as they began their assault on the greatest commercial city in the South.

   (C) The decisive element in the victory of the Union Army was the deployment of the iron-clad ship, the *Manassas.*

   (D) Poor equipment and inadequate training of the all-volunteer army resulted in the defeat of Captain Farragut's troops.

3. In the context of the passage, the word *herculean* (in the second sentence) most nearly means

   (A) mythical

   (B) hasty

   (C) extraordinary

   (D) depressing

Question 4 is based on the following passage.

The history of kite flying begins about 2,800 years ago in China. The first kites, constructed of a bamboo framework covered by thin silk material, were used by ancient people to measure distances, test wind direction, and send signals over long distances. There is evidence that kites were employed as a means of communication in military operations. Kites spread from Asia to Europe when Marco Polo returned from his travels with stories of kites.

4. According to the passage, kites were used for all of the following purposes EXCEPT:

   (A) measuring distances

   (B) figuring out wind direction

   (C) communicating during warfare

   (D) telling stories

Question 5 is based on the following passage.

Eggs tainted with salmonella bacteria pose a significant health hazard. Chickens contract the bacteria from contaminated feed, from rodents, or from their human keepers. The eggs from these infected chickens contain the bacteria. If the eggs are not cooked properly, they can sicken people who eat them.

5. According to the passage, which of the following is a logical conclusion?

(A) Salmonella can only be transferred from chickens to humans, not from humans to chickens.

(B) Keeping rodents out of chicken enclosures is the best way to reduce outbreaks of salmonella.

(C) Properly cooking infected eggs will reduce the health hazard.

(D) A person who never eats eggs will be immune to salmonella.

Question 6 is based on the following passage.

The International Date Line is an imaginary line on the surface of the earth running from the North Pole to the South Pole perpendicular to the equator. The line is on the opposite side of the globe from the Prime Meridian, another imaginary line that runs north-south through Greenwich, England. When travelers cross the International Date Line in an eastward direction, they lose a day; when they are traveling westward, they gain a day.

6. According to the passage, which of the following statements is true?

(A) The International Date Line is an imaginary line that runs parallel to the equator.

(B) A person who crosses the International Date Line while flying east from Vancouver, Canada, to Beijing, China, will lose 24 hours.

(C) A person who flies around the earth in a westerly direction will always lose a day.

(D) The purpose of the International Date Line is to help pilots navigate when they travel from one hemisphere to another.

Question 7 is based on the following passage.

The Congress of the United States is a bicameral legislature. Bicameral means having two houses; the two houses of the U.S. Congress are the Senate and the House of Representatives. Two senators are elected from each of the 50 states, while the number of Representatives is based on each state's population.

7. Which of the following statements can be inferred from the passage?

(A) A bicameral legislature consists of one main house and two lesser houses.

(B) The Senate is comprised of the Congress and the House of Representatives.

(C) California, because it is the most populous state, has the greatest number of senators.

(D) New York State has the same number of senators as North Dakota.

Question 8 is based on the following passage.

Meteorologists define a cyclone as a circular motion of air rotating in the same direction as the earth. It is characterized by high winds spiraling clockwise in the Southern Hemisphere and counterclockwise in the Northern Hemisphere. The formation of cyclones, called cyclogenesis, is the process of cyclone formation and intensification.

8. The best title for this passage is

   (A) A Meteorological Miracle

   (B) Characteristics of a Cyclone

   (C) Weather and Its Wonders

   (D) Movements of the Hemispheres

Question 9 is based on the following passage.

The Art of War, like any other art, is based on certain fixed principles. To learn this art, a student must engage in long and laborious study and avoid the pitfalls along the way. One of these pitfalls is the belief by some that whenever a new war breaks out, all previous warlike knowledge must be discarded and attention paid only to the problem of the hour.

9. The author of this passage would most likely agree with which of the following statements?

   (A) Those who study the art of war can learn much from studying previous battles.

   (B) Every new war requires military leaders to devise a new strategy.

   (C) Because of the constantly changing nature of conflict, leaders must focus their attention on the problem of the hour.

   (D) War is a science rather than an art; thus, its principles are variable.

Questions 10 and 11 are based on the following passage.

When the short days of winter came, dusk fell before we had well eaten our dinners. When we met in the street, the houses had grown somber. The space of sky above us was the color of ever-changing violet and towards it the lamps of the street lifted their feeble lanterns. The cold air stung us and we played till our bodies glowed. Our shouts echoed in the silent street. The career of our play brought us through the dark muddy lanes behind the houses where we ran the gauntlet of the rough tribes from the cottages, to the back doors of the dark dripping gardens where odors arose from the ash pits, to the dark odorous stables where a coachman smoothed and combed the horse or shook music from the buckled harness.

10. It can be inferred that the setting of this passage is most likely

   (A) just before dawn in late March in a small village.

   (B) on a horse farm on a cool September evening.

   (C) in the late afternoon on a December day in a town.

   (D) near midnight on a cold October night in the desert.

11. In the last sentence (*The career . . . buckled harness*), the phrase "we ran the gauntlet" most nearly means which of the following:

    (A) When traveling to distant towns, the narrator endured attacks from tribes of natives.

    (B) The narrator and his friends were forced to run through hostile groups of neighborhood kids.

    (C) Coachmen would launch a surprise ambush as the narrator and his friends ran by the stables.

    (D) The unpleasant smell emitted by the ash pits assaulted the narrator as he and his friends played in the streets.

    Question 12 is based on the following passage.

    Plate tectonics is a relatively new geological theory that proposes that earthquakes, volcanic activity, and mountain creation are the result of the movement of plates in the earth's surface layer. These plates are rigid blocks that rest on the semi-molten layer just under the earth's crust. As gaseous activity in the earth's molten core increases, hot spots are formed that put stress on the plates, causing them to shift. Some plates are pushed under others, pushing them upwards to form mountain ranges.

12. According to the passage, which of the following best describes the sequence of events leading to the creation of mountain ranges?

    (A) The tectonic plates shift; the gaseous activity increases; the surface layer descends.

    (B) The molten core of the earth hardens; the tectonic plates shift upwards; the hot spot activity intensifies.

    (C) An earthquake erupts; the tectonic plates shift upwards; the semi-molten layer sinks.

    (D) The gaseous activity in the earth's core increases; hot spots force the tectonic plates to shift; some plates force others to move upwards.

    Question 13 is based on the following passage.

    Images appear to be three-dimensional (3D) because of the properties of human vision. Our two forward-facing eyes are separated from each other by about 2–3 inches, a distance that causes a slightly different image to be perceived by each eye. Our brain combines these shifted images to perceive depth and distance. Advances in technology have allowed filmmakers to use color-filtered or polarized glasses to trick our eyes into perceiving the illusion of depth. Thus, the monster appears to be leaping off the screen, right into the laps of the screaming audience.

13. Which of the following best states the main idea of the passage?

    (A) Our ability to see images in 3D is a function of human biology.

    (B) In order to see images in 3D, viewers must wear specially designed glasses.

    (C) Without two properly functioning eyes, a spectator will be unable to see 3D images without polarized glasses.

    (D) Advances in technology have made movie watching much more exciting.

Question 14 is based on the following passage.

The pop art movement, which began in the 1950s, challenged the traditional definition of art. The themes and techniques of this art movement, taken from ordinary objects in popular culture, are antithetical to the conventional subject matter of fine art. In pop art, even images from commercial advertising become subjects for artists. Such mundane items as a can of tomato soup or a box of Brillo are transformed into objects of art and adorn the walls of museums of contemporary art.

14. Which of the following is the best title for the passage?

   (A) The Greatest Artists of the Pop Art Movement

   (B) Pop Art: The Unconventional Art Movement

   (C) Using Ordinary Objects to Create Beauty

   (D) Themes and Techniques in Art

Question 15 is based on the following passage.

With regard to marching, General T. J. Jackson once observed, in reply to an allusion to his severe marching, that "it is better to lose one man in marching than five in fighting." Acting on this principle, he invariably surprised his enemy, the most notable instances being his surprise of Milroy at McDowell, of Banks and Fremont in the Valley, of McClellan's right at Gaines's Mill, of Pope at the Second Manassas, and his last and greatest of Hooker at Chancellorsville.

15. Which of the following can be inferred from the passage?

   (A) General T. J. Jackson believed that the movement of soldiers on foot could provide a strategic advantage.

   (B) The loss of troops during a march was unacceptable to General T. J. Jackson.

   (C) The defeat of General T. J. Jackson by the troops of Milroy, Banks, and Freemont was the result of a surprise march.

   (D) When developing tactics for surprising the enemy, General T. J. Jackson minimized the benefits of ambush.

Putting Your Reading Skills to the Test on the ASTB

You have 25 minutes to complete the 27 reading questions on the ASTB. That means you have a bit less than a minute (about 55 seconds) to read each passage and answer the question.

Each question consists of a passage that you should assume to be true. This passage is followed by four possible answers. For each question, select the choice that can be inferred only from the passage itself. Some or all of the choices may be logical and true, but only one can be directly derived from the information contained in the passage.

1. Excavation is the primary method archeologists use to recover information. Although some excavations only uncover, sample, and rebury archeological deposits, all excavations permanently alter the context of archeological resources to some degree. This places archeologists in a unique position — the excavations necessary to recover archeological resources always affect the data they collect.

   (A) Excavation is the only method used by archeologists to unearth artifacts from long-buried civilizations.

   (B) To preserve the integrity of a dig, archeologists always return uncovered objects to their original resting place.

   (C) Once a site has been explored, its context has been irrevocably changed.

   (D) The discovery of archeological deposits is unique in that it provides the only clues scientists have to reconstruct the lives of early human settlements.

2. Every officer in charge of a detached force or flying column, every officer who for the time being has to act independently, every officer in charge of a patrol, is constantly brought face to face with strategical considerations; and success or failure, even where the force is insignificant, will depend upon his familiarity with strategical principles.

   (A) To maintain discipline and order, the practice of strategy in the field is confined to the higher ranks.

   (B) Theoretical training is the most important component in the training of military leaders.

   (C) Regardless of rank, every officer must be capable of making strategic decisions.

   (D) Those who are quick and decisive in their civilian lives will most likely be resolute and daring officers.

3. Unlike many contemporary groups that prohibit audience members from recording live concerts, The Grateful Dead encourages their fans to tape as they listen. Their philosophy stems from the belief that the more people are exposed to their music, the more records they will sell. This is the opposite position of those who feel taping concerts is akin to stealing.

   (A) It is illegal for a member of the audience to tape any live music concert.

   (B) The popularity of The Grateful Dead has declined due to the easy availability of their music.

   (C) Audience members who attend a concert are more likely to purchase the music of a group they have heard live.

   (D) Some musical artists believe that familiarity breeds success.

4. Many new cars come equipped with back-up sensors. These sensors emit a beep as the vehicle approaches an obstacle. Some drivers have become so accustomed to the sound that they find they can no longer accurately judge how close they are to an object.

   (A) New cars that aren't equipped with back-up sensors allow drivers to maintain their ability to judge distance.

   (B) It is not a good idea for a new car buyer to purchase a car with a lot of new technological gadgets.

   (C) It is an accepted truism that old-fashioned methods are often the best methods.

   (D) Sometimes technology that solves one problem may create another.

5. All the members of the Green family were thrilled with their purchase of a 100-year-old house in their hometown even though it clearly needed some work. The project they decided was most essential to tackle first was the old wiring. Many of the rooms also needed a new coat of paint, but that was not a priority for them.

    (A) The Green family had at least two major projects to undertake in their new home.

    (B) Painting the rooms took precedence over repairing the wiring.

    (C) Because of all the work they had to do, the Green family soon regretted their purchase of an old house.

    (D) Once the wiring repair was completed, the Green family would begin immediately on the painting project.

6. The one absolutely unselfish friend that man can have in this selfish world, the one that never deserts him, the one that never proves ungrateful or treacherous is his dog. A man's dog stands by him in prosperity and in poverty, in health and in sickness. He will sleep on the cold ground where the winds blow and snow drives fiercely, if only he may be near his master's side.

    (A) A dog will only sleep on the cold ground if his master is by his side.

    (B) Dogs are used as search and rescue animals because they are fiercely loyal.

    (C) While human companions may prove to be selfish or traitorous, a canine companion will never disappoint.

    (D) It is unwise to keep a sick dog close by because when they are ill, their temperaments are unreliable.

7. If it does not obtain permission to log in national parks, the logging industry is likely to fail. That will not be good for anyone. The forest industry in the United States includes close to 10,000 companies who support many thousands of employees and have an annual payroll of about 2 billion dollars, according to a recent census. Furthermore, logging supports several other industries, from sawmills to pulp and paper production.

    (A) All the logging industry needs to become financially successful are the logging rights to national parks.

    (B) The logging industry deems opening up protected lands to industry important for its employees, for the economy, and for the nation at large.

    (C) The U.S. forest industry employs thousands of workers who contribute about 2 billion dollars a year in tax revenue.

    (D) No industrial development is currently permitted on national park land.

8. According to Theodore Roosevelt, a life of slothful ease, a life of that peace which springs merely from lack either of desire or of power to strive after great things, is as little worthy of a nation as of an individual. He asked that the same dedication to hard work that every self-respecting American demands from himself and from his children should be demanded of the American nation as a whole.

    (A) Theodore Roosevelt asserted that a life of hard work is far more worthy than a life of ease.

    (B) According to Roosevelt, the dream of all Americans to achieve a life of ease drives us to achieve greatness.

    (C) American families must learn to pass on a tradition of values, including patriotism, individualism, and self-respect.

    (D) Dedicated Americans will demand that their leaders embrace the values of Theodore Roosevelt.

9. Golf club heads can be made of many different materials. Stainless steel, titanium, or composite alloys are the most commonly used substances. Many women golfers prefer titanium because it's lightweight and very strong. Stainless steel is cheaper, but heavier.

    (A) Most golf clubs are made of stainless steel because it is cheaper than titanium or composite alloys.

    (B) Stainless steel golf clubs are the best choice for beginners because they are durable and flexible.

    (C) Many female golfers tend to choose golf clubs on the basis of their strength and weight.

    (D) The cost of a new set of golf clubs is an excellent indicator of their superior performance.

10. With computers on every desk and easy access to the Internet, many workers cannot resist the temptation to send personal e-mails, do some Internet browsing, and maybe even shop a bit on company time. Concerned by this personal use of essential and valuable technology and waste of employee time, corporations are fighting back by installing monitoring devices.

    (A) Technology has increased the efficiency of workers to an unforeseen extent.

    (B) The installation of monitoring devices will be an effective deterrent to Internet theft.

    (C) In attempting to update technology, some corporations are using the Internet to simplify their procedures.

    (D) While universally recognized as a boon to businesses, increased technology has created some troublesome issues.

11. A hard, cold man, thus unfortunately situated, seldom or never looking inward, and resolutely taking his idea of himself from what purports to be his image as reflected in the mirror of public opinion, can scarcely arrive at true self-knowledge, except through loss of property and reputation.

    (A) A hard, cold man is rarely prone to self-examination.

    (B) One who is characterized by coldness is often obsessed with his image.

    (C) Public opinion is the only true measure of a person.

    (D) Self-knowledge is essential for maintaining property and reputation.

12. Blu-ray technology (the "blue" refers to the blue laser used to read the disc) is an optical disc storage medium that provides much more storage capacity than traditional DVDs. It was developed to enable recording, rewriting, and playback of high-definition video.

    (A) Blu-ray discs are blue-colored to distinguish them from traditional silver DVDs.

    (B) A traditional DVD is capable of recording and playing back high-definition videos.

    (C) Watching a movie on a Blu-ray-capable player will be a far more enjoyable experience than watching one on a traditional DVD player.

    (D) A traditional DVD has less capacity for storage than some other disc storage media.

13. Recent research has cheered up the spirits of chocoholics: dark chocolate is healthful, perhaps even as good for you as some vegetables. It contains flavonoids, chemicals which act as antioxidants to protect the body from aging and reduce blood pressure.

    (A) All patients who suffer from high blood pressure will markedly improve if they eat several ounces of dark chocolate daily.

    (B) The addition of flavonoids into a daily diet may be a factor in reducing physical signs of aging.

    (C) Children should be encouraged to substitute dark chocolate for vegetables at dinner.

    (D) Chocolate is a major component in one of the daily essential food groups.

14. Frigate birds are fascinating seabirds because they cannot swim. To obtain the sustenance they need, they either snatch their prey from the surface of the ocean using their long, hooked bills or rob other birds of their catch. They harass other birds into dropping their catch of fish or sea turtles; then they swoop down and filch the food.

    (A) Frigate birds can often be seen diving into the sea to capture fish.

    (B) Sea turtles are endangered because too many seabirds prey on their young.

    (C) It would be appropriate to call frigate birds the thieves of the ocean.

    (D) The long, hooked bills of the frigate birds allow them to dig up turtle nests on the beach.

15. Of all Egyptian deities, no god lived so long or had so deep an influence as Osiris. He stands as the prototype of the great class of resurrection gods who die that they may live again. His sufferings, his death, and his resurrection were enacted at the festival of Osiris every year. Small images of the god were made of sand and then cast in a mold of pure gold, representing the god as a mummy. After sunset, the effigy of Osiris was laid in a grave and the image of the previous year was removed.

    (A) The Egyptians believed the god Osiris was the most powerful of all the gods.

    (B) The festival of Osiris was held at the start and at the end of the harvest season.

    (C) The mummy of Osiris was cast in gold and laid in a grave.

    (D) Osiris is an example of a deity who has experienced death and rebirth.

16. The Concorde is a turbojet-powered, supersonic, passenger aircraft. Developed as a joint project between England and France, this thin-winged, delta-shaped plane flew its first commercial flight in 1976. The Concorde flew transatlantic flights in less than half the time of any other passenger airplanes.

    (A) When it was first launched, the Concorde was the fastest commercial transatlantic airplane.

    (B) The main flying route of the Concorde was between England and France.

    (C) Because the Concorde was a supersonic jet, it flew faster than the speed of light.

    (D) The delta shape and extra-thin wings on the Concorde allowed it to cruise at higher altitudes than those of other commercial airliners.

17. Longitude, the distance in degrees, minutes, and seconds east or west of the Prime Meridian, is the most commonly used geographic coordinate for east/west measurement. Unlike latitude, which has the equator as a natural starting point, an arbitrary starting point had to be chosen for longitude. The Prime Meridian (which passes north/south through Greenwich, England) was designated as point zero; all other lines of longitude are measured in their distance from this line.

    (A) Lines of longitude are parallel to the equator.

    (B) All lines of longitude pass through the Prime Meridian.

    (C) Having a "point zero" is essential for both lines of longitude and lines of latitude.

    (D) The Prime Meridian is the only line of longitude that corresponds to a major city.

18. Any sport may be added to the Olympic program if the International Olympic Committee determines that it has worldwide prevalence. For example, rugby sevens and golf will be added to the Olympic Games to be held in Rio de Janeiro in 2016. Sports can also be removed from the Olympic competitions: Baseball and softball were both eliminated in 2006.

    (A) The number of sports contested in the Olympic Games is variable.

    (B) Although individual sports may come and go, the total number of sports in an Olympic program must remain constant.

    (C) Golf and rugby were added to the Olympic program in 2006.

    (D) No sport has ever been included, then excluded, then included again in the history of the Olympics.

19. Rather than the static organ it was previously thought to be, the brain is actually quite dynamic and adaptable. New research shows that when faced with disorder or disease, the human brain is capable of rewiring itself to cope with the injury. These new findings may lead to revolutionary methods of treating brain trauma and mental illness.

    (A) The human brain has a finite number of brain cells.

    (B) Brain damage may be as permanent as scientists previously thought it was.

    (C) Recent research shows that the brain is not immutable.

    (D) Brain injuries may become as obsolete as the Pony Express.

20. Tree squirrels, like the red squirrel and the chickaree, stay alive in the winter by eating stored foods. Ground squirrels, however, must hibernate because their food, mostly acorns or nuts, will germinate if buried in the earth.

    (A) All squirrels must have a larder of stored foods to get them through the cold seasons.

    (B) Squirrels, like most small rodents, are vegetarians.

    (C) Tree squirrels bury each of their nuts or seeds in a separate hole.

    (D) Squirrels have diverse behavior patterns to cope with adverse conditions.

21. Velocardiofacial Syndrome, also called 22Q Syndrome, is a syndrome that affects 1 in 2,000 live births. It is caused by a partial deletion of chromosome 22. Included in its effects are 180 possible symptoms involving every system in the body. Among the most common symptoms are cardiac abnormalities, distinctive facial structure, and palate deformities.

    (A) Patients who have palate deformities are victims of Velocardiofacial Syndrome.

    (B) Chromosomes that are incomplete are capable of causing physical and physiological abnormalities.

    (C) Research shows that screening for genetic abnormalities will reduce the number of instances of birth disorders.

    (D) There are 22 chromosomes in the human genome, each controlling a specific pattern of development.

22. Had the airplane been known in the days of our Civil War, some of its most picturesque figures would have never risen to eminence or at least would have had to win their places in history by efforts of an entirely different sort. There is no place left in modern military tactics for the dashing cavalry scout of the type of Sheridan, Custer, Fitz Lee, or Forrest. The airplane, soaring high above the lines of the enemy, brings back to headquarters in a few hours information that in the old times took a detachment of cavalry days to gather.

    (A) Early airplanes were used during the Civil War to transmit information to headquarters.

    (B) In modern warfare, human scouts have been completely replaced by sophisticated technology.

    (C) During the Civil War years, such men as Custer and Sheridan earned their reputations doing reconnaissance.

    (D) General Robert E. Lee relied on the information of his scouts to plan his strategy.

23. The body mass index (BMI) (which can be simply calculated by dividing weight by height times height and then multiplying the quotient by 703) is widely used by both doctors and laypeople to determine whether a person is overweight, underweight, or normal. This statistic is important because evidence indicates that overweight people have higher risk of heart failure due to high blood pressure. A high BMI is not a death sentence, however, for it can be reduced by diet and exercise.

    (A) Having a low BMI is just as much a cause for alarm as having a high one.

    (B) To calculate BMI, multiply height by weight and divide by 703.

    (C) Maintaining a good BMI will guarantee a person a healthy life.

    (D) One criterion of physical health is BMI.

24. Much controversy in agricultural industries has arisen over genetic modification of crops. When a crop is genetically altered, genes are inserted or deleted. Proponents maintain that genetic modification can lower pesticide use by creating infestation-resistant plants and create larger yields, outcomes which will solve food crises and prevent world hunger. Opponents argue that the modifications are unsafe, but no scientific information to date supports their contention.

    (A) Genetic modification of wheat crops can supply enough bread to solve world hunger problems.

    (B) Scientists have discovered methods of engineering crops that alter their basic properties.

    (C) Most consumers believe genetically altered fruits and vegetables are harmful, especially for young children.

    (D) By experimenting with genetic engineering, agricultural scientists are venturing into dangerous territory.

25. This was Jane's first experience in purchasing a new car, and as she prepared to sign the final papers, her heart was pounding. She was worried about the questionable repair record of the car she had selected. On the other hand, its below-average fuel economy didn't concern her in the least.

    (A) Two issues about the car she was purchasing caused Jane concern.

    (B) The car's reputation for needing repairs troubled Jane.

    (C) Jane traveled 60 miles per day so the cost of fuel was important to Jane.

    (D) Because Jane was purchasing a new car, she was confident it wouldn't need repairs.

26. Carbon monoxide poisoning is the leading cause of accidental poisoning deaths in America, but a simple detector in the home can prevent problems. Because carbon monoxide is an odorless, tasteless, and invisible gas, it can go undetected in the home. A detector reacts to the presence of the gas; an accumulation of carbon monoxide in the air will trigger an alarm and warn of impending danger.

    (A) As soon as you smell carbon monoxide in the home, you should immediately open all windows and exit the premises.

    (B) Homes without carbon monoxide alarms may still be safe if they are equipped with fire alarms.

    (C) A carbon monoxide alarm is incapable of removing the carbon monoxide from the air.

    (D) The installation of carbon monoxide alarms in residences will reduce the number of accidental poisoning deaths in the U.S.

27. Captain Renard, an early inventor of the dirigible balloon, established these specifications: a cigar, or fishlike shape; an internal sack into which air might be pumped to maintain the shape of the balloon; a keel, to maintain the longitudinal stability of the balloon and from which the motor might be hung; a propeller driven by a motor; and a rudder capable of controlling the course of the ship.

    (A) The prototypes of the dirigible balloons were not as spherical in shape as the hot air balloons that preceded them.

    (B) The purpose of the internal sack was to maintain the longitudinal stability of the dirigible.

    (C) The major drawback to the early dirigible was the inability to steer it.

    (D) The addition of a keel allowed the dirigible to ascend and descend at the direction of the pilot.

Checking Your Answers

The following sections provide answers to the two sample Reading Comprehension subtests along with explanations of why each answer is correct. Use these sections to check your answers. If you came up with the wrong answer for a question, read the explanation so you know why the correct answer is accurate and so you can perhaps find out why you chose the wrong answer.

Learn from your mistakes. Try to identify areas of strengths and weaknesses. Do you have more trouble with fact or main-idea and main-purpose questions? Are you choosing an answer before reading all the answer choices? Are you confirming your answers by checking them against content in the passage?

Checking Paragraph Comprehension answers on the sample ASVAB AFQT

1. **B.** The main purpose of the passage is to explain the creation of the Mason-Dixon Line. The writer doesn't argue, Choice (A); propose a solution, Choice (C); or contrast, Choice (D).

2. **B.** The passage details several defensive tactics of the Confederate Army (the mortars, the floating battery). Choice (A) is contradicted by the information in the passage. Choice (C) is inaccurate: The *Manassas* was a Confederate ship. No information in the passage supports Choice (D).

3. **C.** The word *herculean* (related to Hercules, the mythical Roman strongman) most nearly means superhuman or extraordinary in context. The other words don't fit the context of the sentence.

4. **D.** The passage indicates that kites were used for all the choices except telling stories.

5. **C.** The information in the passage indicates that the problem arises when infected eggs are not cooked enough. Choice (A) is incorrect because chickens can contract salmonella from their keepers. No evidence is given in the passage to support Choices (B) or (D).

6. **B.** The passage gives enough information for the reader to infer that traveling east from Canada to China will result in a loss of 24 hours. Choice (A) is inaccurate: The International Date Line is perpendicular to the equator. Choice (C) is contradicted by the information in the passage. Choice (D) can't be supported by any evidence in the passage; in addition, movement from one hemisphere to another is north/south so it would remain unaffected by time difference.

7. **D.** The passage states that all states have two senators. Choices (A), (B), and (C) are all inaccurate based on the information in the passage.

8. **B.** Choice (A) isn't a good title because a cyclone isn't a "miracle." Choice (C) is too general for this passage. Choice (D) has little to do with the passage.

9. **A.** The evidence in the passage suggests the author would agree with Choice (A). He admonishes students of war to recognize that they can avoid the pitfall of the past if they don't discard previous knowledge. Choices (B) and (C) are directly contradicted by the passage. Choice (D) is the opposite of the author's reference to *The Art of War*.

10. **C.** The information in the passage suggests it's set during "the short days of winter" at dusk.

11. **B.** The children are playing in the streets of the town, and they must run through the "rough tribes." The reference to the *gauntlet* (a run between two lines of armed attackers) suggests the hostility of the neighborhood youths. Choice (A) is wrong because the children don't leave their town. Choice (C) is wrong because the coachmen don't attack. Choice (D) is wrong because the gauntlet is the "rough tribes," not the smells.

12. **D.** The passage indicates the order of events: gaseous activity in the earth's core increases; hot spots force the tectonic plates to shift; some plates force others to move upwards.

13. **A.** The main idea of the passage is that eye placement and brain activity create the ability to see 3D images. Choice (B) is a detail, not the main idea. Choice (C) may be true, but it also isn't the main idea. Choice (D) is irrelevant to the main idea.

14. **B.** A good title should reflect the main idea, and the main idea of this passage is that pop art is unconventional. Choice (A) is inaccurate because the passage doesn't discuss great artists. Choice (C) is somewhat relevant, but it isn't the main idea, especially because "beauty" is a subjective term. Choice (D) is too general to be a good title.

15. **A.** The first sentence states Jackson's conviction that marching confers a strategic advantage. Choice (B) is contradicted by the quote from Jackson. Choice (C) misstates the results of the march: Jackson defeated Milroy, Banks, and Freemont. Choice (D) is the opposite of what Jackson believed.

Assessing your reading skills on the ASTB

1. **C.** Choice (C) is supported by the statement "all excavations permanently alter the context of archeological resources to some degree." Choice (A) is incorrect because the passage states excavation is the "primary" not the "only" method. Choice (B) is incorrect because the passage states "some archeologists" rebury artifacts. Insufficient evidence exists in the passage to support Choice (D).

2. **C.** Choice (C) is supported by the statement "every officer in charge of a patrol, is constantly brought face to face with strategical considerations." Choice (A) is contradicted by the information in the passage. Choice (B) is incorrect because theoretical knowledge isn't addressed in the passage. Choice (D) is a fallible conclusion that can't be drawn from the evidence in the passage.

3. **D.** Choice (D) is supported by the phrase "the more people are exposed to their music, the more records they will sell." Choices (A) and (B) aren't supported by evidence in the passage. Choice (C) may be true, but the passage doesn't address the issue.

4. **D.** Choice (D) presents a logical conclusion that may be drawn from the main idea of the passage: The technology that makes it possible for drivers to rely on back-up sensors may cause the drivers to lose their ability to judge distance. No evidence in the passage supports Choice (A). Choices (B) and (C) are unsupported generalizations.

5. **A.** Choice (A) is supported by the two problems mentioned: the wiring and the painting. Choice (B) is contradicted by the passage. No evidence in the passage supports Choices (C) or (D).

6. **C.** The passage is all about how reliable dogs are as companions. Choice (A) is a misreading of the passage. Choices (B) and (D) can't be supported by evidence in the passage.

7. **B.** Choice (B) accurately states the position of the logging industry and evidence in the passage. Choice (A) makes an assumption that goes beyond what's covered in the passage. Choice (C) is inaccurate because $2 billion refers to the payroll, not tax income. You can't know whether Choice (D) is accurate because it's not covered in the passage.

8. **A.** Based on information in the passage, Theodore Roosevelt obviously values a life of hard work over ease. Choice (B) misstates Roosevelt's position. Choice (C) may be a true statement, but it isn't supported by the passage. Choice (D) is an unsupported generalization.

9. **C.** Choice (C) is supported by the phrase "Many women golfers prefer titanium because it's lightweight and very strong. . . ." Choice (A) may be true, but no evidence in the passage suggests that "most golf clubs" are made of stainless steel. The passage doesn't mention beginners, so Choice (B) is incorrect. Choice (D) isn't supported by evidence in the passage.

10. **D.** The passage states that personal use of valuable technology is a "concern" for employers. Choices (A), (B), and (C) are generalizations which may or may not be true, but they can't be supported by any specific evidence in the passage.

11. **A.** Choice (A) is a restatement of the first line of the passage. Choice (B) is a generalization that isn't supported by evidence in the passage. Choice (C) is irrelevant, and Choice (D) is a misreading of the passage.

12. **D.** The passage describes traditional DVDs as having much less storage capacity than newer Blu-ray discs. Choice (A) is inaccurate based on the parenthetical information in the passage. Both Choice (B) and Choice (C) may be true statements, but neither is directly addressed in the passage.

13. **B.** The passage states that flavonoids contain antioxidants that may help reduce the signs of aging. Choice (A) makes a strong assertion ("All patients . . . will markedly improve") that can't be supported by the evidence in the passage. Choice (C) is a fallible conclusion drawn from the passage, and Choice (D) is far too general.

14. **C.** The passage makes clear that frigate birds engage in stealing the catch of other birds. Choice (A) is contradicted by the information in the passage. Choices (B) and (D) are never addressed in the passage.

15. **D.** The passage states that Osiris is an example of a resurrection god, a term defined in the passage. Choice (A) can't be supported because the passage states that Osiris was influential, but it doesn't state that he was the most powerful god. Choice (B) is wrong because the passage states the festival is held once a year. Choice (C) is wrong because the passage states "Small images of the god were made . . . representing the god as a mummy," not that the mummy itself was made.

16. **A.** The last sentence in the passage supports Choice (A). Choice (B) isn't supported by the information in the passage. Supersonic means faster than the speed of sound, so Choice (C) is wrong. Altitude isn't addressed in the passage, so Choice (D) is incorrect.

17. **C.** The passage states that the equator is the natural starting point for latitude and that an arbitrary point had to be chosen for longitude. Choice (A) is wrong because the equator is an east/west line and lines of longitude run north/south. Choice (B) isn't logical; only one line of longitude is the Prime Meridian. Choice (D) also is illogical; any city in the world can be measured by a line of longitude.

18. **A.** Because sports may be added or eliminated from Olympic competition, the total number is variable. The passage contradicts Choice (B). Rugby sevens and golf will be added in 2016, so Choice (C) is wrong. Choice (D) isn't addressed in the passage, but archery, tennis, and golf have been eliminated and then reinstated.

19. **C.** According to the passage, new studies show that the brain is dynamic and capable of change; thus, it isn't immutable (unchanging). Choices (A) and (B) are contradicted by the information in the passage. Choice (D) is illogical because permanently preventing brain injuries is impossible.

20. **D.** The passage states that some squirrels hibernate, and some eat stored food to survive in winter. Thus, their behavior patterns are diverse. Choice (A) is wrong because some squirrels hibernate and have no need for stored foods. Choice (B) can't be inferred because the passage doesn't state that all squirrels are vegetarians. Choice (C) can't be inferred because the passage doesn't address burying patterns.

21. **B.** The passage indicates that the deletion of part of chromosome 22 is the cause of Velocardiofacial Syndrome. Choice (A) is incorrect because it assumes backward from effect to cause. Any number of other causes of palate deformities is possible. No evidence in the passage supports Choice (C); in fact, it's illogical. Choice (D) is incorrect; a human cell contains 46 chromosomes.

22. **C.** The passage makes it clear that these men were well-known scouts. Choice (A) is historically inaccurate. Choice (B) is an inaccurate assumption that can't be inferred from the information in the passage. Choice (D), while certainly true, isn't addressed in the passage.

23. **D.** The passage indicates that a good BMI is one indicator of physical health. Based on the information in the passage, it's impossible to ascertain the accuracy of Choice (A). Choice (B) doesn't accurately state the calculation. Choice (C) is a vague generalization that can't be supported by the evidence in the passage.

24. **B.** *Genetic modifications* (by definition) are changes that alter the basic characteristics of plants. Choice (A) is an unsupported generalization. Choice (C) goes beyond the scope of the passage. Choice (D) can't be supported because no evidence suggests that this procedure is dangerous.

25. **B.** The passage states, "She was worried about the questionable repair record of the car she had selected." Choice (A) is incorrect because only one issue caused her concern. Choice (C) makes a statement about how far Jane traveled that can't be supported by the passage; it also contradicts information in the passage that she wasn't concerned about fuel mileage. Choice (D) can't be supported by the passage.

26. **D.** The passage indicates that carbon monoxide alarms alert residents to the presence of this gas. It's logical that their installation will reduce the hazard of accidental poisonings. Carbon monoxide is odorless, so Choice (A) is wrong. Choice (B) is illogical, and the ability of alarms to remove carbon monoxide, Choice (C), isn't discussed in the passage.

27. **A.** The shape is described in the passage as cigar-like or fish-like. Choice (B) refers to the keel rather than the internal sack. Choice (C) is contradicted by the information regarding the keel. Choice (D) isn't addressed in the passage and can't be inferred.

Part III
Back to School with Math and Science

"This guy writes an equation for over 20 minutes, and he has the nerve to say, 'Voilà'?"

In this part . . .

Chances are pretty good that at one time in your life you knew a great deal of the stuff you're tested on in the math and science portions of the tests. You knew how to use the order of operations, multiply and divide fractions, calculate the area of a triangle, identify the atoms in H_2O, and convert Fahrenheit to Celsius. Maybe you still remember most of what you once knew, but maybe not.

In addition, you need to know about machines, power, and electricity. You don't need to be a mechanical or electrical engineer to do well on these sections of the test, but you do need to know basic physics, the fundamentals of machinery, the various forces that move things, and the gist of electricity and magnetism. And you must know numerous equations for solving basic problems related to mechanics and electronics.

By working through the sample questions and tests in this part, you develop a clearer understanding of what to expect on the test and build your confidence as you add to your knowledge and skills.

Chapter 8

Building Your Math Knowledge

To score well on the Air Force Officer Qualifying Test (AFOQT), Aviation Selection Test Battery (ASTB), or Armed Services Vocational Aptitude Battery (ASVAB), you need quick and clear recall of basic math skills. Whether the test has a mathematical knowledge section, an arithmetic reasoning section, or both, you need to master the core skills of arithmetic, algebra, and geometry to answer the questions you'll face.

In this chapter, you take a short refresher course in the most essential math you learned in school. You start with key concepts from arithmetic; brush up on prime numbers, integers, fractions, and decimals; and hold it all together with the order of operations. You raise numbers to powers and extract roots. You use ratios, proportions, and percentages to describe relationships and solve problems. You review the key skills of algebra, the highlights of geometry, and essential probability and statistics. When all is said and done, you'll be ready for anything you may encounter.

Brushing Up on the Basics

Arithmetic begins with the whole numbers: 0, 1, 2, 3, 4, . . . You count whole numbers and then add, subtract, multiply, and divide them. These fundamental operations form the basis of and gateway to all other arithmetic skills as well as to algebra. The processes you learn for whole numbers lead right into the rules for integers and decimals. After you understand basic arithmetic and a little about prime factors, operations with fractions are an easy next step. In the following sections, you master the fundamentals for acquiring all other arithmetic skills.

Doing basic math with whole numbers and integers

When you learn to count, you work with whole numbers: 0, 1, 2, 3, and so on. Integers are similar to whole numbers, but they include negative values: –1, –2, –3, and so on. Whole numbers are the numbers you use when you first learn basic math — addition, subtraction, multiplication, and division. The integers come later, but the operations are similar. The numbers are easy. You just have to learn how to deal with the positive and negative signs in front of the numbers.

Adding and subtracting

Addition and subtraction are fairly easy in everyday problems like subtracting 50 cents from a dollar. When adding or subtracting negative as well as positive numbers, a sense of balance is important. Knowing how far from zero a number is can help, and absolute value is a way to measure that. The absolute value of a number is the number without its sign. Both +4 and –4 have an absolute value of 4. The symbol for the absolute value of a number, *n,* is $|n|$. So $|{-12}| = 12$, $|43| = 43$, and $|0| = 0$.

With your knowledge of absolute values, you can quickly perform any addition or subtraction problem using the following rules:

- ✔ **To add two integers that have the *same* sign, *add* their absolute values and give your answer the same sign.** For example, 5 + 9 = 14 and –8 + –6 = –14.

- ✔ **To add two numbers with *different* signs, *subtract* the absolute values, and take the sign of the number with the larger absolute value.** For example, to solve –13 + 24, you subtract 13 from 24, which equals 11. You then use the sign from the larger absolute value, which is the plus sign next to 24, so the answer is +11.

- ✔ **When subtracting a negative from a negative, add the two negative numbers.** For example, –29 – 32 is –29 + –32 = –61.

- ✔ **Two negatives equal a positive.** Think of the two minus signs that bump into each other and turn into a plus: –171 – (–38) = –171 + 38 = –133.

The simplest rule for subtracting integers is this: don't. Instead, change subtraction problems to addition by changing the subtraction sign to a plus sign and changing the number following the subtraction sign to the opposite of the number. To subtract a positive number, add a negative. To subtract a negative number, add a positive. Then follow the rules for addition. For example, 20 – 32 = 20 + (– 32). Subtract 20 from 32, which equals 12, and then use the sign from the larger absolute value, which is the minus sign next to 32. Thus, your answer is –12.

After you've changed to addition, you can rearrange if it's more convenient. For example, $5 - 3 \neq 3 - 5$, but $5 + (-3) = -3 + 5$.

Multiplying and dividing

Multiplication and division are opposite or inverse operations, but the rules governing signs are the same for both operations. If both numbers have the same sign, the result is positive — two positives equal a positive and two negatives equal a positive. If the signs of the two numbers are different, the result is negative.

$-12 \times -5 = ?$

Multiply –12 by 5 without worrying about the signs: $12 \times 5 = 60$. Then look at the signs. Because –12 and –5 have the same sign, the result is positive, or 60.

$42 \div -6 = ?$

First, divide without the signs: $42 \div 6 = 7$. Then check the signs. Because 42 is positive and 6 is negative (different signs), the result is negative, or –7.

In division, the dividend is the number that's divided, and the divisor is the number it's divided by. The quotient is the number of times the divisor goes into the dividend. The remainder is what's left over if the dividend isn't a whole-number multiple of the divisor.

Maintaining order in your operations

When a problem involves only addition or only multiplication, you can tackle the numbers in any convenient sequence. As soon as you start to mix up operations, however, you need rules to govern the order in which you perform the operations. Most people remember those rules by the mnemonic PEMDAS. The letters stand for Parentheses, Exponents, Multiplication and Division, Addition and Subtraction.

Parentheses

Do what's in parentheses first. If you have more than one set of grouping symbols, work from the inside out, as explained in the following example.

Simplify $-17 + \left[(-25 - 31) + 48(-2 \div -8) \right]$.

First subtract -25 from 31 in the inner parentheses, and then divide -2 by -8 in the second set of parentheses, as follows:

$$-17 + \left[(-56) + 48(-2 \div -8) \right]$$
$$-17 + \left[(-56) + 48\left(\frac{1}{4}\right) \right]$$

Then multiply $48\left(\frac{1}{4}\right)$ to get $-17 + \left[(-56) + 12 \right]$, add $-56 + 12$, in the brackets, to get $-17 + [-44]$, and finally add $-17 + -44$ to get -61.

Exponents

Deal with exponents next. Exponents are symbols for repeated multiplication. The expression 5^3, for example, means $5 \cdot 5 \cdot 5$. The 5 is the base and the 3 is the exponent.

Don't let the difference in mathematical symbols throw you off your game. A dot, asterisk, or $\times$ are used interchangeably to represent multiplication, so 5×5 is the same as $5 * 5$, which is the same as $5 \cdot 5$.

When working with exponents, remember these three basic rules:

✔ **When you multiply powers of the same base, keep the base and add the exponents.** Check out this example: $3^7 \cdot 3^5 = 3^{7+5} = 3^{12}$.

✔ **When you divide powers of the same base, keep the base and subtract the exponents.** Take a look at this example: $\dfrac{7^{10} \cdot 5^{12}}{7^6 \cdot 5^4} = \dfrac{7^{10}}{7^6} \cdot \dfrac{5^{12}}{5^4} = 7^{10-6} \cdot 5^{12-4} = 7^4 \cdot 5^8$.

✔ **When you raise a power to a power, keep the base and multiply the exponents.** Here's an example: $\left(5^{12}\right)^2 = 5^{12 \cdot 2} = 5^{24}$.

Remember the following two special exponents:

✔ **Raising any number except zero to the power of zero results in 1.** In other words, $a^0 = 1$ (provided $a \neq 0$), so $2379^0 = 1$.

✔ **Raising any number to the power of 1 equals the number itself.** In other words, $a^1 = a$, so $\dfrac{4^3}{4^2} = 4^{3-2} = 4^1 = 4$.

Multiplication and division

After you take care of anything in parentheses and deal with any exponents to make the parentheses and exponents disappear, you're left with the four arithmetic operations: addition, subtraction, multiplication, and division. Multiply and divide first.

Simplify $-7+5\times-2+-12\div-4-3$.

Start from the left and move to the right, performing only the multiplication and division operations. First multiply 5 times negative 2, which equals negative 10, and then divide negative 12 by negative 4 to get positive 3:

$$-7+\underbrace{5\times-2}_{-10}+\underbrace{-12\div-4}_{3}-3$$
$$=-7+-10+3-3$$

Multiplication and division get equal treatment. Don't jump over one to do the other. Deal with them as you meet them from left to right.

Correct: $2\times12\div4\times3=24\div4\times3=6\times3=18$

Incorrect: $2\times12\div4\times3=24\div12=2$

Addition and subtraction

Start from the left again, move to the right, and do addition and subtraction as you meet them. Remember, subtracting a number is the same as adding the opposite of that number. Following is an example:

$$-7+-10+3-3$$
$$-17+3-3$$
$$-14-3$$
$$-17$$

Working with prime and composite numbers

You may encounter questions on the test that deal with prime numbers. A prime number is a whole number that can be evenly divided only by itself and 1. Examples of prime numbers include 2, 3, 5, 7, 11, 13, 17, 19, and 23. Two is the smallest and only even prime number. A composite number is an integer that can be divided by at least one positive integer other than itself and one leaving no remainder; for example, 12 can be divided by 1 and 12, but also by 2, 3, 4, and 6.

One is neither a prime nor a composite number. It has its own category called a *unit*.

Two numbers that are multiplied are called factors, and the result of the multiplication is called the product; for example, in $2\times5=10$, 2 and 5 are factors and 10 is the product. The prime factorization of a number is a rewriting of the number as a product of prime factors; for example, the prime factorization of 18 is $2\times3\times3$, or 2×3^2.

Find the prime factorization of 210.

Start with small primes and work up. Start with 2: $210=2\times105$. You can't divide 105 by 2 again, so try 3: $210=2\times3\times35$, and 35 is divisible by 5 and 7, so the prime factorization of $210=2\times3\times5\times7$.

Figuring fractions

We generally think of a fraction as representing a part of something, which isn't entirely accurate, because fractions can be more than a whole, as in the case of $\frac{3}{2}$, which is $\frac{1}{2}$ more than 1. Fractions can be thought of as statements of division, with the top number (the numerator) divided by the bottom number (the denominator).

Reducing fractions to their lowest terms

A fraction is in lowest terms (simplest form) when the numerator and denominator have no common factors. For example, the fraction $\frac{12}{15}$ is not in its simplest form, because 12 and 15 share the factor 3: $3 \times 4 = 12$ and $3 \times 5 = 15$. To reduce a fraction to its lowest terms, divide the numerator and the denominator by the same number. In this case, you divide the numerator and denominator by 3, and the result is $\frac{4}{5}$. The actual value of the fraction remains the same: $\frac{12}{15} = \frac{4}{5}$.

To reduce quickly, divide by the greatest common factor. If you're not sure what that is, just use numbers you're certain divide both the numerator and denominator, and repeat until no common factors remain.

The primary advantage to having fractions in their simplest form is that you have smaller numbers to work with.

When you're looking at your answer choices, remember that the choices are probably in simplest form, so make sure your answer is, too.

Changing improper fractions to mixed numbers

A fraction like $\frac{13}{12}$ is called an improper fraction because its value is greater than one. You'll often want to turn an improper fraction into a mixed number — a number that has both a whole number part and a fraction part; $\frac{13}{12}$ can become the mixed number $1\frac{1}{12}$ because $\frac{13}{12} = \frac{12}{12} + \frac{1}{12}$ and $\frac{12}{12}$ is equal to one.

The quick rule for changing an improper fraction to a mixed number is to divide the numerator by the denominator. The quotient is the whole number part and the remainder over the divisor gives you the fractional part.

Change $\frac{37}{8}$ to a mixed number.

Remember fractions are division statements, so divide 37 by 8, which gives you 4 with a remainder of 5. The 4 is the whole number part, and the 5 goes over the 8 to give you a fractional part of $\frac{5}{8}$, so $\frac{37}{8} = 4\frac{5}{8}$.

Because working with the improper fraction is often easier, don't rush to change forms. When you're ready to look at your answer choices, make sure the form of your answer matches the form of the choices.

Adding and subtracting fractions

Sometimes adding fractions is as simple as adding whole numbers. Five tables plus four tables is nine tables. Five twelfths plus four twelfths is nine twelfths. The denominator (bottom number) tells you what kind of fraction you have. The numerator (top number) tells you how many of those things you have. If your fractions are the same kind of things — that is, if they have the same denominator — all you have to do is add up the numerators to know how many of those things you have.

The problem arises when you start to add different kinds of things — different denominators. Just as you can't add apples and oranges to find a total number of oranges or a total number of apples, you can't add fractions with different denominators. You must find a common denominator first.

The common denominator is a number divisible by both denominators. Generally, you try to find the least common denominator (LCD) so you have the smallest possible number to deal with. For example, to add $\frac{1}{3} + \frac{1}{2}$, change both fractions to a denominator of 6.

The easiest way to find a common denominator is to multiply the two denominators, but this doesn't always result in the LCD. To find the LCD, list the multiples of each number and then pick the lowest multiple the numbers have in common. For example, the multiples of 3 are 3, 6, 9, 12, and so on, and the multiples of 2 are 2, 4, 6, 8, 12, and so on, so the lowest multiple they have in common is 6.

After you've chosen your common denominator, change each fraction by multiplying it by a disguised 1. (Multiplying a number by one leaves its value unchanged.) The disguise comes from writing the 1 as a number over itself, as in $\frac{2}{2}$ or $\frac{11}{11}$. When you multiply by a disguised one, you change the way the fraction looks, but you don't change its value.

$\frac{3}{5} + \frac{1}{8} = ?$

To solve, use a common denominator of 40, because 40 is divisible by both 5 and 8. Multiply $\frac{3}{5}$ by $\frac{8}{8}$, and multiply $\frac{1}{8}$ by $\frac{5}{5}$:

$$\frac{3}{5} + \frac{1}{8} = \frac{3}{5} \cdot \frac{8}{8} + \frac{1}{8} \cdot \frac{5}{5} = \frac{24}{40} + \frac{5}{40}.$$

Then add the numerators: $\frac{24}{40} + \frac{5}{40} = \frac{29}{40}$.

Subtracting fractions is just like adding fractions, except you subtract. Yes, that's a silly statement, but you convert to a common denominator, and then subtract the numerators.

$\frac{7}{12} - \frac{2}{5} = ?$

First, change to a common denominator of 60:

$$\frac{7}{12} - \frac{2}{5} = \frac{7}{12} \cdot \frac{5}{5} - \frac{2}{5} \cdot \frac{12}{12} = \frac{35}{60} - \frac{24}{60}.$$

Then subtract the numerators: $\frac{35}{60} - \frac{24}{60} = \frac{11}{60}$.

When you subtract mixed numbers, you may encounter an extra complication, however. If the fraction part of the first number is smaller than the fraction part of the second number, you may have to borrow from the whole number and regroup.

$6\frac{1}{8} - 2\frac{3}{4} = ?$

First, change to a common denominator: $6\frac{1}{8} - 2\frac{3}{4} = 6\frac{1}{8} - 2\frac{6}{8}$. In theory, you subtract the whole numbers, $6 - 2$, and subtract the fractions, but $\frac{1}{8} - \frac{6}{8}$ is a problem. Take $6\frac{1}{8}$ and rewrite it as $5 + 1 + \frac{1}{8} = 5 + \frac{8}{8} + \frac{1}{8} = 5\frac{9}{8}$. Now your subtraction becomes $5\frac{9}{8} - 2\frac{6}{8} = 3\frac{3}{8}$.

Multiplying and dividing fractions

The basic rule for multiplying fractions is very simple. Multiply numerator times numerator and denominator times denominator, like this: $\frac{3}{5} \times \frac{2}{3} = \frac{6}{15} = \frac{2}{5}$.

In this example, you multiply the numerators ($3 \times 2 = 6$) and the denominators ($5 \times 3 = 15$). You can then simplify $\frac{6}{15}$ by dividing the numerator and denominator by 3: $6 \div 3 = 2$, and $15 \div 3 = 5$.

If you follow this rule faithfully, however, you'll find yourself working with much larger numbers than necessary, and reducing a lot of answers to their simplest form. The better way to proceed is to simplify early. First, make sure that each fraction is in its lowest term. Then, reduce even further using common factors in the numerators and denominators of the different fractions.

$$\frac{6}{49} \times \frac{14}{15} = ?$$

Multiplying 6 by 14 and 49 by 15 and then reducing would take far too long. Instead, cancel first, using common factors in the numerators and denominators. Six and 15 are both divisible by 3, and 49 and 14 can be divided by 7:

$$\frac{6}{49} \times \frac{14}{15} = \frac{\overset{2}{\cancel{6}}}{\underset{7}{\cancel{49}}} \times \frac{\overset{2}{\cancel{14}}}{\underset{5}{\cancel{15}}} = \frac{2 \times 2}{7 \times 5} = \frac{4}{35}$$

This works because common factors in the numerator and denominator equal 1, so they cancel out one another. Look at it this way:

$$\frac{6}{49} \times \frac{14}{15} = \frac{\cancel{3} \times 2 \times \cancel{7} \times 2}{7 \times 7 \times \cancel{3} \times 5} = \frac{4}{35}$$

To multiply mixed numbers, your best strategy is to change the mixed numbers to improper fractions first. Multiply the improper fractions and then convert back to a mixed number, if necessary.

$$5\frac{4}{7} \times 4\frac{2}{3} = ?$$

Convert $5\frac{4}{7}$ to $\frac{39}{7}$ and $4\frac{2}{3}$ to $\frac{14}{3}$. Then multiply $\frac{39}{7} \times \frac{14}{3} = \frac{\overset{13}{\cancel{39}}}{\underset{1}{\cancel{7}}} \times \frac{\overset{2}{\cancel{14}}}{\underset{1}{\cancel{3}}} = 26$.

Avoid the temptation to multiply the whole number by the whole number and the fraction by the fraction. That strategy of separation works for addition, but not for multiplication.

The rule for dividing by fractions is simple and familiar: don't. You never actually divide by a fraction. To divide fractions, invert the divisor and multiply. In the following example, the divisor is $\frac{3}{4}$. You invert it to make $\frac{4}{3}$ and then multiply:

$$\frac{5}{7} \div \frac{3}{4} = \frac{5}{7} \times \frac{4}{3} = \frac{20}{21}$$

To find the reciprocal of a whole number or a mixed number, first write it as a fraction and then invert. After rewriting the problem as a multiplication problem, simply follow the rules for multiplying fractions.

$$4\frac{3}{8} \div 1\frac{7}{8} = ?$$

Change $4\frac{3}{8}$ to $\frac{35}{8}$ and $1\frac{7}{8}$ to $\frac{15}{8}$, and then invert the divisor and multiply:

$$\frac{35}{8} \div \frac{15}{8} = \frac{\overset{7}{\cancel{35}}}{\cancel{8}} \times \frac{\cancel{8}}{\underset{3}{\cancel{15}}} = \frac{7}{3} = 2\frac{1}{3}$$

Taking command of decimals

Decimals are fractions with a denominator (the number on the bottom) that's a power of ten. For example, ten cents is 0.1 or one tenth of a dollar. A penny is 0.01 or one hundredth of a dollar. The arithmetic of decimals — or more accurately, decimal fractions — follows the same rules as the arithmetic of whole numbers. The only additional concern is making sure the decimal point is in the right place. As you move to the right of the decimal, the denominator increases by one power of ten: one tenth, one hundredth, one thousandth, and so on, as shown here:

$$0.62345 = \underset{\text{ones}}{0} \cdot \underset{\text{tenths}}{6} \quad \underset{\text{hundredths}}{2} \quad \underset{\text{thousandths}}{3} \quad \underset{\text{ten-thousandths}}{4} \quad \underset{\text{hundred-thousandths}}{5}$$

Rounding decimals up or down

If you're asked to round a number to a particular decimal place, look one place to the right of that. If the digit is 5 or higher, add one to the digit in your desired place and drop all the following digits. If the digit in that next place is 4 or lower, leave the digit in your desired place as is and drop all the following digits.

Round 372.98147 to the nearest hundredth.

To round to the nearest hundredth, or two places to the right of the decimal point, look at the third digit after the decimal point. Because that digit is 1, leave the digit in the hundredths place as is and drop all the digits that follow: 1, 4, and 7. The correct answer is 372.98.

Lining up decimals to add and subtract

To add or subtract numbers with decimals, stack the numbers so the decimal points align. Doing so ensures that to the left of the decimal point you're subtracting ones from ones, tens from tens, and hundreds from hundreds and to the right of the decimal point, you're subtracting tenths from tenths, hundredths from hundredths, and thousandths from thousandths. After you've lined up the decimal points, you can add the numbers just as if they were whole numbers. If it makes your work easier, once the decimal points are aligned, you can add zeros to the end of any number to fill out the columns of digits.

128.37 + 42.9 + 1602.539 = ?

Line up the decimal points. Add zeros if it helps you. Add down the columns carrying carefully, as shown here:

$$
\begin{array}{r}
\overset{1\ 1\ 1}{128.37}0 \\
42.900 \\
1602.539 \\
\hline
1773.809
\end{array}
$$

Adding zeros

When subtracting decimals, adding zeros so that the numbers have the same number of places becomes more important.

Subtract 23.48 from 45.927.

Line up the decimals. Add a zero, if you like, and subtract as follows:

$$
\begin{array}{r}
45.927 \\
-23.480 \\
\hline
22.447
\end{array}
$$

This subtraction could be completed without adding a zero, if you remember to bring down the seven. Seven minus the unseen zero at the end of 23.48 is seven. The next example really needs the added zero.

Subtract 371.934 from 839.5.

Line up the decimals and add zeros, as shown:

$$839.500$$
$$-371.934$$

If you don't add the two extras zeros to 839.5, you may be tempted to "bring down" the three and the four from 371.934, which would be incorrect. Those digits need to be subtracted from something. You need the zeros so you have something to subtract them from.

Because you can't subtract nonzero numbers from zero, you need to borrow and regroup, like so:

$$
\begin{array}{ccccccc}
\overset{7}{\cancel{8}} & {}^{1}3 & \overset{8}{\cancel{9}} & . & \overset{{}^{1}4}{\cancel{5}} & \overset{9}{{}^{1}\cancel{0}} & {}^{1}0 \\
3 & 7 & 1 & . & 9 & 3 & 4 \\
\hline
4 & 6 & 7 & . & 5 & 6 & 6 \\
\end{array}
$$

Multiplication of decimals follows the same patterns as multiplication of whole numbers, but when that work is done, you have to place the decimal point correctly. The rule says to count the number of digits after the decimal point in each of the factors, add those counts, and place the decimal point in the product so that many places follow the decimal point.

$4.83 \times 2.1 = ?$

Multiply these numbers just the way you would multiply 483 by 21. You should get 10,143. Then count the digits to the right of the decimal point in each number and add them. The answer must have 3 decimal places. Count back three digits from the right and place the decimal point as shown here:

$$4.83 \times 2.1 = 4.\underset{2}{\underline{83}} \times 2.\underset{1}{\underline{1}} = 10.\underset{3}{\underline{143}}$$

Estimating (calculating a ballpark figure) can help you place the decimal point as well. In the example above, 4.83 rounds to 5, and 2.1 to 2, so you should expect an answer around 10.

Need to divide decimals? Don't. At least, never divide by a decimal. Instead, adjust the problem so that the divisor is a whole number. You're actually multiplying both the dividend and the divisor by a power of ten.

$5.48 \div 0.004 = ?$

Move the decimal point to the end of the divisor (0.004 in this case) and the same number of places in the dividend (5.48). This makes your divisor a whole number (4) and your dividend 5,480. Divide, and place the decimal point in the quotient directly above the point in the dividend, like this:

$$0.\underline{004})5.\underline{480} \Rightarrow 4\overline{)5480.}^{\,1370.}$$

The whole number division problem 5,480 ÷ 4 has exactly the same value as 5.48 ÷ 0.004 because you've multiplied both numbers by 1,000.

Keeping Ratios and Percents in Proportion

Many of the questions you'll encounter on the Officer Candidate Tests (OCT) deal in one way or another with proportional thinking. Sometimes it's packaged as a percentage question, but percent problems come back to proportions anyway. Regardless of whether your focus is on proportions or percentages, the following sections help you answer correctly.

Preparing proportions

A *ratio* is a comparison of two numbers by division. If one number is three times the size of another, we say the ratio of the larger to the smaller is "3 to 1," or the ratio of the smaller to the larger is "1 to 3." A *proportion* is a statement that two ratios are equal, as in $\frac{1}{3} = \frac{2}{6}$.

To solve ratio or proportion problems, assign a variable to both numbers in the ratio. Suppose you're told that the ratio of one number to another is 5:2. As long as you multiply both numbers by the same value, the resulting ratio remains the same. For example, $5x:2x = 5:2$.

If the ratio of two numbers is 7:3 and their sum is 50, what are the two numbers?

You can easily solve this problem using $7x$ and $3x$ to stand for the two numbers:

$$7x + 3x = 50$$
$$10x = 50$$
$$x = 5$$
$$7x = 35$$
$$3x = 15$$

The ratio of three angles of a triangle is 2:3:5. If the total of the three angles is 180 degrees, find the measure of the largest angle.

Add a variable to each number in the ratio, and the measures of the three angles become $2x$, $3x$, and $5x$. The three angles add up to 180, so $2x + 3x + 5x = 180$. That means $10x = 180$, so $x = 18$, making the largest angle $5x$ or 5×18, which equals 90 degrees.

In any proportion, the products of diagonally opposite terms are equal. In the proportion $\frac{5}{8} = \frac{15}{24}$, the product of 5 and 24 is equal to the product of 8 and 15. Whenever you have two equal ratios, you can cross-multiply.

If $\frac{7}{4} = \frac{x}{14}$, find the value of x.

Cross-multiplying produces $4x = 7 \cdot 14$. Solving this equation gives you $x = \frac{7 \cdot 14}{4} = \frac{98}{4} = 24.5$.

Find the value of x if $\frac{16}{x} = \frac{80}{75}$.

Cross-multiply to get $80x = 16 \cdot 75$, but don't spend time multiplying out 16 times 75. Move right to the division: $x = \frac{16 \cdot 75}{80\,_5} = \frac{75}{5} = 15$.

Calculating percentages

The word *percent* means "out of a hundred" or "for every hundred," so you solve most percent problems by the proportion $\frac{\text{part}}{\text{whole}} = \frac{\%}{100}$. Percentage questions supply two of the three pieces: part, whole, and percent. Fill in the two you know, and solve the proportion to find the other one.

If you scored 360 points out of a possible 480 points on a test, what percent did you score?

The equation $\frac{\text{part}}{\text{whole}} = \frac{\%}{100}$ becomes $\frac{360}{480} = \frac{x}{100}$. You can reduce $\frac{360}{480} = \frac{36}{48} = \frac{3}{4}$, giving you $\frac{3}{4} = \frac{x}{100}$. Cross-multiply and $4x = 300$, so $x = 75$. The correct answer is 75%.

Find 32% of 800.

$\frac{\text{part}}{\text{whole}} = \frac{\%}{100}$ becomes $\frac{x}{800} = \frac{32}{100}$. Cross-multiply to get $100x = 800 \cdot 32$, and divide to get $x = \frac{800 \cdot 32}{100} = 8 \cdot 32 = 256$.

Sixteen is 30% of what number?

The equation $\frac{\text{part}}{\text{whole}} = \frac{\%}{100}$ becomes $\frac{16}{x} = \frac{30}{100}$ or $\frac{16}{x} = \frac{3}{10}$. Cross-multiply to get $3x = 160$ and $x = \frac{160}{3} = 53\frac{1}{3}$.

Dealing with decimals

Change percents to decimal form by dropping the percent sign and moving the decimal point two places to the left. For example, 15% = 0.15.

Change decimals to percents by moving the decimal point two places to the right and adding a percent sign, like this: 0.817 = 81.7%.

If you prefer to work percent problems with decimals rather than fractions, the rule you want to remember is whole × percent = part.

Twelve percent of 300 is what percent of 240?

Change 12% to 0.12 and multiply: $300 \times 0.12 = 36$. To answer the question, "Thirty-six is what percent of 240?", set up $240x = 36$ and solve by dividing: $x = \frac{36}{240} = \frac{3}{20} = 0.15$. Change 0.15 to a percent: 0.15 = 15%.

Digging Up Roots and Radicals

The *square root* of a number is a value that when squared (multiplied by itself) produces the number. The square root of 4 is 2 because $2 \times 2 = 4$. The square root of 49 is 7 because $7 \times 7 = 49$. To indicate the square root of a number, use the radical sign; for example, to indicate the positive square root of 49, you write $\sqrt{49}$ (pronounced "radical forty-nine").

Perfect squares, such as 4, 16, and 81, have square roots that are integers. Some numbers have square roots that are fractions. For example, the square root of $\frac{4}{9}$ is $\frac{2}{3}$.

A great many numbers have square roots that are not integers, fractions, or even nice decimals. When the square root of a number is a messy decimal that goes on forever and doesn't repeat, leaving the number in its radical form is more convenient and exact. Working with $\sqrt{2}$ is easier than trying to deal with 1.41421356 . . . .

Leaving square roots in radical form, however, opens up a whole new set of rules for arithmetic, including simplifying radicals, as explained in the following sections.

Simplifying radicals

Before you try to deal with radicals in an expression, try to simplify the radical. Look for factors of the number under the radical that are perfect squares.

Put $\sqrt{48}$ in simplest form.

First, consider that $\sqrt{48} = \sqrt{16 \cdot 3}$. Give each factor its own radical: $\sqrt{16} \cdot \sqrt{3}$. Then, because you know $\sqrt{16} = 4$, $\sqrt{48} = \sqrt{16}\sqrt{3} = 4\sqrt{3}$.

Most people don't know the square roots of large numbers, but if you look for factors of the number that are perfect squares and use the technique for simplifying radicals, you may be able to figure out the square root of the larger number. Take a look at this example: $\sqrt{72,900} = \sqrt{729 \cdot 100} = \sqrt{9 \cdot 81 \cdot 100} = \sqrt{9} \cdot \sqrt{81} \cdot \sqrt{100} = 3 \times 9 \times 10 = 270$.

Adding and subtracting radicals

You can add and subtract only like radicals; for example, you can add $2\sqrt{5} + 7\sqrt{5} = 9\sqrt{5}$, but you can't add or subtract unlike radicals, such as $2\sqrt{5} + 7\sqrt{11}$. Add or subtract like radicals by adding or subtracting the coefficients indicating how many of that radical you have. (A *coefficient* is a multiplier, so in the case of $7\sqrt{11}$, 7 is the coefficient of $\sqrt{11}$.) Here are a couple examples: $5\sqrt{3} + 3\sqrt{3} = 8\sqrt{3}$ and $6\sqrt{7} - 2\sqrt{7} = 4\sqrt{7}$.

If you're asked to add or subtract unlike radicals, first put each radical in simplest form to try to transform unlike radicals into like radicals. Then, if you have multiples of the same radical, you can add or subtract the coefficients.

$\sqrt{32} + \sqrt{50} = ?$

Simplify each radical as follows: $\sqrt{32} = \sqrt{16}\sqrt{2} = 4\sqrt{2}$ and $\sqrt{50} = \sqrt{25}\sqrt{2} = 5\sqrt{2}$, so $\sqrt{32} + \sqrt{50} = 4\sqrt{2} + 5\sqrt{2} = 9\sqrt{2}$.

Multiplying and dividing radicals

When you multiply or divide expressions involving radicals, multiply or divide numbers under the radical with numbers under the radical, and numbers outside the radical with numbers outside the radical. Check out these examples: $4\sqrt{3} \cdot 5\sqrt{2} = 4 \cdot 5 \cdot \sqrt{3} \cdot \sqrt{2} = 20\sqrt{3 \cdot 2} = 20\sqrt{6}$, and $14\sqrt{6} \div 7\sqrt{3} = (14 \div 7) \cdot (\sqrt{6} \div \sqrt{3}) = 2\sqrt{6 \div 3} = 2\sqrt{2}$.

Getting Up to Speed with Basic Algebra

The minute you start to use a *variable* (a letter or other symbol to stand for a number), you're technically in the world of algebra. Algebra problems typically provide you with known values and challenge you to use the known values to calculate unknown values represented by variables.

First encounters

An algebraic expression is simply an arithmetic problem that involves one or more variables. To evaluate an expression, find its value when the variable is replaced with a particular number. For example, to evaluate $3x + 5$ when $x = -2$, you rewrite it with -2 in place of x, and do the arithmetic: $3(-2) + 5 = -6 + 5 = -1$.

Remember the order of operations when evaluating expressions: PEMDAS (Parentheses, Exponents, Multiplication and Division, Addition and Subtraction).

Whenever possible, put variable expressions in simplest form. Generally, an expression is in simplest form when it has as few terms as possible and no parentheses. Usually, you use the distributive property to remove parentheses; then you combine *like terms* — terms with the same variable — by adding or subtracting.

According to the distributive property, multiplication distributes across addition, so $5 \times (3 + 5x + 7x) = (5 \times 3) + (5 \times 5x) + (5 \times 7x)$.

Simplify $3(2x - 7) + 5(x + 3)$.

First, use the distributive property to eliminate the parentheses: $3(2x - 7) + 5(x + 3) = 6x - 21 + 5x + 15$. Then add the variable terms: $6x - 21 + 5x + 15 = 11x - 21 + 15$. Finally, add the constant terms: $11x - 21 + 15 = 11x - 6$.

Solving equations

Before you begin the actual work of solving an equation, make the equation as simple as possible. Focus on one side of the equation at a time, and if parentheses or other grouping symbols are present, perform the steps necessary to remove them: Simplify the expression inside the parentheses using the distributive property, or, if the parentheses aren't necessary, just remove them. For example, $5(x + 3) = 4 - (5 - x)$ becomes $5x + 15 = 4 - 5 + x$.

After clearing the parentheses, combine like terms (and only like terms). Never begin solving with more than two terms on either side of the equal sign. Now $5(x + 3) = 4 - (5 - x)$ becomes $5x + 15 = 4 - 5 + x$ or $5x + 15 = -1 + x$.

In solving an equation, your job is to undo the arithmetic that's been performed and isolate the variable on one side of the equation. Undoing means doing the opposite of what has been done. To keep the equation balanced, you perform the same operation on both sides of the equation:

1. **If the variable is on both sides of the equation, add or subtract to eliminate the variable on one side of the equation.**

2. **Add or subtract to eliminate the constant term that is on the same side as the variable term. You want to have one variable term equal to one constant term.**

3. **Divide both sides by the coefficient of the variable term.**

In the equation $5x + 15 = -1 + x$, the variable is on both sides, so subtract x from both sides: $5x + 15 - x = 4x + 15$, and $-1 + x - x = -1$, which leaves $4x + 15 = -1$.

Remove the constant from the side that still has a variable by subtracting 15 from both sides: $4x + 15 - 15 = 4x$, and $-1 - 15 = -16$, so $4x = -16$.

Divide both sides by 4 to isolate the variable, and $x = -4$.

Solving inequalities

An *inequality* is similar to an equation, except that the equal sign is replaced with an inequality sign: greater than (>), greater than or equal to (≥), less than (<), or less than or equal to (≤). The rules for solving inequalities are the same as those for solving equations (see the preceding section), except at the last step. When you divide both sides of an inequality by the coefficient of the variable term, you must make a decision about the inequality sign.

If you multiply or divide both sides of an inequality by a negative number, reverse the direction of the inequality sign. If you divide by a negative number, a < sign becomes a > sign, and a > sign turns into a < sign. If you divide both sides of an inequality by a positive number, leave the inequality sign as is.

Solve $5t - 9 \leq 8t + 15$.

Subtract 8t from both sides to get $-3t - 9 \leq 15$, and then add 9 to both sides to get $-3t \leq 24$. Divide both sides by –3 and, because you're dividing by a negative, reverse the direction of the inequality sign: $t \geq -8$.

Solving compound inequalities

A compound inequality consists of two inequalities in a single statement. If you know that the value of x is greater than 3 but less than 9, you could write $x > 3$ and $x < 9$, or you could compress that information into the statement $3 < x < 9$.

If you're asked to solve a compound inequality, simply break it into its two components and solve each inequality separately. Then, if you want to, you can compress the two answers into a compound inequality.

Solve $-5 < 2x - 3 < 7$.

Rewrite as two inequalities: $-5 < 2x - 3$ and $2x - 3 < 7$. Solve both inequalities. First, add three to both sides of the first inequality to get $-2 < 2x$, so $x < -1$. Then, add three to both sides of the second inequality to get $2x < 10$, so $x < 5$.

Then you can compress the two solutions, $-1 < x$ and $x < 5$, into $-1 < x < 5$.

Calculating slopes of lines on a graph

A single equation with two variables doesn't have one correct answer. Its solutions are pairs of numbers representing the two variables, x and y. Each ordered pair of numbers that solves the equation can be represented by a point in the coordinate plane (a two-dimensional graph with an x axis and a y axis). The collection of all those points forms the graph of the equation. You won't be asked to draw graphs on the OCT, but you may be asked questions about graphs — specifically about the slopes of lines formed by x,y points plotted on a graph.

Slope

The slope of a line tells whether the line is rising or falling and how quickly. Slope can be expressed as the ratio of rise to run; that is, the amount of vertical change (in the y direction) to the amount of horizontal change (in the x direction). If two points on the line are $\left(x_1, y_1\right)$ and $\left(x_2, y_2\right)$, then the slope, m, of the line is $m = \frac{y_2 - y_1}{x_2 - x_1}$. For example, the slope of the line through

the points (–4,–4) and (7,3) is $m = \frac{y_2 - y_1}{x_2 - x_1} = \frac{3 - -4}{7 - -4} = \frac{7}{11}$.

A horizontal line has a slope of 0. The slope of a vertical line is undefined. The correct way to express this is to say that a vertical line has no slope.

The equation of a line can take several forms, including slope-intercept and point-slope, which are covered in the following sections. Slope-intercept form is most useful for graphing, and point-slope form is most useful for writing the equation.

Slope-intercept form

The slope-intercept form of a linear equation is $y = mx + b$, where m is the slope and b is the y-intercept — the point at which the line crosses the y axis. If the slope and y-intercept of a line are known, you can write the equation by plugging the two numbers into the equation. For example, the equation of a line with a slope of -5 and a y-intercept of $(0, 2)$ is $y = -5x + 2$.

Point-slope form

The point-slope form $y - y_1 = m(x - x_1)$ is used to write the equation of a line with slope m through the point (x_1, y_1).

Find the equation of the line through the points $(2, 5)$ and $(-7, 23)$.

Use the slope formula to find the slope from the two points: $m = \dfrac{y_2 - y_1}{x_2 - x_1} = \dfrac{23 - 5}{-7 - 2} = \dfrac{18}{-9} = -2$.

Using $(2, 5)$ and the slope of -2, the point-slope form becomes $y - 5 = -2(x - 2)$. You can simplify to slope-intercept form if you like: $y = -2x + 9$.

Parallel and perpendicular lines

Parallel lines have the same slope, but if two lines are perpendicular, their slopes are negative reciprocals; that is, they're numbers that multiply to negative one, like -2 and $\dfrac{1}{2}$, or $\dfrac{3}{4}$ and $-\dfrac{4}{3}$.

Get with the systems: Solving systems of equations

A *system of equations* is a set of two equations with two variables. To solve a system of equations, you find the values of the two variables that make both equations true. A system of equations may have one solution, no solution, or infinitely many solutions.

To solve a system of equations, use either the substitution method or the elimination method, as explained in the following sections.

Substitution

To solve a system by substitution, choose one equation and isolate a variable. Doing so tells you that, for example, y is equal to some expression involving x. Use that information to replace the y in the other equation with the equivalent expression. You should get an equation involving only one variable, which you can solve. When you know the value of one variable, plug that back into one of the equations, and solve for the other variable.

Solve $\begin{cases} 3x - y = -15 \\ 5x + 2y = -14 \end{cases}$

Begin by isolating y in the first equation:

$$-y = -3x - 15$$
$$y = 3x + 15$$

Replace y with $3x + 15$ in the second equation:

$$5x + 2y = -14$$
$$5x + 2(3x + 15) = -14$$

Clear the parentheses, combine like terms, and then solve:

$$5x + 6x + 30 = -14$$
$$11x + 30 = -14$$
$$11x = -44$$
$$x = -4$$

When you know the value of x, substitute into one of the original equations:

$$3x - y = -15$$
$$3(-4) - y = -15$$
$$-12 - y = -15$$
$$-y = -3$$
$$y = 3$$

The solution of the system is $x = -4$, $y = 3$.

Elimination

The elimination method of solving a system uses addition or subtraction to eliminate one of the variables. If the coefficient of one variable is the same in both equations, subtracting one equation from the other will eliminate that variable. If the coefficients are opposites, adding will eliminate the variable. When you have eliminated one variable, solve and then use substitution to find the value of the other variable.

Solve $\begin{cases} 8a - 2b = 18 \\ 3a + 2b = -7 \end{cases}$

Add the equations to eliminate b:

$$8a - 2b = 18$$
$$\underline{3a + 2b = -7}$$
$$11a \quad\ = 11$$

Solving the equation tells you that $a = 1$. Substitute 1 for a in the second equation, and solve for b:

$$3(1) + 2b = -7$$
$$3 + 2b = -7$$
$$2b = -10$$
$$b = -5$$

The solution of the system is $a = 1$, $b = -5$.

Coming to terms with polynomials

Polynomials include constants, such as 6 or –12, variable terms, such as $3x$ or $-7y$, and sums and differences of such terms. A sum or difference of two terms is called a binomial, and three terms make a trinomial. The equation $3x - 7$ is a binomial and $4x^2 - 9x + 3$ is a trinomial. The following sections explain various ways to make polynomial expressions more manageable.

Simplifying like terms

To add or subtract polynomials, add or subtract like terms and only like terms. (The phrase "like terms" means terms that contain the same variable, raised to the same power. The terms differ only in the coefficient.) To add or subtract like terms, add or subtract the coefficients. In the expression $9y^2 + 4x - 3y^2 + 2x^2$, only the y^2 terms are like and can be combined: $9y^2 + 4x - 3y^2 + 2x^2 = 6y^2 + 4x + 2x^2$.

Distributing the minus in front of parentheses

Parentheses may appear in an algebraic expression to make it clear that one polynomial is to be subtracted from another.

Simplify $4x + 3 - (x + 5)$.

You need to subtract $x + 5$ from $4x + 3$. Do that by adding the opposite. Distribute the minus sign over all the terms in the parentheses, and then add: $4x + 3 - (x + 5) = 4x + 3 - x - 5 = 3x - 2$.

Making greater use of the distributive property

Removing parentheses from a variable expression usually involves performing some kind of multiplication. To multiply a single term times a polynomial, distribute the multiplication to each term of the polynomial.

Simplify $-7x^2 (5x^3 - 4x^2 + 8x - 1)$.

Multiply $-7x^2$ by each of the four terms in the parentheses. Simplify each term, paying attention to signs:

$$-7x^2 (5x^3 - 4x^2 + 8x - 1)$$
$$(-7x^2 \cdot 5x^3) - (-7x^2 \cdot 4x^2) + (-7x^2 \cdot 8x) - (-7x^2 \cdot 1)$$
$$-35x^5 - -28x^4 + -56x^3 - -7x^2$$
$$-35x^5 + 28x^4 - 56x^3 + 7x^2$$

Multiplying binomials: The FOIL rule

To multiply two binomials, use the FOIL rule. The letters in FOIL stand for First, Outer, Inner, and Last, and they refer to the four multiplications you must do. To multiply the binomials $(x + 5)(x - 3)$, follow these steps:

1. **Multiply the first terms of the binomials.**

$$\left(\underset{\text{First}}{x} + 5 \right) \left(\underset{\text{First}}{x} - 3 \right)$$

$$x \cdot x = x^2$$

2. **Multiply the outer terms.**

$$\left(\underset{\text{Outer}}{x} + 5\right)\left(x \underset{\text{Outer}}{-3}\right)$$

$$-3 \cdot x = -3x$$

3. **Multiply the inner terms.**

$$\left(x + \underset{\text{Inner}}{5}\right)\left(\underset{\text{Inner}}{x} - 3\right)$$

$$5 \cdot x = 5x$$

4. **Multiply the last terms of the binomials.**

$$\left(x + \underset{\text{Last}}{5}\right)\left(x \underset{\text{Last}}{-3}\right)$$

$$5 \cdot -3 = -15$$

5. **Combine like terms (usually the inner and the outer terms).**

$$x^2 - 3x + 5x - 15 = x^2 + 2x - 15$$

Breaking it down by factoring

Factoring asks you to go in the opposite direction from multiplication, starting with a single polynomial and rewriting it as the product of two or more factors. The following sections introduce you to the fundamentals of factoring.

Greatest common factor

To factor out a common monomial factor, take the following steps:

1. **Determine the largest number that divides the numerical coefficient of every term.**

   The numeric coefficient is the number that accompanies the variable; for example, in $9x^2$, 9 is the numeric coefficient.

2. **Determine the highest power of the variable that is common to all terms.**

3. **Place the common factor outside the parentheses.**

4. **Simplify the original polynomial by dividing each term of the original by the common factor.**

5. **Place the simpler polynomial inside.**

Factor $6x^5 - 9x^4 + 27x^3$.

To solve, implement the steps from the preceding list as follows:

1. The numeric coefficients are 6, 9, and 27. The largest number that divides 6, 9, and 27 is 3.

2. The largest power of x common to all terms is x^3.

3. Place the greatest common factor of $3x^3$ in front of a set of parentheses: $3x^3()$.

4. Divide each term of $6x^5 - 9x^4 + 27x^3$ by $3x^3$: $\frac{6x^5}{3x^3} = 2x^2$, $\frac{-9x^4}{3x^3} = -3x$, and $\frac{27x^3}{3x^3} = 9$.

5. Place the simpler polynomial inside the parentheses: $6x^5 - 9x^4 + 27x^3 = 3x^3\left(2x^2 - 3x + 9\right)$.

FOIL factoring for trinomials

A trinomial of the form $ax^2 + bx + c$ can often, though not always, be factored into the product of two binomials. To factor a trinomial into the product of two binomials, follow these steps:

1. **Put the trinomial in standard form ($ax^2 + bx + c$).**

2. **List pairs of factors for the squared term.**

3. **List pairs of factors for the constant term.**

4. **Try different arrangements of these factors, checking with the FOIL rule to see whether the inner and outer products produce the desired middle term.**

5. **Place the positive and negative signs and check the answer.**

Factor $13x + 6x^2 - 8$.

Implement the steps from the preceding list as follows:

1. Put the trinomial in a standard form:

   $$6x^2 + 13x - 8$$

2. List factors of $6x^2$.

3. List factors of 8. Don't worry about signs yet.

   Table 8-1 lists all the factors of $6x^2$ and all the factors of 8, and it assembles all the possible factors of the trinomial for you to test.

4. Set up two sets of parentheses and try various pairs of factors, as shown in Table 8-1, to see whether they produce the middle term of $13x$. The inner of $16x$ and the outer of $3x$ could make a middle term of $13x$ if the signs are right. To get $+13x$, you need $+16x$ and $-3x$.

5. Put a plus in front of 8 and a negative in front of 1, and then check by multiplying (see Table 8-1):

   $$(3x + 8)(2x - 1)$$
   $$6x^2 - 3x + 16x - 8$$
   $$6x^2 + 13x - 8$$

Table 8-1		Factors of $6x^2$ and 8			
Factors of $6x^2$	Factors of 8	Basic Setup	Inner Product	Outer Product	Possible Middle Term
3x and 2x	1 and 8	$(3x+1)(2x+8)$	$2x$	$24x$	26x or 22x
	8 and 1	$(3x+8)(2x+1)$	$16x$	$3x$	19x or 13x
	2 and 4	$(3x+2)(2x+4)$	$4x$	$12x$	16x or 8x
	4 and 2	$(3x+4)(2x+2)$	$8x$	$6x$	14x or 2x
6x and x	1 and 8	$(6x+1)(x+8)$	x	$48x$	49x or 47x
	8 and 1	$(6x+8)(x+1)$	$8x$	$6x$	14x or 2x
	2 and 4	$(6x+2)(x+4)$	$2x$	$24x$	26x or 22x
	4 and 2	$(6x+4)(x+2)$	$4x$	$12x$	16x or 8x

If the constant term is positive, both signs are the same as the sign of the middle term, and the inner and outer products add up to the middle term. If the constant term is negative, place the sign of the middle term on the larger of the two products, and the middle term is the difference of the inner and outer products.

Trying the difference of squares

The product of two binomials usually produces a trinomial, but in one case, the inner and the outer terms add to zero, leaving only two terms — the difference of squares. Consider this example: $x^2 - 36 = (x+6)(x-6)$. The inner term, $6x$, and the outer one, $-6x$, add to zero.

Squaring off with quadratic equations

A *quadratic equation* is one in which the highest power of the variable is 2; that is, x^2. Solving a quadratic equation requires some special techniques.

If a variable expression squared equals a constant term, you can solve by taking the square root of both sides. For example, if you know that $x^2 = 9$, then $x = \pm\sqrt{9} = \pm3$. If this gives you a messy result, leave your answer in simplest radical form.

Solve $3(x+1)^2 - 48 = 0$.

Add 48 to both sides, and divide both sides by 3:

$$3(x+1)^2 - 48 = 0$$
$$3(x+1)^2 = 48$$
$$(x+1)^2 = 16$$

Take the square root of both sides and then solve two equations:

$$(x+1)^2 = 16$$
$$x+1 = \pm4$$

$$x+1 = 4 \qquad x+1 = -4$$
$$x = 3 \qquad x = -5$$

Don't forget that when you take the square root of both sides, you always get the positive and the negative square root.

Equations that have a quadratic expression equal to zero are common. The key to solving such equations is to remember that if the product of two factors is zero, then at least one of the factors is zero. Sometimes, the solutions of a "quadratic = 0" equation is obvious. Consider this one: $(x-5)(x-7) = 0$. For the product of $(x-5)(x-7)$ to equal 0, either $(x-5)$ or $(x-7)$ has to equal 0, so x is either 5 or 7. You would write the answer as $x = 5, 7$.

The solutions of quadratic equations are not always so easy to spot. Here's an example of one that's not so obvious.

Solve $3x^2 + 2x - 6 = 2x^2 - 12 - 3x$.

The first step is to simplify the equation by moving the variable terms to one side. After you simplify, the "quadratic = 0" equation is clear: $x^2 + 5x + 6 = 0$.

You factor the quadratic into two expressions that, when multiplied together, equal zero: $3x^2 + 2x - 6 = 50 - 3x - 3x^2$. For the product of $(x + 3)(x + 2)$ to equal 0, either $(x + 3)$ or $(x + 2)$ must equal zero, so x is either -3 or -2. The answer is $x = -3, -2$.

Factoring in rational expressions

Rational expressions, sometimes called algebraic fractions, are the quotient of two polynomials. To simplify a rational expression, factor the numerator and the denominator and cancel any factors that appear in both.

Simplify $\dfrac{x^2 - x - 2}{x^2 - 4}$.

Factor $\dfrac{x^2 - x - 2}{x^2 - 4} = \dfrac{(x-2)(x+1)}{(x-2)(x+2)}$. The factor $x - 2$ appears in both the numerator and denominator, so it can be cancelled, leaving $\dfrac{x+1}{x+2}$.

Multiplying and dividing rational expressions

When multiplying or dividing rational expressions, you can save time and effort by canceling before multiplying, just as you do with regular fractions.

To multiply rational expressions, here's what you do:

1. **Factor all numerators and denominators.**

2. **Cancel any factor that appears in both a numerator and a denominator.**

3. **Multiply numerator times numerator and denominator times denominator.**

To divide rational expressions, invert the divisor and then follow the preceding steps.

Divide $\dfrac{x+5}{x^2 + 8x + 15} \div \dfrac{x+5}{x^2 + 6x + 9}$

Invert the divisor: $\dfrac{x+5}{x^2 + 8x + 15} \cdot \dfrac{x^2 + 6x + 9}{x+5}$. Factor all numerators and denominators, cancel, and then multiply:

$$\frac{\cancel{(x+5)}}{\cancel{(x+3)}(x+5)} \cdot \frac{\cancel{(x+3)}(x+3)}{\cancel{(x+5)}} = \frac{(x+3)}{(x+5)}$$

Adding and subtracting rational expressions

Adding and subtracting algebraic fractions requires a common denominator. If the fractions have the same denominator, you add or subtract the numerators, and keep the same denominator. Adding the numerators just means combining like terms.

When you subtract, remember that the fraction bar acts like a set of parentheses grouping everything in the numerator, so change all the signs in the second numerator. Here's an example:

$$\frac{2x+7}{x+5} - \frac{x-8}{x+5} = \frac{2x+7-(x-8)}{x+5} = \frac{2x+7-x+8}{x+5} = \frac{x+15}{x+5}$$

If the fractions have different denominators, take the following steps:

1. **Factor the denominators.**

2. **Identify the common factors in the denominators. Note the factors that don't appear in all the denominators.**

3. **Multiply each fraction's numerator and denominator by any factors that appear in other denominators but not in this one, to make the denominators identical.**

4. **Add or subtract the numerators.**

Subtract $\dfrac{5x-1}{3x-3} - \dfrac{3x+4}{2x-2}$.

First, factor each denominator: $\dfrac{5x-1}{3(x-1)} - \dfrac{3x+4}{2(x-1)}$. The denominators have the factor $x-1$ in common, but they don't have the factors 3 and 2 in common. The LCD is $2 \cdot 3(x-1) = 6(x-1)$. To make the denominators identical, multiply the first fraction by $\frac{2}{2}$ and the second fraction by $\frac{3}{3}$.

$$\dfrac{5x-1}{3(x-1)} \cdot \dfrac{2}{2} - \dfrac{3x+4}{2(x-1)} \cdot \dfrac{3}{3}$$

$$\dfrac{10x-2}{6(x-1)} - \dfrac{9x+12}{6(x-1)}$$

$$\dfrac{10x-2-(9x+12)}{6(x-1)}$$

$$\dfrac{10x-2-9x-12}{6(x-1)}$$

$$\dfrac{x-14}{6(x-1)}$$

Solving rational expression equations

You can solve some equations that involve algebraic fractions by cross-multiplying, as you do with a proportion. (See "Preparing proportions," earlier in this chapter, for details.) If the equation is two equal fractions (fractions on opposite sides of an equal sign) or can easily be simplified to two equal fractions, then you can cross-multiply.

Solve for x: $\dfrac{x-3}{7} = \dfrac{6}{7}$.

The solution looks like this:

$$7x - 21 = 42$$
$$7x = 21$$
$$x = 3$$

If it's more complicated, start by factoring each of the denominators, and determine the LCD of all the fractions. Multiply both sides of the equation by the LCD, distributing if necessary, and cancel. All denominators should disappear.

Solve $\dfrac{4}{x+1} + \dfrac{2}{3} = \dfrac{5}{3x+3}$.

Factor the denominators. In this case, only the denominator on the right side of the equal sign needs to be factored: $\dfrac{5}{3x+3} = \dfrac{5}{3(x+1)}$.

Identifying the LCD in this case, is easy, because multiplying the first denominator by the second denominator results in the third (common) denominator: $(x+1) \times 3 = 3(x+1)$.

Now, multiply each term of the equation by the LCD $3(x+1)$ and cancel where possible to simplify:

$$3\cancel{(x+1)}\left(\dfrac{4}{\cancel{x+1}}\right) + 3(x+1)\left(\dfrac{2}{3}\right) = 3\cancel{(x+1)}\left(\dfrac{5}{\cancel{3(x+1)}}\right)$$

$$12 + 2(x+1) = 5$$
$$12 + 2x + 2 = 5$$
$$2x + 14 = 5$$
$$2x = -9$$
$$x = -4.5$$

When you solve rational equations, be careful not to say that a value that makes the denominator zero is a solution. Solutions like this pop up sometimes, but they're called *extraneous solutions*. Ignore them.

Shaping Up with Geometry

A lot of the geometry you learned in high school was really aimed at teaching you to make a convincing argument by reasoning from the facts at hand. You use that reasoning skill in several sections of the test, and you need to recall some of the facts you learned in your high school geometry course. In the sections that follow, you review all the vocabulary you need for the geometry questions and refresh your memory of lines, angles, and polygons and their properties and relationships. After some practice with area and volume, you'll be ready for any geometry questions you meet.

Talking about lines

For questions about geometry, you need to know the concepts and the terms and symbols that describe those concepts. Here's what you need to know about lines:

- **Line:** A straight, infinite length with no width or height. The term "straight line" is redundant, because "line" means "straight."
- **Line segment:** A portion of a line between two endpoints.
- **Parallel lines:** Lines that are always the same distance apart and therefore never intersect. The symbol for parallel is ∥.
- **Perpendicular lines:** Lines that intersect at right angles. The symbol for "is perpendicular to" is ⊥.
- **Midpoint:** A point on a line segment that divides the segment into two pieces of equal length. Any line, ray, or segment that passes through the midpoint of a segment is a *bisector* of the segment.
- **Perpendicular bisector:** A line that passes through the midpoint of a segment and is perpendicular to the segment.
- **Ray:** A part of a line that extends from one point and goes on forever.

Coming 'round the bend: Angles

An angle is made of two rays or segments that meet at a point, called the *vertex*. Angles are measured by the amount of rotation between the rays, like the movement of a door on a hinge. The wider the door is opened, the bigger the angle. As with lines, you must understand basic concepts and terms about angles. The following sections bring you up to speed.

Identifying the four angle types

In geometry, angles are measured in degrees and classified by size. A full rotation — all the way around the circle — is 360 degrees. Angles fit in four categories, as listed in Table 8-2.

Table 8-2	The Four Types of Angles
Angle Type	*Size*
Acute angle	0° to 90°
Right angle	90°
Obtuse angle	Greater than 90° but less than 180°
Straight angle	180°

Angle bisectors

An *angle bisector* is a line that divides an angle into two angles of equal size, each half the size of the original.

Complementary angles

Complementary angles are two angles whose measurements total 90 degrees. If two angles are complementary, each is the complement of the other. To find the complement of an angle of 25 degrees, subtract from 90 degrees: $90° - 25° = 65°$.

Supplementary angles

Supplementary angles are two angles whose measurements total 180 degrees. If two angles are supplementary, each is the supplement of the other. To find the supplement of an angle of 32 degrees, subtract from 180 degrees: $180° - 32° = 148°$.

Vertical angles

Two intersecting lines form four angles. Each pair of angles across the "X" from one another is a pair of vertical angles, which are always the same size, as shown in Figure 8-1.

Figure 8-1:
Two inter-
secting lines
form two
sets of verti-
cal angles.

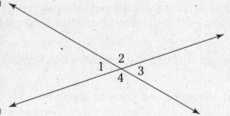

In Figure 8-1, if ∠1 measures 53 degrees, the measure of ∠3 is also 53 degrees. Because ∠1 and ∠3 are vertical angles, they're the same size.

Parallel lines

A line that cuts a pair of parallel lines is called a *transversal*. Eight angles, in two groups of four, are created by the transversal, as shown in Figure 8-2. Table 8-3 lists the different names for the various angle pairs that are formed. The symbol ≅ means "is congruent to," indicating that the angles are the same number of degrees.

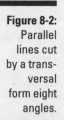

Figure 8-2:
Parallel
lines cut
by a trans-
versal
form eight
angles.

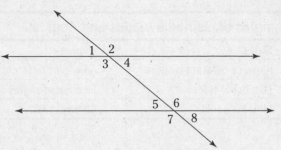

Table 8-3	Angle Pairs Created by a Transversal
Angle Pair Name	*Angle Pairs*
Corresponding angles	$\angle 1 \cong \angle 5$, $\angle 2 \cong \angle 6$, $\angle 3 \cong \angle 7$, $\angle 4 \cong \angle 8$
Alternate interior angles	$\angle 3 \cong \angle 6$, $\angle 4 \cong \angle 5$
Alternate exterior angles	$\angle 1 \cong \angle 8$, $\angle 2 \cong \angle 7$

Add the fact that $\angle 1$ and $\angle 2$ are supplementary, and it becomes possible to assign each of the angles one of two measurements. For example, in Figure 8-3, if $\angle 1 = 37°$, $\angle 4$, $\angle 5$ and $\angle 8$ are also $37°$, and $\angle 2$, $\angle 3$, $\angle 6$ and $\angle 7$ are all $143°$ ($180° - 37° = 143°$).

Exploring the many sides of polygons

Polygons are closed figures made up of line segments. The most common polygons are triangles (three-sided) and quadrilaterals (four-sided). The following sections introduce you to these two common shapes and the key details you need to know about each of them.

Many of the larger polygons can be divided into triangles or quadrilaterals, so you can use the knowledge and skills you gain in the following sections to solve problems related to other polygons.

Finding your way around triangles

A *triangle* is a polygon with three sides and three angles. In any triangle, the sum of the measures of the three angles is 180 degrees.

Triangles are classified by their sides and by their angles. See Tables 8-4 and 8-5.

Table 8-4	Triangles Classified by Angles
Triangle Type	*Angles*
Acute	All acute angles
Right	One right angle
Obtuse	One obtuse angle (greater than 90°)

Table 8-5	Triangles Classified by Sides and Angles	
Triangle Type	*Sides*	*Angles*
Scalene	All sides different lengths	All angles different sizes
Isosceles	Two equal sides	Two equal angles
Equilateral	All sides equal	All angles 60°

An exterior angle of a triangle is formed by extending one side of the triangle and is supplementary to the interior angle at the same vertex. (See Figure 8-3.) The measure of an exterior angle of a triangle is equal to the sum of the two remote interior angles.

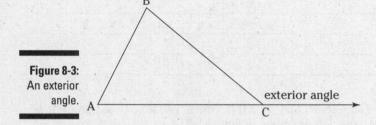

Figure 8-3:
An exterior
angle.

An *altitude* is a line or segment from a vertex perpendicular to the opposite side. (See Figure 8-4.) In an isosceles triangle, the altitude drawn from the vertex angle to the base bisects the base and the vertex angle.

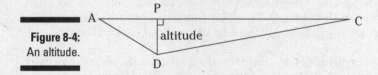

Figure 8-4:
An altitude.

A *median* of a triangle is a line segment that connects a vertex of the triangle to the midpoint of the opposite side. A median divides the triangle into two triangles of equal area. (See Figure 8-5.)

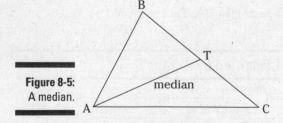

Figure 8-5:
A median.

A segment that joins the midpoints of two sides of a triangle is called a *midsegment* of the triangle. It's parallel to the third side and half as long. (See Figure 8-6.)

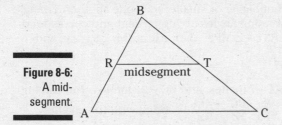

Figure 8-6:
A mid-
segment.

In any triangle, the sum of the lengths of any two sides is greater than the length of the third. Put another way, the length of any side of a triangle is less than the sum of the other two sides but more than the difference between them.

Consider this example: Gretchen lives 5 miles from the library and 2 miles from the supermarket. If Gretchen's house, the library, and the supermarket are the vertices of a triangle, then the distance from the library to the supermarket must be greater than 5 – 2 and less than 5 + 2, so the distance is between 3 and 7 miles.

Grasping the basics of the Pythagorean Theorem

A right triangle contains one right angle, and the side opposite the right angle is called the *hypotenuse.* The other two sides, which form the right angle, are called *legs.* The Pythagorean Theorem states that in any right triangle, the square of the hypotenuse is equal to the sum of the squares of the other two sides. Most people remember it in symbolic form. If the legs of the right triangle are a and b and the hypotenuse is c, then $a^2 + b^2 = c^2$.

To find the length of the hypotenuse of a right triangle whose legs measure 5 yards and 12 yards, as shown in Figure 8-7, use the Pythagorean Theorem: $5^2 + 12^2 = c^2$, so $c^2 = 25 + 144 = 169$, and $c = 13$ yards.

Figure 8-7:
Calculate
the length of
the hypot-
enuse using
the lengths
of the other
two sides.

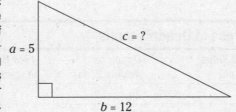

Sets of three whole numbers that fit the Pythagorean Theorem are called *Pythagorean Triples.* Common Pythagorean Triples are 3, 4, 5 and 5, 12, 13. Multiples of Pythagorean Triples are also Pythagorean Triples, so 6, 8, 10 or 25, 60, 65 also fit the Pythagorean Theorem.

Analyzing congruence and similarity

Geometry is involved in relationships between polygons as well as their individual properties. Congruence and similarity are the two fundamental relationships.

Triangles are congruent if they're the same shape and the same size. When the congruent triangles are named, the order in which the vertices are listed tells you what matches up. If you're told that $\triangle ABC \cong \triangle RST$, the angles match up as $\angle A \cong \angle R$, $\angle B \cong \angle T$, and $\angle C \cong \angle S$, and the sides as $\overline{AB} \cong \overline{RS}$, $\overline{BC} \cong \overline{ST}$, and $\overline{AC} \cong \overline{RT}$.

Triangles are similar if they're the same shape, but bigger or smaller than one another. Triangle similarity is indicated with the ~ sign. Corresponding angles are congruent and corresponding sides are in proportion. If you know that △RST ~ △MPN, then $\angle R \cong \angle M$, $\angle S \cong \angle P$, and $\angle T \cong \angle N$, and the proportion is $\frac{RS}{MP} = \frac{ST}{PN} = \frac{RT}{MN}$.

In Figure 8-8, △ABC ~ △XYZ. If XY = 4 inches, YZ = 7 inches, and BC = 21 inches, you can find the length of AC by setting up the proportion $\frac{AB}{XY} = \frac{BC}{YZ} = \frac{AC}{XZ}$. Working with the given lengths, $\frac{AB}{4} = \frac{21}{7}$. Using $\frac{AB}{4} = \frac{21}{7}$ and cross-multiplying, $7 \cdot AB = 4 \cdot 21$, so AB = 12 inches.

Figure 8-8:
Similar triangles are the same shape but different sizes.

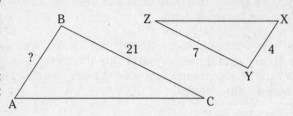

Quadrilaterals

The term *quadrilateral* denotes any four-sided figure, but most of the attention falls on the four members of the parallelogram family (see Table 8-6):

- **Parallelogram:** A quadrilateral with two pairs of opposite sides parallel.

- **Rhombus:** A parallelogram with four equal sides.

- **Rectangle:** A parallelogram with four right angles.

- **Square:** A parallelogram that is both a rhombus and a rectangle.

Table 8-6	Types of Quadrilaterals			
Quadrilateral Type	**Opposite Sides Equal**	**All Sides Equal**	**Opposite Angles Equal**	**Four Right Angles**
Parallelogram	✓		✓	
Rhombus	✓	✓	✓	
Rectangle	✓		✓	✓
Square	✓	✓	✓	✓

Trapezoids

A *trapezoid* is a quadrilateral with one pair of parallel sides and one nonparallel pair. In trapezoids, the parallel sides are called the *bases,* and the nonparallel sides are called *legs*.

If the nonparallel sides of a trapezoid are congruent, the trapezoid is an isosceles trapezoid. In an isosceles trapezoid, base angles are equal.

The line segment joining the midpoints of the nonparallel sides is called the *midsegment* of the trapezoid. The midsegment is parallel to the bases, and its length is the average of the lengths of the bases.

Polygons with more than four sides

While most of the attention focuses on triangles and quadrilaterals, many polygons have more than four sides. You should know their names and some general properties they share. Like triangles and quadrilaterals, other polygons take their names from the number of sides they have. For example, a polygon with five sides is a pentagon, six sides is a hexagon, and eight sides is an octagon.

The total of the measures of the three angles in a triangle is 180 degrees. Because any quadrilateral divides into two triangles when you draw a diagonal connecting two opposite vertices, the total of the four angles in a quadrilateral is 360 degrees. If a polygon with more than three sides is divided into triangles by drawing all the possible diagonals from a single vertex, the number of triangles is two less than the number of sides. Each triangle has angles totaling 180 degrees, so the sum of the interior angles of any polygon can be found with the formula $s = 180° (n - 2)$, where n is the number of sides.

Here are a couple examples of this equation in action. The total of the measures of the five interior angles of a pentagon is $180 \times (5 - 2)$, or 540 degrees. The total of the measures of the ten interior angles of a decagon is $180 \times (10 - 2)$ or 1,440 degrees.

Calculating perimeter and area

On the OCT, you're almost certain to encounter questions asking you to calculate the perimeter or area of a polygon. The following sections provide everything you need to know to ace these questions.

Perimeter of a polygon

The perimeter of a polygon is the distance around it. You can generally find the perimeter by simply adding the lengths of all the sides. To calculate the perimeter of a rectangle more simply, use the equation $P = 2l + 2w$; that is, perimeter is equal to twice the length plus twice the width.

Area of a parallelogram

To find the area of a parallelogram, multiply its base times the height: $A = bh$. The height must be measured as the perpendicular distance between the bases. Don't confuse the side with the height.

Area of a rectangle

Because a rectangle is a parallelogram, its area is also base times height. But because the adjacent sides of the rectangle are perpendicular, the length and width are the base and the height, so $A = lw$.

Area of a triangle

Every triangle is half of some parallelogram, so the area of a triangle is half the product of the base and the height: $A = \frac{1}{2} bh$.

If the area of a triangle is 88 square feet and the base is 16 feet, you can find the height of the triangle by plugging the known values into the formula, $A = \frac{1}{2} bh$. If $88 = \frac{1}{2}(16)h$, then $88 = 8h$ and $h = 11$ feet.

Area of a trapezoid

If you draw a diagonal in a trapezoid, you create two triangles. The area of one triangle is half the top base times the height, and the area of the other triangle is half the bottom base times the height. The area of a trapezoid is equal to the areas of the two triangles added together, $\frac{1}{2} b_1 h + \frac{1}{2} b_2 h$ or $A = \frac{1}{2} h (b_1 + b_2)$.

For example, if the area of a trapezoid is 40 cm^2, and the bases are 3 cm and 5 cm, you can find the height by substituting into the formula $A = \frac{1}{2}h(b_1 + b_2)$ to get $40 = \frac{1}{2}h(3+5)$. Simplify, and you get $40 = 4h$, so $h = 10$.

Centering on circles

A *circle* is the set of all points at a fixed distance, called the *radius,* from a given point, called the *center*. For questions about circles, you need to know some basics about the parts of a circle and how to calculate circumference (perimeter), area, arc length, and the area of a sector. The following sections cover these basics.

Circumference and area

The *circumference* of a circle is the distance around the circle. The formula for the circumference of a circle is $C = 2\pi r = \pi d$, where r is the radius of the circle, d is the diameter of the circle, and π is a constant approximately equal to 3.14159.

The area of a circle is the product of π and the square of the radius: $A = \pi r^2$.

Here's an example. If the circumference of a circle is 32π centimeters, the diameter is 32 centimeters and the radius is 16 centimeters. The area is $A = \pi r^2 = \pi(16)^2 = 256\pi$ cm^2.

Arc length and area of a sector

If you draw an angle inside a circle with its vertex at the center, as shown in Figure 8-9, the measure of the angle is equal to the measure of the arc cut off, in this case, 50 degrees. (A full circle is 360 degrees.) If the vertex is on the circle, the angle is half the size of the arc, in this case, 25 degrees.

When a central angle is drawn in a circle, it cuts off a section of the circle — a wedge like a piece of pie — called a *sector*. The area of the sector is a fraction of the area of the circle equal to the measure of the central angle in degrees over 360.

The area of a sector that has a central angle of 54 degrees would be $\frac{54°}{360°}$ the area of the circle.

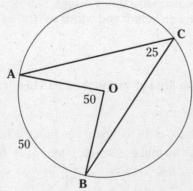

Figure 8-9:
Measuring
angles
and arcs.

You can use this to calculate other unknowns in related questions, as shown in the following example. Suppose the area of the sector defined by a central angle of 72 degrees is 5π in^2. The fraction of the circle cut off by a central angle of 72 degrees is $\frac{72}{360} = \frac{1}{5}$. Because the 5π in^2 is only $\frac{1}{5}$ of the area, the total area of the circle is 5 times 5π in^2, or 25π in^2. Knowing this, you can determine the radius of the circle, because $A = \pi r^2$. With 25π in^2 = πr^2, you divide both sides by π to find 25 in^2 equal to r^2. Take the square root of both sides of the equation, and $r = 5$. Because circumference equals $2\pi r,$ the circumference of the circle is $2 \times \pi \times 5 = 10\pi$, and because the angle intercepts an arc whose length is $\frac{1}{5}$ of that circumference, the circumference of the arc is $10\pi \times \frac{1}{5} = 2\pi$ inches.

Solid information on volume

The *volume* of a solid is a measurement of the space inside it, or the amount it holds, and is measured in cubic units. Calculating area is key to finding volume easily:

- ✔ The volume of a prism (including a cube) or a cylinder is equal to the area of its base times its height.

- ✔ The volume of a pyramid or cone is one-third of the product of the base area and the height.

To find the volume of a square prism 4 inches high, whose base edges are 6 inches long, as shown in Figure 8-10, first find that the area of the base is 36 square inches. Multiply that by the height of 4 inches and you discover that the volume is 144 cubic inches.

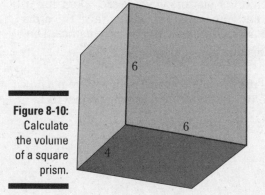

Figure 8-10:
Calculate the volume of a square prism.

Mastering Math That Counts

If you've wondered about your chances of scoring well on the AFOQT or about what kind of scores people earn on the ASVAB, you've used probability and statistics. The math that lets you talk about things that aren't certain requires you to count large numbers of events in a very quick and organized fashion. In the following sections, you master the basic counting principle and techniques for counting the number of arrangements and combinations. You practice the fundamentals of probability and review the three types of averages.

Counting all the possibilities

If you were asked about the probability of a particular number coming up when you roll a die, you'd want to know how many sides the die had (and what numbers are printed on it). If you were asked about the probability of pulling a certain two-card combination from a standard deck of 52 cards, you'd want to know how many different ways there are to pull two cards. In some situations, like the die, you can quickly list all the possible outcomes, but listing all the two-card combinations you could possibly draw would take too long. When it's too difficult or time consuming to list all the possibilities, the basic counting principle provides a convenient alternative.

The basic counting principle instructs you to

1. **Create a space for each choice that needs to be made or event that needs to happen.**

2. **Fill each space with the number of options for making that choice or the number of ways that event can happen.**

3. **Multiply the numbers you've entered to find the total number of ways choices can be made or events can happen.**

If Susan has 4 skirts, 7 blouses, and 3 jackets, how many different outfits, each consisting of a skirt, a blouse, and a jacket, can Susan create?

Susan must choose three items of clothing, so you need three slots: (_)(_)(_). She has 4 options for the skirt, 7 options for the blouse, and 3 options for the jacket, so $(4)(7)(3)$. Multiply the numbers you've entered to find the total number of combinations: $(4)(7)(3) = 84$ different outfits.

Permutations

A *permutation* is an arrangement of items in which order matters. If you were asked, for example, how many different ways John, Martin, and Andrew could finish a race, the order of finish would matter, so you would want all the permutations of these three names. The formula for the number of permutations of n things taken t at a time is $_nP_t = \dfrac{n!}{(n-t)!}$.

! is the symbol for factorial. n! instructs you to find the product of whole numbers from n down to 1. 4! would be $4 \times 3 \times 2 \times 1 = 24$. 0! doesn't fit that rule; it's defined as being equal to 1.

How many different ways could John, Martin, and Andrew finish a race?

The solution looks like this:

$$_3P_3 = \frac{3!}{(3-3)!}$$

$$\frac{3!}{0!} = \frac{3!}{1} = 3! = 3 \times 2 \times 1 = 6$$

Combinations

A *combination* is a group of objects in which the order doesn't matter. If you're asked to select a team of 5 people to represent your office of 20 people, the order in which you choose the five doesn't matter, so the number of different teams is the combinations of 20 people taken 5 at a time.

The formula for the number of combinations of n things taken t at a time is $_nC_t = \dfrac{n!}{(n-t)!\,t!}$.

How many different teams of 5 people would be possible if you select combinations from 20 people?

The formula becomes:

$$_{20}C_5 = \frac{20!}{(20-5)!\,5!} = \frac{20!}{15!\,5!}$$

If you expand 20! out, you see that 15! can cancel:

$$\frac{20\cdot19\cdot18\cdot17\cdot16\cdot\cancel{15!}}{\cancel{15!}\,5!} = \frac{20\cdot19\cdot18\cdot17\cdot16}{5!}$$

Expand 5! in the denominator and cancel with the numbers in the numerator wherever you can:

$$\frac{\cancel{20}^{4}\cdot19\cdot\cancel{18}^{6}\cdot17\cdot\cancel{16}^{4}}{\cancel{5}\cdot\cancel{4}\cdot\cancel{3}\cdot2\cdot1} = \frac{4\cdot19\cdot6\cdot17\cdot\cancel{4}^{2}}{\cancel{2}} = 15{,}504$$

Taking a chance on probability

The *probability* of an event is a number between zero and one that indicates how likely the event is to happen. An impossible event has a probability of zero. An event with a probability of one is certain to happen. The following sections explain how to calculate probability, which is likely to help not only on your test but during your next trip to Vegas.

Simple probability

The probability of an event is the number of successes — the things you want to happen — divided by the number of possible outcomes — all the things that can happen.

The probability of choosing the ace of spades from a standard deck of 52 cards is $\frac{1}{52}$, because the deck contains only one ace of spades, but the probability of choosing any ace is $\frac{4}{52} = \frac{1}{13}$, because the deck has four aces.

Probability of compound events

The probability of two events both occurring is the probability of the first times the probability of the second. Be sure to think about whether the first event affects the probability of the second.

Suppose a card is drawn from a standard deck of 52 cards, recorded, and then replaced in the deck. The deck is shuffled and a second card is drawn. The probability that both cards are hearts is $P(\text{heart}) \times P(\text{heart}) = \frac{13}{52} \times \frac{13}{52} = \frac{1}{4} \cdot \frac{1}{4} = \frac{1}{16}$. Because the first card drawn is replaced before the second draw, the probability of drawing a heart on the second try is the same.

If the first card isn't returned to the deck before the second card is drawn, the probability of the first card being a heart is $\frac{13}{52} = \frac{1}{4}$, but the probability of drawing a heart on the second try is $\frac{12}{51} = \frac{4}{17}$ because 12 hearts are left among the 51 remaining cards. The probability of drawing two hearts without replacement is $\frac{1}{4} \cdot \frac{4}{17} = \frac{1}{17}$, slightly less than with replacement.

The probability that one event or another will occur is basically the probability that the first will occur plus the probability that the second will occur, but in some cases, that requires a little adjustment.

Suppose a card is drawn at random from a standard deck. What is the probability that the card is either a king or a queen?

The probability that the card is a king is $\frac{4}{52} = \frac{1}{13}$. The probability that it's a queen is $\frac{4}{52} = \frac{1}{13}$. The probability of drawing a king or a queen is $\frac{4}{52} + \frac{4}{52} = \frac{8}{52} = \frac{2}{13}$. Now you probably could have figured that out by simply counting 4 kings and 4 queens, for 8 successes out of 52 possibilities. But look at a slightly different question.

Suppose a card is drawn at random from a standard deck. What is the probability that the card is either an ace or a heart?

The probability that the card is an ace is $\frac{4}{52} = \frac{1}{13}$. The probability that it's a heart is $\frac{13}{52} = \frac{1}{4}$. One card, however, fits into both categories — the ace of hearts — so it gets counted twice. To eliminate that duplication, subtract $\frac{1}{52}$, the probability of pulling a card that is both an ace and a heart. The probability that the card is an ace or a heart is $\frac{4}{52} + \frac{13}{52} - \frac{1}{52} = \frac{16}{52} = \frac{4}{13}$.

Rising above the average

Statistics are numbers that represent collections of data or information. They make it easier to draw conclusions about the data. One of the ways you can represent a set of data is by giving an average of the data. The mean, mode, and median are all ways of representing the average. The following sections describe each.

Mean

The mean is the number most people think of when they hear "average." The mean is found by adding all the data items and dividing by the number of items. If the data set is large, this can be a nasty calculation. Remember the mean is the average with the mean, nasty arithmetic.

Here's an example. The mean of the odd numbers between 2 and 10 is the sum of the odd numbers between 2 and 10, divided by the number of odd numbers between 2 and 10. That's $\frac{3+5+7+9}{4} = \frac{24}{4} = 6$.

Mode

The phrase "a la mode" really doesn't mean "with ice cream." It means "according to the fashion." The mode is the most fashionable value, the one that occurs most often. The mode of the set of numbers 1, 2, 3, 3, 5 is 3, because 3 occurs twice, whereas each of the other numbers occurs once.

Median

The median is the middle value when a set of data has been ordered from smallest to largest or largest to smallest. Remember the median is that strip of grass in the middle of the highway. If the number of data points is even, and two numbers seem to be in the middle, the mean of those two is the median.

Find the median of the even numbers between 1 and 9.

Start by listing the numbers in order: 2, 4, 6, 8. Because there are four numbers, no true middle exists, so average the two in the middle: $\frac{4+6}{2} = \frac{10}{2} = 5$.

Chapter 9

Putting Your Math Skills to the Test

● ●

The Air Force Officer Qualifying Test (AFOQT), Armed Services Vocational Aptitude Battery (ASVAB), and Aviation Selection Test Battery (ASTB) all include sections of questions designed to test your knowledge of the math that most people learn in high school. If your memory of some (or all) of that material is fuzzy, Chapter 8 brings you up to speed on the topics you're likely to encounter and the skills you need to succeed.

This chapter gives you the opportunity to test your knowledge of that math on a collection of questions similar to what you see on the test. The chapter is organized into four sections:

- ✐ **AFOQT Mathematics Knowledge** has 25 multiple choice questions like the ones you'll find on the AFOQT.

- ✐ **ASVAB Mathematics Knowledge** consists of another group of 25 questions, also multiple-choice, designed to mimic the ASVAB Mathematics Knowledge section.

- ✐ **ASTB Math Skills** is a little longer. This section has 30 questions, and, like the ASTB test, is a blend of math knowledge and reasoning.

- ✐ **The answer key,** the final part of the chapter, provides answers and solutions for each group of questions so you can check your work and learn from any mistakes you may make.

AFOQT Mathematics Knowledge

Choose the best answer for each question from the answer choices provided.

1. Simplify: $-25 - 18 \div -6 \times -21 - -7$

   (A) −81

   (B) −31

   (C) 45

   (D) 12

2. Evaluate $(x+z)^2 + 4y$ when $x = 4$, $y = 2$, and $z = 3$.

   (A) 20

   (B) 21

   (C) 48

   (D) 57

3. If $\frac{x}{y} = \frac{3}{5}$, then $y =$

   (A) $\frac{5x}{3}$

   (B) $\frac{3x}{5}$

   (C) $\frac{15}{x}$

   (D) $\frac{x}{15}$

4. Which of the following is the equation of a line with a slope of -3 and a y-intercept of 7?

   (A) $y = 7x - 3$

   (B) $y = 3x - 7$

   (C) $y = -3x + 7$

   (D) $y = -7x + 3$

5. Solve: $\frac{x}{16} = \frac{4}{x}$

   (A) $x = 8, x = -8$

   (B) $x = 8, x = 0$

   (C) $x = 4, x = 16$

   (D) $x = 4, x = -16$

6. Solve: $3(x - 5) + 4(2x - 1) = 47$

   (A) $x = -5.6$

   (B) $x = -13.2$

   (C) $x = 1$

   (D) $x = 6$

7. Solve: $9y - 6 > 2y + 15$

   (A) $y > 3$

   (B) $y < -3$

   (C) $y > 15$

   (D) $y < 15$

8. Simplify: $(5t + 2)(t - 8)$

   (A) $5t^2 - 16$

   (B) $5t^2 - 42t - 16$

   (C) $5t^2 + 42t - 16$

   (D) $5t^2 - 38t - 16$

9. Factor $x^2 - 9x + 14$.

   (A) $(x-7)(x+2)$

   (B) $(x-7)(x-2)$

   (C) $(x+7)(x+2)$

   (D) $(x+7)(x-2)$

10. Solve: $x^2 - 7 = 18$

    (A) $x = 7,\ x = -7$

    (B) $x = -1,\ x = -4$

    (C) $x = 2,\ x = 16$

    (D) $x = 5,\ x = -5$

11. Simplify: $\dfrac{2x-1}{x-7} + \dfrac{3x+5}{x-7}$

    (A) $\dfrac{5x+4}{x-7}$

    (B) $\dfrac{5x-6}{x-7}$

    (C) $\dfrac{5x+4}{2(x-7)}$

    (D) $\dfrac{5x-6}{2(x-7)}$

12. Solve: $\begin{cases} y = 2x - 1 \\ x + y = 14 \end{cases}$

    (A) $x = 5,\ y = 9$

    (B) $x = 5,\ y = 11$

    (C) $x = 7.5,\ y = 6.5$

    (D) $x = 15,\ y = -1$

13. Simplify: $\sqrt{27} + \sqrt{75}$

    (A) $\sqrt{102}$

    (B) $3\sqrt{8}$

    (C) $8\sqrt{3}$

    (D) $15\sqrt{3}$

14. In how many ways can you answer a five-question, multiple-choice test if each question has four choices?

    (A) 4

    (B) 5

    (C) 20

    (D) 1,024

15. A bag contains 20 marbles, of which 10 are red, 2 are white, and 8 are blue. What is the probability that a marble selected at random will be blue?

    (A) $\frac{1}{2}$

    (B) $\frac{1}{10}$

    (C) $\frac{2}{5}$

    (D) $\frac{1}{5}$

16. Ten high school students were asked how much money they were carrying. Their responses are shown in the following table. Find the difference between the mean and the median values.

$5.00	$16.00	$25.00	$18.50	$7.00	$5.00	$1.50	$3.00	$12.00	$9.00

    (A) $2.20

    (B) $8.00

    (C) $10.20

    (D) $12.20

17. Find the supplement of an angle of 15 degrees.

    (A) 15 degrees

    (B) 30 degrees

    (C) 75 degrees

    (D) 165 degrees

18. M is the midpoint of $\overline{XY}$. If XM = 3 centimeters, what is the length of $\overline{XY}$?

    (A) 3 centimeters

    (B) 4 centimeters

    (C) 5 centimeters

    (D) 6 centimeters

19. $\triangle RST$ is a right triangle with a right angle at R. If RS = 12 and RT = 16, find the length of $\overline{TS}$.

    (A) 18

    (B) 20

    (C) 24

    (D) 28

20. A rectangle has a side of 15 inches and a diagonal of 39 inches. Find the length of the other side.

    (A) 48 inches

    (B) 36 inches

    (C) 24 inches

    (D) 12 inches

21. A parallelogram has a base of 12 inches. If its area is 96 square inches, find the height of the parallelogram.

    (A) 8 inches

    (B) 16 inches

    (C) 42 inches

    (D) 84 inches

22. If $\triangle ARM \sim \triangle LEG$, RM = 9 inches, AM = 15 inches, and EG = 21 inches. Find the length of $\overline{LG}$.

    (A) 15 inches

    (B) 21 inches

    (C) 27 inches

    (D) 35 inches

23. Chords $\overline{DU}$ and $\overline{UG}$ are drawn in circle O. If central angle $\angle DOG$ measures 84 degrees, find the measure of $\angle DUG$.

    (A) 21 degrees

    (B) 42 degrees

    (C) 63 degrees

    (D) 84 degrees

24. The circumference of a circle is 40π centimeters. Find its area.

    (A) 20π square centimeters

    (B) 40π square centimeters

    (C) 400π square centimeters

    (D) $1,600\pi$ square centimeters

25. A prism is constructed with a base that is a square with a side of 10 centimeters. If the prism is 20 centimeters high, find its volume.

    (A) 200 cubic centimeters

    (B) 400 cubic centimeters

    (C) 2,000 cubic centimeters

    (D) 4,000 cubic centimeters

ASVAB Mathematics Knowledge

Choose the best answer for each question from the answer choices provided.

1. Simplify: $-13 \times 20 + -35 + -15 - -48 \div 16$

    (A) −307

    (B) −577

    (C) 583

    (D) 683

2. Evaluate $x - 7(y + 3z)$ when $x = 4$, $y = 2$, and $z = 3$.

   (A) 3

   (B) -1

   (C) -33

   (D) -73

3. In the senior class, the ratio of boys to girls is 7:8. If there are 300 students in the senior class, how many are girls?

   (A) 15

   (B) 20

   (C) 140

   (D) 160

4. Solve: $-8 + 9t > 10t - 23$

   (A) $t < -15$

   (B) $t > -15$

   (C) $t < 15$

   (D) $t > 15$

5. Solve: $(6 + a) - (5 - 2a) = -2$

   (A) $a = -13$

   (B) $a = -3$

   (C) $a = -1$

   (D) $a = -\frac{1}{3}$

6. Find the equation of a line through the point $(1, 1)$ and parallel to $y = 5x - 7$.

   (A) $y = 5x - 4$

   (B) $y = -5x - 6$

   (C) $y = 0.2x - 6$

   (D) $y = -0.2x - 1$

7. Solve: $x^2 = 4 + 3x$

   (A) $x = -4$, $x = 1$

   (B) $x = 4$, $x = -1$

   (C) $x = 3$, $x = -1$

   (D) $x = -3$, $x = 1$

8. Simplify: $5t^2(3t - 9)$

   (A) $15t^3 - 45$

   (B) $15t^3 - 9$

   (C) $15t^3 - 45t^2$

   (D) $8t^3 - 14t^2$

9. Factor $9x^2 - y^2$.

   (A) $(3x + y)^2$

   (B) $(3x - y)^2$

   (C) $(3x + y)(3x - y)$

   (D) $(9x - y)(x + y)$

10. Simplify: $\sqrt{63} \cdot \sqrt{44}$

    (A) $6\sqrt{18}$

    (B) $18\sqrt{6}$

    (C) $77\sqrt{6}$

    (D) $6\sqrt{77}$

11. Simplify: $\dfrac{x}{3a} - \dfrac{y}{5a}$

    (A) $\dfrac{x - y}{8a}$

    (B) $\dfrac{x - y}{15a}$

    (C) $\dfrac{5x - 3y}{15a}$

    (D) $\dfrac{5x - 3y}{8a}$

12. Solve: $\dfrac{5}{x} - \dfrac{3}{2x} = \dfrac{1}{2}$

    (A) $x = 2$

    (B) $x = 4$

    (C) $x = 7$

    (D) $x = 13$

13. Solve: $\begin{cases} x + y = 4 \\ x - y = 2 \end{cases}$

    (A) $x = 4, y = 2$

    (B) $x = 1, y = 3$

    (C) $x = 3, y = 1$

    (D) $x = 2, y = -4$

14. Ten contestants are in a talent competition. Prizes will be awarded for first, second, and third places. How many different choices are possible for the top three finishers?

    (A) 30

    (B) 120

    (C) 720

    (D) 1,000

15. If a card is selected at random from a standard deck of 52 cards, what is the probability that it is either a queen or a king?

    (A) $\frac{1}{26}$

    (B) $\frac{2}{13}$

    (C) $\frac{1}{4}$

    (D) $\frac{1}{169}$

16. Set D = {2, 2, 3, 4, 5} and set E = {1, 3, 5, 5}. Find the mean of the medians of sets D and E.

    (A) 3

    (B) 3.5

    (C) 4

    (D) 4.5

17. If $\angle A$ measures 42 degrees, what is the measure of the complement of $\angle A$?

    (A) 42 degrees

    (B) 48 degrees

    (C) 84 degrees

    (D) 138 degrees

18. If $\overline{AB}$ is the perpendicular bisector of $\overline{XY}$ and $\overline{AX}$ is 7 centimeters long, how long is $\overline{AY}$?

    (A) 3.5 centimeters

    (B) 7 centimeters

    (C) 10.5 centimeters

    (D) 14 centimeters

19. Placidville is 43 miles from Aurora, and Aurora is 37 miles from Lake Grove. Which of the following could be the distance from Placidville to Lake Grove?

    (A) 85 miles

    (B) 5 miles

    (C) 108 miles

    (D) 28 miles

20. Find the length of a diagonal of a rectangle if its sides measure 15 centimeters and 20 centimeters.

    (A) 15 centimeters

    (B) 18 centimeters

    (C) 20 centimeters

    (D) 25 centimeters

21. The base of a triangle is twice its height. If the area is 64 square inches, what is the length of the base?

    (A) 4 inches

    (B) 8 inches

    (C) 16 inches

    (D) 32 inches

22. $\triangle MNP \sim \triangle XYZ$ and MN = 12 inches, NP = 8 inches, and XY = 18 inches. Find the length of $\overline{YZ}$.

    (A) 8 inches

    (B) 12 inches

    (C) 16 inches

    (D) 18 inches

23. Chords $\overline{RS}$, $\overline{SV}$, and $\overline{VU}$ are drawn in circle O. If $\overset{\frown}{RV}$ measures 100 degrees and $\overset{\frown}{SU}$ measures 20 degrees, find the difference between the measure of $\angle RSV$ and the measure of $\angle SVU$.

    (A) 20 degrees

    (B) 40 degrees

    (C) 60 degrees

    (D) 80 degrees

24. Find the circumference of a circle whose area is 36π square inches.

    (A) 12π inches

    (B) 18π inches

    (C) 36π inches

    (D) 72π inches

25. Find the volume of a cylinder with a radius of 2 centimeters and a height of 8 centimeters.

    (A) 6π cubic centimeters

    (B) 16π cubic centimeters

    (C) 32π cubic centimeters

    (D) 64π cubic centimeters

ASTB Math Skills

Choose the best answer for each question from the answer choices provided.

1. When John purchased a used car, it showed that it had been driven 48,391 miles. Today, it shows 87,294 miles. How far has John driven the car?

    (A) 39,903 miles

    (B) 39,197 miles

    (C) 38,903 miles

    (D) 38,197 miles

2. In the most recent census, the population of a town was recorded as 13,472. In the prior census, it had been 11,398. By how much did the population increase?

   (A) 2,174

   (B) 2,074

   (C) 2,070

   (D) 2,026

3. Olivia painted $8\frac{1}{2}$ feet of fence, and Omar painted $6\frac{2}{3}$ feet of fence. How much more did Olivia paint?

   (A) $1\frac{5}{6}$ feet

   (B) $1\frac{11}{12}$ feet

   (C) $2\frac{1}{6}$ feet

   (D) $2\frac{5}{6}$ feet

4. The perimeter of a triangle is 94.27 centimeters. If two of the sides total 73.8 centimeters, what is the length of the third side?

   (A) 20.47 centimeters

   (B) 20.53 centimeters

   (C) 21.47 centimeters

   (D) 21.53 centimeters

5. If there are 365 days in a year and 24 hours in a day, how many hours are in a year?

   (A) 2,190

   (B) 1,582

   (C) 7,446

   (D) 8,760

6. The gravity on the moon is approximately $\frac{1}{6}$ of that on earth. If an astronaut weighs 189 pounds on earth, what will he weigh on the moon?

   (A) $31\frac{1}{2}$ pounds

   (B) 33 pounds

   (C) 133 pounds

   (D) 1,134 pounds

7. Simplify: $-21 \times 3 + 84 \div -12$

   (A) −14

   (B) 14

   (C) −70

   (D) 70

8. Simplify: $\sqrt{23,716}$

   (A) 154

   (B) 176

   (C) 298

   (D) 539

9. A pizza shop offers eight toppings. Determine the number of different two-topping pizzas available.

   (A) 16

   (B) 28

   (C) 56

   (D) 112

10. Find the probability of choosing a red ace from a standard deck of 52 cards.

    (A) $\frac{1}{52}$

    (B) $\frac{1}{26}$

    (C) $\frac{1}{13}$

    (D) $\frac{1}{4}$

11. Find the mean of set A if A = {32, 34, 36, 38}

    (A) 33

    (B) 34

    (C) 35

    (D) 36

12. Find the median of set B if B = {33, 34, 35, 36, 37, 38, 39}

    (A) 33

    (B) 34

    (C) 35

    (D) 36

13. Evaluate $-t^2$ when $t = 5$.

    (A) 10

    (B) –10

    (C) 25

    (D) –25

14. Solve: $(2x + 5) - 4 = 7$

    (A) $x = 4$

    (B) $x = -3$

    (C) $x = -4$

    (D) $x = 3$

15. Solve: $5x - 3 \le 7$

    (A) $x \le 0.8$

    (B) $x \ge 0.8$

    (C) $x \le 2$

    (D) $x \ge 2$

16. Solve: $\begin{cases} 2x + y = 1 \\ x - y = -7 \end{cases}$

    (A) $x = -2,\ y = 9$

    (B) $x = -2,\ y = 5$

    (C) $x = -6,\ y = 1$

    (D) $x = 8,\ y = 1$

17. Simplify: $-4(3t + 2) - (7 - t)$

    (A) $-11t - 15$

    (B) $-13t - 15$

    (C) $-13t + 1$

    (D) $-11t + 1$

18. Solve: $x^2 + x = 12$

    (A) $x = -4,\ x = -3$

    (B) $x = 4,\ x = 3$

    (C) $x = -4,\ x = 3$

    (D) $x = 4,\ x = -3$

19. Simplify: $\dfrac{x^3 - 4x^2}{x - 4}$

    (A) x

    (B) x^2

    (C) $x^3 - x$

    (D) $x^3 - x^2$

20. If $\dfrac{3}{5} = \dfrac{x}{70}$, find x.

    (A) 116.7

    (B) 42

    (C) 14

    (D) 4.2

21. Solve: $\dfrac{x}{x-1} + \dfrac{12}{x-1} = \dfrac{6}{x-1}$

    (A) $x = -12$

    (B) $x = -6$

    (C) $x = 6$

    (D) $x = 12$

22. Find the slope of a line perpendicular to $y = x - 4$.

    (A) 1

    (B) –1

    (C) –4

    (D) 4

23. If $\overline{YW}$ bisects $\angle XYZ$, and $\angle XYZ$ measures 86 degrees, find the measure of $\angle XYW$.

    (A) 4 degrees

    (B) 43 degrees

    (C) 86 degrees

    (D) 94 degrees

24. P, Q, and R are the midpoints of sides $\overline{AB}$, $\overline{BC}$, and $\overline{AC}$ respectively. If $AB = 20$ centimeters, $BC = 24$ centimeters, and $AC = 30$ centimeters, find the perimeter of $\triangle PQR$.

    (A) 20 centimeters

    (B) 24 centimeters

    (C) 30 centimeters

    (D) 37 centimeters

25. $ABCD$ is a trapezoid with $\overline{BC} \parallel \overline{AD}$. If $BC = 14$ inches and the midsegment of the trapezoid measures 18 inches, find AD.

    (A) 22 inches

    (B) 20 inches

    (C) 18 inches

    (D) 16 inches

26. The legs of a right triangle have lengths of 12 centimeters and 16 centimeters. Find the area of the triangle.

    (A) 192 square centimeters

    (B) 96 square centimeters

    (C) 48 square centimeters

    (D) 36 square centimeters

27. If $\triangle ARM \sim \triangle LEG$, $RM = 9$ inches, $EG = 21$ inches, and the perimeter of $\triangle ARM$ is 24 inches, find the perimeter of $\triangle LEG$.

    (A) 24 inches

    (B) 56 inches

    (C) 72 inches

    (D) 168 inches

28. Find the circumference of a circle if the radius is 11 inches.

    (A) 11π inches

    (B) 22π inches

    (C) 121π inches

    (D) 484π inches

29. A can is made in the shape of a cylinder with a radius of 4 inches and a height of 10 inches. In square inches, how much metal is needed to make the can?

    (A) 400π square inches

    (B) 112π square inches

    (C) 56π square inches

    (D) 40π square inches

30. Find the height of a square pyramid with a volume of 108 cubic centimeters and a base edge of 9 centimeters.

    (A) 2 centimeters

    (B) 4 centimeters

    (C) 8 centimeters

    (D) 12 centimeters

Answer Key

Following are the answers to the AFOQT, ASVAB, and ASTB practice questions along with explanations as to how the problems are solved. If you miss a question, check the explanation to see where you went astray. If you need to review a concept further, see Chapter 8.

AFOQT

Here are the answers to the AFOQT Mathematics Knowledge questions.

1. **A.** Do your division and multiplication first: $-25 - ((18 \div -6) \times -21) - -7 = -25 - -3 \times -21 - -7 = -25 - 63 - -7 = -88 + 7 = -81$.

2. **D.** Substitute 4 for x, 2 for y, and 3 for z: $(x+z)^2 + 4y = (4+3)^2 + 4 \cdot 2 = (7)^2 + 4 \cdot 2 = 49 + 4 \cdot 2 = 49 + 8 = 57$.

3. **A.** If $\frac{x}{y} = \frac{3}{5}$, cross-multiplying gives you $5x = 3y$. Dividing both sides by 3, you have $y = \frac{5x}{3}$.

4. **C.** Use the slope-intercept form $y = mx + b$ and replace m with -3 and b with 7: $y = -3x + 7$.

5. **A.** Cross-multiply for $x^2 = 64$ and take the square root of both sides to get $x = \pm 8$.

6. **D.** Distribute $3(x-5) + 4(2x-1) = 47$ to get $3x - 15 + 8x - 4 = 47$. Combine like terms, making the equation $11x - 19 = 47$. Add 19 to both sides, for $11x = 66$, and then divide both sides by 11 to arrive at $x = 6$.

7. **A.** Subtracting $2y$ from both sides makes the inequality $7y - 6 > 15$, and adding 6 to both sides makes it $7y > 21$. Divide both sides by 7 to get the solution of $y > 3$. The divisor is positive, so the inequality remains the same.

8. **D.** $(5t + 2)(t - 8) = 5t^2 - 40t + 2t - 16 = 5t^2 - 38t - 16$.

9. **B.** Basic FOIL factoring solves this problem. The paired factors for the squared term are easy because both factors are 1, but this doesn't help. The paired factors for the constant are 2 and 7, which also add up to 9: $x^2 - 9x + 14 = (x-7)(x-2)$.

10. **D.** Use the square root method. Add seven to both sides to get $x^2 = 25$, and then take the square root of both sides to get $x = \pm 5$.

11. **A.** Add the numerators: $\frac{2x-1}{x-7} + \frac{3x+5}{x-7} = \frac{2x-1+3x+5}{x-7} = \frac{5x+4}{x-7}$.

12. **A.** Use the first equation to substitute $2x-1$ for y in the second equation. $x+2x-1=14$ becomes $3x-1=14$. Add 1 to both sides for $3x=15$. Dividing by 3 gives you $x=5$. Return to the first equation, replacing x with 5. From this, $y=2(5)-1=9$, so $x=5$, $y=9$.

13. **C.** First, simplify each radical; then add the coefficients of the like radicals.
$\sqrt{27}+\sqrt{75}=\sqrt{9\cdot3}+\sqrt{25\cdot3}=\sqrt{9}\cdot\sqrt{3}+\sqrt{25}\cdot\sqrt{3}=3\sqrt{3}+5\sqrt{3}=8\sqrt{3}$.

14. **D.** Five questions, with 4 choices for each, means $4\times4\times4\times4\times4$, which equals 1,024.

15. **C.** Of the 20 total marbles, 8 are blue: $\frac{8}{20}=\frac{2}{5}$.

16. **A.** To find the mean, add the amounts and divide by the number of amounts given: $5.00 + 16.00 + 25.00 + 18.50 + 7.00 + 5.00 + 1.50 + 3.00 + 12.00 + 9.00 = 102 \div 10 = 10.20$. To find the median, put the numbers in order as shown in the following table.

$1.50	$3.00	$5.00	$5.00	$7.00	$9.00	$12.00	$16.00	$18.50	$25.00

The median is midway between the two middle numbers, $7.00 and $9.00, so the median is $8.00. The difference between the mean and the median is $10.20 – $8.00, or $2.20.

17. **D.** The supplement of an angle of 15 degrees = $180 - 15 = 165$ degrees.

18. **D.** If M is the midpoint of $\overline{XY}$, $\overline{XM}$ and $\overline{MY}$ are equal in length and each is half of $\overline{XY}$. If $XM = 3$ centimeters, $\overline{XY}$ measures 6 centimeters.

19. **B.** Use the Pythagorean Theorem, with $a=12$ and $b=16$. $c^2=12^2+16^2$ becomes $c^2=144+256=400$. TS will be 20.

20. **B.** If a rectangle has a side of 15 inches and a diagonal of 39 inches, you can find the other side with the Pythagorean Theorem, or you can recognize that $15 = 3\times5$ and $39 = 3\times13$, and spot the 5, 12, 13 Pythagorean Triple. The other side of the rectangle = 3×12, or 36 inches.

21. **A.** The area of a parallelogram is base times height, so the height is equal to the area divided by the base: $96 \div 12 = 8$ inches.

22. **D.** If $\triangle ARM \sim \triangle LEG$, $\frac{RM}{EG}=\frac{AM}{LG}$, so $\frac{9}{21}=\frac{15}{LG}$. Simplify and cross multiply: $\frac{3}{7}=\frac{15}{LG}$, so $3LG = 105$ and $LG = 35$.

23. **B.** If central angle $\angle DOG$ measures 84 degrees, then the measure of $\widehat{DG}$ is 84 degrees, and inscribed angle $\angle DUG$ measures half of 84 degrees, or 42 degrees.

24. **C.** $C = \pi d = 40\pi$ centimeters, so the diameter must be 40 centimeters and the radius 20 centimeters. Therefore, the area of the circle is $\pi r^2 = \pi 20^2 = 400\pi$ square centimeters.

25. **C.** The area of the base is 100 square centimeters, and the volume is equal to the area of the base times the height, so the volume is 2,000 cubic centimeters.

ASVAB

Following are the answers to the ASVAB Mathematics Knowledge questions.

1. **A.** Do your multiplication and division first: $(-13\times20) + -35 + -15 - -(48 \div 16) = -260 + -35 + -15 - -3 = -310 + 3 = -307$.

2. **D.** Substitute 4 for x, 2 for y, and 3 for z: $x-7(y+3z) = 4 - 7(2 + 3\cdot3) = 4 - 7(2 + 9) = 4 - 7(11) = 4 - 77 = -73$.

3. **D.** $7x + 8x = 300$, so $15x = 300$, and $x = 20$. Therefore, there are 7×20, or 140, boys and 8×20, or 160, girls.

4. **C.** Subtracting $10t$ from both sides gives you $-8 - t > -23$. Next, add 8 to both sides and the inequality becomes $-t > -15$. Finally, divide both sides by -1 and reverse the inequality: $t < 15$.

5. **C.** The second set is preceded by a minus sign, which changes the signs of that second expression. The equation becomes $6 + a - 5 + 2a = -2$. Combine like terms, making the equation $3a + 1 = -2$. Subtract 1 from both sides, for $3a = -3$, and divide by 3 to get $a = -1$.

6. **A.** The slope-intercept form of a linear equation is $y = mx + b$, so the slope of $y = 5x - 7$ is 5. The new line should also have a slope of 5. Use the point-slope form and plug in 5 for m, 1 for x_1, and 1 for y_1 because the line passes through the point (1, 1). Thus, $y - 1 = 5(x - 1)$ becomes $y - 1 = 5x - 5$, or $y = 5x - 4$.

7. **B.** To solve $x^2 = 4 + 3x$, move everything to one side so you have $x^2 - 3x - 4 = 0$, which factors as $(x - 4)(x + 1) = 0$. This gives you solutions of $x = 4$ or $x = -1$.

8. **C.** $5t^2(3t - 9) = 5t^2 \cdot 3t - 5t^2 \cdot 9 = 15t^3 - 45t^2$.

9. **C.** Factor the difference of squares: $9x^2 - y^2 = (3x + y)(3x - y)$.

10. **D.** Simplify each radical before trying to multiply: $\sqrt{63} \cdot \sqrt{44} = \sqrt{9 \cdot 7} \cdot \sqrt{4 \cdot 11} = \sqrt{9}\sqrt{7} \cdot \sqrt{4}\sqrt{11} = 3\sqrt{7} \cdot 2\sqrt{11} = 6\sqrt{77}$.

11. **C.** Use a common denominator of $15a$: $\frac{x}{3a} - \frac{y}{5a} = \frac{5x}{15a} - \frac{3y}{15a} = \frac{5x - 3y}{15a}$.

12. **C.** Multiply through by $2x$. $2x\left(\frac{5}{x} - \frac{3}{2x} = \frac{1}{2}\right)$ becomes $10 - 3 = x$, so $x = 7$.

13. **C.** Adding the equations eliminates y and leaves $2x = 6$ or $x = 3$. Substituting 3 for x in the first equation yields $3 + y = 4$. Subtract 3 from both sides for $y = 1$.

14. **C.** There are 10 choices for first place, leaving 9 for second, and 8 for third — and order matters — so $10 \times 9 \times 8 = 720$.

15. **B.** There are 4 queens and 4 kings, so you have 8 successes out of 52 cards: $\frac{8}{52} = \frac{2}{13}$.

16. **B.** The median of set D = {2, 2, 3, 4, 5} is 3, and the median of set E = {1, 3, 5, 5} is midway between 3 and 5, so it's 4. The mean of 3 and 4 is 3.5.

17. **B.** The complement of $\angle A = 90° - 42° = 48°$.

18. **B.** If $\overline{AB}$ is the perpendicular bisector of $\overline{XY}$, $\overline{AX}$ and $\overline{AY}$ are equal in length. If $\overline{AX}$ is 7 centimeters long, $\overline{AY}$ is also 7 centimeters.

19. **D.** If the three cities are arranged in a triangle, the distance from Placidville to Lake Grove will be greater than $43 - 37$ and less than $43 + 37$, or between 6 and 80.

20. **D.** Use the Pythagorean Theorem with $a = 15$ and $b = 20$, and you find that $c^2 = 15^2 + 20^2 = 225 + 400 = 625$, and $c = 25$. Or, recognize that 15 and 20 are 5×3 and 5×4, so the Pythagorean Triple would be completed by 5×5, or 25.

21. **C.** If $b = 2h$, the area of the triangle becomes $A = \frac{1}{2}bh = \frac{1}{2}(2h)h = h^2$, so $64 = h^2$. Take the square root of both sides and $h = 8$. The base is $2h$, or 2×8, which is 16 inches.

22. **B.** If $\triangle MNP \sim \triangle XYZ$, $\frac{MN}{XY} = \frac{NP}{YZ}$, so $\frac{12}{18} = \frac{8}{YZ}$. Simplify and cross multiply: $\frac{2}{3} = \frac{8}{YZ}$ so $2YZ = 24$ and $YZ = 12$.

23. **B.** $\angle RSV$ is an inscribed angle equal to half of $\overarc{RV}$, so $\angle RSV$ is 50 degrees. $\angle SVU$ is also inscribed and equal to half of $\overarc{SU}$, or 10 degrees. The difference is $50° - 10°$, or $40°$.

24. **A.** If $A = \pi r^2 = 36\pi$, then the radius is the square root of 36, which is 6 inches. $C = 2\pi r = 2 \times 6 \times \pi = 12\pi$ inches.

25. **C.** The volume of the cylinder is the area of the base times the height, so $4\pi \cdot 8 = 32\pi$ cubic centimeters.

ASTB

This section provides the answers for the ASTB math skills questions.

1. **C.** This is a simple subtraction problem: $87,294 - 48,391 = 38,903$. The numbers are large, but you can "make change" as we explain in Chapter 10. Start with 48,391, and add 3 to make 48,394. An extra 900 puts you at 49,294, another 1,000 is 50,294, and 37,000 gets you to 87,294. Add $3 + 900 + 1,000 + 37,000$ and you get 38,903.

2. **B.** A quick estimate says 13,000 minus 11,000 is 2,000. Look at the other digits: $472 - 398$ is $472 - 400 + 2 = 72 + 2 = 74$. Add the 2,000 and you get 2,074.

3. **A.** Your common denominator is 6, and you need to borrow 1 from the 8:
$$8\frac{1}{2} - 6\frac{2}{3} = 8\frac{3}{6} - 6\frac{4}{6} = 7\frac{9}{6} - 6\frac{4}{6} = 1\frac{5}{6}.$$

4. **A.** Annexing a zero on 73.8 is optional, but be sure to line up the decimal points. $94.27 - 73.8 = 20.47$.

5. **D.** It's possible to do $365 \times 20 + 365 \times 4$ if you don't want to use the standard algorithm. It's a little bit too much to hold in your head, so you need to jot down the partial products. $365 \times 20 + 365 \times 4 = (6,000 + 1,200 + 100) + (1,200 + 240 + 20) = 7,300 + 1,460 = 8,760$. So $365 \times 24 = 8,760$.

6. **A.** Gravity acting on mass determines weight, so $\frac{1}{6}$ the gravity means $\frac{1}{6}$ the weight:
$\frac{1}{6} \times 189 = 189 \div 6 = 31\frac{3}{6} = 31\frac{1}{2}$ pounds.

7. **C.** Do your multiplication and division first: $(-21 \times 3) + (84 \div -12) = -63 + -7 = -70$.

8. **A.** Don't be discouraged by the size of the number, but look for perfect square factors: $\sqrt{23,716} = \sqrt{4 \cdot 5,929} = \sqrt{4 \cdot 7 \cdot 847} = \sqrt{4 \cdot 7 \cdot 7 \cdot 121} = \sqrt{4 \cdot 49 \cdot 121}$. Take the square root of each perfect square and multiply: $\sqrt{4} \cdot \sqrt{49} \cdot \sqrt{121} = 2 \cdot 7 \cdot 11 = 154$.

9. **B.** Use the formula for calculating combinations, because the order in which they're combined doesn't matter: $_nC_t = \frac{n!}{(n-t)!t!}$, $_8C_2 = \frac{8 \cdot 7 \cdot 6!}{(8-2)!2!} = \frac{56 \cdot 6!}{6! \cdot 2!} = \frac{56}{2 \cdot 1} = \frac{56}{2} = 28$ possibilities.

10. **B.** There are 4 aces but only 2 are red, so $\frac{2}{52}$, or $\frac{1}{26}$.

11. **C.** $32 + 34 + 36 + 38 = 140$. Divide by 4 to find that the mean is 35.

12. **D.** The numbers {33, 34, 35, 36, 37, 38, 39} are in order, so find the middle value. The median is 36.

13. **D.** $-5^2 = -(5 \cdot 5) = -25$.

14. **D.** Simplify first: $(2x + 5) - 4 = 2x + 1 = 7$. If $2x + 1 = 7$, $2x = 6$ and $x = 3$.

15. **C.** If $5x - 3 \le 7$, $5x \le 10$ and $x \le 2$.

16. **B.** Adding the equations eliminates y, leaving $3x = -6$, or $x = -2$. Replacing x with -2 in the first equation gives you $2(-2) + y = 1$, or $-4 + y = 1$. Add 4 to both sides for $y = 5$, so $x = -2$, $y = 5$.

17. **A.** $-4(3t + 2) - (7 - t) = -12t - 8 - 7 + t = -12t + t - 8 - 7 = -11t - 15$.

18. **C.** Subtract 12 from both sides for $x^2 + x - 12 = 0$ and factor. $(x + 4)(x - 3) = 0$, so $x + 4 = 0$ yields $x = -4$, and $x - 3 = 0$ yields $x = 3$.

19. **B.** Factor and cancel: $\frac{x^3 - 4x^2}{x - 4} = \frac{x^2(x - 4)}{x - 4} = x^2$.

20. **B.** Cross-multiply for $5x = 210$ and solve to get $x = 42$.

21. **B.** Multiply through by $x - 1$ to cancel out all the denominators, and
$(x-1)\left(\frac{x}{x-1} + \frac{12}{x-1}\right) = (x-1)\left(\frac{6}{x-1}\right)$ becomes $x + 12 = 6$, so $x = -6$.

22. **B.** From the slope-intercept form $y = mx + b$ with m representing slope, you know that the slope of the given line is 1. The slope of a line perpendicular to the given line would be -1, because perpendicular lines have slopes that are negative reciprocals.

23. **B.** If $\overline{YW}$ bisects $\angle XYZ$, and $\angle XYZ$ measures 86 degrees, the measure of $\angle XYW$ is half of 86 degrees, or 43 degrees.

24. **D.** The sides of $\triangle PQR$ are all midsegments of $\triangle ABC$, so they measure half of the sides of $\triangle ABC$. The perimeter of $\triangle PQR = 10 + 12 + 15 = 37$ centimeters.

25. **A.** Remember from Chapter 8 that the midsegment of the trapezoid is the line segment that joins the midpoints of the nonparallel sides. The median of the trapezoid is half the sum of the lengths of the bases, so if the median is 18, the bases must total 36. Because $BC = 14$, AD must be $36 - 14$, or 22.

26. **B.** In a right triangle, because the legs are perpendicular to one another, the lengths of the legs can be used as the base and the height. The area of the triangle is half the base times the height, and half of $12 \times 16 = 96$ square centimeters.

27. **B.** If the triangles are similar in a ratio of $9:21 = 3:7$, then the ratio of the perimeters is also $3:7$. If the perimeter of $\triangle ARM$ is 24 inches, then the perimeter of $\triangle LEG$ can be found by solving $\frac{24}{P} = \frac{3}{7}$. $P = \frac{24 \cdot 7}{3} = 56$ inches.

28. **B.** Circumference $= 2\pi r$, so the circumference is 22π.

29. **B.** The metal needed to make the can is the surface area of the cylinder. Each of the two circular bases has an area of 16π. The curved surface of the can unrolls to a rectangle whose base is the circumference of the circular base, 8π, and whose height is 10. The total surface area is $2 \cdot 16\pi + 80\pi = 32\pi + 80\pi = 112\pi$ square inches.

30. **B.** The volume is $V = \frac{1}{3}Bh$, and the area of the base is 81 square centimeters because the edge is 9 centimeters. $108 = \frac{1}{3} \cdot 81 \cdot h$ means that $108 = 27h$ and $h = 4$.

Chapter 10

Solving Arithmetic Word Problems

● ●

In This Chapter

▶ Understanding the language of word problems

▶ Using recognizable problem types to your advantage

▶ Strategies for performing calculations more quickly

● ●

The Arithmetic Reasoning sections of the Air Force Officer Qualifying Test (AFOQT) and Armed Services Vocational Aptitude Battery (ASVAB) challenge you to use your arithmetic skills to reason from problem to solution. To do that, you must be able to analyze the problem, identify the information you need, and use your numerical skills as quickly and accurately as possible.

This chapter explains how to solve word problems faster and improve your chances of answering correctly. You discover how to translate word problems into mathematical expressions, approach common types of word problems more effectively, and solve problems more quickly so you don't run out of time.

You will have scratch paper to do your calculations, but no calculators are allowed on the test.

Translating Word Problems into Mathematical Language

Learning to make sense of word problems is a little like learning a new language. Before you can do anything with your new language, you need to acquire a basic vocabulary and an understanding of grammar. As you begin to communicate, you translate sentences word by word, but in time you become more fluent. When you first tackle word problems, you may find yourself doing a lot of that word-by-word work, but with practice you'll find that you can read the whole problem and restate it in mathematical symbols more comfortably. The following sections reveal a few strategies to make your task easier.

Read right to the end

You want to work quickly on the Arithmetic Reasoning subtests but not so quickly that you read the first phrases of a question and jump to conclusions about what you're being asked. Take the time to read the question all the way to the end. If you don't, you may actually waste time doing things you weren't asked to do. Consider the following problems.

Javier lost 12 pounds and Angel lost 18 pounds. How much more weight did Angel lose?

(A) 6 pounds

(B) 15 pounds

(C) 18 pounds

(D) 30 pounds

Javier lost 12 pounds and Angel lost 18 pounds. What was their combined weight loss?

(A) 6 pounds

(B) 15 pounds

(C) 18 pounds

(D) 30 pounds

Javier lost 12 pounds and Angel lost 18 pounds. What was their average weight loss?

(A) 6 pounds

(B) 15 pounds

(C) 18 pounds

(D) 30 pounds

Each one of the preceding examples is a reasonably simple arithmetic problem: $18 - 12$, $18 + 12$, and $(18 + 12) \div 2$, respectively. But if you read only the first sentence of the problem, your guess about which calculation to do may not be accurate, and you may end up answering the wrong question. The time you thought you were saving is wasted. Read right to the end of a question before you start to work.

Identify the goal

When you get to the end of the question, you should know what you're looking for. If you don't, double back, read again, and look for key words, like "total" or "average," that may tell you what you need to do.

You must identify the unknown, the quantity that needs to be calculated. You may think of that quantity as a variable, which you denote by a letter or symbol, or simply as the result of a particular calculation. If your goal, for example, is to find the total weight loss of two people, you could call the total T, and write $T = 12 + 18$.

On the other hand, if you're told that a certain number was multiplied by seven, four was added to that answer, and the result was 46, you'll probably want to write x to stand for that certain number while you sort out what's happened and what you need to do. In this case, your equation would be $(x \times 7) + 4 = 46$.

Identify the goal. If you don't know what you're looking for, you'll never find it.

Javier and Angel lost a total of 37 pounds. If Angel lost 22 pounds, how much did Javier lose?

(A) 6 pounds

(B) 15 pounds

(C) 18 pounds

(D) 30 pounds

The unknown here is Javier's weight loss — the number of pounds he lost. You could call it x (or p, or J, or whatever), but what's important is that you realize that the variable represents what you're looking for. Notice that they lost a *total* of 37 pounds. *Total* means *add,* so $x + 22 = 37$. You want to get back to the individual weight losses, so work backward; subtract 22 from 37 to find the unknown. Javier lost $37 - 22 = 15$ pounds, so Choice (B) is the correct answer.

Collect the pieces of the puzzle

Ever work for hours on a jigsaw puzzle and then find out pieces were missing? Having *most* of the puzzle won't get you to the ultimate solution, and missing pieces will likely get you confused along the way. When you tackle the mathematical puzzles called *word problems,* make sure you have all the pieces before you start trying to put them together.

In the case of word problems, you must have all the numerical information you need and an understanding of the relationship that ties it all together. You've read right to the end, and you've identified your goal. Now what do you need to know to get there? In the example presented in the preceding section, you need to know the total weight loss and Angel's individual weight loss, and you need to recognize that *total* means Angel's loss and Javier's loss are added to get 37 pounds. Then you can work backward, or subtract, to find the unknown.

If you were trying to find the area of a rectangle, you'd need to know the length and the width and know that you would multiply them to find the area. The measurements would have to be somewhere in the problem. (The fact that you need to multiply them should be in your store of knowledge.) If the information you think you need isn't in the problem, think about whether you can tackle the task a different way or whether you need to take another step first.

Take a look at the following example. Read right to the end, identify the goal, and name the unknown with a variable, if you find it helpful. Then check to see whether you have all the pieces of the puzzle.

Javier and Angel lost an average of 18 pounds. If Angel lost 21 pounds, how much did Javier lose?

(A) 6 pounds

(B) 15 pounds

(C) 18 pounds

(D) 30 pounds

For this example, you probably want to use a variable to stand for the unknown quantity. The variable is still Javier's weight loss, but finding it is a two-step process. Using a variable can help you keep track of what has been done and what you still need to do. So let x stand for Javier's weight loss. The tip-off word here is *average*. Out of your store of knowledge comes the fact that to find the average of two numbers, you add them and divide by two. What do you need to know? Angel's weight loss and the average. Angel's weight loss is 21 pounds, and the average is 18 pounds, so your equation looks like this: $\frac{x+21}{2} = 18$. To find x, first multiply both sides by 2, which gives you $x + 21 = 36$. Then subtract 21 from 36: $x = 36 - 21 = 15$. Javier lost 15 pounds, so the correct answer is Choice (B).

Okay, enough of that. Let Angel and Javier go have a burger and fries, while you move on to more strategies for translating English into math.

Convert for compatibility if necessary

Word problems often trip up test-takers by mixing units of measure; for example, feet and inches or hours and minutes. If you're not careful, you can mix these units of measure in your calculations and arrive at the wrong answer, which is almost always included in the list of answer choices.

Before you begin writing out your equation, identify the units of measure and perform any necessary conversions; for example, converting feet to inches or inches to feet. Following is an example.

If carpet costs $20 per square yard, how much will it cost to carpet a room that measures 12 feet wide x 15 feet long?

(A) $400

(B) $1,080

(C) $1,200

(D) $3,600

You read right to the end, so you know what you're looking for: the cost of the carpet. Do you have the information you need? You have the dimensions of the room, 12 x 15 feet, and the cost of the carpet, $20 per square yard. And yet a lot of people still get the wrong answer. Why? Because the measurements of the room are in feet, but the cost of the carpet is in dollars per square yard. You need to convert a measurement to make the units compatible. Either convert the cost from square yards to square feet or the room dimensions from feet to yards.

In this example, your best bet is to convert the feet to yards first. Then you can find the number of square yards of carpeting needed and the cost. Instead of thinking of the room as 12 x 15 feet, change the feet to yards by dividing by three (because 3 feet = 1 yard). The room is 4 x 5 yards, or 20 square yards. Twenty square yards at $20 per square yard is $400. The correct answer is Choice (A).

When you need to convert a quantity from one unit of measurement to another, target the simplest unit. It's easier to convert a simple unit — such as feet or miles — than it is to convert a square or cubic unit, such as square feet, or a rate, such as feet per minute or miles per hour. Likewise, most people can remember that 1 yard is 3 feet, but they may have trouble remembering that 1 square yard is 9 square feet or that 1 cubic yard is 27 cubic feet. So you're better off converting everything to yards from the start.

Memorize some conversion factors, but don't worry about remembering them all. You only need common conversions, including the ones in Table 10-1. You won't be expected to know how many furlongs equal one astronomical unit.

Table 10-1	Common Conversion Factors		
Length	*Time*	*Liquid*	*Weight*
12 inches = 1 foot	60 seconds = 1 minute	8 ounces = 1 cup	16 ounces = 1 pound
3 feet = 1 yard	60 minutes = 1 hour	4 quarts = 1 gallon	2,000 pounds = 1 ton
5,280 feet = 1 mile	24 hours = 1 day		
	7 days = 1 week		
	365 days = 1 year		

When doing conversions, do you get confused about whether to multiply or divide? Don't worry. Here's a tip: It's all about balance. Consider the following:

- **Bigger unit, smaller number:** If you're changing to a bigger unit, say going from feet to yards, you should get a smaller number, so divide; 12 feet ÷ 3 feet per yard = 4 yards.

- **Smaller unit, bigger number:** If you're going to a smaller unit, say feet to inches, you should expect a bigger number, so multiply; 12 feet × 12 inches per foot = 144 inches.

Converting rates requires more thought, but if you must do it, take it one step at a time and let the units help you out. Suppose you need to change 20 miles per hour to feet per minute. Write the rates as fractions: $\frac{20 \text{ miles}}{1 \text{ hour}} \Rightarrow \frac{? \text{ feet}}{\text{minute}}$. First, you want the miles to change to feet, so write the miles-to-feet conversion factor as a fraction, with the miles placed diagonally so they'll cancel. Multiply to get feet per hour:

$$\frac{20 \text{ miles}}{1 \text{ hour}} \times \frac{5,280 \text{ feet}}{1 \text{ mile}} = \frac{105,600 \text{ feet}}{1 \text{ hour}}$$

Then use the hours-to-minutes conversion factor, cancel the hours, and divide 105,600 by 60:

$$\frac{\overset{1,760}{105,600} \text{ feet}}{1 \text{ hour}} \times \frac{1 \text{ hour}}{60 \text{ minutes}} = \frac{1,760 \text{ feet}}{1 \text{ minute}}$$

We told you that the simple units were easier to convert, right?

Choose wisely

When you've found your answer, make sure that after all your careful work you're not misled by crafty wrong answer choices. Does the question ask for the total of a purchase including the tip? You can bet the total without the tip will be another answer choice. If your answer is 500 feet per minute, don't be surprised to find an option of 500 feet per second as well. Read the answer choices carefully and make sure you're choosing the answer your work produced.

Solving Predictable Problems

Familiar conversations, practiced again and again, help to develop fluency with a language. In the language of word problems, these take the form of *type problems,* common situations frequently encountered and solved by a few standard techniques. We show you some of these problems in the following sections.

Determining distance, rate, and time

Problems involving some kind of travel follow the basic rule that the distance (D) traveled is equal to the rate (R) of speed multiplied by the time (T) spent traveling, or $D = R \times T$. If you're asked to find a distance, multiply the speed by the time.

Check the units to make sure you're calculating correctly. Miles per hour times hours gives you miles. Feet per second times seconds gives you feet. If your units don't simplify nicely, you know you need to convert something.

A new robot can move forward at 15 feet per second. How far can it travel in 30 minutes?

(A) 7.5 feet

(B) 45 feet

(C) 450 feet

(D) 27,000 feet

You're looking for "how far," or the distance (D). You have a rate (R) of speed, 15 feet per second, and a time (T), 30 minutes. You know that $D = R \times T$ (the distance traveled = the rate times the time), but the units aren't compatible. 15 feet per second × 30 minutes doesn't simplify nicely, so you have to change 30 minutes to 30 × 60 seconds, or 1,800 seconds. And then you can find the distance: 15 feet per second × 1,800 seconds = $10 \times 1,800 + 5 \times 1,800 = 18,000 + 9,000 = 27,000$ feet. The correct answer is Choice (D).

Not all distance problems ask for the distance, of course. If you're asked for a rate of speed, divide the distance by the time. If you're asked for the time, divide the distance by the rate of speed:

$$D = R \times T$$
$$R = D \div T$$
$$T = D \div R$$

Check the units again. If you're looking for a speed, you can substitute the word "per" for the division symbol between the unit of distance and the unit of time. For example, miles divided by hours gives you miles per hour, and feet divided by seconds gives you feet per second. If you need a time, think of dividing distance by speed as dividing by a fraction:

$$\text{miles} \div \frac{\text{miles}}{\text{hour}} = \cancel{\text{miles}} \; ? \; \frac{\text{hour}}{\cancel{\text{miles}}} = \text{hours}$$

If you drive 135 miles in 90 minutes, what is your speed in miles per hour?

(A) 1.5 miles per hour

(B) 15 miles per hour

(C) 45 miles per hour

(D) 90 miles per hour

You're looking for speed in miles per hour. You have a distance, 135 miles, and a time, 90 minutes. First change 90 minutes to $90 \div 60 = 1\frac{1}{2}$ hours. Then divide the distance, 135 miles, by the time, $1\frac{1}{2}$ hours, to find the speed:

$$135 \div 1\frac{1}{2} = \frac{135}{1} \div \frac{3}{2} = \frac{\overset{45}{135}}{1} \times \frac{2}{\cancel{3}} = 90 \text{ mph}$$

The correct answer is Choice (D).

Figuring tax, tip, and interest

Many common problems are just different ways to ask you to find a percent of a number. When you make a purchase, you often pay a sales tax — a percent of the sale. You frequently leave a tip for service, usually a percent of the bill. You may pay interest on a loan or receive interest on your savings or investment. What all these have in common is that each of them is calculated as a percentage of some quantity. Sales tax is a percentage of the amount purchased, a tip is usually a percentage of the price of the service, and interest is a percentage of the amount borrowed, saved, or invested.

Change percents to decimals or fractions before doing any calculations. Percent literally means "out of 100," so 6% is $\frac{6}{100}$ and 15% is $\frac{15}{100}$. If you prefer to work with decimals, drop the percent sign and move the decimal point two places to the left. So 6% = 0.06 and 15% = 0.15.

To calculate the tax (or tip or interest), change the percent to a decimal or fraction and then multiply by the amount of the purchase (or the price of the service or the amount of the loan or investment).

If you buy a circular saw for $199 in a city where the sales tax is 7%, how much tax do you pay?

(A) $7.99

(B) $13.93

(C) $14.00

(D) $139.30

Change 7% to 0.07 and multiply by $199. (Because $199 is just under two hundred and 7% means 7 for each hundred, expect your answer to be a little less than $14.) $0.07 \times 199 = $13.93, so Choice (B) is the correct answer.

Interest is paid at an annual rate, 4% per year, for example. The interest for one year is just a percent of the amount invested (called the *principal*), but when you look at an investment that earns interest for more than one year, you need to include that length of time in your calculation. The rule for simple interest is $I = P \times R \times T$, or interest equals principal times rate (of interest) times time. Remember that this formula only calculates the interest, not the total amount of your investment.

If you invest $5,000 at an interest rate of 2.5% interest per year, how much interest will you receive in one year?

(A) $10.50

(B) $102.50

(C) $125.00

(D) $1,250.00

Change 2.5% to a decimal by dropping the percent sign and moving the decimal point two places to the left: 2.5% = 0.025. Multiply 0.025 by $5,000 to get interest of $125, which is Choice (C).

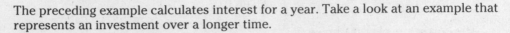

Because finding 10% of a number is easy — you just move the decimal point one place left — you can use that fact to help you with other percents: 10% of $64 is $6.40; 5% of $64 is half as much, $3.20. You also could work through the preceding example by thinking that 10% of $5,000 is $500, so 5% is half of that, or $250, and 2.5% is half of that, or $125.

The preceding example calculates interest for a year. Take a look at an example that represents an investment over a longer time.

If you invest $5,000 at an interest rate of 2.5% interest per year for 10 years, how much interest will you receive?

(A) $10.50

(B) $102.50

(C) $125.00

(D) $1,250.00

Because this example deals with a 10-year investment, multiply principal times rate times time ($I = P \times R \times T$): $I = \$5,000 \times 0.025 \times 10 = \$1,250$. The correct answer is Choice (D).

You've earned all that interest; now you can go out to eat to celebrate! You may want to leave a tip; the following example shows you how.

If you like to leave a 15% tip for service, how much of a tip should you leave on a check of $48?

(A) $3.20

(B) $5.04

(C) $7.20

(D) $9.00

Choose your favorite way to do this one. If you like fractions, change 15% to $\frac{15}{100}$ and reduce to $\frac{3}{20}$. Multiply $\frac{3}{20_5} \times \$\cancel{48}^{12} = \frac{36}{5} = \$7.20$. If you prefer decimals, change 15% to 0.15 and multiply by $48. Hopefully, you still get $7.20. Or, think that 10% of $48 is $4.80 and 5% of $4.80 is half of that, or $2.40, so 15% is $4.80 + $2.40 = $7.20. Any way you figure it, the correct answer is Choice (C).

To find the total bill, including tax or tip — or the new balance, including interest — calculate the tax (or tip or interest) and add it to the original amount. To get the job done in one step, remember that the original amount is 100% of the original amount. The total bill for a $40 meal plus 6% tax is 100% of the $40 plus 6% of the $40, or 106% of $40. Change that percent to a decimal and you get 1.06 × $40 or $42.40.

Computing discount and depreciation

You can work problems involving discount and depreciation in a fashion similar to tax, tip, and interest problems. However, unlike tax and tips that are added to the bill, discounts are amounts subtracted from the price of a purchase. While interest adds to the value of an investment, depreciation reduces the value.

To find just the discount or depreciation, change percents to decimals or fractions and multiply by the original amount, just as you did with tax in the earlier section "Figuring tax, tip, and interest."

The value of a new car depreciates 11% in the first year. If the car sells for $20,000, how much does the value decrease in the first year?

(A) $22

(B) $220

(C) $2,200

(D) $17,800

Change 11% to 0.11 and multiply by $20,000. The decrease in the value of the car is 0.11 × $20,000 = $2,200, or Choice (C).

To find the final cost of an item or the final value of an investment, you can use either of two methods. In one method, you find the discount or depreciation and subtract that discount or depreciation from the original cost or value. In the other, you subtract the percent of the discount or depreciation from 100% and multiply that result by the original value. The following example shows you both methods.

Rachel buys a new coat that lists for $150, but she receives a 20% discount. What does she pay for the coat?

(A) $80

(B) $110

(C) $120

(D) $130

For the first method, you find 20% of $150, which is $30, and then subtract that from $150 to end up with $120. For the second method, you change 20% to 0.20, and subtract that from 1 (representing 100%) to get 0.80. Multiply 0.80 by $150: 0.80 × $150 = $120. Either way, the correct answer is Choice (C).

Calculating commission

Commission is calculated as a percentage of sales. Problems involving commission are a little different because a worker generally receives a salary as well as commission, so the two amounts must be calculated separately and then added together.

Mr. Ellison earns $18 an hour plus a 2% commission on his sales. How much does he earn in a week when he works 40 hours and sells $80,000 worth of merchandise?

(A) $1,440

(B) $1,600

(C) $2,320

(D) $3,200

Mr. Ellison's salary amounts to $18 per hour × 40 hours = $720. His commission is 0.02 × $80,000 = $1,600. Add salary plus commission to find that he earns $720 + $1,600 = $2,320 for the week. The correct answer is Choice (C).

Finding perimeter and area

Calculating perimeter and area are common challenges on tests of arithmetic reasoning. The problems may be presented in words or pictures or both. Some problems combine two or more simple figures. For more on area and perimeter, see the geometry section of Chapter 8.

Perimeter is simply the distance around the outside of an area, so you can find it by adding the lengths of the sides. Perimeter is measured in linear units, including feet, inches, meters, and centimeters. For rectangles, where opposite sides are the same length, you may remember using the formula $P = 2w + 2l$, or $P = 2(w + l)$.

Find the perimeter of a rectangle that is 4 feet wide and 7 feet long.

(A) 11 feet

(B) 22 feet

(C) 28 feet

(D) 56 feet

The perimeter is the sum of the lengths of the sides, so $P = 4 + 7 + 4 + 7 = 2(4) + 2(7) = 22$ feet. The correct answer is Choice (B).

Here's another example that requires a little more thinking.

How many meters of fencing are needed to enclose the field shown in the figure?

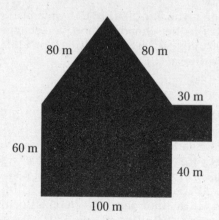

80 m   80 m

30 m

60 m

40 m

100 m

(A) 390 meters

(B) 440 meters

(C) 450 meters

(D) 620 meters

Asking for the amount of fencing needed is just another way to ask for the perimeter, and you can find the perimeter by adding up all the sides. But be careful! Not all the sides of the field are actually labeled with a measurement. Before you can find the perimeter, you need to figure out the length of those sides. You're missing one short vertical side and one short horizontal side, over on the right side of the field. The opposite horizontal side is labeled, so you can conclude that the missing horizontal side is also 30 meters, but don't assume that the vertical side is 30 meters, too. Use the 60-meter vertical side and the vertical side labeled 40 meters to determine that the unlabeled vertical side is 20 meters long. Then the perimeter, and therefore the amount of fencing needed, is $60 + 80 + 80 + 30 + 20 + 30 + 40 + 100 = (60 + 40) + (80 + 20) + 100 + 80 + 30 + 30 = 300 + 140 = 440$ meters. The correct answer is Choice (B).

If you're given the perimeter of a rectangle and one dimension, you can calculate the other dimension by working backward. The perimeter is $P = 2(w + l)$, so divide the perimeter by two and subtract the known dimension to find the other.

Find the width of a rectangle 12 inches long if its perimeter is 76 inches.

(A) 64 inches

(B) 32 inches

(C) 26 inches

(D) 16 inches

The perimeter of 76 inches is equal to twice the sum of the length and the width, so the length plus the width equals 38 inches. Because the width is 12 inches, the length is $38 - 12 = 26$ inches. Choice (C) is the correct answer.

Area measures the space inside a figure. To find the area of a rectangle, multiply length by width:

$$A = lw$$

If the area and one dimension of a rectangle are provided, you can find the unknown dimension by dividing the area by the known dimension:

$$l = A \div w$$
$$w = A \div l$$

Area is always measured in square units.

Find the length of a rectangle that is 21 centimeters wide if the area is 231 cm^2.

(A) 11 centimeters

(B) 110 centimeters

(C) 189 centimeters

(D) 210 centimeters

The area is 231 cm^2 and the width is 21 centimeters, so divide 231 by 21 to get 11 centimeters as the length. Don't be fooled by the fact that all the other answer choices are larger. Choice (A) is correct.

The area of a triangle is half of its base times its height:

$$A = \tfrac{1}{2}bh$$

Find the area of a triangle with a base of 14 inches and a height of 11 inches.

(A) 36 in^2

(B) 50 in^2

(C) 77 in^2

(D) 154 in^2

The area of a triangle is half the product of the base and the height, so $A = \frac{1}{2} \times 14 \times 11 = 7 \times 11 = 77$ in^2. The correct answer is Choice (C).

Feeding the Need for Speed

On a test that asks you to answer 25 questions in 29 minutes (the AFOQT) or 30 questions in 36 minutes (the ASVAB), you can't linger over any question. That doesn't mean you have to rush mindlessly through the test, though. Stop and watch the clock tick off 69 to 72 seconds (the approximate amount of time you have per problem on the test). Most people get bored around the 20-second mark. You can answer an arithmetic word problem in 69 seconds if you work efficiently. You just don't want to waste time, so consider some of the tricks we provide in the following sections to speed up your work.

Don't abandon your word problem strategy out of fear of the clock. You have enough time to read right to the end, identify your goal, collect all the pieces of the puzzle, and make necessary conversions.

Deal with the compatible numbers first

When you add a list of numbers, look for compatible numbers — pairs that add to ten or another repeating sum. It's quicker to tote up those repeated sums and then add on any extras than to juggle the numbers in whatever order they occur. If you add $5 + 4 + 9 + 1 + 6$ in the order listed, it's $5 + 4 = 9$, plus 9 is 18, plus 1 is 19, plus 6 is 25. Certainly, that's doable, but $5 + 4 + 9 + 1 + 6$ is easier if you make groups of ten, and then add on the extra five: $(4 + 6) + (9 + 1) + 5 = 10 + 10 + 5 = 25$.

If you don't see pairs that make tens, go with what you do see. Any patterns you recognize speed the process. The equation $3 + 7 + 6 + 2 + 3$ has two nines and an extra three. $(7 + 2) + (6 + 3) + 3 = 9 + 9 + 3 = 18 + 3 = 21$. You may see $4 + 5 + 3 + 2$ as two sevens. Any repeating element you can find makes your computation easier.

Make minor adjustments

You can speed up addition by estimating with round numbers and then adjusting. To add 39 and 47, think $40 + 50$. That answer of 90 puts you in the right neighborhood. Sometimes that's enough to rule out all but one answer. If you need the exact answer, take the 90 and adjust. Because 39 is one less than 40 and 47 is three less than 50, the exact total is 4 units less than 90, or 86.

Make change

Subtraction is the opposite of addition, so one way to do it quickly is the *adding back* technique often used by cashiers when giving change. If you make a $12.49 purchase and give the cashier a $20 bill, you may be given your change with an explanation like this: "1 makes 50, and 50 makes $13, and 7 makes $20." Take your $12.49 and add a penny to make $12.50, add 50 cents to make $13, and then another $7 to make $20. Thus, $20 − $12.49 = $7.51.

Zero in on numbers

Need to multiply a whole number by 10? Add a zero. If you need to multiply by a power of ten, such as 100 or 1,000, just add one zero for each zero in your multiplier. $567 \times 10,000$ is 567 followed by four zeros, or 5,670,000. Need to multiply by 5? Add a zero and then divide by two. 48×5 is $480 \div 2$ or 240, and $67 \times 5 = 670 \div 2 = 335$.

Divide and conquer

No, we're not talking about division, but multiplication. Mental multiplication gets easier if you use the distributive property, which is just a tactic for breaking the multiplication into small, easy-to-handle problems and then putting the answers together. So 5×12 is equal to 5×10 plus 5×2. Because $50 + 10 = 60$, $5 \times 12 = 60$.

You can use this principle for larger numbers, too. Need to solve 14×325? Try it as $14 \times 300 + 14 \times 20 + 14 \times 5$. 14×3 is $30 + 12$ ($14 = 10 + 4$; $10 \times 3 = 30$ and $4 \times 3 = 12$) or 42, so 14×300 is 4,200. 14×20 is 280, and $14 \times 5 = 140 \div 2$ ($14 \times 10 = 140$; 5 is half of 10) or 70. Add it up, and $4,200 + 280 + 70 = 4,550$.

Use double digits to your advantage

Eleven times a single digit number is easy multiplication: $7 \times 11 = 77$; $4 \times 11 = 44$. But did you know you also can use a shortcut for multiplying a two-digit number by eleven? Separate the two digits, making space for one digit between them. For example, if you have the problem 27×11, write 2_7. Then add the digits and place the sum in the empty space. In this case, $2 + 7 = 9$, so you place the 9 in the empty space to get 2_9_7. Now you have your answer: $27 \times 11 = 297$. If the sum is two digits, put the ones digit in the space and carry the tens. Here's an example:

$$85 \times 11 \Rightarrow 8 \underline{\quad} 5 \Rightarrow (8 + 5 = 13) \Rightarrow 8^{+1}\underline{3}5 = 935$$

Master the bowtie

A quick shortcut exists for adding two fractions with different denominators. This shortcut is nicknamed "the bowtie." The following figure uses arrows to show you what to multiply, and the arrows look a little like a bowtie.

$$\frac{3}{4} + \frac{1}{3} = \overset{3 \times 3 = 9}{\underset{4 \times 3 = 12}{\frac{3}{4} \bowtie \frac{1}{3}}}^{4 \times 1 = 4} = \frac{9}{12} + \frac{4}{12} = \frac{13}{12}$$

First, multiply the bottom right by the upper left and write the result over the left fraction. Multiply up diagonally from the left to the right and write the answer above the right fraction. Then multiply the two denominators and use that product as the denominator of your answer. Add the two numbers you wrote above the fractions to form the numerator of your answer.

See Chapter 8 if you need to brush up on your fractions a bit more.

Borrow properly or avoid it improperly

Subtracting mixed numbers can present a problem. When you add mixed numbers, you add the whole numbers and add the fractions. You may have to simplify when you're done, but that's all there is to it. When you're working with mixed numbers and try to subtract the whole numbers and subtract the fractions, say, in a calculation like $6\frac{1}{4} - 2\frac{3}{4}$, you bump into a problem when you try to subtract $\frac{3}{4}$ from $\frac{1}{4}$.

Officially, you borrow 1 from 6 and regroup it as $\frac{4}{4}$, so that $6\frac{1}{4}$ becomes $\cancel{6}^{5} + \frac{4}{4} + \frac{1}{4} = 5\frac{5}{4}$. Then you can subtract $5\frac{5}{4} - 2\frac{3}{4} = 3\frac{2}{4} = 3\frac{1}{2}$. The other possibility is to change both mixed numbers to improper fractions, subtract, and convert back. $6\frac{1}{4} - 2\frac{3}{4} = \frac{25}{4} - \frac{11}{4} = \frac{14}{4} = 3\frac{2}{4} = 3\frac{1}{2}$. Either method does the job, but in different situations one may be faster than the other. The improper fraction method gets tedious if the numbers are large, but for many people it's faster than regrouping.

Chapter 11

Testing Your Arithmetic Reasoning Skills

● ●

*T*he Air Force Officer Qualifying Test (AFOQT) and the Armed Services Vocational Aptitude Battery (ASVAB) include sections that test arithmetic reasoning. Your arithmetic skills are the tools to solving the problems, but your reasoning is what's really being tested. You're unlikely to see a naked arithmetic problem. All the questions are presented as word problems, and your job is to collect the pertinent information, determine what needs to be done, and accomplish it as quickly as possible.

You need to work efficiently, because these tests give you just slightly more than a minute per question. But don't feel you have to rush. A minute should be enough to answer most of these questions. You'll have scratch paper to do your calculations, but calculators aren't permitted. If you don't find an answer for a question quickly, circle it to come back to later, and then move on.

Review the tips in Chapter 10 for quick calculation, and make sure you're comfortable with standard types of problems, including distance, area, and percent problems. Then test your skills with these practice problems. You can check your answers in this chapter as well.

AFOQT Practice Questions

This test has 25 questions, and you have 29 minutes to complete them. Choose the best answer for each question from the choices provided.

1. The weather service recorded 12 inches of snow in January, 18 inches in February, and 6 inches in March. What is the total snowfall for the first quarter of the year?

    (A) 26 inches

    (B) 30 inches

    (C) 34 inches

    (D) 36 inches

2. According to the mission schedule, astronauts planned to work outside the shuttle for 390 minutes. If they have been outside for 158 minutes, how much longer do they plan to work?

    (A) 132 minutes

    (B) 148 minutes

    (C) 232 minutes

    (D) 248 minutes

3. Jim needs to move 22 cinder blocks. If each block weighs 42 pounds, how much will the entire load weigh?

   (A) 964 pounds

   (B) 924 pounds

   (C) 804 pounds

   (D) 168 pounds

4. An office purchases shipments of 576 reams of paper at a time. If they use 9 reams of paper per day, how many days will the shipment last?

   (A) 66 days

   (B) 64 days

   (C) 62 days

   (D) 60 days

5. John bought $\frac{1}{2}$ pound of roast beef, $\frac{3}{4}$ pound of ham, $1\frac{1}{4}$ pounds of turkey, $2\frac{1}{2}$ pounds of American cheese, and $1\frac{3}{4}$ pounds of Swiss cheese. How many pounds of cold cuts did he buy?

   (A) $6\frac{3}{4}$ pounds

   (B) $6\frac{1}{4}$ pounds

   (C) $5\frac{3}{4}$ pounds

   (D) $5\frac{1}{4}$ pounds

6. If you're making a trip that takes $8\frac{1}{2}$ hours and you've been traveling for $5\frac{3}{4}$ hours, how much longer do you need to travel?

   (A) $3\frac{3}{4}$ hours

   (B) $3\frac{1}{4}$ hours

   (C) $2\frac{3}{4}$ hours

   (D) $2\frac{1}{4}$ hours

7. What is the area of a room that measures $10\frac{2}{3}$ feet by $12\frac{3}{4}$ feet?

   (A) 136 square feet

   (B) $128\frac{1}{2}$ square feet

   (C) 128 square feet

   (D) $120\frac{1}{2}$ square feet

8. If Jack hiked $39\frac{3}{8}$ miles in $5\frac{1}{4}$ hours, what was his average speed?

   (A) $7\frac{3}{7}$ miles per hour

   (B) $7\frac{1}{2}$ miles per hour

   (C) $9\frac{3}{10}$ miles per hour

   (D) 15 miles per hour

9. Jason bought a circular saw for $269.97, a set of wrenches for $54.96, and a pair of safety goggles for $11.47. What is his total bill?

   (A) $334.00

   (B) $336.91

   (C) $336.40

   (D) $337.00

10. You earn $478.29 a week, but $86.09 of federal tax is withheld. How much do you actually take home?

    (A) $392.20

    (B) $392.38

    (C) $391.80

    (D) $400.39

11. A fertilizer manufacturer recommends using 6.25 pounds of fertilizer per 1,000 square feet. How much fertilizer do you need for 2,100 square feet?

    (A) 13.125 pounds

    (B) 131.25 pounds

    (C) 1,312.5 pounds

    (D) 13,125 pounds

12. The area of a rectangle is 42.9 square inches. If the length of the rectangle is 7.15 inches, find the width.

    (A) 5.8 inches

    (B) 6 inches

    (C) 6.1 inches

    (D) 6.8 inches

13. If you have $327 in your checking account, deposit $415, and then write checks for $38 and $105, how much will you have left in your account?

    (A) $272

    (B) $599

    (C) $742

    (D) $885

14. Olivia painted $8\frac{1}{2}$ feet of fence, and Omar painted $6\frac{2}{3}$ feet of fence. If the fence is 20 feet long, how many feet of fence are left to paint?

    (A) $5\frac{5}{6}$

    (B) $5\frac{1}{6}$

    (C) $4\frac{5}{6}$

    (D) $4\frac{1}{6}$

15. Kevin bought a pen for $1.25, a notebook for $2.87, and computer software for $31. If he gave the cashier a $50 bill, how much change did he receive?

    (A) $5.70

    (B) $14.88

    (C) $26.88

    (D) $45.57

16. How far can a train travel in 7 hours at an average speed of 85 miles per hour?

    (A) 595 miles

    (B) 92 miles

    (C) 78 miles

    (D) 12 miles

17. A trip of 840 miles requires a total of 14 hours of driving. What is the average rate of speed?

    (A) $16\frac{2}{3}$ miles per hour

    (B) 60 miles per hour

    (C) 66 miles per hour

    (D) $166\frac{2}{3}$ miles per hour

18. If a runner completes a 10,000 meter run in 40 minutes, what is his speed in meters per hour?

    (A) 250 meters per hour

    (B) 1,500 meters per hour

    (C) 2,500 meters per hour

    (D) 15,000 meters per hour

19. Find the total cost of a new car that lists for $24,000 if a sales tax of 5% is added.

    (A) $25,200

    (B) $27,400

    (C) $28,600

    (D) $36,000

20. Machinery purchased for a factory depreciates at a rate of 8% per year. If the factory owner installs $50,000 in new equipment, what will it be worth at the end of the first year?

    (A) $4,000

    (B) $40,000

    (C) $46,000

    (D) $54,000

21. Mrs. Anderson earns $11 per hour plus 2.5% commission on her sales. Find her total earnings for a week in which she works 40 hours and sells $1,200 worth of merchandise.

   (A) $440

   (B) $443

   (C) $470

   (D) $740

22. Find the area of a triangle with a base of 18 feet and a height of 9 feet.

   (A) 45 square feet

   (B) 54 square feet

   (C) 81 square feet

   (D) 162 square feet

23. Find the length of a rectangle 3.2 meters wide if the area of the rectangle is 64 square meters.

   (A) 57.6 meters

   (B) 32 meters

   (C) 30.4 meters

   (D) 20 meters

24. If you borrow $300 at 6% interest per year for 5 years, how much interest will you pay?

   (A) $18

   (B) $90

   (C) $318

   (D) $390

25. At 8 a.m. there were 7 cars in the parking lot. If 13 more cars entered over the next hour and 3 left, how many cars were in the lot at 9 a.m.?

   (A) 4

   (B) 6

   (C) 10

   (D) 17

ASVAB Practice Questions

This test has 30 questions, and you have 36 minutes to complete them. Choose the best answer for each question from the choices provided.

1. A recipe for a party punch calls for 46 ounces of pineapple juice, 12 ounces of lemon juice, 12 ounces of orange juice, 112 ounces of sparkling water, and 32 ounces of ginger ale. How many ounces of punch will the recipe make?

   (A) 102

   (B) 190

   (C) 202

   (D) 214

2. If you're making a trip of 810 miles and the trip odometer reads 623 miles, how many more miles do you have to drive?

   (A) 213 miles

   (B) 187 miles

   (C) 97 miles

   (D) 93 miles

3. If a charter company has 138 buses and each bus can hold 45 people, what is the greatest number of passengers the buses can transport?

   (A) 6,210

   (B) 5,565

   (C) 5,525

   (D) 1,242

4. The mess hall used 1,147 pounds of potatoes in 31 days. How many pounds of potatoes did it use on average each day?

   (A) 34 pounds

   (B) 35 pounds

   (C) 36 pounds

   (D) 37 pounds

5. Hector worked on Mr. Collins' car for $4\frac{1}{2}$ hours on Tuesday and finished the job in $6\frac{3}{4}$ hours on Wednesday. How many hours did Hector work on the car?

   (A) $10\frac{3}{4}$

   (B) $11\frac{1}{4}$

   (C) $11\frac{1}{2}$

   (D) $11\frac{3}{4}$

6. A fence post $8\frac{3}{4}$ feet long is driven $1\frac{1}{8}$ feet into the ground. How much of the fence post remains above ground?

   (A) $7\frac{5}{8}$ feet

   (B) $7\frac{1}{2}$ feet

   (C) $7\frac{1}{4}$ feet

   (D) $6\frac{5}{8}$ feet

7. A radio-controlled airplane uses $\frac{3}{8}$ of a gallon of fuel each hour. How much fuel will it use in $\frac{1}{4}$ hour?

   (A) $\frac{1}{8}$

   (B) $\frac{3}{32}$

   (C) $\frac{1}{4}$

   (D) $\frac{3}{8}$

8. If the area of a rectangle is $60\frac{1}{2}$ square feet and the length is $14\frac{2}{3}$ feet, find the width.

   (A) $3\frac{5}{8}$ feet

   (B) $3\frac{7}{8}$ feet

   (C) 4 feet

   (D) $4\frac{1}{8}$ feet

9. If the airfare to your vacation spot is $125.10 and the return flight costs $193.60, what is the price of the round trip?

   (A) $387.20

   (B) $320.00

   (C) $318.70

   (D) $250.20

10. If you have saved $372.39 and want to buy a flat-screen TV that costs $693.89, how much more do you need to save?

   (A) $322.38

   (B) $321.59

   (C) $321.50

   (D) $320.96

11. A company sells 3.6 million widgets for $2.50 per widget. What is its revenue from the sale?

   (A) $1.44 million

   (B) $6.3 million

   (C) $8.1 million

   (D) $9 million

12. A defensive lineman was credited with 16.5 sacks in 11 games. What was his average number of sacks per game?

(A) 1.5

(B) 1.55

(C) 1.6

(D) 1.65

13. Jason lifts weights and is increasing the amount he can lift. He's currently lifting a bar that weighs 54 pounds with a 50-pound plate on each end. If he increases the weight by 10 pounds per week, how much will he lift in 8 weeks?

(A) 134

(B) 180

(C) 184

(D) 234

14. Jeff stacks two boards and glues them together. One is $\frac{3}{4}$ inch thick and the other is $\frac{1}{2}$ inch thick. What is the thickness of the resulting board?

(A) $\frac{7}{8}$

(B) $1\frac{1}{8}$

(C) $1\frac{1}{4}$

(D) $1\frac{3}{8}$

15. Jason bought a circular saw for $269.97, a set of wrenches for $54.96, and a pair of safety goggles for $11.47. A 6% sales tax was added to his bill. What is his total bill?

(A) $201.84

(B) $336.40

(C) $356.58

(D) $538.24

16. A train travels at an average speed of 72 miles per hour. How far will it travel in 45 minutes?

(A) 16 miles

(B) 54 miles

(C) 96 miles

(D) 324 miles

17. The driving distance between New York and Los Angeles is estimated to be 2,451 miles. If you can make the drive at an average speed of 50 miles per hour, how long will the trip take?

(A) 4.902 hours

(B) 12.225 hours

(C) 49.02 hours

(D) 122.55 hours

18. The International Space Station orbits the earth every 90 minutes. If the orbital speed is about 26,720 kilometers per hour, what is the length of its orbit?

    (A) 2,404,800 kilometers

    (B) 40,080 kilometers

    (C) $17,813\frac{1}{3}$ kilometers

    (D) $296\frac{8}{9}$ kilometers

19. A restaurant adds an 18% tip to the bill for parties of eight or more. How much is the tip added to a check of $220?

    (A) $1.44

    (B) $14.40

    (C) $26.00

    (D) $39.60

20. If you invest $10,000 at 4% per year for 3 years, how much interest will you earn?

    (A) $300

    (B) $400

    (C) $700

    (D) $1,200

21. If a $540 refrigerator is on sale at a 20% discount, how much will you save on the purchase?

    (A) $54

    (B) $108

    (C) $432

    (D) $648

22. Equipment valued at $120,000 depreciates at 7% per year. How much of its value does it lose in the first year?

    (A) $8,400

    (B) $36,000

    (C) $84,000

    (D) $111,600

23. You hike to a position $1\frac{1}{2}$ miles from base, and then continue $2\frac{2}{3}$ miles to a rendezvous point. If you maintain an average speed of $2\frac{1}{2}$ miles per hour, how long does the trip take?

    (A) $1\frac{1}{15}$ hours

    (B) $1\frac{2}{3}$ hours

    (C) $2\frac{1}{12}$ hours

    (D) $2\frac{1}{2}$ hours

24. An aquarium contains 117 fish, and 35 new fish are introduced. All of them survive. If the volume of the tank is 76 cubic feet, what is the number of fish per cubic foot of space?

    (A) 1

    (B) 2

    (C) 3

    (D) 4

25. A recipe for a party punch calls for 46 ounces of pineapple juice, 12 ounces of lemon juice, 12 ounces of orange juice, 112 ounces of sparkling water, and 32 ounces of ginger ale. If 1 cup equals 8 ounces, how many cups of punch will you have?

    (A) $25\frac{1}{4}$

    (B) 26

    (C) $26\frac{3}{4}$

    (D) 27

26. What is the final price of a washer that lists for $590 if it is on sale at a 15% discount?

    (A) $88.50

    (B) $501.50

    (C) $505.00

    (D) $575.00

27. Mrs. Anderson earns $12.50 per hour plus 3% commission on her sales. Find her total earnings for a week in which she works 30 hours and sells $800 worth of merchandise.

    (A) $240.00

    (B) $375.00

    (C) $377.40

    (D) $399.00

28. Find the area of a square that measures 12 inches on each side.

    (A) 144 square inches

    (B) 120 square inches

    (C) 48 square inches

    (D) 24 square inches

29. A company produced 428.5 million transistors last year and 649.75 transistors this year. What was the average number of transistors produced per year?

    (A) 538.75 million

    (B) 539.125 million

    (C) 539.25 million

    (D) 589.125 million

30. In 2001, a tree was 14.86 meters tall. By 2006, it was 18.75 meters. On average, how much did the tree grow each of those five years?

    (A) 0.778 meters

    (B) 1.995 meters

    (C) 6.722 meters

    (D) 16.805 meters

Answers to the AFOQT Practice Questions

This section contains the answers for the AFOQT arithmetic reasoning practice problems. We suggest you read the explanation that follows the answer if you didn't come up with the correct answer (or if you just want to reinforce how to solve a particular type of problem).

1. **D.** Take the 2 from the 12 and the 8 from 18 to make a 10: $12 + 18 + 6 = (10 + 2) + (10 + 8) + 6 = 10 + 10 + (2 + 8) + 6 = 36$ inches.

2. **C.** They're at 158 now, 2 minutes will make 160, and 30 more will make 190. Another 200 minutes will make 390. Add $2 + 30 + 200$ to get 232.

3. **B.** There's a multiple of eleven, so think about it this way: $22 \times 42 = 11 \times 2 \times 42 = 11 \times 84$. Add $8 + 4$ to get 12. Separate the 8 and the 4, put down the 2 from the 12, and add the 1 from the 12 to the 8: $22 \times 42 = 11 \times 84 = 924$.

4. **B.** Short division should do the job: $576 \div 9 = 64$.

5. **A.** The idea of compatible numbers works for fractions as well as for whole numbers. Here, group the halves and the numbers for which the quarters will add to one:
   $\frac{1}{2} + \frac{3}{4} + 1\frac{1}{4} + 2\frac{1}{2} + 1\frac{3}{4} = \left(\frac{1}{2} + 2\frac{1}{2}\right) + \left(\frac{3}{4} + 1\frac{1}{4}\right) + 1\frac{3}{4}$. Then, $\frac{1}{2} + 2\frac{1}{2}$ gives you 3 and $\frac{3}{4} + 1\frac{1}{4}$ gives you 2, so you have $3 + 2 + 1\frac{3}{4} = 6\frac{3}{4}$.

6. **C.** Borrow 1 from the 8, and change to a common denominator of 4: $8\frac{1}{2} - 5\frac{3}{4} = 7 + 1 + \frac{1}{2} - 5\frac{3}{4} = 7\frac{3}{2} - 5\frac{3}{4} = 7\frac{6}{4} - 5\frac{3}{4} = 2\frac{3}{4}$.

7. **A.** The area is $10\frac{2}{3}$ times $12\frac{3}{4}$, which is $10\frac{2}{3} \times 12\frac{3}{4} = \frac{\overset{8}{\cancel{32}}}{\cancel{3}} \times \frac{\overset{17}{\cancel{51}}}{\cancel{4}} = 136$.

8. **B.** Distance divided by time gives you speed: $39\frac{3}{8} \div 5\frac{1}{4} = \frac{315}{8} \div \frac{21}{4} = \frac{\overset{45}{\cancel{315}}}{\underset{2}{\cancel{8}}} \times \frac{\cancel{4}}{\underset{3}{\cancel{21}}} = \frac{45}{6} = 7\frac{3}{6} = 7\frac{1}{2}$ miles per hour.

9. **C.** Round to get an estimate: $270 + 55 + 11 \approx 270 + 66 \approx 336$. Adjust down 3 cents, down 4 cents, and up 47 cents for a net change of 40 cents up: $\$269.97 + \$54.96 + \$11.47 = \$336.40$.

10. **A.** Estimation may help you solve this problem. The $86 withheld takes away the $78 plus another $8, so expect an answer around $392. The 9 cents come off the 29 cents. The solution is as follows: $\$478.29 - \$86.09 = \$392.20$.

11. **A.** First, 2,100 square feet is 2.1 thousands ($2,100 \div 1,000$). Continue solving as follows: $2.1 \times 6.25 = (2 \times 6.25) + (0.1 \times 6.25) = 12.5 + 0.625 = 13.125$. Or use estimation to eliminate answers. Because 2,100 is approximately twice as much as 1,000, you would need approximately twice as much fertilizer. As a result, you know you can eliminate Choices (B), (C), and (D), which are too big.

12. **B.** The number of places you move the decimal point is determined by the divisor. In this case, the divisor is 7.15, so move the decimal point two places. Your problem becomes 4,290 divided by 715. Because $4,200 \div 700 = 6$, you should expect an answer around 6. You can use the distributive property to check: $6 \times 715 = 6 \times 700 + 6 \times 15 = 4,200 + 90 = 4,290$.

13. **B.** You begin with \$327 and deposit \$415, bringing the total in your account to \$742 (\$327 + \$415). You then write checks for \$38 and \$105, for a total of \$143 (\$38 + \$105). That \$143 is deducted from the \$742: \$742 − \$143 = \$599.

14. **C.** Together, Olivia and Omar painted $8\frac{1}{2}+6\frac{2}{3}=8\frac{3}{6}+6\frac{4}{6}$ feet of fence. $8\frac{3}{6}+6\frac{4}{6}=8+6+\frac{3}{6}+\frac{4}{6}$ $=14+\frac{7}{6}=14+1\frac{1}{6}=15\frac{1}{6}$. Use estimation to avoid mistakes. They painted a little more than 15 of the 20 feet of fence, so they have a little less than 5 feet left. In fact, they have $20-15\frac{1}{6}=19\frac{6}{6}-15\frac{1}{6}=4\frac{5}{6}$ feet left to paint.

15. **B.** Add the smaller dollar and cents amounts first, and then break them up to use mental math: \$1.25 + \$2.87 = 1 + 2 + (0.20 + 0.80) + (0.05 + 0. 07) = 3 + 1 + 0.12 = 4.12. Add the \$31 to the \$4.12 to get \$35.12. Subtract \$35.12 from \$50 to get \$14.88.

16. **A.** Multiply 85 miles per hour by 7 hours to get 595 miles. But here's a hint: If you realize that the necessary operation is multiplication, you can see that Choice (A) is the only reasonable answer.

17. **B.** Divide 840 miles by 14 hours to get 60 miles per hour.

18. **D.** First, convert 40 minutes to $\frac{40}{60}=\frac{2}{3}$ of an hour. Then divide 10,000 meters by $\frac{2}{3}$ of an hour to get $10,000\div\frac{2}{3}=10,000\times\frac{3}{2}=\frac{30,000}{2}=15,000$ meters per hour.

19. **A.** Ten percent of \$24,000 would be \$2,400, so 5% is half of that, or \$1,200. The total cost is \$24,000 plus the \$1,200 tax, or \$25,200.

20. **C.** If the equipment loses 8% of its value, it loses \$4,000 the first year. At the end of that year, it will be worth \$50,000 − \$4,000, or \$46,000.

21. **C.** Mrs. Anderson's base salary is 40 hours times \$11 per hour, or \$440. However, that amount doesn't include her commission, so you can eliminate Choice (A). Commission of 2.5% on sales of \$1,200 = 0.025 × 1,200 = 2.5 × 12 = 2.5 × 10 + 2.5 × 2 = 25 + 5 = \$30. Her base salary of \$440 plus \$30 commission gives her \$470.

22. **C.** The area of a triangle is half the product of the base and the height, so multiply $\frac{1}{2}\times18$ feet × 9 feet = 9 × 9 = 81 square feet.

23. **D.** Divide to find the length: 64 m^2 ÷ 3.2 meters = 20 meters.

24. **B.** The formula to use is $I = PRT$, so \$300 × 0.06 × 5 = 300 × 0.3 = \$90.

25. **D.** The hour starts with 7 cars. Then 13 cars are added and 3 are subtracted: 7 + 13 = 20 and 20 − 3 = 17.

Answers to the ASVAB Practice Questions

Following are the answers to the ASVAB arithmetic reasoning practice questions. We also provide guidance on how to get the correct answer in case you need help figuring out where you went wrong.

1. **D.** You may want to stack the numbers in this problem to add them, but the two 12s make 24, which adds nicely with the 46. You can solve the problem like this: 46 + (12 + 12) + 112 + 32 = 46 + 24 + 112 + 32 = 70 + 32 + 112 = 102 + 112 = 214.

2. **B.** Make change the way a cashier would to do this mentally. Start with 623. Seven makes 630, 70 more puts you at 700, another hundred makes 800, and then you need 10 more to reach 810. 7 + 70 + 100 + 10 = 187.

3. **A.** Factor and rearrange the numbers to make the multiplication easier. 138 is 69×2 and 45 is 5×9. Because the whole problem is multiplication, you can rearrange to a more convenient order. $138 \times 45 = (69 \times 2) \times (5 \times 9) = (69 \times 9) \times (2 \times 5) = (621) \times 10 = 6{,}210$. So $138 \times 45 = 6{,}210$.

4. **D.** Estimate $1{,}147 \div 31$ as $1{,}200 \div 30$, which equals 40. Check to see that $40 \times 31 = 1{,}240$, and $1{,}240 - 1{,}147 = 93$. Because 93 is 3×31, $1{,}147 \div 31 = 40 - 3 = 37$.

5. **B.** First, add the whole numbers: $4\frac{1}{2} + 6\frac{3}{4} = 4 + 6 + \frac{1}{2} + \frac{3}{4} = 10 + \frac{1}{2} + \frac{3}{4}$. Change the $\frac{1}{2}$ to $\frac{2}{4}$ and add the fractions: $10 + \frac{2}{4} + \frac{3}{4} = 10 + \frac{5}{4}$. Lastly, change the improper fraction to a mixed number: $10 + \frac{5}{4} = 10 + 1\frac{1}{4} = 11\frac{1}{4}$.

6. **A.** Change the denominator of the first fraction to 8, and you don't have to borrow: $8\frac{3}{4} - 1\frac{1}{8} = 8\frac{6}{8} - 1\frac{1}{8} = 7\frac{5}{8}$.

7. **B.** The airplane will use $\frac{1}{4}$ of $\frac{3}{8}$ of a gallon, which is $\frac{1}{4} \times \frac{3}{8} = \frac{3}{32}$ of fuel in a quarter of an hour. Resist the temptation to cancel two denominators. You may only cancel a numerator with a denominator.

8. **D.** Divide the area by the known dimension: $60\frac{1}{2} \div 14\frac{2}{3} = \frac{121}{2} \div \frac{44}{3} = \frac{\overset{11}{\cancel{121}}}{2} \times \frac{3}{\underset{4}{\cancel{44}}} = \frac{33}{8} = 4\frac{1}{8}$ feet.

9. **C.** If you estimate this as $125 + 200$, two answer choices seem unreasonable: Choice (A), \$387.20, because it seems too big, and Choice (D), \$250.20, because it seems too small. You rounded \$193.60 up several dollars and \$125.10 down only a few cents, so your actual answer should be a few dollars less than the estimate of \$325. The correct answer is Choice (C): $\$125.10 + \$193.60 = \$318.70$.

10. **C.** No borrowing is needed: $\$693.89 - \$372.39 = \$321.50$.

11. **D.** Just carry the million along. Do a little regrouping and this one gets easier: 3.6 million $\times$ \$2.50 = (1.8 million $\times$ 2) $\times$ \$2.50 = 1.8 million $\times$ (2 $\times$ \$2.50) = 1.8 million $\times$ \$5.00 = \$9 million.

12. **A.** Remember the trick for multiplying by 11? You can work it backward, too. It looks like the solution to 16.5 divided by 11 is one-point-something, and the 5 on the end makes you guess at 1.5: $15 \times 11 = 165$, so $16.5 \div 11 = 1.5$.

13. **D.** You need to add 10 pounds per week times 8 weeks to his current $54 + 2 \times 50$ pounds. Save the 54 for last: $54 + (2 \times 50) + (8 \times 10) = 54 + 100 + 80 = 54 + 180 = 234$ pounds.

14. **C.** Change the $\frac{1}{2}$ to $\frac{2}{4}$, add, and then change to a mixed number: $\frac{3}{4} + \frac{1}{2} = \frac{3}{4} + \frac{1}{2} \cdot \frac{2}{2} = \frac{3}{4} + \frac{2}{4} = \frac{5}{4} = 1\frac{1}{4}$.

15. **C.** Add the costs of the items purchased: $269.97 + 54.96 + 11.47 = \$336.40$. To find the total bill, multiply \$336.40 by 1.06 (1 for 100% of the original bill plus 0.06 for the 6% tax): $\$336.40 \times 1.06 = \$356.58$.

16. **B.** Change 45 minutes to $\frac{3}{4}$ hour. Then, 72 miles per hour $\times \frac{3}{4}$ hour = 54 miles.

17. **C.** The solution looks like this: 2,451 miles $\div$ 50 miles per hour = 49.02 hours.

18. **B.** Change 90 minutes to 1.5 hours and then multiply it out: 26,720 kilometers per hour $\times$ 1.5 hours = 40,080 kilometers.

19. **D.** You were only asked to find the tip, not the total bill, so multiply 0.18 by \$220 and you get \$39.60.

20. **D.** To find the interest on \$10,000 at 4% per year for 3 years, remember that $I = PRT$, so $10{,}000 \times 0.04 \times 3 = \$1{,}200$.

21. **B.** Ten percent of $540 is $54, so 20% is $108. You save $108.

22. **A.** The equipment loses 7% of its value, and $0.07 \times \$120,000 = \$8,400$.

23. **B.** You need to add the distances and then divide the total by your speed, so it may be easier to work with improper fractions. You travel $1\frac{1}{2} + 2\frac{2}{3} = \frac{3}{2} + \frac{8}{3} = \frac{9+16}{6} = \frac{25}{6}$ miles. Divide that by $2\frac{1}{2} = \frac{5}{2}$ miles per hour: $\frac{25}{6} \div \frac{5}{2} = \frac{\overset{5}{\cancel{25}}}{\underset{3}{\cancel{6}}} \times \frac{\cancel{2}}{\cancel{5}} = \frac{5}{3} = 1\frac{2}{3}$ hours.

24. **B.** Add $117 + 35$ to find the number of fish in the tank: 152. Read the question carefully. "Fish per cubic foot" tells you to divide 152 fish by 76 cubic feet: $152 \div 76 = 2$ fish per cubic foot.

25. **C.** Find the total number of ounces: $46 + 12 + 12 + 112 + 32 = 214$ ounces. Then divide the total ounces by the 8 ounces in 1 cup to get the number of cups: $214 \div 8 = 26\frac{3}{4}$ cups.

26. **B.** If the washer is discounted by 15%, you pay 85% of the price: $0.85 \times \$590 = \$501.50$.

27. **D.** First, find Mrs. Anderson's base pay, and then add to that the amount of commission she earns: $12.50 per hour $\times$ 30 hours $+ 0.03 \times \$800 = \$375 + \$24 = \$399$.

28. **A.** The area of a square equals length $\times$ width, but because length and width are the same in this case, the area is the length of one side squared: $12 \times 12 = 144$ square inches.

29. **B.** The "million" just tags along and has no effect on your calculation. Add $649.75 + 428.5$ to get 1,078.25, and then divide by 2 to get 539.125 million.

30. **A.** Start by finding the total growth for the five years. You're taking a little less than 15 away from 18.75. Expect an answer a bit bigger than 3.75. In fact, $18.75 - 14.86 = 3.89$. Then divide by 5 to find the average growth per year: $3.89 \div 5 = 0.778$.

Chapter 12

Grasping the Specifics of General Science

General science covers a whole lot of ground — biology, botany, chemistry, physics, human anatomy, earth science, oceanography, astronomy, genetics, agriculture, nutrition, and a host of other subjects you may or may not have encountered in high school. This range represents volumes of information that a single chapter of a single book can't possibly cover in any detail, but that's not the point. The purpose of the General Science subtest is not to stump you with obscure scientific trivia questions. Instead, it's meant to determine whether you have a solid grasp of general scientific knowledge and are able to demonstrate logical problem-solving skills.

This chapter provides a refresher course on life sciences, chemistry, earth sciences, and the solar system — four general categories that encompass almost every facet of scientific knowledge. It also helps you bone up on the metric system, which scientists are partial to, and the scientific method. Consider this your general science *CliffsNotes* — a condensed survey of general science designed specifically to prepare you for the General Science subtest of the Officer Candidate Tests (OCT). For coverage of physics, see Chapter 14.

Exploring the Diversity of Scientific Fields

The diversity of scientific study ranges from micro to macro, from the smallest of organisms and particles of matter in the universe to infinity and beyond. Science encompasses far too many fields to cover in such a brief amount of space, so in this section we focus on a few of the most important and prevalent areas of study (at least regarding what's on the test): the natural sciences.

The term *natural science* means a study of the world with respect to how everything in nature follows a certain natural order or law. In a broad sense, natural science is the study of how things work. Specifically, natural sciences include life science, chemistry, physics, and earth science.

Looking at life science from A to Z

Life science is the study of living things — plants and animals (including humans). Table 12-1 lists a few of the more familiar life sciences covered in this chapter and provides a brief description of each.

Table 12-1	Familiar Life Sciences
Life Science	*Study of*
Anatomy	The structure of living organisms
Biology	Living organisms and their lives
Botany	Plants
Ecology	The interaction of organisms with their environment
Genetics	Heredity
Physiology	The function of living systems
Zoology	Animals

Elementary, my dear Watson: Chemistry

Chemistry is the study of matter and how it changes. More specifically, chemistry explores matter's composition, structure, properties, and changes that occur in chemical reactions. For the test, you need to know the basics of how atoms are structured; the roles that electrons, protons, and neutrons play inside an atom; the difference between atoms, molecules, and compounds; differences in chemical states; what makes an acid an acid (and a base a base); how to make sense of the periodic table, and the two types of chemical reactions. You discover all this and more in the later section "Cracking Open the Chemistry Kit."

Exploring energy and matter: Physics

Physics is another study of matter that differs from chemistry in that it examines how matter exists in the physical world. The big difference between physics and chemistry is that physics examines how matter changes with forces and energy exchange, whereas chemistry studies changes in the chemical composition of matter. For more about physics, turn to Chapter 14.

Digging into the earth sciences

The *earth sciences* slice and dice your home planet into a variety of scientific studies. Table 12-2 introduces you to the earth sciences you're most likely to encounter on the tests.

Table 12-2	A Selection of Earth Sciences
Earth Science	*Study of*
Astronomy	The physical universe beyond earth's atmosphere
Geography	Earth's inhabitants and environments
Geology	Earth's composition
Hydrology	Water
Meteorology	Weather
Mineralogy	Minerals

Brushing Up on the Metric System

The United States is one of the few countries in the world that uses units of measure other than the metric system. In scientific circles, however, measurements are always in metric, so you need to know how to work with metric units. The good news is that the metric system is all about the number 10, which greatly simplifies calculations. The following sections bring you up to speed on the metric system.

Metric measures

To understand the metric system, you need to shift your thinking from inches and feet to centimeters and meters and from ounces and gallons to centiliters and liters. The following information should help ease the transition:

- **Length:** Length is measured in meters, centimeters, millimeters, and kilometers. A meter is a little longer than a yard. A kilometer is a little more than 0.6 mile.

- **Volume:** Volume is measured in liters and milliliters. A liter is slightly more than a quart.

- **Mass (weight):** Mass is measured in grams and kilograms. A kilogram is about 2.2 pounds. One ounce is slightly more than 28 grams.

- **Temperature:** Temperature is measured in Celsius with a freezing point of 0° (versus 32° in Fahrenheit) and a boiling point of 100° (versus 212° in Fahrenheit).

See "Conversion factors," later in this chapter, for details on converting U.S. measurement units to their metric equivalents.

Prefixes and abbreviations

In the metric system, you tack on a prefix to a general unit of measure to make the unit more specific. For example, the prefix *centi-* means 1/100th (or .001). A centimeter is 1/100th of a meter. A centiliter is 1/100th of a liter. Table 12-3 lists the metric prefixes you should know, along with their symbols and multiplication factor.

Table 12-3	Metric Prefixes, Symbols, and Multiplication Factors	
Prefix	Symbol	Multiplication Factor
tera-	T	$10^{12} = 1\ 000\ 000\ 000\ 000$
giga-	G	$10^{9} = 1\ 000\ 000\ 000$
mega-	M	$10^{6} = 1\ 000\ 000$
kilo-	k	$10^{3} = 1\ 000$
hector-	h	$10^{2} = 100$
deka-	da	$10^{1} = 1$
deci-	d	$10^{-1} = 0.1$
centi-	c	$10^{-2} = 0.01$
milli-	m	$10^{-3} = 0.001$
micro-	μ	$10^{-6} = 0.000\ 001$
nano-	n	$10^{-9} = 0.000\ 000\ 001$
pico-	p	$10^{-12} = 0.000\ 000\ 000\ 001$

To change between quantities of units, multiply or divide by the specified multiple of 10. For example:

$$1 \text{ centimeter} = 1 \text{ meter} \times 10^{-2} = 0.01 \text{ meters}$$

$$10 \text{ kilogram} = 1 \text{ gram} \times 10^{3} = 1{,}000 \text{ grams}$$

Test questions may include metric abbreviations, such as cm and kg. To understand what the most common metric abbreviations stand for, check out Table 12-4.

Table 12-4		Metric Abbreviations	
Abbreviation	Stands for	Abbreviation	Stands for
m	meter	ml	milliliter
mm	millimeter	m^2	square meter
cm	centimeter	m^3	cubic meter
km	kilometer	km^2	square kilometer
g	gram	cc	cubic centimeter
mg	milligram	t	metric ton (1,000 kilograms)
kg	kilogram	ha	hectare
l	liter	C	Celsius

A milliliter (ml) is equivalent to a cubic centimeter (cc).

Conversion factors

Some questions may require converting a standard U.S. unit of measure into its metric equivalent. Table 12-5 provides the conversion factors for the most common units of measure.

Table 12-5	U.S.-to-Metric Conversion Factors	
Multiply . . .	*By . . .*	*To Get . . .*
inches	2.54	centimeters
feet	0.305	meters
miles	1.6	kilometers
pounds	2.2	kilograms
ounces	28	grams
fluid ounces	30	milliliters
gallons	3.8	liters

To convert metric measurements to U.S. units of measure, reverse the operation — divide by the number in the center column of Table 12-5 instead of multiplying.

Temperature scales and conversions

Throughout the U.S., people measure temperature in degrees Fahrenheit, with water freezing at 32 and boiling at 212. In scientific work and in most other countries, people measure temperature in degrees Celsius, with water freezing at 0 and boiling at 100. To convert a temperature from one system to the other, use the following formulas:

$$°C = \frac{5}{9} \times (°F - 32°)$$

$$°F = \frac{9}{5} \times °C + 32°$$

A third scale, also commonly used in scientific work, is the Kelvin scale, in which water freezes at 273 and boils at 373 degrees. It starts at absolute zero — the temperature when matter has no thermal energy. To convert a temperature from Celsius to Kelvin, add 273 degrees:

$$°K = °C + 273°$$

Celsius or centigrade?

You may encounter the word "centigrade" instead of "Celsius," but they both reference the temperature scale that represents 100 degrees between water's freezing and boiling points. Scientists in the U.S. used the term "centigrade" from approximately 1742 to 1948 when the Conference General des Poids et Measures (CGPM) officially adopted the name "Celsius" (for the scientist who invented it).

The two scales have some slight differences, but for the most part, "centigrade" and "Celsius" are interchangeable.

Wrapping Your Brain around the Scientific Method

You may encounter one or more questions that require a basic understanding of the *scientific method* — a systematic approach for solving a problem or answering a question in science. Following are the steps that comprise the scientific method:

1. **State the purpose.**

   The *purpose* is a specific description of what a scientist hopes to accomplish through a particular experiment.

2. **Perform research.**

   Thorough research helps prevent redundant experiments and helps refine the purpose statement and hypothesis.

3. **Formulate a hypothesis.**

   A *hypothesis* is scientist's best guess as to what the results of the experiment will prove. It's normally worded like this:

   "If _____, then _____."

   The first space contains the *independent variable* — what the scientist can control. The second space contains the *dependent variable* — what the scientist believes will happen as a result of the independent variable.

4. **List required materials.**

   This list is the detailed shopping list for all the stuff required to perform the experiment.

5. **Establish the procedure.**

   The procedure is the step-by-step instruction manual for performing the experiment.

6. **Record the results.**

   Results are anything you can observe or measure, including changes in color, texture, or temperature; funny smells; explosions; or perhaps nothing at all.

7. **Draw a conclusion based on the results.**

   The conclusion summarizes what happened; for example, "When _____ was done, _____ happened."

 The scientific method helps to ensure the validity of experimental evidence. If a scientist follows the scientific method in performing an experiment, anyone should be able to repeat the experiment and reach the same conclusion.

Cramming Life Science Essentials

Life sciences cover a lot of ground — everything from microscopic, single-celled organisms to plants and animals with numerous cell types and complex biological systems. You can't possibly know everything about the life sciences that you *may* encounter on the OCT, but you can cram some essential information into your brain to better prepare yourself. The following sections cover the fundamentals.

Classifying all living things

In an attempt to organize nature, humans have developed a system of classifying all living things called a *taxonomy*. The most widely accepted taxonomy divides all living things into broad categories, or *kingdoms,* based on their structure. Kingdoms are the broadest category for classifying plants and animals. Don't be surprised if you get a question asking which kingdom a particular organism belongs to. Following is a list of the five kingdoms with a brief description of each:

- ✔ **Monera:** Simple, single cells that don't have membrane-bound nuclei, such as parasitic bacteria and photosynthesizing blue-green algae.

- ✔ **Protista:** Complex single-celled organisms that have distinct nuclei, including slime molds, protozoa, and single- or multiple-cell algaes. Members of this group are distinguished from one another by whether they feed off of other organisms or perform photosynthesis.

- ✔ **Fungi:** Immobile, multicelled organisms that can't perform photosynthesis and must decompose other dead organisms for food. Fungi include mushrooms, yeasts, and molds.

- ✔ **Planta:** Multicelled organisms that can perform photosynthesis to create food, such as mosses and plants. Two categories of plants exist: Bryophyta that do not have a vascular system, and Tracheophyta that do.

- ✔ **Animalia:** Mobile, multicelled organisms that feed on other organisms (plant or animal) for food. The main division within this kingdom is between *vertebrates* (with a backbone) and *invertebrates* (without a backbone).

Six more categories further subdivide the kingdoms. Each subcategory contains a progressively smaller number of different organisms. Here's a complete list of categories in increasing specificity:

- ✔ **A kingdom** contains several related phyla.

- ✔ **A phylum** contains several related classes.

- ✔ **A class** contains several related orders.

- ✔ **An order** contains several related families.

- ✔ **A family** contains several related genera.

- ✔ **A genus** contains several related species.

- ✔ **A species** contains organisms so similar that they can reproduce together.

For human beings, classification goes like this:

- ✔ **Kingdom:** Animalia

- ✔ **Phylum:** Chordata (vertebrate)

- ✔ **Class:** Mammalia

- ✔ **Order:** Primate

- ✔ **Family:** Hominidae

- ✔ **Genus:** Homo

- ✔ **Species:** Sapiens

Everything you wanted to know about cells — and then some

Among living things, a cell is the smallest, but the body of information that surrounds it is huge. The following sections present the need-to-know information to get you through any questions you're likely to encounter concerning cells and cell theory.

Passing the life test

Cells are the most basic form of life, which leads to the question: What exactly is life? Something is determined to be living only if it has the following characteristics:

- **Homeostasis:** The ability to regulate its own internal environment to maintain a cell or body at a relatively constant state.

- **Organization:** Being composed of one or more cells.

- **Metabolism:** The transfer of energy by consumption of matter or chemicals or through photosynthesis.

- **Growth:** The ability of all or some of its parts to increase in size, not just acquire more matter.

- **Adaptation:** The ability to adjust to a changing external environment.

- **Response to stimuli:** The ability to react to external stimuli, including light, sound, and heat. Responses may vary from the most basic chemical response of a single cell organism to motion resulting from the perception of a complex sensory system.

- **Reproduction:** The ability to reproduce either sexually or *asexually* (without sex).

Viruses straddle the line between living and nonliving organisms. Because they require a host cell to reproduce, many scientists consider them nonliving organisms that deserve a class of their own — *infectious agents*.

Understanding cell theory

According to *cell theory,* cells are the base unit of every living organism from single-celled to complex organisms, such as humans or trees. The development of this theory began with the invention of the microscope and the science of *microscopy*. Cell theory is one of the principal theories in modern biology.

Naming cell parts

Although cells are tiny, they comprise even tinier parts that you may need to identify on the OCT. The following list, along with Figure 12-1, should help you pick the parts out of a lineup:

- **Cytoplasm:** The fluid membrane that holds and supports all of a cell's components.

- **Endoplasmic reticulum (ER):** An extensive network of sac-like structures that synthesize proteins and lipids and assist in folding and transporting manufactured proteins.

- **Golgi bodies (Golgi apparatus):** Layers of membrane-bound structures that modify, sort, and package complex molecules (*macromolecules*) to be used within the cell or to be secreted by the cell.

- **Lysosomes:** Cube-shaped structures that contain enzymes to help break down cell waste and prepare it for excretion. These structures are found only in animal cells.

- **Vacuoles:** Found only in plant cells, vacuoles are the equivalent of the lysosomes found in animal cells.

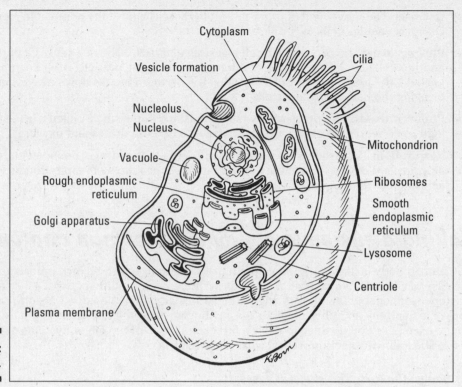

Figure 12-1:
Cell parts.

✔ **Membrane (wall):** The protein layer that surrounds the cell, giving it form and protecting it from its external environment. The membrane is *selectively permeable* to allow food and other desirables into the cell, while keeping harmful matter outside. (*Permeable* means water or gas can pass through it, like a coffee filter.)

✔ **Mitochondria:** The membrane-enclosed structures wherein cell respiration occurs. These structures are commonly described as the cell's "power plants." The activity and number of mitochondria within a cell determine the cell's metabolism.

✔ **Chloroplasts:** Found only in plant cells, chloroplasts are the equivalent of the mitochondria in animal cells. Chloroplasts capture light energy and convert it into free energy within the cell.

✔ **Nucleus:** The part of a cell that contains its DNA and controls reproduction.

✔ **Organelle:** Any of the many subunits within a cell, including ribosomes, mitochondria, and lysosomes.

✔ **Ribosomes:** Components within a cell that form proteins from amino acids.

Knowing how cells survive and thrive

Cells live, breathe, and procreate by engaging in various cellular processes. You won't be asked to describe these on the OCT, but you may encounter questions that require you to know what a specific process is all about. Following are the names of the different cellular processes along with a brief description of each:

✔ **Metabolism:** Chemical reactions that occur within a living cell that maintain the cell's life. Metabolism is broken down into two functions:

  • *Catabolism* breaks down organic matter to create energy.

  • *Anabolism* constructs proteins and nucleic acids to grow and repair the cells.

✔ **Osmosis:** The movement of water molecules across a partially permeable membrane. Osmosis enables cells to "drink."

✔ **Phagocytosis:** The process of a cell ingesting a particle. The cell senses a particle or another cell near its membrane and then surrounds the particle. After surrounding the particle, the *phagocyte* (the cell ingesting the particle) breaks down its own membrane, bringing the particle inside itself.

✔ **Photosynthesis:** The process by which plants and some single-celled organisms use light to convert water and carbon dioxide into carbohydrates and oxygen.

✔ **Respiration:** The process of converting nutrients in the form of amino acids, proteins, glucose, and oxygen into energy for a cell. The byproducts of respiration are carbonic acids and carbon dioxide.

Taking a systemic approach to human anatomy

The human body is like a large metropolitan area complete with its own infrastructure. In the case of a human body, several complex systems work simultaneously 24/7 to maintain existence and enable the body to engage in various activities. You don't need to take a course in anatomy and physiology to ace any human anatomy questions you may encounter on the exam, but you do need to know a little about each of the major systems in the human body. The following sections reveal what you need to know.

No bones about it: The skeletal system

The *skeletal system* is the frame that gives your body its shape; it's the structure that supports you and everything beneath your skin. Without your skeleton, you would be little more than a big bag of jelly. The skeletal system is made of bones and *cartilage* — the softer, more flexible material found in places like your nose and ears.

Oh, and if you're asked what connects the knee bone to the hip bone, the answer is the *ligament* — special tissue that forms the connections between bones. Figure 12-2 introduces the bones that comprise the human skeletal system.

Putting some muscles on them bones

Your *muscular system* enables you to move your bag of bones. Tendons attach muscles to bones. Muscles come in two basic types, depending on their function:

✔ **Voluntary:** You consciously contract or relax the muscle, as you may do when you smile.

✔ **Involuntary:** Your brain instructs the muscle to contract or relax without any conscious intervention on your part, as in the case of your heart muscle.

Getting around with the circulatory system

Think of the *circulatory system* as a vast transportation system inside your body that's in charge of pickups and deliveries. The central hub is the heart, which pumps the blood to deliver essential nutrients to cells and carry waste products from them.

As shown in Figure 12-3, the human heart has four main *chambers* — two *atriums* (upper chambers) and two *ventricles* (lower chambers). Deoxygenated blood enters the right atrium from the *superior vena cava* and then moves to the right ventricle, which pumps the blood to your lungs through your *pulmonary artery*. After the blood is oxygenated in the lungs, it returns to the left atrium via the *pulmonary vein* and then drops into the left ventricle. Finally, it exits the heart through the *aorta* and other arteries and delivers oxygen to all parts of your body before returning to the heart to repeat the cycle.

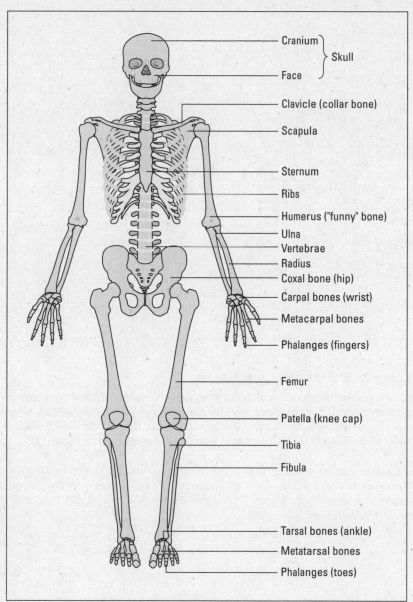

Cranium ⎤
              ⎬ Skull
Face   ⎦

Clavicle (collar bone)

Scapula

Sternum

Ribs

Humerus ("funny" bone)

Ulna

Vertebrae

Radius

Coxal bone (hip)

Carpal bones (wrist)

Metacarpal bones

Phalanges (fingers)

Femur

Patella (knee cap)

Tibia

Fibula

Tarsal bones (ankle)

Metatarsal bones

Phalanges (toes)

Figure 12-2:
The human
skeletal
system.

From LifeART,® Super Anatomy 1, © 2002, Lippincott Williams & Wilkins

Arteries carry blood *away* from the heart, when it is rich and bright red with oxygen. Veins carry blood *to* the heart, when it is dark due to a lack of oxygen. *Capillaries* are cells with thin walls that facilitate the exchange of nutrients between your blood and cells. Blood has several components: *plasma* is the liquid part; *red cells* carry oxygen; *white cells* fight infections; and *platelets* make blood clot (to stop a wound from bleeding).

The four types of blood are A, B, AB, and O. People with O blood are *universal donors;* they can give blood to a person with any blood type. People with AB blood are *universal recipients;* they can receive blood from a person with any blood type.

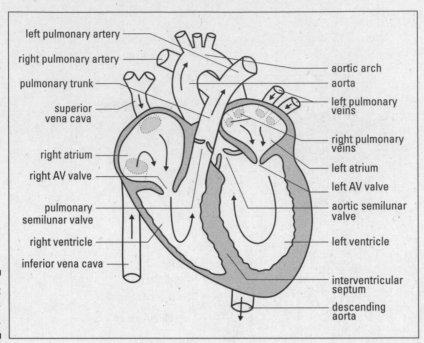

Figure 12-3:
The circulatory system.

Breathing easy with the respiratory system

Your *respiratory system* teams up with your circulatory system to deliver oxygen to cells throughout your body. It begins when you inhale through your nose, which filters, warms, and moistens the air. Air travels down your *trachea* (throat) and divides between your left and right *bronchi,* leading into your left and right *lungs,* as shown in Figure 12-4.

Inside your lungs are even smaller branches of bronchioles that have small sacs at their ends called *alveoli,* which contain the capillaries where oxygen enters the bloodstream. Your *diaphragm* is a large muscle that forces you to breathe in and out by relaxing and contracting beneath your lungs.

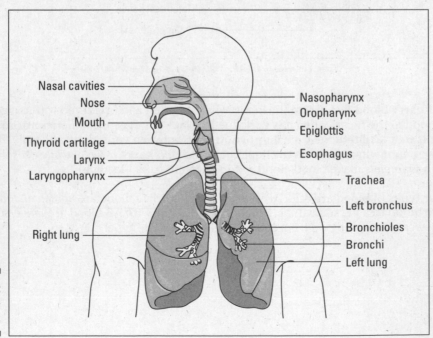

Figure 12-4:
The respiratory system.

From LifeART,® Super Anatomy 1, © 2002, Lippincott Williams & Wilkins

Nervous? That's your nervous system talking

The *nervous system* is the body's communication network, transporting messages throughout your body even faster than e-mail. The *central nervous system* includes the brain and spinal cord. *Peripheral nervous systems,* comprised of nerve cells (*neurons*), are located throughout the rest of the body. Knowing the four parts of the central nervous system may come in handy on the OCT (see Figure 12-5):

- ✔ **Cerebrum:** The largest part of your brain, the cerebrum controls senses and thoughts.

- ✔ **Cerebellum:** The cerebellum is the lower, back side of your brain that controls balance and movement through communications with muscles.

- ✔ **Medulla or brain stem:** Located in front of the cerebellum, the medulla controls involuntary functions such as breathing and heartbeat. It's quite literally the stem that connects your brain to your spinal cord.

- ✔ **Spinal cord:** Running vertically up and down your spine, the spinal cord functions as the main highway for messages between the neurons located all over your body and the brain. The spinal cord also controls simple reflexes, like those the doctor tests when banging on your knee with that rubber hammer.

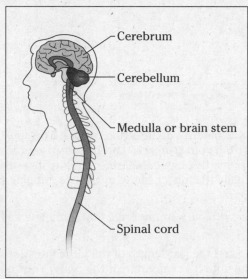

Cerebrum

Cerebellum

Medulla or brain stem

Spinal cord

Figure 12-5:
The human
nervous
system.

Feeding your curiosity about the digestive system

The *digestive system* is in charge of squeezing energy and nutrients out of all that stuff you eat and drink and then expelling all waste products. Your digestive system is hard at work right now. As it does its job, introduce yourself to its various parts so you have a clearer understanding of what's going on inside you this very minute (see Figure 12-6):

- ✔ **Mouth:** This is where the process begins. It starts with your teeth, which slice, dice, and mash food into small particles and mix the food with saliva. Saliva contains enzymes that help break down starches.

- ✔ **Esophagus:** This muscular tube connects your mouth to your stomach; contractions in the muscle push the contents from your mouth downward into your stomach.

- ✔ **Stomach:** A muscular bag in which food collects after being swallowed. Your body releases gastric acids and pepsin into the stomach to digest the proteins in the food and prepare it to move into the intestines.

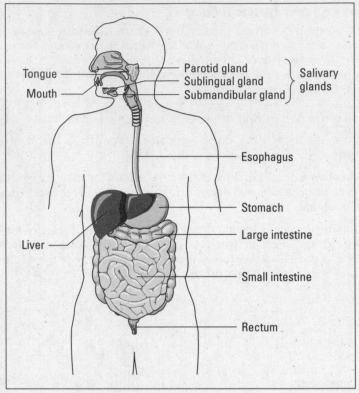

From LifeART.® Super Anatomy 1, © 2002, Lippincott Williams & Wilkins

Figure 12-6:
The human
digestive
system.

✔ **Small intestine:** The place where the majority of digestion occurs. The small intestine breaks down food, using enzymes from your pancreas and bile from your liver and gall-bladder, before absorbing the nutrients through capillaries that line its walls. (Despite its name, the small intestine is actually the longer of the intestines, ranging an average of 16 feet in adult humans.)

✔ **Large intestine:** Absorbs any water, vitamins, or minerals that remain in solid waste after it leaves the small intestine.

✔ **Rectum:** The last leg of the journey and the last length of the large intestine, this is where your body stores solid waste until it's ready to exit the body. Your body stores liquid waste in the bladder.

✔ **Anus:** The place where solid waste exits the body. Liquid waste exits through the urethra.

The endocrine system: It's a hormone thing

The *endocrine system* consists of numerous glands, as shown in Figure 12-7, that release hormones into the body. *Hormones* are chemicals that act as messengers in the body, regulating metabolism, growth, tissue function, and reproductive needs. The main glands to be familiar with are the following:

✔ **Pituitary:** A pea-size gland located at the bottom of the brain, the pituitary helps control blood pressure and growth.

✔ **Thyroid:** Located at the front of the throat, the thyroid is mainly responsible for producing hormones that regulate the body's metabolism.

✔ **Thymus:** Located at the back of the chest, the thymus is part of the immune system.

✔ **Adrenal glands:** Located at the top of the kidneys, these glands produce adrenaline, which controls heart rate, blood pressure, and other important bodily functions.

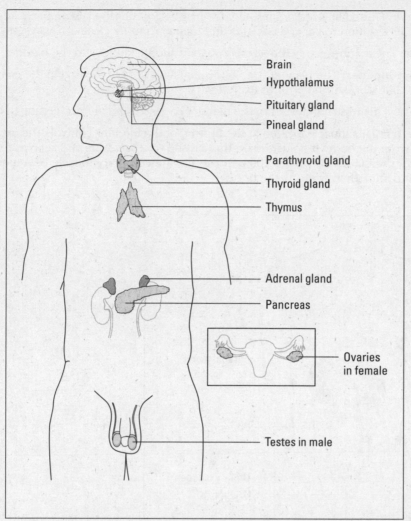

Brain
Hypothalamus
Pituitary gland
Pineal gland
Parathyroid gland
Thyroid gland
Thymus
Adrenal gland
Pancreas
Ovaries in female
Testes in male

Figure 12-7:
The human endocrine system.

From LifeART,® Super Anatomy 1, © 2002, Lippincott Williams & Wilkins

✔ **Pancreas:** Located behind the stomach, the pancreas produces enzymes to digest food and regulate blood sugar and insulin levels in your body.

✔ **Ovaries (in women) and testes (in men):** Located in the lower part of the abdomen, the ovaries and testes are responsible for reproductive functions.

Making babies: The reproductive system

The *reproductive system* is what separates men from women . . . and generally connects them, too. As covered in the preceding section, women have ovaries and men have testes, so what else do you need to know? Every 28 days or so, a woman's ovaries release an egg that travels down the fallopian tube to the uterus. During the reproductive act, the male's penis ejaculates sperm into the woman's vagina. The sperm cells travel up into the uterus. If the timing is right (or wrong, depending on the situation), a single sperm cell penetrates the egg and fertilizes it, which results in pregnancy.

Flushing the system: The urinary system

The *urinary system* consists of only a few organs that filter, store, and eliminate liquid waste from the human body in the form of urine, as shown in Figure 12-8. Urine is the sterile fluid excreted from the body. It consists primarily of water with small amounts of chloride, sodium, and potassium. The main organs and parts to be familiar with are the following:

✔ **Kidneys:** These fist-sized organs, located just below the rib cage on both sides of your spine, filter blood to separate wastes and toxins from the circulatory system.

✔ **Ureter:** These tubes carry the filtered waste from the kidneys to the bladder.

✔ **Urinary bladder:** The bladder is a hollow, muscular organ located in the center of your pelvis that stores urine prior to excretion.

✔ **Urethra:** This tube connected to the bladder carries urine out of the human body.

✔ **Sphincter:** This muscle located at the bottom of the bladder controls the excretion of urine from the body. It holds the urethra closed to store urine and relaxes to excrete urine. If the bladder becomes 100 percent full, the voluntary muscle becomes involuntary and immediately ejects the urine.

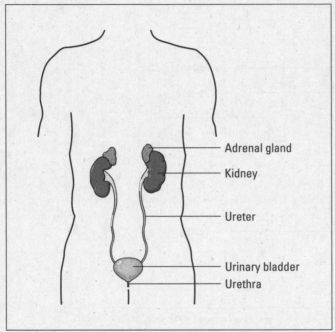

Figure 12-8: The urinary system.

Adrenal gland

Kidney

Ureter

Urinary bladder

Urethra

From LifeART,® Super Anatomy 1, © 2002, Lippincott Williams & Wilkins

Fighting infection with the lymphatic system

The *lymphatic system* consists of numerous glands, capillaries, and nodes, as shown in Figure 12-9. The system's primary functions are to trigger immune system response, transport immune cells to and from the lymphatic system into bones, remove swelling and fluid from tissues, and absorb and transport fatty acids. This system is critical for the body's immune system response to infection and also helps eliminate swelling and, in some cases, tumors and cancerous cells. The main components to be familiar with are the following:

✔ **Lymph:** Lymph is a clear liquid that contains white blood cells and moves through the lymphatic system. The fluid travels in only one direction, towards the heart.

✔ **Lymphatic vessels:** Located throughout the body, lymphatic vessels transport lymph to lymph nodes and to almost every organ and tissue.

✔ **Lymph nodes:** Glands located throughout the body where lymph is filtered free of infection before returning to the circulatory system to maintain the hydration of the system. These glands are located throughout the body and are in particularly high concentration in the chest, neck, throat, and abdominal regions. Lymph nodes are the battleground where the immune system fights off many infections.

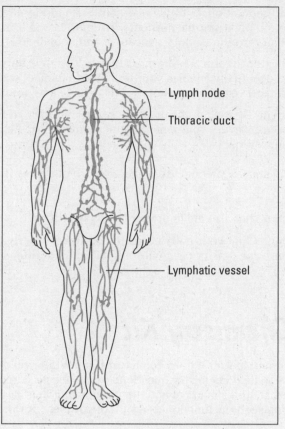

Figure 12-9:
The
lymphatic
system.

From LifeART,® Super Anatomy 3, © 2002, Lippincott Williams & Wilkins

- ✔ **Tonsils:** Located in the back of the throat, these glands are the body's first-line defense against infections that enter the body through ingestion or inhalation.

- ✔ **Thymus:** Located in the upper chest, between the lungs, the thymus holds the body's *T cells,* which are responsible for the body's adaptive immune response.

- ✔ **Spleen:** Located in the upper left quadrant of the abdomen, the spleen not only stores extra blood for the circulatory system, but also removes antibody-coated bacteria and blood cells from the circulatory system. The spleen essentially is a gigantic lymph node that also stores extra blood for the body.

Getting your fill of nutrition

The human body is a complex machine that requires fuel to keep it going and provide the essential components to build cells. You don't need to be a nutritionist to handle the one or two nutrition questions you may encounter on the exam, but you do need a general understanding of the macro- and micronutrients required by the human body. Start with the *macronutrients:*

- ✔ **Carbohydrates:** Starches and sugars that supply energy and usually make food taste a whole lot better. Breads, cereals, pastas, potatoes, beans, and baked desserts are the primary sources of carbohydrates. The body converts any excess starches and sugars into fat.

- ✔ **Proteins:** Present in almost every part of the human body, proteins are used in repairing and growing cells. You find protein in animal products, including meat, eggs, milk, and cheese as well as in beans, nuts, grains, and some vegetables.

✔ **Lipids (fats):** Fats have a bad reputation, but they're essential (in moderation) for energy, growth, and adsorption of fat-soluble nutrients. You find fats in lots of foods, including bacon and eggs, dairy products, nuts, avocados, and cooking oils.

✔ **Fiber:** Fiber teams up with water to form a bulky mass that helps move nutrients through your intestines and eventually enables your body to rid itself of waste. Good sources of fiber are raw fruit and vegetables, whole grains, beans, and potatoes.

✔ **Water:** Water is a vital nutrient. By weight, it's the most prevalent nutrient in the human body, and it's required by every component of the human body. All beverages and almost all foods contain water.

Micronutrients are essential but in smaller amounts than macronutrients. They include the following:

✔ **Vitamins:** Organic compounds that also aid in proper bodily functions.

✔ **Minerals:** Chemical compounds that your body needs to function properly. Some of the more familiar minerals are calcium, potassium, sodium, iron, fluoride, chlorine, iodine, magnesium, and zinc.

Cracking Open the Chemistry Kit

Chemistry is the study of matter, and matter it does come test time. While you don't need a bachelor's degree in chemistry to field chemistry questions on the exam, you do need a fundamental understanding of what stuff's made of and the various building blocks that comprise all matter. The following sections function as a suitable primer for the test.

Knowing what stuff's made of

Chemistry is the study of little stuff that makes up big stuff — electrons, protons, and neutrons that comprise atoms; atoms that combine to form molecules; and molecules that collect in large numbers to form materials as we know them. Before getting too involved in a study of chemistry, familiarize yourself with the following key terminology related to matter:

✔ **Matter:** Stuff, including air, water, food, earth, plants, animals, you name it.

✔ **Elements:** Categories of matter, including oxygen, gold, silver, sodium, nitrogen, and so on.

✔ **Atoms:** Building blocks of matter that make up the material world.

✔ **Electrons:** Negatively charged particles that orbit the nucleus of an atom. (The nucleus is comprised of protons and neutrons.)

✔ **Protons:** Positively charged particles that reside in the nucleus of atoms.

✔ **Neutrons:** Uncharged particles in the nucleus of atoms that provide additional mass, defining the atom's isotope and stability.

✔ **Isotopes:** Atoms of the same element that have different numbers of neutrons. An element is defined by the number of protons it has, so atoms with the same number of protons belong to the same element, but different isotopes of the same element have different numbers of neutrons.

Better living through chemistry

Our modern lifestyle and standard of living owes a great deal to chemistry. Without the discoveries cooked up in labs around the world, modern civilization wouldn't be so modern. Just think of life without computers, cellphones, cellophane, plexiglass, or disposable diapers!

In addition, many things we take for granted are made possible by advances in chemistry, including medications, the foods we eat, and the clothes we wear. Without modern fertilizers, herbicides, pesticides, and preservatives, the world food supply would very likely be incapable of sustaining the world population.

Mixing it up with molecules and compounds

Although atoms of a particular element hang out with one another, they often combine with atoms of different elements to form molecules. A single molecule of water (H_2O), for example, consists of two hydrogen atoms and one oxygen atom bound together. This tendency introduces a few more key terms and concepts you need to know:

- **Compound:** A substance that has a specific ratio of different elements in a particular organization that makes it unique. This arrangement and ratio gives a compound specific chemical properties. Examples of compounds include water, ammonia, chlorine, gasoline, and countless others.

- **Molecule:** The smallest indivisible particle of a compound, which gives it its chemical properties. For example, water is a compound, and H_2O is the molecule.

- **Ions:** Charged particles that form bonds. Positively charged *cations,* such as Na^+ (sodium), bond with negatively charged *anions,* such as Cl^- (chlorine), to form molecules. In the solid state, these molecules usually form in a crystal lattice structure. In water or in a solvent, they behave as a *solute* and separate into pairs of positively- and negatively-charged ions. In gaseous form, they're most often found as *plasma* — a gas in which a certain portion of the particles are ionized.

Not all molecules remain bonded in all states. For example, NaCl, or sodium chloride (table salt), is bonded with an ionic bond in its solid form, but when mixed with water, the sodium and chlorine atoms separate.

Recognizing the different chemical states

Substances exist in different states. Water, for example, may exist as water (liquid), ice (solid), or steam (gas). The state of a substance is a factor of the substance itself along with pressure and temperature. Be aware of the following four states (phases):

- **Solid:** A solid substance is rigid and resistant to changes in shape and volume. This phase occurs with lower temperature and higher pressure relative to the liquid phase. The molecules of the substance are very close together and are arranged in a highly organized pattern.

✔ **Liquid:** In a liquid, molecules are close together and have order but aren't composed in a rigid structure. This phase generally occurs at higher temperatures and lower pressures than solids, but at lower temperatures and higher pressures than the gaseous phase. Liquid substances conform to the shape of their container but are still highly resistant to changes in volume. Most fluids are considered *incompressible fluids,* such as hydraulic oil or water.

✔ **Gas:** Molecules in the gaseous phase have a much larger separation from each other than molecules in the solid and liquid phases, and they're highly disordered. The molecules occupy a space where they may change volume and shape with relative ease. High temperature and/or low pressure transition a substance from liquid to gas.

✔ **Plasma:** This phase is similar to the gaseous phase, but the molecules of a given plasma substance are ionized (split into cations and anions). Like a gas, the substance has no defined shape or volume. But, unlike gas, plasma is highly conductive and susceptible to electronic or magnetic fields.

Temperature and pressure combine to influence the state of a substance. As pressure increases, more heat is required to change the state of a substance from solid to liquid to gas to plasma. Likewise, as pressure decreases, less heat is needed for a substance to change states. In a pressure cooker, for example, water can be heated above its boiling point and still retain its liquid state due to the high-pressure condition inside the pot.

As shown in the phase diagram in Figure 12-10, although substances can have vastly different melting and boiling points, the pressure-to-temperature ratio required for a change from one state to another remains nearly the same. Two points on the phase diagram are most important:

✔ **Triple point:** At the triple point, the substance can be solid, liquid, or gas and has a tendency to periodically change between phases.

✔ **Critical point:** At the critical point, the properties of liquid and gas become indistinguishable. A fluid phase exists that contains properties of both a gas and a liquid.

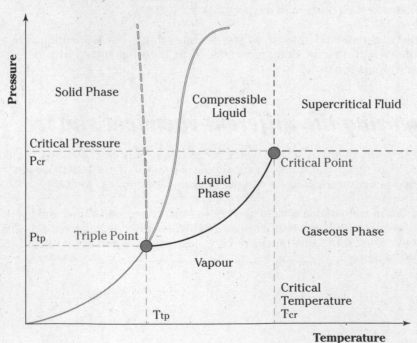

Figure 12-10:
Phase
diagram.

Making sense of the periodic table and atomic notation

Hanging in every chemistry classroom in every country in the world is the periodic table — a chart of all known elements. You don't need to memorize it for the test, but you do need to know a little bit about the information it contains, how it presents that information, and how to decipher the atomic notation it contains. (*Atomic notation* is shorthand for describing an element.)

Perusing the periodic table

The periodic table presents each element in its own box that includes the following information from top to bottom, as shown in Figure 12-11:

- **Element name:** The full name of the element, such as "lead" or "silver."

- **Atomic number:** Each element has an atomic number representing the number of protons it has in its nucleus. Hydrogen (H), for example, has one proton. Gold (Au) has 79. The periodic table organizes elements by atomic number.

- **Atomic symbol:** The one- or two-letter symbol for the element; for example H for hydrogen, O for oxygen, and Li for lithium.

- **Atomic mass:** The mass of a single atom of the element. For some of the large elements, atomic mass is estimated (and appears in parentheses) due to the element's relatively short half-life. Many of the elements with large masses are man-made or experimentally determined, because they're not found in nature.

The periodic table generally groups elements by their chemical properties. The noble gases are at the far right. Reactive metals are on the far left (below hydrogen). Metals and metalloids make up the center. And nonmetals and halogens make up the remaining elements located between the noble gasses and metals.

Taking a closer look at atomic notation

Atomic notation, an example of which is shown in Figure 12-12, is an important standard for representing key properties of an element. Each element's atomic notation includes the following details:

- **Mass number (atomic weight):** The total number of protons and neutrons that comprise one atom of the element.

- **Atomic number:** The number of protons in the atom.

- **Symbol:** The abbreviation of the element's name, which doesn't always make much sense; for example, "Na" stands for "sodium."

- **Charge:** A plus or minus sign denoting whether the charge is positive, negative, or neutral (indicated by the absence of a sign). A neutral atom has an equal number of protons and electrons. A positive charge indicates more protons than electrons, and a negative charge indicates more electrons than protons. A number next to the sign denotes how negative or positive the charge is. For example, if an atom has one less electron than proton, the charge is + or +1. If an atom has three more electrons than protons, the charge is –3.

PERIODIC TABLE OF THE ELEMENTS

	1 IA	2 IIA	3 IIIB	4 IVB	5 VB	6 VIB	7 VIIB	8 VIIIB	9 VIIIB	10 VIIIB	11 IB	12 IIB	13 IIIA	14 IVA	15 VA	16 VIA	17 VIIA	18 0
1	1 H Hydrogen 1.00797																	2 He Helium 4.0026
2	3 Li Lithium 6.939	4 Be Beryllium 9.0122											5 B Boron 10.811	6 C Carbon 12.0115	7 N Nitrogen 14.0067	8 O Oxygen 15.9994	9 F Fluorine 18.9984	10 Ne Neon 20.183
3	11 Na Sodium 22.9898	12 Mg Magnesium 24.312											13 Al Aluminum 26.9815	14 Si Silicon 28.086	15 P Phosphorus 30.9738	16 S Sulfur 32.064	17 Cl Chlorine 35.453	18 Ar Argon 39.948
4	19 K Potassium 39.102	20 Ca Calcium 40.08	21 Sc Scandium 44.956	22 Ti Titanium 47.90	23 V Vanadium 50.942	24 Cr Chromium 51.996	25 Mn Manganese 54.9380	26 Fe Iron 55.847	27 Co Cobalt 58.9332	28 Ni Nickel 58.71	29 Cu Copper 63.546	30 Zn Zinc 65.37	31 Ga Gallium 69.72	32 Ge Germanium 72.59	33 As Arsenic 74.9216	34 Se Selenium 78.96	35 Br Bromine 79.904	36 Kr Krypton 83.80
5	37 Rb Rubidium 85.47	38 Sr Strontium 87.62	39 Y Yttrium 88.905	40 Zr Zirconium 91.22	41 Nb Niobium 92.906	42 Mo Molybdenum 95.94	43 Tc Technetium (99)	44 Ru Ruthenium 101.07	45 Rh Rhodium 102.905	46 Pd Palladium 106.4	47 Ag Silver 107.868	48 Cd Cadmium 112.40	49 In Indium 114.82	50 Sn Tin 118.69	51 Sb Antimony 121.75	52 Te Tellurium 127.60	53 I Iodine 126.9044	54 Xe Xenon 131.30
6	55 Cs Cesium 132.905	56 Ba Barium 137.34	57 La Lanthanum 138.91	72 Hf Hafnium 179.49	73 Ta Tantalum 180.948	74 W Tungsten 183.85	75 Re Rhenium 186.2	76 Os Osmium 190.2	77 Ir Iridium 192.2	78 Pt Platinum 195.09	79 Au Gold 196.967	80 Hg Mercury 200.59	81 Tl Thallium 204.37	82 Pb Lead 207.19	83 Bi Bismuth 208.980	84 Po Polonium (210)	85 At Astatine (210)	86 Rn Radon (222)
7	87 Fr Francium (223)	88 Ra Radium (226)	89 Ac Actinium (227)	104 Rf Rutherfordium (261)	105 Db Dubnium (262)	106 Sg Seaborgium (266)	107 Bh Bohrium (264)	108 Hs Hassium (269)	109 Mt Meitnerium (268)	110 Uun Ununnilium (269)	111 Uuu Unununium (272)	112 Uub Ununbium (277)	113 Uut §	114 Uuq Ununquadium (285)	115 Uup §	116 Uuh Ununhexium (289)	117 Uus §	118 Uuo Ununoctium (293)

Lanthanide Series

58 Ce Cerium 140.12	59 Pr Praseodymium 140.907	60 Nd Neodymium 144.24	61 Pm Promethium (145)	62 Sm Samarium 150.35	63 Eu Europium 151.96	64 Gd Gadolinium 157.25	65 Tb Terbium 158.924	66 Dy Dysprosium 162.50	67 Ho Holmium 164.930	68 Er Erbium 167.26	69 Tm Thulium 168.934	70 Yb Ytterbium 173.04	71 Lu Lutetium 174.97

Actinide Series

90 Th Thorium 232.038	91 Pa Protactinium (231)	92 U Uranium 238.03	93 Np Neptunium (237)	94 Pu Plutonium (242)	95 Am Americium (243)	96 Cm Curium (247)	97 Bk Berkelium (247)	98 Cf Californium (251)	99 Es Einsteinium (254)	100 Fm Fermium (257)	101 Md Mendelevium (258)	102 No Nobelium (259)	103 Lr Lawrencium (260)

§ Note: Elements 113, 115, and 117 are not known at this time, but are included in the table to show their expected positions.

Figure 12-11:
The periodic table.

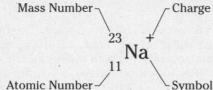

Figure 12-12: Atomic notation.

If you know an atom's mass number and atomic number, you can easily figure out the number of neutrons it contains. Simply subtract the atomic number (protons) from the mass number (neutrons and protons). In the case of sodium, shown in Figure 12-12, you do this math to find the number of neutrons: 23 – 11 = 12.

You may notice in the periodic table that atomic weights are not whole numbers. Isotopes are responsible for this. Chlorine, for example, has two isotopes — Chlorine-35 with 17 protons and 18 neutrons, weighing in with an atomic weight of 35, and Chlorine-37 with 17 protons and 20 neutrons, tipping the scales with an atomic weight of 37. Chlorine consists of about 75 percent Chlorine-35 and 25 percent Chlorine-37. Do the math to determine the relative atomic mass:

$$(0.75 \times 35) + (0.25 \times 37) = 26.25 + 9.25 = 35.5$$

Grasping the different types of chemical reactions

A *chemical reaction* is any change in which a new substance is formed. Reactions are often categorized as endothermic or exothermic, depending on whether they absorb or give off heat:

- **Endothermic:** A chemical reaction that absorbs heat from its surroundings. The prefix "endo" is Latin for "into," and "thermal" is Latin for "heat." Mix ammonium nitrate with water, for example, as you do when you pop the bubble in an ice pack, and you have an endothermic reaction.

- **Exothermic:** A chemical reaction that releases heat. The prefix "ex" is Latin for "out of." An example of an exothermic reaction is fuel combustion — it's what fuels our cars and the world around us. Although a small amount of energy may be required to trigger the combustion, the actual combustion releases much more energy than is required to start it.

Think of reactions in terms of heat transfer. Things don't radiate cold. If something "feels" cold, it's absorbing heat from its surroundings (endothermic). Ice, for example, sucks the heat out of your soft drink to make it cold. If it's radiating heat, it's exothermic.

Avoiding the chemical burn: Acids and bases

You've heard about acids and bases, but how much do you really know about these common classifications for substances? Well, you're about to find out.

Both acids and bases are *caustic,* meaning they burn or destroy living tissue.

With a pH of 7.0, water sets the standard for acids and bases. Anything with a pH of less than 7.0 is an acid. Above 7.0, it's a base.

Below the cut: Acids

Acids are substances with a pH less than 7.0. Like vinegar and lemon juice, they taste sour, corrode metals, and turn litmus paper red. By nature, when in solution, acids lose their hydrogen atom, which combines with water molecules to become hydronium (H_3O^+). The six strong acids are hydrochloric (HCl), nitric (HNO_3), sulfuric (H_2SO_4), hydrobromic (HBr), hydroiodic (HI), and perchloric ($HClO_4$). These acids are so strong because they completely dissociate their H^+ ion in water.

Above the cut: Bases

Bases are substances with a pH greater than 7. Like bleach and ammonia, they feel slippery and turn litmus paper blue. A base accepts hydronium ions in water, thereby reducing the concentration of hydronium ions while increasing the concentration of hydroxide ions (OH^-). Strong bases that completely dissociate their hydroxide ion in water include lithium hydroxide (LiOH), sodium hydroxide (NaOH), potassium hydroxide (KOH), rubidium hydroxide (RbOH), and cesium hydroxide (CsOH).

Getting Down to Earth Sciences

You're likely to encounter at least a couple questions on the General Science subtest that deal with the big blue marble we call earth. To assist you in answering those questions, the following section presents some basic key facts about the earth. Subsequent sections focus on the three big components that comprise the earth — land, sea, and air.

Brushing up on earth trivia

Before cracking into the crust of the earth sciences, brush up on some key facts about the earth that may be helpful going into the exam. Tables 12-6, 12-7, and 12-8 reveal notable characteristics you should know about your home planet. You don't need to memorize these characteristics, but do know the approximations and be aware of how they are relative to one another.

Table 12-6	Fast Facts about the Earth
The Earth's . . .	**Is . . .**
Diameter	12,742 km
Circumference	40,008 km
Distance from the sun	Just under 150 million km
Distance to the moon	384,400 km
Highest elevation	Mt. Everest at 29,028 ft
Lowest elevation	Dead Sea at 1,371 ft
Water to land ratio	70.8:29.2
Age	Approximately 4.5 billion years
Rotation period	23 hr, 56 m, 4.1 s
Orbit period	365.256 days

Table 12-7	Earth's Chemical Composition
Chemical	*Percentage*
Silica	≈60%
Alumina	≈16%
Lime	≈8%
Iron oxide	≈7%
Magnesia	≈5%

Table 12-8	Earth's Atmospheric Composition
Gas	*Percentage*
Nitrogen	≈78%
Oxygen	≈21%
Argon	≈1%

Cracking the rocks: Geology

An old TV show refers to earth as the "third rock from the sun" for good reason — earth is essentially a big rock covered with lots of water that has stuff growing on it and crawling around on it and in it. Geology focuses on the rock part. You're likely to encounter at least one science question that requires a basic knowledge of geology or at least an understanding of key terminology, as presented in the following sections.

Identifying the three types of rock

Pick up any rock, and you can classify it as belonging to at least one of the three following categories:

- **Igneous:** Formed when magma or lava cools near the earth's surface. A few examples of these types of rocks are granite, pumice, basalt, and obsidian.

- **Sedimentary:** Formed by deposits of minerals, organic matter, or chemical precipitates compacted either over a long period of time at the earth's surface or under the pressure of the ocean. Sedimentary rocks are sources of important resources, including coal and ore. Other examples of sedimentary rock are sandstone, limestone, shale, and clay stone.

- **Metamorphic:** Formed by taking any rock and subjecting it to pressures and temperatures that it was not subjected to when it originally formed. These pressures and temperatures must be high enough to change the structure of the original rock, so these types of rocks don't form near the surface of the earth. Some examples of these rocks are slate, marble, quartzite, and gneiss.

A rock may fit into more than one category.

Knowing what makes gems and minerals so special

Minerals are naturally occurring chemical substances that have a specific chemical makeup and a highly organized atomic structure, usually in a crystallized form. Gems are simply valuable minerals based on their aesthetics, rareness, and hardness. Common minerals are salts and silicates. Some rarer minerals (gemstones) are diamonds, rubies, aquamarine, and many others — they're most commonly used for jewelry.

Exploring earth's layers and plate tectonics

The earth is structured like an onion with multiple layers, as shown in Figure 12-13. The following list names and describes each layer starting from the inside and working outward:

- **Inner core:** The solid part of the core at center of the earth, composed mostly of an iron-nickel alloy.

- **Outer core:** Primarily iron and nickel in a liquid state. The outer core surrounds the inner core.

- **Mantle:** Layers surrounding the outer core. The mantle has varying degrees of *viscosity,* meaning some parts of it are more fluid than others. The outer layers are actually less *viscous,* meaning they're more fluid-like. This viscosity is due to the fact that the outer layer is under less pressure than the layers deeper in the mantle, which are more likely to be solid. Because the mantle is comprised mainly of silicates, its melting point is higher than that of the fluid, iron-nickel core.

- **Lithosphere:** The boundary layer between the mantle and the crust. The lithosphere comprises large rock islands called *tectonic plates* that more or less float on top of the mantle. These plates move continuously, forming new earth in places like the mid-ocean ridges as old crust is melted back down into liquid mantle at the *convergent boundaries* (where plates meet) or *underwater trenches* (where one plate slides under another). The movement of tectonic plates causes earthquakes and volcanoes. Active volcanoes and earthquake fault lines follow the convergent boundaries around all the tectonic plates.

- **Crust:** The outermost, coolest layer of the earth, which contains all the earth's surface features. The crust is where we live.

The deeper you dig into the earth, the hotter and more pressurized it gets. The inner core is estimated to be about as hot as the surface of the sun and is under tremendous pressure.

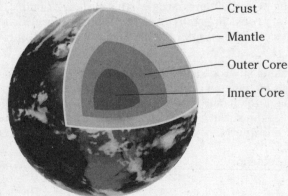

Crust

Mantle

Outer Core

Inner Core

Figure 12-13:
Earth's
layers.

Calming the storm: Meteorology

You can't prep for the OCT simply by watching the Weather Channel for a couple hours. Meteorology is much more involved, as you discover in the following sections. Here you find out all about the different layers of the atmosphere, weather patterns, types of clouds, and the all-important water cycle.

Flying through the five atmospheric layers

The big rock isn't the only thing in geology that comes in layers. The atmosphere has layers, too: five to be precise. Four of these layers are shown in Figure 12-14. The following list names and describes all five atmospheric layers, starting farthest from the earth and working down:

- ✔ **Exosphere:** This far-out layer contains mostly hydrogen and helium atoms — you wouldn't want to spend a lot of time here.

- ✔ **Thermosphere:** This layer is toasty — up to 1,200 degrees Celsius. It has a higher temperature at higher altitudes, but due to the lower pressure and the fact that molecules are so far apart, the "air" doesn't feel as hot as it would at lower altitudes.

- ✔ **Mesosphere:** This layer extends up from the stratosphere, and the temperature decreases as the altitude increases. Most meteors burn up in the mesosphere before they have a chance to crash into the earth, because the density of the atmosphere rises considerably closer to the earth's surface.

- ✔ **Stratosphere:** The stratosphere is best known for the company it keeps. This is where the ozone layer hangs out. The ozone layer is comprised of *triatomic oxygen* (O_3), meaning each molecule consists of three oxygen atoms instead of the standard two in the normal *diatomic oxygen* (O_2) that we breathe. The ozone layer is great for blocking ultraviolet radiation from space, but this form of oxygen is toxic closer to the earth's surface because it is harmful to breathe and can burn plants. In the stratosphere, temperature increases the higher you fly.

- ✔ **Troposphere:** This is where you live and breathe. The troposphere begins at the earth's surface and extends up to the stratosphere. It contains roughly 80 percent of the mass of the entire atmosphere and is where most familiar weather patterns form.

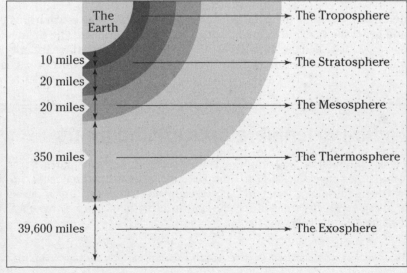

Figure 12-14: The first four of earth's five atmospheric layers.

Stepping behind the scenes with the weather

You won't be asked to predict the weather, but you may need to know about the forces that drive the weather and the characteristics of clouds and weather fronts.

Major weather fronts and patterns occur in the troposphere.

You can tell a lot about the weather by examining cloud formations. The following list explains the differences among the three types of cloud formations and how *convection*, or vertical air movement, plays a part in their formation:

- **Cirriform:** *Cirrus* clouds are generally detached and wispy. They fly high and are generally nonconvective, meaning they form when air movement due to temperature differences at different altitudes is minimal. Because of this, cirrus clouds are a sign of less turbulent weather conditions.

- **Cumuliform:** *Cumulus* clouds are mostly detached and fluffy. They're a product of local convective lift and indicate a more turbulent condition in the atmosphere.

- **Stratiform:** *Stratus* clouds are continuous for the most part and may have a somewhat rippled form, sort of like a blanket. These clouds usually form on slow-moving fronts with high levels of convective lift and float a bit lower in the sky than their cumulus cousins. The convection of stratus clouds spans a much larger area than the conditions that form cumulus clouds. It indicates turbulent atmospheric conditions.

Although the skies are often clear and sunny, people are most excited by weather events triggered by *fronts* — the leading edges of air masses that differ in temperature and pressure. Fronts are considered the weather makers, so to understand the weather you need to understand the four types of fronts:

- **Cold front:** *Cold fronts* occur where colder, denser air pushes under warmer, thinner air. Cold fronts travel faster than warm fronts and usually form more violent storm conditions and higher amounts of precipitation.

- **Warm front:** *Warm fronts* occur where warmer air forms a wedge over colder air and slowly advances, pushing the cold air out. Warm fronts sometimes have thunderstorms on their leading edge, but more often form fog.

- **Stationary front:** When fronts stop moving, they're said to be *stationary,* and you experience little, if any, change in the weather until another front pushes it out of the way.

- **Occluded front:** *Occluded fronts* form when cold fronts overtake warm fronts or vice versa and generally result in a rapid mixing of cold and warm air. The point where the two fronts meet is called the *triple point.* An occluded front may have thunderstorms, but it normally forms around more mature low pressure or high pressure areas and is dry.

Predicting temperatures around fronts

Winds generally flow clockwise around a high pressure system. As a result, the leading edge of the system draws cold air down from the north, making temperatures drop. As the high pressure system passes over an area, the trailing edge draws warm air up from the south, making temperatures rise.

Winds around a low pressure system generally flow in the opposite direction — counterclockwise. As a result, the western edge of the cold front draws the cold air down while the eastern edge draws warm air up.

Hurricanes, tornados, and other violent storms usually form when a cold air mass is above a warm water or land mass. This placement of the cold air mass causes violently convective conditions that lead to violent storms. A front or a consistent wind generally triggers the spinning effects, but the true nature of how these storms are formed is still somewhat of a mystery.

Following the water cycle

The *water cycle* is essentially a story illustrating that what goes up must come down, as shown in Figure 12-15. The water cycle is a continuous process in which water *evaporates* from the earth's surface, *condenses* to form clouds, and then falls back to earth in some form of *precipitation.* Just remember the differences between evaporation, condensation, and precipitation, and you'll do fine.

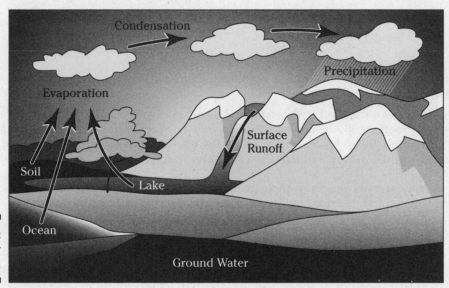

Figure 12-15: The water cycle.

Taming the motion in the ocean: Oceanography

A sea of knowledge swirls around the topic of earth's oceans — far too much to cover in one section of one chapter of a book. *Oceanography* covers everything from marine life to underwater ecosystems to currents and waves and sea floor features. Instead of trying to cover everything you need to know in 500 words or less, the following sections focus on the key topics of the oceans, currents, and underwater geographical features.

Sailing through the seven seas . . . and four or five oceans

Knowing at least the four (or is it five?) oceans and at least a few seas is most important, especially if you're taking a test for the Navy. Here's a list of the five oceans ranked by surface area, from largest to smallest:

- ✔ Pacific
- ✔ Atlantic
- ✔ Indian
- ✔ Southern
- ✔ Arctic

The Southern Ocean was officially recognized in the year 2000. It is the band of water that extends from the coast of Antarctica north to 60 degrees south latitude.

In addition to the five oceans, the earth has seven seas. According to the National Ocean Service, "A *sea* is a part of the ocean partially enclosed by land." Following is a list of the seven seas ranked by surface area, from largest to smallest:

- Arabian Sea
- South China Sea
- Caribbean Sea
- Mediterranean Sea
- Bering Sea
- Bay of Bengal
- Gulf of Mexico

Investigating current events

The ocean isn't a stagnant body of water. It's constantly in motion, flowing in various directions all around the globe in the form of *currents*. The two currents that have the greatest effect on the earth's ecosystem at large are the warm and cold currents that circulate around the globe — rivers of warm or cold water that travel great distances:

- **Warm currents** generally originate near the equator and travel toward the poles. They travel along the surface of the ocean because warm water is less dense.

- **Cold currents** form near the poles and travel toward the equator. They move along the bottom of the ocean because cold water is denser.

As currents flow north and south, trade winds on the surface may deflect the currents, so they tend to flow counterclockwise in the southern hemisphere and clockwise in the northern hemisphere. (*Trade winds* blow steadily from east to west near the equator.) Not all currents follow these trade wind patterns; in fact, several cold currents travel deeper in the ocean and flow underneath warm currents that may be traveling in the opposite direction.

Currents have a powerful influence on the world's ecosystem. They influence migratory patterns of fish, whales, and some sea turtles. Currents also help regulate the global temperature, moderating temperature extremes. The Gulf Stream, for example, carries warm water from the Gulf of Mexico across the Atlantic Ocean to the British Isles and is primarily responsible for the relatively mild winters in England and Ireland compared to Poland and central Russia, which are no farther north.

Navigation at sea also largely depends on currents for transoceanic passages. Many mariners over the centuries have used currents, along with trade winds, to speed their travel across oceans. Even merchants today use currents to save time and fuel.

Diving down to the ocean floor

The ocean floor isn't as smooth as your average beach. When you hit bottom, it's still the earth, complete with mountains, valleys, and canyons. The only difference is that it's under water. You don't need to know much about the ocean floor, but following are some details to pin to your brain for test day:

- Depths range from mere inches along coastlines to more than 6.85 miles deep (35,480 feet) at the deepest point — the Marianas Trench, which is deeper than Mount Everest is high.

✔ The mid-ocean *rifts* in the Atlantic, Indian, and Pacific Oceans are where some of the earth's newest land is formed, as magma pushes up through the lithosphere and the crust, pushing apart the tectonic plates.

✔ Trenches such as the Marianas Trench and the Peru-Chile Trench are *subduction zones,* where old sea floor pushes underneath the continental plates where the sea floor melts into magma as it enters the earth's mantle.

Exploring the Solar System

Regardless of whether you're an amateur astronomer, you need to know a bit about the solar system to answer related questions on the General Science subtest. Most of what you need to know is about the earth's relationship to the sun and moon, but you may also encounter questions about other planets and heavenly bodies.

First you need a working definition of the *solar system,* which is shown in Figure 12-16. The solar system consists of the sun and the heavenly bodies that orbit it. Eight planets revolve around the sun — four inner planets and four outer planets.

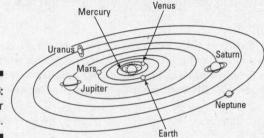

Figure 12-16:
The solar
system.

Mercury, Venus, Earth, and Mars are the *inner* planets, often called *terrestrial* planets, because they have a rocky surface with similar features, including rifts, valleys, mountains, impact craters, and volcanoes. They all have refractory metals and minerals, such as silicates, that make up the majority of their crusts and mantles, and they all have cores that are composed of metals such as iron and nickel. (The term *refractory* means stable at high temperatures.) Three of the four planets (Venus, Earth, and Mars) have substantial enough atmospheres to generate winds and weather. The term *inner planet* or *terrestrial planet* shouldn't be confused with the term *inferior planet,* which refers to the planets that are closer to the sun than earth — Mercury and Venus. Following are some key facts about the inner planets:

✔ **Mercury:** Close proximity to the sun makes Mercury the hottest planet. It's also the smallest — slightly larger than earth's moon. Speaking of moons, Mercury has none.

✔ **Venus:** Commonly considered earth's sister planet, Venus is only slightly smaller than earth, but it's a whole lot hotter. In fact, its claim to fame is that it has the hottest average temperature of all the planets at 855 degrees Fahrenheit. It's also moonless.

✔ **Earth:** The largest of the inner planets, this is the only planet in our solar system that supports life . . . although the jury is still out on that. Earth has one moon.

✔ **Mars:** Commonly known as the red planet, Mars is most like earth. Because it's farther from the sun, it's much colder and requires about twice the time to travel around the sun. Mars has two moons.

Jupiter, Saturn, Uranus, and Neptune are the *outer planets,* also known as *gas giants* because they're primarily composed of the gases hydrogen and helium and are all bigger than the inner planets. The outer two gas giants, Uranus and Neptune, have more hydrocarbons and ices than Jupiter and Saturn and so are often referred to as the *ice giants.* Following are some additional important details about each of the outer planets:

- **Jupiter:** Jupiter is huge — 318 times the mass of the earth and 2.5 times the mass of all the other planets combined. Jupiter's high internal heat is responsible for creating its characteristic cloud bands, and it has 63 known moons.

- **Saturn:** Saturn is a little over half the size of Jupiter in volume but less than a third of its size in mass, making it the least dense of the planets. Its characteristic rings are formed by ice and rock particles that circle the planet. Saturn has 62 confirmed moons, one of which (Titan) is larger than Mercury.

- **Uranus:** This planet's claim to fame is that it's the coldest in the solar system with a temperature of about −322 degrees Fahrenheit. It also spins on its side like a yo-yo, unlike most planets, which spin upright like tops. Because of this, a day or night on Uranus may last more than 40 years. Uranus has 27 known moons.

- **Neptune:** Neptune is the farthest from the sun — 30 times farther than the earth — and it orbits the sun once every 165 earth-years. Its deep blue color is due to the blue light reflecting off the methane gas in its atmosphere. Even though it's farther from the sun, Neptune is slightly warmer than Uranus because it generates more internal heat. It has eight known moons.

Beyond the outer planets is the zone known as the *trans-Neptune region* or the *outer solar system.* A few "dwarf" planets — such as Pluto, which was considered a planet until 2006 — reside in this region. This region also is believed to hold many other smaller asteroids and comets, such as Halley's Comet, that periodically venture into the inner solar system.

Basking in sun facts and figures

The sun is classified as a G2V yellow dwarf star. G2 classifies the surface temperature of the sun as approximately 5,500 degrees Celsius, or almost 10,000 degrees Fahrenheit, based on its yellow appearance. The sun is by far the chief component of the solar system, containing 99.9 percent of all mass in the solar system. The sun is 332,900 earth masses, its diameter is 100 times that of earth, and its surface area is almost 12,000 times that of earth.

The sun is a huge ball of gas composed primarily of hydrogen (approximately 73 percent) and helium (approximately 25 percent), with smaller amounts of oxygen, iron, sulfur, neon, nitrogen, silicone, and magnesium. Even though these other elements occur in smaller amounts relative to the mass of the sun, the amount of oxygen in the sun is more than 2,500 times the mass of earth.

From inside out, the sun is composed of a core, radiative zone, convective zone, photosphere, chromosphere, and corona. The core is the hottest area of the sun and is where 99 percent of the fusion reaction takes place, generating heat and energy. The core is estimated to be about 15 million degrees Celsius.

Zooming in on the earth

Earth is close to home and may be nearer and dearer to the test developers, so pay particular attention to facts about the earth. The most basic thing you need to know is that the earth *rotates* on its axis and *revolves* around the sun. One rotation takes a little less than 24 hours, while a trip around the sun takes a little less than a year.

The earth's axis is tilted at an angle of about $23\frac{1}{2}$ degrees and wobbles during the trip around the sun. As the North Pole tilts toward the sun during part of the earth's orbit, the northern hemisphere experiences summer, while the southern hemisphere experiences winter. During the second half of earth's orbit, the southern hemisphere is closer to the sun. This tilt also explains why night and day are not equal throughout the year. The vernal (spring) and autumnal (fall) equinoxes are the only two days of the year when day and night are of equal duration.

The earth's relative position to the sun and moon explains two key phenomena — tides and eclipses:

- **Tides:** The sun and moon team up to create tides, with the moon playing a larger role. As the sun sets and the moon rises, the gravitational pull of the moon causes the ocean nearest the moon to bulge out toward the moon. As a result, the tide rises locally and falls everywhere else around the globe.

- **Solar eclipse:** A *solar eclipse* occurs when the moon passes between the earth and the sun, partially or totally blocking the rays of the sun.

- **Lunar eclipse:** A *lunar eclipse* occurs when the earth passes between the sun and the moon, partially or totally preventing the rays of the sun from striking and reflecting off of the moon.

One of the most important stars in the sky is the North Star, or "Polaris." The North Star is virtually stationary in the night sky in the northern hemisphere and points north because it's almost exactly in line with the North Pole. Due to its stationary appearance, it has been used as an aid to navigation throughout history.

Chapter 13

Testing Your General Science Skills

● ●

*T*he Air Force Officer Qualifying Test (AFOQT) and the Armed Services Vocational Aptitude Battery (ASVAB) include sections that test general science knowledge and the ability to reason scientifically. You need to work efficiently on these tests, because you have only about 30 seconds per question, but don't feel you have to rush. A half minute or so should be enough to answer most of these questions. If you don't find an answer for a question quickly and you're taking the paper and pencil (P&P) version of the exam, circle the question to come back to later and move on.

Prior to taking this practice exam, you may want to consider reading or reviewing Chapter 12 for a refresher course on general science. Or, just take the practice test cold to identify general science topics you need to work on.

General Science Practice Questions

This section presents 25 questions that challenge a broad range of general science knowledge and skills. These questions reflect the depth and level of difficulty you may encounter on a military exam. Give yourself approximately 11 minutes to complete the test. Choose the best answer for each question from the choices provided.

1. What area of science is defined as the study of rocks?

    (A) geography

    (B) zoology

    (C) geology

    (D) genealogy

2. What kingdom of life does bacteria belong to?

    (A) monera

    (B) protista

    (C) fungi

    (D) planta

3. What subdivision of life contains several related species?

    (A) family

    (B) class

    (C) order

    (D) genus

4. Which of the following is NOT a defining characteristic of a living organism?

   (A) consumption

   (B) homeostasis

   (C) metabolism

   (D) adaptation

5. Which of the following is NOT a living organism?

   (A) mushroom

   (B) influenza virus

   (C) German shepherd

   (D) orangutan

6. Which cell organelle converts light into usable energy?

   (A) photosynthesis

   (B) chlorophyll

   (C) chloroplast

   (D) chloroform

7. What is the function of the cell membrane?

   (A) It holds and supports all of the cell organelles.

   (B) It contains DNA and controls cell reproduction.

   (C) It modifies, sorts, and packages complex molecules.

   (D) It controls what enters and exits, and it protects the cell from the outside environment.

8. Which of the following characterizes a virus?

   (A) a small infectious agent containing DNA that can replicate only inside a living cell

   (B) a small infectious agent containing RNA that can replicate only inside a living cell

   (C) a small infectious agent containing DNA that can replicate only inside the nucleus of a living cell

   (D) a small infectious agent containing RNA that can replicate only inside the nucleus of a living cell

9. Which of the following would NOT be considered a significant source of carbohydrates?

   (A) bread

   (B) cereal

   (C) pasta

   (D) steak

10. 38°C is ____ °F.

   (A) 21

   (B) 53

   (C) 68

   (D) 100

11. Which of the following is NOT a cell function?

    (A) osmosis

    (B) metabolism

    (C) perspiration

    (D) respiration

12. Your cerebrum is a part of what system in your body?

    (A) digestive

    (B) respiratory

    (C) circulatory

    (D) nervous

13. Where does food go immediately after leaving the stomach in the normal digestive cycle?

    (A) esophagus

    (B) small intestine

    (C) large intestine

    (D) liver

14. A substance is considered to be an acid if its pH level is what?

    (A) greater than 7

    (B) less than 7

    (C) 7

    (D) between 6 and 8

15. A reaction that gives off heat is considered to be _____.

    (A) endothermic

    (B) endomorphic

    (C) exothermic

    (D) isomorphic

16. If you saw the following symbol: $^{238}_{92}U$, how many neutrons would the atom have?

    (A) 92

    (B) 238

    (C) 146

    (D) 126

17. About how old is the earth?

    (A) 4.5 billion years

    (B) 4.5 million years

    (C) 2 billion years

    (D) 2,000 years

18. About how long does it take the earth to make a full orbit around the sun?

(A) 264 days

(B) 364 days

(C) 365 days

(D) 24 hours

19. What type of rock is formed by dried lava?

(A) sedimentary

(B) metamorphic

(C) marble

(D) igneous

20. The solid core of the earth is composed primarily of what?

(A) silicates

(B) iron-nickel alloy

(C) titanium-nickel alloy

(D) iron-manganese alloy

21. Which surface feature is farthest from sea level?

(A) Mount Everest

(B) Mid-Atlantic rift

(C) Mount McKinley

(D) Marianas Trench

22. All of the following are oceans EXCEPT which of the following?

(A) Indian

(B) Arabian

(C) Arctic

(D) Southern

23. Which of the following is NOT an atmospheric layer?

(A) stratosphere

(B) cumulosphere

(C) thermosphere

(D) mesosphere

24. Which planet is farthest from the sun?

(A) Neptune

(B) Venus

(C) Uranus

(D) Jupiter

25. Which planet has the shortest orbital period?

    (A) Mercury

    (B) Saturn

    (C) Mars

    (D) Earth

General Science Answers

1. **C.** The word "geology" literally means "study of rocks." Geography, Choice (A), is similar to geology, but is more specifically a study of the earth's shape and inhabitants, including civics, borders, and social aspects. Choice (B), zoology, is the study of the structure, function, and behavior of animals, and Choice (D), genealogy, is the study of ancestry.

2. **A.** Two kingdoms should immediately be eliminated — Choices (C) and (D), fungi and planta — because these two kingdoms are comprised only of multicelled living organisms, and bacteria are single-celled organisms. Distinguishing between Choices (A) and (B), monera and protista, is a little more difficult. Because bacteria don't have a membrane-bound nucleus in most cases, the best answer is Choice (A), monera. All protista have distinct nuclei.

3. **D.** For the answer to this question, review the section in Chapter 12 that explains the breakdown and classification of all living things. There, you find that the order of the categories is as follows, from largest to most specific: kingdom, phylum, class, order, family, genus, and species. Therefore, the subdivision genus contains one or more species.

4. **A.** All living things have the following characteristics in common: homeostasis, organization, metabolism, growth, adaptation, response to stimuli, and reproduction. Among the choices given, the only choice that isn't one of these characteristics is Choice (A), consumption. Although consumption is a form of metabolism, plants don't consume sunlight — they transfer the energy through photosynthesis.

5. **B.** This question is somewhat tricky if you don't eliminate obvious answers. You know that Choices (C) and (D), German shepherds and orangutans, are animals, so cross those off the list. Mushrooms, Choice (A), are fungi, which are classified as living things, so cross those off the list, too. The only choice remaining is Choice (B), influenza virus. Because viruses can't reproduce without host cells, they're considered to be only partially living organisms.

6. **C.** In this question, you can immediately eliminate Choice (A), because photosynthesis is a process, not a part of a cell. The remaining choices are designed to confuse you. Again, only one of these choices is actually an organelle in a cell. Chlorophyll, Choice (B), is the green pigment found in plant cells (oddly enough, inside the chloroplasts). Chlorophyll itself isn't an organelle. You can also eliminate Choice (D), chloroform, fairly easily because it has nothing to do with plants; it's an organic compound that's a precursor to refrigerants and Teflon. You're left with only Choice (C), chloroplast.

7. **D.** If you get tripped up on this question, review the cell parts and illustration in Chapter 12. All the choices are correct descriptions of cell parts, but only Choice (D) describes the membrane. Remember, the cell membrane is a semipermeable wall. It gives the cell its shape, protects it from the outside world, and selectively allows materials to flow into the cell.

8. **A.** All the incorrect answer choices in this question are designed to throw you off and test your knowledge of two facts about viruses: that viruses contain DNA, not RNA; and that viruses can reproduce only within other cells, not outside living cells.

9. **D.** If you have trouble with this question, you may want to refer to the nutrition section in Chapter 12. That section lists several good sources of carbohydrates. The section also reveals several other essential nutrients, including proteins, fats, and fibers. Steak, Choice (D), is a good source of protein, not carbohydrates.

10. **D.** To get the correct answer for this problem, you need to know the equation for converting Celsius into Fahrenheit:

$$°C = \frac{5}{9} \times (°F - 32°)$$

Change °C to 38, and then solve for °F as follows:

$$38 = \frac{5}{9} \times (°F - 32) = 38 \times \frac{9}{5} + 32 = \frac{342}{5} + 32 = 68.4 + 32 = 100.4°F$$

11. **C.** If you have trouble with this question, refer to the section in Chapter 12 on how cells survive and thrive. In that section, you find that the basic cell functions are metabolism, osmosis, phagocytosis, photosynthesis, and respiration. The only answer choice that isn't one of these is Choice (C), perspiration.

12. **D.** The cerebrum is part of your brain, and your brain is part of your nervous system. If you have difficulties with this question or are a little fuzzy on human anatomy, take another look at the anatomy section in Chapter 12.

13. **B.** To answer this question correctly, you need to understand the flow paths in the different systems in your body — in this case, the digestive system. The normal flow path for food is mouth to esophagus to stomach to small intestine to large intestine to rectum, and then excretion through the anus. This means the correct answer to this question is Choice (B), small intestine.

This type of anatomy question requires a higher level of understanding. Get used to questions like this one, because they're more common than those that just involve relating organs to systems.

14. **B.** Take a look in the chemistry section of Chapter 12. An acid is a substance with a pH that's less than 7. A base is a substance with a pH higher than 7.

15. **C.** For this question, you can immediately eliminate two answer choices — Choices (B) and (D), endomorphic and isomorphic, because they have nothing to do with the exchange of heat during chemical reactions. The correct answer is Choice (C), exothermic, because exothermic reactions release heat, whereas endothermic reactions, Choice (A), absorb heat from the surroundings.

16. **C.** This question may be a little tricky, but remember the correct notation for atoms shows the atomic mass in the upper half of the fraction left of the element's abbreviation, and the number of protons (or atomic number) in the lower half. In this case, the uranium atom has an atomic mass of 238 and has 92 protons. The number of neutrons isn't given, so to find it, you must subtract the atomic number (92) from the atomic mass (238). That calculation leaves 146, which is the number of neutrons in this atom.

17. **A.** This question is taken directly from the geology coverage in Chapter 12. The correct answer is 4.5 billion years.

18. **C.** Make sure you read the question correctly. If you answered Choice (D), 24 hours, you mistakenly responded with the rotational period for the earth. The question asks how long it takes the earth to make one orbit around the sun. The correct answer is about 365 days, Choice (C).

19. **D.** The three different types of rocks are igneous, sedimentary, and metamorphic. The type of rock formed by volcanic activity is igneous.

20. **B.** Earth is composed primarily of silicates, Choice (A), but the earth's *core* is different. It's primarily composed of an iron-nickel alloy, Choice (B).

21. **D.** This question is a little tricky, because it doesn't ask you for the deepest point in the ocean or the highest point above sea level. It asks for the *farthest* from sea level, which can mean either up or down. Mount Everest, Choice (A), is the highest point on earth, but the Marianna's Trench, Choice (D), is much farther from sea level at its deepest point than Mount Everest.

22. **B.** The five oceans are the Pacific, Atlantic, Indian, Southern, and Arctic. The only body of water listed in the answer choices that's not one of these oceans is the Arabian Sea, indicated by Choice (B).

23. **B.** This question is a little tricky, because cumulous clouds exist in the troposphere. However, the layers of the earth's atmosphere are troposphere, stratosphere, mesosphere, thermosphere, and exosphere. Cumulosphere isn't one of the earth's atmospheric layers.

24. **A.** The planets in order from closest to farthest from the sun are Mercury, Venus, Earth, Mars, Jupiter, Saturn, Uranus, and Neptune. Therefore, the farthest planet from the sun is Neptune, Choice (A).

25. **A.** The orbital period is the time it takes a planet to make one full revolution around the sun. In general, planets closer to the sun have shorter orbital periods, while those farther away have longer orbital periods. Mercury has the shortest orbital period of any planet in our solar system and is also closest to the sun.

Chapter 14

Brushing Up on Mechanics

● ●

In This Chapter

▶ Getting to know essential physics formulas

▶ Reviewing pressure problems

▶ Grasping the fundamentals of simple machines

▶ Working with rotational forces

● ●

If you're applying for the Navy OCS (Officer Candidate School) or striving to become an aviator in the Marine Corps or Coast Guard, you can count on taking a Mechanical Comprehension subtest to prove your knowledge of basic mechanical principles and the math behind them. To do well on this subtest, you first need a solid foundation in math. If you don't have that, be sure to work through Chapter 8. You also need a clear understanding of how machines work to make lifting, pulling, pushing, twisting, and other physically challenging tasks easier to perform. So you must have a firm grasp of *physics* — the science of matter and energy and how they interact. Finally, you need to know how basic machines do their thing — how pulleys make lifting heavy objects easier, how an ax splits wood, how levers give you leverage, how gears turn other gears, and so on.

This chapter delivers everything you need in one small package. We can't guarantee this information will help you ace the test, but we're certain it will help boost your score.

It's All About Physics (and Math)

Physics pretty much covers everything, because it's the study of mass and energy and how the two interact. Physics is deeply rooted in math. In fact, you may think of physics as an attempt to discover mathematical explanations for everything — mechanics, optics, electricity, magnetism, aviation, acoustics, heat, meteorology, chemistry, and so on.

But that's only half the story. From understanding comes application. Grasping the theories allows you to leverage the power of physics to innovate and solve real-world problems. Most of the mechanics test questions relate to applying physics to the real world — and the following sections are here to help.

Weighing in on mass

Mass is the amount of matter an object has. Sometimes, people mistakenly equate mass with weight, but an important difference exists between the two. Keep the following in mind:

✔ **Mass:** The mass of an object can't change unless you remove some of it or convert it to energy.

✔ **Weight:** The weight of an object varies according to gravity or other forces acting on the object. (You can read more about force in the upcoming section "Understanding the fundamentals of force.")

The preceding definition of mass doesn't fully describe all its different characteristics and properties, but it's all you need to know right now. When you take your first course in quantum physics, you can study the finer characteristics of matter.

Understanding the fundamentals of force

Force is any influence that imparts acceleration on a free body; it's expressed with the following formula:

Force = mass × acceleration

Forces are measured in newtons (N) or $kg \times \frac{m}{s^2}$, where 1 newton = $1\, kg \times \frac{m}{s^2}$. In English, that means 1 kilogram times meters per second per second.

The force acting on a body always has a magnitude and direction represented by an arrow, called a *vector*. As explained later in this chapter, vector magnitude and direction are equally important in solving many physics problems.

Pay close attention to the direction in which forces are applied. A force may accelerate an object in the direction of its original motion, slow down acceleration from the opposite direction, be perpendicular to a moving body, or strike it at an angle. All these have very different effects.

Putting mass in motion with force

Old-school physics focuses a great deal on putting mass in motion or accelerating mass with a force. These remain fundamental concepts today. Problems associated with putting mass in motion, pushing objects across frictionless surfaces, and dropping objects from certain heights to find their velocities or displacement are classic physics problems you'll learn to love . . . or at least master. Check out the following sections to get started.

Noting the difference between potential and kinetic energy

Physics distinguishes between two types of energy — potential and kinetic. Here's a rundown of each:

- **Potential energy:** This type of energy is that which is stored within an object due to its position in a given field of force. In other words, given the gravitational field on earth, a bobsled at the top of a run has more potential energy than a bobsled of equal mass halfway down the run. This relationship is shown with the following equation:

  $E_p = m \times g \times h$, where E_p is potential energy, m is mass, g is acceleration due to gravity, and h is the altitude of the object.

  Altitude is always a distance from some point of reference. For most examples in physics, the reference point is sea level, but you can use any reference height as long as you use the same point through the duration of a problem.

- **Kinetic energy:** This is energy an object possesses due to its motion. In other words, if an object is in motion, its kinetic energy is equal to the amount of energy required to bring the object to rest. For instance, a semi-truck traveling on the interstate at 50 miles per hour has much more kinetic energy than a man running 12 miles per hour. Both the velocity and mass of the semi-truck are much greater than that of the man running. The equation for kinetic energy is

  $E_k = \frac{1}{2} m \times v^2$, where E_k is kinetic energy, m is mass, and v is the relative velocity.

A 10 kilogram ball is dropped from a height of 20 meters. What is the initial potential energy of the ball at the height from which it is dropped?

The very first step in solving any problem is to draw a picture (if one isn't provided). Then jot down the known values. This information can provide guidance on exactly what you need to do to solve the problem. See Figure 14-1 for a visual of the preceding example.

Figure 14-1:
A 10 kilogram ball dropped from 20 meters.

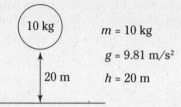

$m = 10$ kg

$g = 9.81$ m/s^2

$h = 20$ m

After you consult your visual and note your known values, jot down the formula you're going to use, plug in the values, and work the equation. Here's how it would look:

$$E_p = m \times g \times h$$
$$E_p = (10 \text{ kg})(9.81 \text{ m}/\text{s}^2)(20 \text{ m})$$
$$E_p = 1962 \text{ J or } 2.0 \text{ kJ}$$

Changing potential energy to kinetic and vice versa

Although energy can be potential or kinetic, it also can change from one to the other and back again.

A roller coaster is a great example of the way energy can change. Suppose a roller coaster car starts at the bottom of the first hill — the lowest point on the track. Until a force acts upon it to put it in motion, the car has zero energy, kinetic or potential. A force is applied to push the car to the top of the first hill — the highest point on the track — where it now sits, perfectly still. The car isn't moving, so its kinetic energy is still zero. However, due to its newly acquired altitude, it has potential energy: $E_p = m \times g \times h$.

As the roller coaster car slowly starts to move and then drop, its energy is transferred from potential to kinetic energy. The farther down the hill it rolls, the less potential energy it has and the more kinetic energy it has. Discounting other forces acting on the car, including wind and friction, the total energy remains the same: $E_{total} = E_p + E_k$.

Remember: According to the law of *conservation of energy*, the total amount of energy in a closed system remains constant. Potential energy in the system can transform into kinetic and vice versa, but the total amount of energy remains constant.

A 10 kilogram ball is dropped from a height of 20 meters. What is the velocity of the ball when it is 2 meters from the ground, assuming no friction or wind resistance?

To answer this question, first calculate the potential energy of the ball before it was dropped, as in the previous example:

$$E_p = (10 \text{ kg})(9.81 \text{ m}/\text{s}^2)(20 \text{ m})$$
$$E_p = 1962 \text{ J or } 2.0 \text{ kJ}$$

All the energy at this point is potential, because the ball isn't in motion. So kinetic energy is zero. Due to conservation of energy, as the ball drops, potential energy is converted into kinetic energy. However, the total energy remains constant:

$$E_{p(\text{init})} + E_{k(\text{init})} = E_{p(2\,\text{m})} + E_{k(2\,\text{m})}$$

Next, you need to determine how much of that potential energy has been converted. Start by solving to find the potential energy at 2 meters. Use the same equation you used to calculate potential energy at the height of 20 meters, changing the height to 2 meters:

$$E_{p(2\,\text{m})} = (10\text{ kg})(9.81\text{ m}/\text{s}^2)(2\text{ m})$$
$$E_{p(2\,\text{m})} = 196.2\text{ J}$$

Now substitute the values you know into the balanced energy equation and do the math to find the kinetic energy at 2 meters:

$$E_{p(\text{init})} + E_{k(\text{init})} = E_{p(2\,\text{m})} + E_{k(2\,\text{m})}$$
$$1962\text{ J} + 0\text{ J} = 196.2\text{ J} + E_{k(2\,\text{m})}$$
$$E_{k(2\,\text{m})} = 1962\text{ J} - 196.2\text{ J}$$
$$E_{k(2\,\text{m})} = 1765.8\text{ J}$$

Knowing the kinetic energy at 2 meters and the mass of the ball, you have everything you need to find its velocity:

$$E_{k(2\,\text{m})} = \frac{1}{2}mv^2$$
$$1765.8\text{ J} = \frac{1}{2}(10\text{ kg})(v^2)$$
$$v^2 = \frac{1765.8\text{ J} \times \frac{2}{1}}{10\text{ kg}}$$
$$v = \sqrt{353.16\text{ m}^2/\text{s}^2}$$
$$v = 18.79\text{ m}/\text{s, or approximately } 19\text{ m}/\text{s}$$

So, as you can see, the velocity at 2 meters is approximately 19 meters per second.

The origins of physics

The word "physics" comes from the Greek word "physis," meaning nature. The ancient Greeks recognized physics as the key to unlocking the mysteries of the universe. Physics existed before anyone realized it or thought of naming it, but it wasn't a formal discipline until the pre-Socratic philosopher Thales, the "Father of Science," declared that every event had a natural cause. No more of that mythological nonsense.

Later, Aristotle came along and wrote the first physics textbook entitled, surprisingly enough, *Aristotle's Physics*. Back then, however, everything in science was considered physics. Nowadays physics has a somewhat narrower niche, focusing on math, matter, motion, energy, and force.

Exploring types of force

You're almost certain to encounter the different types of forces on the Mechanical Comprehension subtest: fundamental and nonfundamental forces and the subcategories of each of those two types. An ability to recognize the different forces and know which formulas apply to each is key to solving quantitative force-related problems on the exam. We explain everything you need to know in the following sections.

Fundamental forces

In physics, you encounter four fundamental forces: strong and weak (both nuclear forces), electromagnetic, and gravitational. The following sections describe each of these forces in greater detail.

You should know and memorize the fundamental forces so you can differentiate between them and the nonfundamental forces on an exam.

Nuclear

Strong and weak forces are the two nuclear forces that affect objects on a subatomic level. Strong forces preserve the structural integrity of an atom's nucleus, and weak forces are responsible for the decay of *nuclides* (an atom specified by its atomic mass, for example carbon-14 or oxygen-18). Weak forces cause radiation emission as an atom decays. Unless you're studying to become a nuclear physicist, all you really need to know is that these forces exist.

Electromagnetic

Electromagnetic forces are associated with charged particles. For more about electricity, magnetic forces, and charged particles, check out Chapter 16.

Gravitational

Gravitational force, or gravity, is the force that keeps your feet firmly planted on the earth. It's also the most prevalent force on the exam (and in classical physics as well). For the test, memorize the following two tidbits:

- The earth's gravitational constant is calculated with this equation: $g = 9.81$ m/s^2.

- The force imparted on an object by gravity is directly proportional to the object's mass. In mathematical terms, this means:

  $F = m \times g$, where F is force, m is mass, and g is acceleration due to gravity.

You may not encounter a pure gravity question, such as one that provides the mass of an object and asks you to solve for F. What's more likely is a problem in which you must determine F from the mass of an object as the first step in finding some other unknown, such as the displacement of a spring. You can read through an example in the later section on elastic force.

Nonfundamental forces

Nonfundamental forces are a consequence or combination of fundamental forces. They include elastic force, normal force, frictional force, buoyancy, tension, rotational force, and centripetal force. The following sections introduce the nonfundamental forces and provide the related formulas you may need on the test.

Elastic

An elastic force works like an ideal spring — to restore the spring to its original form. Ideal springs pull when extended and push when contracted. Therefore, elastic force most often acts in the opposite direction of an applied force, such as a bungee jumper hanging from a cord. Mathematically speaking, elastic force can be written like this:

$$F = -k \times \Delta x$$

where F is the elastic force, $-k$ is the spring constant (or k constant), and Δx is the displacement. The minus represents the tendency of the spring to act in opposition to the load.

A typical elastic force test question has an object of a certain mass hanging from an ideal spring. The question provides you with the mass and k constant and asks you to find the displacement. *Displacement* is a vector quantity that represents the distance and direction that an object moves.

If a 5 kilogram weight is hung from a spring with a spring constant of 3.5, how far does the spring stretch?

To solve this problem, you need to know that the earth's gravitational constant is 9.81 m/s² and that the formula for force is $F = m \times g$. Then you simply plug in the numbers:

$$(5 \text{ kg})(9.81 \text{ m/s}^2) = (3.5 \text{ kg/s}^2)(\Delta x)$$

$$49.05 \text{ N} = (3.5 \text{ kg/s}^2)(\Delta x)$$

$$\frac{49.05 \text{ N}}{3.5 \text{ kg/s}^2} = \Delta x$$

$$\Delta x = 14 \text{ m}$$

A variation on this type of question may provide you with the k constant and displacement and ask for the mass of the object hanging from the spring.

Normal

The normal force of an object is a result of the repulsive forces of atoms when objects come in contact with one another. The resulting force is always perpendicularly away from the point or plane of contact of the two objects. As a result, the direction of a normal force always points perpendicularly away from the surface an object rests or moves on, as shown in Figure 14-2.

The formula for finding the normal force goes like this:

$$F_n = mg\cos(\text{incline}\angle)$$

where Fn is normal force, m is mass, g is gravity, and $\cos(\text{incline}\angle)$ is the cosine of the acute angle at the base of the ramp.

Figure 14-2:
Normal
force.

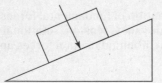

Assuming you have the angle of incline, calculating the normal force is relatively easy. Suppose, for example, you're pushing a 25 kilogram object up a 30-degree incline. Here's what the calculation would look like:

$$F_n = (25 \text{ kg})(9.81 \text{ m} / \text{s}^2)\cos(30°) = 245.25 \times 0.87 = 213.37 \text{ N}$$

However, if you aren't given the angle and are only provided with the length and height of the ramp, you first need to calculate the angle of incline. For example, if the ramp is 20 meters long and 6 meters high, here's how you'd find the angle:

$$\text{incline}\angle = \sin^{-1}(7 \text{ m} / 20 \text{ m})$$
$$\text{incline}\angle = 20.5°$$

You can then plug the angle into the normal force equation.

Frictional

Frictional force is the force that resists motion, always operating in the opposite direction of motion. It's derived as a fraction of the normal force of an object, like this:

$$F_f = \mu F_n$$

where F_f is frictional force, μ is the coefficient of friction, and F_n is the normal force. The higher the coefficient of friction, the greater the frictional force. See the later section "Working with the formula for the coefficient of friction" for more on the coefficient of friction.

Buoyancy

Buoyancy is the upward acting force in a fluid. It's caused by fluid pressure opposing an object's weight. If the object is less dense than the fluid or shaped appropriately (like a boat), the fluid can keep the object afloat. Buoyant force is the density of the fluid times gravity times the volume displaced by an object. For an object to float, its mass times gravity must be equal to that of the buoyant force. Here's buoyancy force in equation form:

$$B = \rho_f V_{\text{disp}} g$$
$$F_{\text{net}} = 0 = mg - \rho_f V_{\text{disp}} g$$

where B is buoyant force, ρ_f is the fluid density, V_{disp} is the volume displaced by the object, g is gravity, and m is the mass of the object.

Tension

Tension is the magnitude of pull exerted by a string, cable, line, or other similar tool onto a load. Tension is most commonly examined when looking at the strength of cables or the ability of cranes or other lifting machines to carry a load.

$\Sigma \vec{F} = \vec{T} + mg = 0$ or $\vec{T} = -mg$ for a system in equilibrium (constant velocity), where ΣF is the sum of all forces, T is the tension force, m is mass, and g is gravity.

Rotational

Otherwise known as *torque,* rotational force spins an object about an axis. Linear forces are seen as pushing, pulling, or lifting forces, while torque is a twisting or turning force. Torque can be represented in equation form as

$$\tau = r \times F \text{ or}$$
$$\tau = rF \sin\theta$$

where τ is torque, r is the radius about the axis, × is the mathematic symbol for *cross,* F is the linear force vector, and θ is the angle between the force vector and the lever arm. These two equations are the same but written in different notation. The first is in linear notation, and the second is in radian notation, with × represented by $\sin\theta$.

To find out more about torque, see "Taking a Spin with Rotational Motion and Forces" later in this chapter.

Centripetal

Centripetal force makes a body follow a curved path through space and is always pointed in toward the axis around which the object moves, as shown in Figure 14-3.

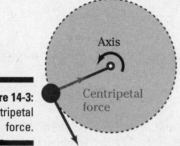

Figure 14-3:
Centripetal
force.

Axis

Centripetal
force

Centripetal force is represented in equation form with the following equations:

$$F = ma_c = \frac{mv^2}{r} \text{ or}$$

$$F = mr\omega^2$$

where F is the magnitude of centripetal force, m is the mass of the moving object, a_c is the centripetal acceleration, v is the straight-line or tangential velocity of the object, r is the radius of the curve, and ω is the angular velocity. For more about centripetal force, check out the later section "Taking a Spin with Rotational Motion and Forces."

Coming to terms with Newton's laws of motion

Newton's laws of motion are fundamental to understanding the relationships between mass, force, and motion. The following sections briefly explain these three laws.

You should know and be able to recognize Newton's three laws in written form and in equation form for the test.

Newton's First Law

Newton's First Law says that objects at rest will remain at rest unless acted upon by an outside force. Conversely, objects in motion will remain in a constant state of motion unless acted upon by an outside force.

Newton's Second Law

In his second law, Newton states that the rate of change of an object or its acceleration (a) is directly proportional to the magnitude of a net force (F_{net}) and indirectly proportional to the object's mass (m). Here's the law in equation form:

$$a = \frac{F_{net}}{m}$$

However, it's most commonly written as:

$$F_{net} = m \times a$$

Newton's Third Law

Newton's Third Law maintains that all actions have an equal and opposite reaction. This means that for every force (F) that's applied to an object, there's a reciprocal force ($-F$) that's exactly equal in magnitude to the original force but acting in the exact opposite direction.

Calculating work

In physics, *work* is defined as the amount of energy a force transfers over a distance. Assuming the force moves on a plane, the formula looks like this:

$$W = F \times d$$

where W is work, F is force, and d is distance.

The metric unit for work is newton-meter (N-m) or joule (J), and the British unit for work is the foot-pound (ft-lb).

A 15 kilogram object is sitting at the bottom of a ramp that's 13 meters long and rises 5 meters. How much force is required to push the object to the top of the ramp assuming no friction?

The absence of friction is key here, because without friction the 15 kilogram object is essentially being lifted 5 meters. At rest, the object's potential energy is zero. When it's lifted 5 meters, its potential energy is:

$$E_p = (15 \text{ kg})(9.81 \text{ m} / \text{s}^2)(5 \text{ m})$$
$$E_p = 735.75 \text{ J}$$

This potential energy also represents the amount of work required to lift the object, so

$$E_p = W = 735.75 \text{ J}$$

After you determine the value for work, you can use the work equation to find the applied force required to move the object up the 13 meter ramp to a height of 5 meters. Here's how the calculation would look:

$$W = F \times d$$
$$735.75 \text{ J} = F \times 13 \text{ m}$$
$$F = \frac{735.75 \text{ J}}{13 \text{ m}}$$
$$F = 56.60 \text{ N}$$

Working with the formula for the coefficient of friction

The *coefficient of friction* is just a ratio that relates the normal force exerted on the object due to gravity or whatever else is pushing or pulling the object toward a surface and the amount of force required to overcome the surface's tendency to prevent the object from being moved. The coefficient of friction is always less than or equal to one. In other words, it's never easier to pick up an object and move it than to move it across a surface — unless, of course, the object is glued or physically attached to the surface. But in that case, you have to overcome different forces besides friction.

A 15 kilogram object is sitting at the bottom of a ramp that's 13 meters long and rises 5 meters. The force required to move the object to the top of the ramp is 1032 joules. What's the coefficient of friction working against motion?

To solve this problem, the first step is to use the formula for the coefficient of friction:

$$F_f = \mu F_n$$

To calculate μ (coefficient of friction), find F_f (force frictional) and F_n (force normal). Start with F_f:

$$W = F \times d$$
$$F = \frac{W}{d}$$

The question includes the value for d (distance): The ramp is 13 meters long. Now you need to find the value for W (work). First calculate the work required when friction isn't involved, which, in this case, is the same as in the example in the previous section:

$$E_p = (15 \text{ kg})(9.81 \text{ m}/\text{s}^2)(5 \text{ m})$$
$$E_p = 735.75 \text{ J}$$
$$E_p = W = 735.75 \text{ J}$$

Without friction, it took 735.75 joules of work to move the object up the ramp. With friction, 296.25 joules more energy is required (1032 joules – 735.75 joules). Because friction acts in a direction opposite to motion, you have to make it a negative value: –296.25 joules. Using the values for distance and work, you can find F_f:

$$F_f = \frac{-296.25 \text{ J}}{13 \text{ m}}$$
$$F_f = -22.7 \text{ N}$$

Next, you find F_n using the formula for normal force:

$$F_n = mg \cos(\text{incline}\angle)$$

Because the question doesn't provide the angle of incline, you need to figure it out yourself using the inverse sine function ($\sin^{-1}$), which calculates the angle using the length of the opposite side of a right triangle divided by the hypotenuse. Check out the calculation:

$$\text{incline}\angle = \sin^{-1}(5 \text{ m}/13 \text{ m})$$
$$\text{incline}\angle = 23°$$

Now you have everything you need to find F_n. Plug in the values and do the math:

$$F_n = mg \cos(\text{incline}\angle)$$
$$F_n = (15 \text{ kg})(9.81 \text{ m}/\text{s}^2)\cos(23°)$$
$$F_n = 135.45 \text{ N}$$

Time for the grand finale:

$$F_f = \mu F_n$$

$$-22.7 \text{ N} = \mu \times 135.45 \text{ N}$$

$$\frac{-22.7 \text{ N}}{135.45 \text{ N}} = -0.17$$

Thus, the frictional coefficient is –0.17. The fact that the answer is a negative number may seem strange, but remember that the direction of frictional forces is always opposite the direction of motion.

The test designers won't try to trick you by providing a positive and negative version of the correct number. As long as the number is correct, you're good to go. But do remember that friction is always opposite the direction of motion.

Here's a sample question that challenges your ability to use two equations together — the equations for centripetal force and friction — to solve a problem.

A car of a certain mass is making a turn on a curve with a radius of 24 meters. The coefficient of friction between the car's tires and the road is 0.35. If the car doesn't slide, find the tangential velocity of the car.

Start by writing down the two equations you're going to use — the equation for frictional force and the equation for centripetal force:

$$F_f = \mu F_n$$

$$F_{\text{centripetal}} = \frac{mv^2}{r}$$

Because the car doesn't slip,

$$F_f = F_{\text{centripetal}}$$

So

$$\mu F_n = \frac{mv^2}{r}$$

$$0.35(m)(g) = \frac{(m)(v^2)}{24 \text{ m}}$$

$$v^2 = \frac{(0.35)(m)(9.81 \text{ m} / \text{s}^2)(24 \text{ m})}{m}$$

$$v^2 = (0.35)(9.81 \text{ m} / \text{s}^2)(24 \text{ m}) = 82.4 \text{ m}^2 / \text{s}^2$$

$$v = 9.1 \text{ m} / \text{s}$$

Surviving collision problems

As you know, collisions occur when objects smash into one another. Aside from explosions, collisions are probably the most exciting way energy is transferred from one object to another. But even in explosions, the most dynamic part is when objects collide. Collisions come in three types: elastic, inelastic, and a combination of the two. On the test, you can expect all collision problems you encounter to be entirely one or the other (not a combo). The following sections provide coverage for both.

Elastic collisions

A purely elastic collision is one in which the objects involved bounce off one another — sort of like billiard balls do. In an elastic collision, kinetic energy and momentum (mass × velocity) are conserved, although energy may be transferred to other objects. As a result, the total amount of momentum and of kinetic energy in the system is the same before and after the collision. In perfectly elastic collisions, the energy of one object is completely transferred to the other object and vice versa.

In equation form, conservation of momentum looks like this:

$$m_1 v_{1_i} + m_2 v_{2_i} = m_1 v_{1_f} + m_2 v_{2_f}$$

where m is mass, v is volume, 1 and 2 are the two objects, i is the initial velocities, and f is the final velocities.

The conservation of kinetic energy formula looks like this:

$$\frac{m_1 v_{1_i}^2}{2} + \frac{m_2 v_{2_i}^2}{2} = \frac{m_1 v_{1_f}^2}{2} + \frac{m_2 v_{2_f}^2}{2}$$

The variables represent the same items as in the conservation of momentum formula.

Elastic collision problems often include billiard balls, leading many to believe that physics professors are really pool-hall junkies. To keep with tradition, we'll stick with that theme and add a couple minor variations. Instead of assuming you have one stationary ball, for instance, assume both balls are in motion. And instead of colliding in three-dimensional space, assume the balls remain on a linear course — this way you don't have to deal with x, y, and z axes.

Two balls are moving in opposite directions on a collision course. One ball, 15 kilograms in mass, is moving at a velocity of 10 m/s. The other ball, 10 kilograms in mass, is moving at a velocity of –5 m/s. What's the total amount of kinetic energy in the system before and after the collision?

You know that kinetic energy in the system remains constant, so it's the same before and after the collision. All you need to do to solve this problem is add the kinetic energy of each ball before the collision using this formula:

$$E_{k_i} = \frac{m_1 v_{1_i}^2}{2} + \frac{m_2 v_{2_i}^2}{2}$$

$$E_{k_i} = \frac{(15 \text{ kg})(10 \text{ m}/\text{s})^2}{2} + \frac{(10 \text{ kg})(-5 \text{ m}/\text{s})^2}{2}$$

$$E_{k_i} = 875 \text{ J}$$

Using the scenario from the previous example, what are the final velocities of both balls assuming a completely elastic collision?

Having a visual on hand often makes problems easier to solve. So to solve this one, first draw a picture on scratch paper of what's going on, as shown in Figure 14-4. (On test day, the test center provides you scratch paper and pencils.)

Figure 14-4:
A picture of
the collision.

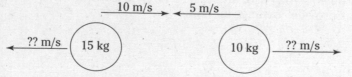

Because this question is about velocity, it's about momentum. Keeping in mind that the mass of the objects remains constant, use the conservation of momentum formula to find the new velocities.

Because each ball transfers its energy to the other ball in perfectly elastic collisions, assume the second ball starts with zero velocity and the first ball transfers all its kinetic energy to the second ball. Here's what your calculation will look like:

$$(15 \text{ kg})(10 \text{ m/s}) + (10 \text{ kg})(0 \text{ m/s}) = (15 \text{ kg})(0 \text{ m/s})(10 \text{ kg})(v_{2_f})$$

$$v_{2_f} = \frac{(15 \text{ kg})(10 \text{ m/s})}{10 \text{ kg}}$$

$$v_{2_f} = 15 \text{ m/s}$$

To find the velocity of the first ball, assume it starts with zero velocity and the second ball transfers all its kinetic energy to the first ball. Check it out:

$$(15 \text{ kg})(0 \text{ m/s}) + (10 \text{ kg})(-5 \text{ m/s}) = (15 \text{ kg})(v_{1_f}) + (10 \text{ kg})(0 \text{ m/s})$$

$$v_{1_f} = \frac{(10 \text{ kg})(-5 \text{ m/s})}{15 \text{ kg}}$$

$$v_{1_f} = -3.33 \text{ m/s}$$

Inelastic collisions

In purely inelastic collisions, the two colliding objects essentially become one big mass . . . or mess, depending on the situation. Think head-on car collision without all the glass and plastic flying everywhere, and you have a pretty clear idea of what an inelastic collision is all about.

In an inelastic collision, kinetic energy isn't conserved, but momentum is always conserved. Here's the equation for a totally inelastic collision:

$$m_1 v_{1_i} + m_2 v_{2_i} = (m_1 + m_2) v_f$$

The following is an example of an inelastic problem like one you may encounter on the test. To keep it simple, the example is of a perfectly inelastic, linear collision. If you're a physics buff, you can find more challenging questions, but this example is more on the level with questions you're likely to encounter on the test.

A speeding semi-truck and a car are on a head-on collision course. The semi-truck weighs 10,000 kilograms, and the car weighs 2,000 kilograms. The semi is traveling with a velocity of 40 m/s and the car is traveling at −25 m/s. (The car is traveling in the opposite direction of the semi, so its velocity is negative.) If the collision of the two objects is completely inelastic, what's the final velocity of the pile of mangled vehicles?

Knowing the formula for inelastic collisions, all you need to do is plug in the numbers and do the math. Look at the calculations:

$$m_1 v_{1_i} + m_2 v_{2_i} = (m_1 + m_2) v_f$$

$$(20,000 \text{ kg})(40 \text{ m/s}) + (2,000 \text{ kg})(-25 \text{ m/s}) = (20,000 \text{ kg} + 2,000 \text{ kg}) v_f$$

$$v_f = \frac{(20,000 \text{ kg})(40 \text{ m/s}) + (2,000 \text{ kg})(-25 \text{ m/s})}{(20,000 \text{ kg} + 2,000 \text{ kg})}$$

$$v_f = 34.1 \text{ m/s}$$

Building on the previous example, what are the initial kinetic energy, the final kinetic energy, and the amount of kinetic energy lost from the collision?

Because these questions deal with kinetic energy, use the formula for kinetic energy to solve them. Here's how to find the initial kinetic energy:

$$E_k = \frac{mv^2}{2}$$

$$E_{k_i} = \frac{(20{,}000 \text{ kg})(40 \text{ m/s})^2}{2} + \frac{(2{,}000 \text{ kg})(-25 \text{ m/s})^2}{2}$$

$$E_{k_i} = 16625000 \text{ J or } 16.6 \text{ kJ}$$

To calculate the final kinetic energy, first calculate the final velocity, as you did in the previous example. Then use the final velocity along with the total mass of the two objects to determine final kinetic energy, like so:

$$E_{k_f} = \frac{(20{,}000 \text{ kg} + 2{,}000 \text{ kg})(34.1 \text{ m/s})^2}{2}$$

$$E_{k_f} = 12791000 \text{ J or } 12.8 \text{ kJ}$$

If you know the initial and final kinetic energies, calculating the loss of kinetic energy is a snap. Take a look:

$$E_{k_{loss}} = E_{k_i} - E_{k_f}$$

$$E_{k_{loss}} = 16.6 \text{ kJ} - 12.8 \text{ kJ}$$

$$E_{k_{loss}} = 3.8 \text{ kJ}$$

Say Watt? Examining Power and Horsepower

Power is the rate at which work is done or energy is converted. For the mechanical portion of the test, all you really need to know about power is the formula and how to use it. Here it is:

$$P = \frac{W}{t}$$

The metric unit for power is the watt (W) or joule per second (J/s). The standard unit for power is horsepower (hp). The conversion is 1 hp = 745.7 W, but you don't need to memorize it for the test. If you're given metric units for everything else and asked to express a value in horsepower, the exam will supply you with the conversions required.

Sounds pretty simple, right? Well, unfortunately, power is more involved than that. You can have different types of power, including electrical and mechanical. Because this chapter is dedicated to mechanical stuff, however, simply focus on mechanical power and the power equation for now. And keep in mind that questions don't always provide you with watts wrapped in a neat little package; for example, you may need to solve for W first using mass, gravity, and height to find the value you need to plug into the equation.

Using the formula for power, you can solve for watt or time, too. Here are the formulas:

$$P = \frac{W}{t}$$

$$W = Pt$$

$$t = \frac{P}{W}$$

What exactly is horsepower?

Engineer James Watt came up with the horsepower unit of measure to help describe the power of steam engines in a way that most people at the time could understand — as relative to the amount of work that draft horses could perform. Watt estimated that a horse could do 22000 foot-pounds of work in a minute. He increased that estimate by 50 percent to 33000 foot-pounds and called it 1 horsepower. His estimate was a bit arbitrary, but that's how the unit came into being. Horsepower, especially in physics and engineering is considered too imprecise a unit, so stick with watts or joules per second.

Over the course of 30 seconds, a crane lifts a 20 kilogram object to the roof of a 55 meter building. How much power did the crane use, assuming no friction or other mechanical or thermal losses?

This question gives you the time but not the value you need for W. So you first need to determine that using your handy-dandy potential energy equation from earlier in this chapter (see the section "Noting the difference between potential and kinetic energy" for more info). Check it out:

$$E_p = mgh$$
$$E_p = (20 \text{ kg})(9.81 \text{ m} / \text{s}^2)(55 \text{ m}) = 10791 \text{ J}$$

For all practical purposes, $W = E$, so $W = 10791$ J. You now have what you need to solve the equation for power:

$$P = \frac{W}{t}$$
$$P = \frac{10791 \text{ J}}{30 \text{ s}} = 359.7 \text{ W}$$

Watch out for misleading information when working test power problems. Some questions may include information you don't need to solve the problem.

Finding Relief from Pressure Problems

The relationship of gasses with pressure, volume, and temperature boils down to three laws that provide the two equations you need to solve any pressure problems on the mechanics test. Here are the three laws:

- **Ideal Gas Law:** $pV = nRT$, where p is pressure, V is volume, n is the amount of the substance, R is the gas constant (always provided unless you're asked to solve for it), and T is the absolute temperature. Absolute temperature means that you must use Kelvin instead of Celsius. Fortunately, questions on the test include temperature in Kelvin or supply the conversion factor you need to figure it out.

- **Boyle's Law (Pressure and Volume relation)/Charles's Law (Volume and Temperature relation):** $\frac{p_1 V_1}{T_1} = \frac{p_2 V_2}{T_2}$, where p is pressure, V is volume, and T is the absolute temperature. And again, temperature must be in Kelvin.

Boyle's Law and Charles's Law work only for a closed system, meaning you can't add or remove any type of gas from the system. The amount of gas must be the same, only undergoing a pressure, volume, or temperature change or some combination of the three.

Exploring Different Types of Machines

All machines are composed of one or more of the six simple machines: lever, inclined plane, wheel (and axle), screw, wedge, and pulley. (Electronics adds another facet to the whole machine thing, but that's covered in Chapter 16.) All other machines — including most tools you find in your garage, many appliances in your kitchen, and bicycles, cars, and airplanes — employ the principles of these six simple machines.

The following sections describe the six simple machines along with a couple that are variations or combinations of simple machines. But before we explain how these machines work, you first need to know how to calculate how much effort a machine saves you.

Show me the benefit: Grasping mechanical advantage

Mechanical advantage describes the quality of a machine that enables you to do more work with less force. In mathematical terms, mechanical advantage is the ratio of force a machine exerts to the force applied to it. For all simple machines, the mechanical advantage translates into the following equations (ignoring friction and other losses):

$$MA = \frac{F_{out}}{F_{in}}$$

$$MA = \frac{d_{in}}{d_{out}}$$

$$F_{in}d_{in} = F_{out}d_{out}$$

where MA is mechanical advantage, F_{out} is output force, F_{in} is input force, d_{in} is the distance over which the input force is applied, and d_{out} is the distance over which the output force is applied. To guide you in answering test questions, the next several sections show how this mechanical advantage equation applies to different types of simple machines.

Mechanical advantage is all about distributing force over a greater distance. If you increase the distance over which the force is applied, you decrease the amount of force you need to apply.

Looking into levers

A *lever* uses a rigid arm and a fulcrum (pivot point) to multiply mechanical force. Levers come in three classes, as described in Table 14-1.

Table 14-1		Classes of Levers
Class	*Examples*	*Description*
1	Scissors, pliers, seesaw	The force is applied on the opposite side of the fulcrum as the load.
2	Nutcracker	The load is between the force applied and the fulcrum.
3	Tweezers	The force applied is between the load and the fulcrum.

Some machines may use more than one class of levers. Nail clippers, for example, use a Class 1 and a Class 3 lever. The lever you push down on is Class 1, and the part that does the actual clipping functions more like tweezers (Class 3).

The simplified equation for calculating the mechanical advantage of a lever is:

$$M = F \times d$$

where M is the turning force (moment or torque) exerted on the load, F is the force applied, and d is the distance between the force and the fulcrum. Therefore, the force multiplied by distance at one end of the fulcrum is equal to the turning force.

Ramping up or down with inclined planes

The *inclined plane* is one of the oldest simple machines. It was even used in ancient Egypt as a ramp to lift huge stone blocks to high altitudes using less force. The mechanical advantage of the inclined plane is calculated as the ratio of the length of the sloped surface to the height that the plane spans. Here's the formula:

$$MA = \frac{l}{h}$$

where l is length and h is height.

Whether you're lifting an object or sliding it up a ramp, the amount of energy required to move the object to its new height is the same (ignoring resistance from friction). When using a ramp, however, you apply less force over a greater distance. That's the mechanical advantage.

Splitting and cutting with wedges

A *wedge* is a triangular splitting and cutting tool with a skinny back end and longer, slanted sides. Examples include axes and knives. It's essentially a moveable inclined plane and has the same mechanical advantage as an inclined plane. As a force is exerted on the back end of a wedge, the force is transferred into normal forces perpendicular to the slanted faces of the wedge. (See Figure 14-5.)

The mechanical advantage is due to the fact that energy applied to the back of the wedge is conserved and the resulting normal forces are exerted over a longer distance on the slanted sides. If the back of the wedge were longer than the slanted sides, a mechanical disadvantage would exist.

In equation form, mechanical advantage of a wedge looks like this:

$$MA = \frac{S}{W}$$

where S is the length of the slanted side and W is the width of the back of the wedge.

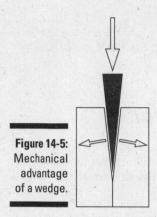

Figure 14-5:
Mechanical advantage of a wedge.

Easing the load with pulleys

Mechanical advantage results when you apply force over a greater distance. In the case of pulleys, the extra distance consists of extra rope or cable, as shown in Figure 14-6. A single pulley that changes the direction of force (you pull down and the object goes up) has a mechanical advantage of 1, meaning no advantage at all. Mechanical advantage increases by one for each additional pulley.

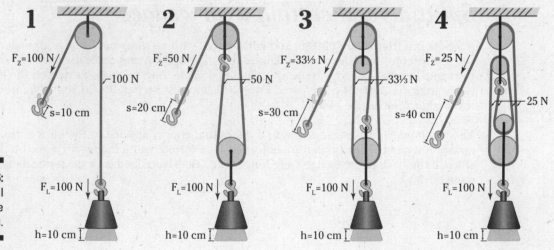

Figure 14-6:
Mechanical advantage of pulleys.

The more pulleys you add, the more rope you need to pull to lift the object the same distance. As with all simple machines, pulleys allow you to apply less force over a greater distance. Mathematically, the mechanical advantage of pulleys looks like this:

$$F_z s = F_L h$$
$$F_L = MA(F_z)$$
$$s = MA(h)$$

where F_z is the applied force, F_L is the load, s is the distance over which the applied force is exerted, h is the distance the load is moved, and MA is mechanical advantage.

Tapping the mechanical advantage of screws

A *screw* is a mechanical device that converts rotational motion into linear motion. Here's how it works for your average hardware store screw: As you rotate the screw, its tip is driven deeper in a linear direction into the surface. In the case of a screw-type jack, you rotate the screw to lift up a load linearly.

The screw acts as an inclined plane wrapped helically around an axis. Think of it as a circular ramp or winding staircase. When you apply a torque to the screw, it converts the radial force into a linear force along the screw's axis. Here's the mechanical advantage of a screw in equation form:

$$MA = \frac{\pi d_m}{l}$$

where MA is mechanical advantage, d_m is the mean diameter of the screw lead, and l is the lead of the screw. (*Lead* is how far the axle or length of the screw advances for each rotation. *Mean diameter* or *pitch diameter* is the difference between the smallest and largest diameters of the screw — the inside and outside of the threads.)

To remember this formula, consider it a modified version of the formula for an inclined plane. (Flip to the earlier section "Ramping up or down with inclined planes" for more information.) The mechanical advantage in both is length divided by height. The length for a screw is its circumference ($C = \pi d$), and the height is the height of the lead.

Improving movement with wheels and axles

Wheels are dual-use machines. When they're used in carts, cars, wagons, and so on, wheels reduce friction because the bottom of the wheel is the only thing touching the ground. As a result, they provide less surface area for friction to operate on.

A wheel also works like a Class 1 lever, with the fulcrum (or pivot point) at the very center of the axle, as shown in Figure 14-7. Note that the distance from the fulcrum to the edge of the wheel (where force is applied) is much shorter than the distance from the fulcrum to the edge of the axle (where the load is positioned). Mechanical advantage is the radius of the wheel divided by the radius of the axle, or in equation form:

$$MA = \frac{r_{\text{wheel}}}{r_{\text{axle}}}$$

MA is mechanical advantage, r_{wheel} is the radius of the wheel, and r_{axle} is the radius of the axle.

The larger the wheel and/or the smaller the axle, the easier it is to turn. However, in this case, you need to turn the wheel more to lift a load a certain distance.

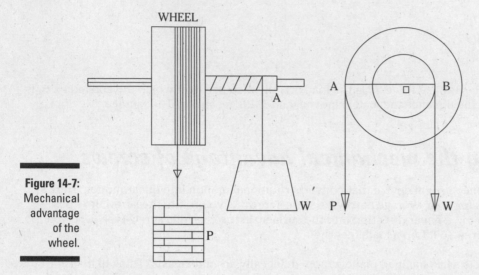

Figure 14-7:
Mechanical advantage of the wheel.

Gears are wheels with teeth. Why use gears sometimes instead of smooth wheels? Gears provide traction. The teeth on gears engage to avoid wasting energy to slippage. Avoiding slippage also is important for ensuring precision, which is why gears are preferred in nondigital watches and clocks.

Crossing a lever with a gear: Winches

A *winch* is a tool consisting of a gear and a lever that's used to wind up or let out rope or cable. The combination of a lever and a gear increases the device's mechanical advantage. The formulas for calculating mechanical advantage of a winch are the same as those used in a lever and wheel and axle (see earlier sections for the equations). To find the mechanical advantage of a winch, simply add the mechanical advantage of the parts: the lever plus the wheel and axle. Winches have many real world applications, including ratchets, cranes, anchor winches, and line winches.

Pumping up with hydraulic jacks

Hydraulic machines use the properties of incompressible fluids to create a mechanical advantage through differences in surface area. Figure 14-8 illustrates how this works. If, for instance, you depress the piston in either cylinder, the piston in the other cylinder rises. If you depress the piston in the small cylinder, you apply pressure measured in force per unit area to the other piston. Because the large piston has more surface area, this force per unit area is magnified, moving the load more easily. However, to move the load a small distance in the large cylinder, you must depress the piston a much larger distance in the small cylinder.

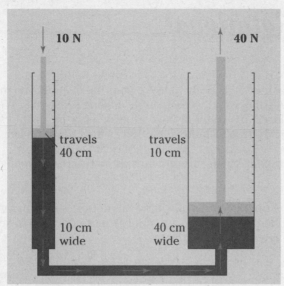

Figure 14-8:
Mechanical
advantage
hydraulics.

The mechanical advantage of hydraulics is a ratio between surface area of where the force is applied and the load. Here's what the equation looks like:

$$\frac{F_{applied}}{A_{applied}} = \frac{F_{load}}{A_{load}}$$

where F is force and A is area.

A hydraulic system comprises two square water columns. One column has a surface area of 1 meter x 1 meter, and the other has a surface area of 10 meters x 10 meters. If a force of 10 newtons is applied to the piston in the smaller water column, what's the force to the load in the larger column?

To solve this problem, you need to use the mechanical advantage of hydraulics formula to find the value for F_{load}. Here's what the calculations would look like:

$$\frac{10 \text{ N}}{1 \text{ m}^2} = \frac{F_{load}}{100 \text{ m}^2}$$
$$F_{load} = \frac{(10)(100)}{1} = 1000 \text{ N}$$

Building on the previous example, how far would you need to depress the piston in the smaller column to raise the piston in the larger column 5 meters?

In order to displace 5 meters of the water in the larger column, you need to displace the same volume of water in the smaller water column. To determine how far you need to depress the piston in the smaller column, you must find how much volume is displaced in the smaller column. So start with the equation for volume (base times height or surface area times height), like so:

$$V = Ah$$
$$V_{load} = (100 \text{ m}^2)(5 \text{ m})$$
$$V_{load} = 500 \text{ m}^3$$
$$V_{load} = V_{applied}$$
$$500 \text{ m}^3 = (1 \text{ m}^2)(h)$$
$$h = \frac{500 \text{ m}^2}{1 \text{ m}}$$
$$h = 500 \text{ m}$$

Taking a Spin with Rotational Motion and Forces

If you're like most folks, rotational motion is likely to make your head spin. Even math majors who spend an entire semester wrestling with it have trouble making sense of it. We can't promise to make you a rotational motion master in the course of a few pages, but we can make the subject easier. The key is to treat rotational motion as linear motion in a circle.

Rotational motion is linear motion that's going around an axis instead of traveling on a plane.

The following sections explain the fundamentals of rotational motion — angular velocity and angular acceleration — and then show you how to apply these concepts to solving problems similar to those you may encounter on the test.

Angular velocity

Angular velocity is the change in angular position of an object relative to an axis over time. For instance, if an object travels along the circumference of the circle in Figure 14-9 from Point A to Point B, it travels the angular distance equivalent to ϕ or a distance along the circumference equivalent to θ.

Its angular velocity can then be expressed as:

$$\omega = \frac{\phi}{t}$$

or

$$\omega = \frac{\theta}{t}$$

where ω represents angular velocity, ϕ represents the angular distance traveled (in degrees), θ represents the distance traveled along the circumference (in radians), and *t* represents time. A *radian* is a distance along the circumference equivalent to the length of the radius.

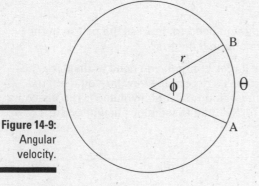

Figure 14-9:
Angular
velocity.

Radians provide a way to convert angular distance into distance along the circumference. Circumference = $2\pi r$, whether r stands for radius or radian. $360° = 2\pi r$. $180° = 1\pi$ radians. Knowing this, you can express the angular velocity of the earth in either degrees per hour or radians per hour, for example:

$$\frac{360°}{24 \text{ hours}} = \frac{15°}{\text{hour}}$$

$$\frac{2\pi}{24 \text{ hours}} = \frac{\pi}{12} \text{ radians / hour}$$

A fan spins at 75 revolutions per minute. What is its angular velocity in radians and in degrees?

You know that 1 revolution = 2π radians, so the fan spins at 75 rpm $\times 2\pi = 150\pi$ radians per minute. To convert radians per minute into degrees per minute, multiply by the conversion factor of $\frac{180°}{\pi}$. Here are the calculations:

$$\frac{150\pi}{\text{min}} \times \frac{180°}{\pi} = 27,000° / \text{min}$$

To determine the linear velocity of a point revolving around an axis, simply multiply the angular velocity in radians by the radius, like this:

$$v = \frac{r\theta}{t}$$

where v is linear velocity, r is radius, θ is the angular measure in radians, and t is time.

You also may look at angular velocity as *rotational velocity,* which is complicated even for the most advanced budding physicists. To keep it simple, memorize the following mathematical expression for rotational velocity:

$$\omega = \frac{|v|\sin(\theta)}{|r|} = \frac{2\pi}{T} = 2\pi f$$

where ω is angular velocity, v is linear velocity vector, θ is the angle between the radial velocity vector ($v_{||}$) and the linear velocity vector (v), r (radius) is the distance between the object and the axis, T is the period, and f is frequency. The last two equalities show the relationship between angular velocity, period, and frequency.

A ball tethered to a pole is being swung around the pole at a rate of 6 revolutions per second. What's the angular velocity of the ball expressed in radians per second (rad/s)?

This is the simplest type of angular velocity problem you're likely to encounter. To solve, use the relationship between angular velocity and frequency, like so:

$$\omega = 2\pi f$$
$$\omega = 2\pi(6 \text{ hz}) = 12\pi \text{ rad / s} = 37.7 \text{ rad / s}$$

Angular acceleration

Angular acceleration is the rate of change of angular velocity with respect to time. The unit for angular acceleration is radians per second squared (rad/s²). Mathematically, angular acceleration is written like this:

$$\alpha = \frac{d\omega}{dt} = \frac{a_T}{r}$$

where α is angular acceleration, $d\omega$ is change in angular velocity, dt is change in time, a_T is tangential acceleration, and r is the radius.

An object is rotating around an axis with an initial angular velocity of 20 radians per second. Two seconds later, the same object has an angular velocity of 25 radians per second. What's the angular acceleration of the object?

You know the initial and final angular velocities and the time it took the object to accelerate from 20 to 25 radians per second, so all you have to do is plug them into the equation and do the math:

$$\alpha = \frac{d\omega}{dt}$$
$$\alpha = \frac{\omega_f - \omega_i}{dt}$$
$$dt = 2s \ \omega_f = 25 \ \text{rad}/s \ \omega_i = 20 \ \text{rad}/s$$
$$\alpha = \frac{25 \ \text{rad}/s - 20 \ \text{rad}/s}{2 \ s}$$
$$\alpha = 2.5 \ \text{rad}/s^2$$

An object is traveling with a linear velocity of 25 meters per second past a stationary object. The object in motion crosses the stationary object at 2 meters at their closest distance. What's the angular velocity between the two objects when they're 2 meters away from each other? What's the angular velocity when they're 4 meters away from each other?

To solve this problem, first draw a picture like the one shown in Figure 14-10, and then jot down the known values: r = 2 meters (the distance between the objects at their closest point), θ = 90° (because the object in motion is passing the stationary object at a 90° angle), and v = 25 meters per second.

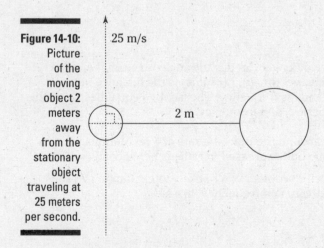

Figure 14-10: Picture of the moving object 2 meters away from the stationary object traveling at 25 meters per second.

After a quick glance at the values, you know you have everything you need to solve for angular velocity (see the preceding section for details). Plug in the numbers and do the math:

$$\omega = \frac{|v|\sin(\theta)}{|r|}$$
$$r = 2 \ m \ \theta = 90° \ v = 25 \ m/s$$
$$\omega = \frac{|25 \ m/s|\sin(90°)}{|2 \ m|} = 12.5 \ \text{rad}/s$$

For the second part, draw another sketch, as shown in Figure 14-11.

Figure 14-11: Picture of the moving object 4 meters away from the stationary object traveling at 25 meters per second.

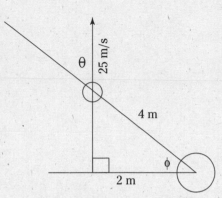

Find angle θ first; then you can solve this problem using the same equation you used to solve the first part. As you may know, θ is equal to the angle opposite θ. You can figure out that angle with basic geometry and trigonometry. You know the angle where the two bodies crossed paths at their closest points is 90°. Find ϕ, and you'll have the two angles you need to find the angle opposite θ. To find ϕ, use the sin function along with the lengths of the two sides of the triangle adjacent to ϕ, like so:

$$\sin\phi = \frac{2 \text{ m}}{4 \text{ m}}$$

$$\phi = \sin^{-1}\left(\frac{2 \text{ m}}{4 \text{ m}}\right)$$

$$\phi = 30°$$

Given $\phi = 30°$ and one angle of 90°, you can now determine θ:

$$180° - 90° - 30° = 60° = \theta$$

Now you can plug your values into the same equation you used to solve the first part of the problem. Check out the calculations:

$$\omega = \frac{|25 \text{ m}/\text{s}|\sin(60°)}{|4 \text{ m}|} = 5.4 \text{ rad}/\text{s}$$

Chapter 15

Testing Your Mechanical Comprehension

• •

The Armed Services Vocational Aptitude Battery (ASVAB) and Aviation Selection Test Battery (ASTB) include sections that test your mechanical knowledge and your ability to reason mechanically. You need to work efficiently on these tests, because you have only about 30 to 45 seconds per question (depending on the test). However, don't feel you have to rush. You may be able to answer some of the fact questions in just a few seconds, whereas the math problems may take you 60 seconds or more. If you don't find an answer for a question quickly and you're taking the P&P (pencil and paper) version of the exam, circle the question to come back to later and then move on. (See Chapter 3 for more details on the P&P version.)

Prior to taking this practice exam, you may want to consider reading or reviewing Chapter 14 to brush up on basic mechanics and some of the more common formulas. Or you can take the practice test cold to identify mechanical topics you need to work on.

Checking Out ASVAB or ASTB Mechanical Comprehension Practice Questions

This section presents 30 questions that challenge a broad range of mechanical knowledge, skills, and reasoning. Questions reflect the depth and level of difficulty you may encounter on a military exam. If you're taking the ASTB, give yourself about 15 minutes to complete the test. If you're taking the ASVAB, give yourself about 23 minutes. Choose the best answer for each question from the choices provided.

1. What is mass?

    (A) the amount an object weighs on earth

    (B) the amount of matter an object has

    (C) an amount that varies depending on other forces acting on an object

    (D) the amount of energy stored within an object due to its position in space

2. What is kinetic energy?

    (A) the amount of energy stored within an object due to its position in a given field of force

    (B) the amount of matter an object has

    (C) the amount of energy that an object possesses due to its motion

    (D) the amount of energy an object has due to its position as well as motion

3. If an object has a mass of 5 kilograms and is at a height of 10 meters, what is the total potential energy of the object, assuming acceleration due to gravity is 9.81 m/s^2?

    (A) 50 newtons

    (B) 50 joules

    (C) 491 newtons

    (D) 491 joules

4. An object with a mass of 10 kilograms is dropped from a height of 20 meters. The initial velocity of the object is 0 m/s. Assuming the acceleration due to gravity is 9.81 m/s^2, what would be the total amount of kinetic energy in the system when the object reaches a height of 5 meters?

    (A) 530 joules

    (B) 1050 newtons

    (C) 1471.5 joules

    (D) 2.32 newtons

5. An object with a mass of 15 kilograms is dropped from a height of 15 meters. The initial velocity of the object is 0 m/s. Assuming the acceleration due to gravity is 9.81 m/s^2, what would be the velocity of the object just prior to striking the ground?

    (A) 5 m/s

    (B) 12 m/s

    (C) 17 m/s

    (D) 147 m/s

6. A cannon pointing directly to the sky shoots a cannonball that has 30 kilograms of mass. The initial velocity of the cannonball is 100 m/s. Assuming the acceleration due to gravity is 9.81 m/s^2, what is the highest point the cannonball will reach?

    (A) 34 meters

    (B) 510 meters

    (C) 10 meters

    (D) 1020 meters

7. All the following are considered fundamental forces except _____.

    (A) normal

    (B) gravitational

    (C) electromagnetic

    (D) nuclear

8. What is frictional force?

    (A) force that is perpendicular to the point or plane of contact between two objects

    (B) force that acts in the opposite direction of an applied force and resists motion

    (C) upward acting force in a fluid caused by the pressure of the fluid around an object

    (D) the magnitude of pull exerted by a string, cable, line, or similar type of object

9. What is the normal force acted on an object with a mass of 30 kilograms on an incline that. has an angle of 30°? Assume acceleration due to gravity is 9.81 m/s².

   (A) 588 newtons

   (B) 354 newtons

   (C) 255 newtons

   (D) 147 newtons

10. What are nonfundamental forces?

    (A) forces that govern the physical world

    (B) forces that do not behave in the same way as fundamental forces

    (C) forces that are similar to fundamental forces but are more complex and cannot be explained by known physics

    (D) forces that are a consequence or combination of fundamental forces

11. What is Newton's First Law?

    (A) All actions have an equal and opposite reaction.

    (B) The rate of change of an object is directly proportional to the magnitude of a net force and indirectly proportional to that object's mass.

    (C) Objects at rest will stay at rest unless acted upon by an outside force, and objects in motion will stay in motion unless acted upon by an outside force.

    (D) $E = mc^2$

12. What force causes objects to follow a curved path through space and always points toward the axis about which the object moves?

    (A) centripetal force

    (B) centrifugal force

    (C) torque

    (D) normal force

13. What is the amount of energy transferred by a force over a distance?

    (A) energy

    (B) effort

    (C) efficiency

    (D) work

14. A 50 kilogram box is at the bottom of a ramp. The ramp is 20 meters long and rises 5 meters. How much force is required to push the box to the top of the ramp? Assume that there are no frictional forces and that the acceleration due to gravity is 9.81 m/s².

    (A) 32 newtons

    (B) 123 newtons

    (C) 234 newtons

    (D) 174 newtons

15. What force is required to push a 20 kilogram box up a ramp with an incline angle of 25°, given a coefficient of friction of 0.13? Assume that acceleration due to gravity is 9.81 m/s^2.

    (A) 106 newtons

    (B) 83 newtons

    (C) 23 newtons

    (D) 178 newtons

16. In an inelastic collision, the objects involved in the collision do what?

    (A) bounce off each other and move in opposite directions

    (B) fragment and move apart in many different directions

    (C) combine and come to a complete stop

    (D) combine and move in the direction proportional to the direction of force in the system

17. A 15 kilogram object is traveling at a speed of 5 m/s straight toward another object. The second object has a mass of 30 kilograms and is traveling at a speed of 10 m/s toward the first object. Assuming a completely elastic collision, what is the final velocity of the 15 kilogram object?

    (A) 5 m/s

    (B) 10 m/s

    (C) 20 m/s

    (D) 40 m/s

18. What is power?

    (A) the total amount of matter an object has

    (B) the rate at which work is done or energy is converted

    (C) the amount of energy required to move an object over a distance

    (D) the rate at which potential energy is converted to kinetic energy

19. An elevator has a capacity of 30,000 kilograms. The elevator is filled to capacity and then travels from the 1st floor to the 22nd floor (or 200 feet up). It takes the elevator 30 seconds to reach the 22nd floor. How much power did the elevator use for one trip up? Assume the acceleration due to gravity is 9.81 m/s^2.

    (A) 1962 kilowatts

    (B) 58860 kilowatts

    (C) 200 kilowatts

    (D) 1842 kilowatts

20. What law in physics relates pressure and volume of gases?

    (A) Charles's Law

    (B) Boyle's Law

    (C) Ideal Gas Law

    (D) Newton's Third Law

21. If a balloon is filled with helium and occupies a volume of 1 liter at 280° Kelvin, what volume would the helium occupy if the temperature is raised to 320° Kelvin? Assume pressure remains the same.

    (A) 2 liters

    (B) 1.4 liters

    (C) 1.24 liters

    (D) 1.14 liters

22. What is the term that is defined by allowing more work to be done with less force?

    (A) lever

    (B) friction

    (C) mechanical advantage

    (D) electrical advantage

23. Which of the following is NOT a simple machine?

    (A) lever

    (B) wheel and axle

    (C) inclined plane

    (D) winch

24. In a pulley system, three pulleys provide a total mechanical advantage of 3. The load force is 600 newtons. What force must be applied to lift the load?

    (A) 200 newtons

    (B) 300 newtons

    (C) 600 newtons

    (D) 1800 newtons

25. Given a wheel and axle, if the wheel radius is 5 meters and the axle radius is 2 meters, what is the mechanical advantage?

    (A) 2.5

    (B) 2

    (C) 1.5

    (D) 0.4

26. If a ball is tethered to a pole and then swung around the pole at a frequency of 9 revolutions per minute, what is its angular velocity expressed in rad/s? Assume the value of π is 3.14.

    (A) 1.43 rad/s

    (B) 56.52 rad/s

    (C) 28.26 rad/s

    (D) 0.94 rad/s

27. A 45 kilogram box is resting on a sidewalk. How much force is exerted on the object due to the acceleration of gravity? Assume acceleration due to gravity is 9.81 m/s^2.

(A) 9.81 newtons

(B) 441 newtons

(C) 458 newtons

(D) 254 newtons

28. What is another name for rotational force?

(A) centripetal force

(B) centrifugal force

(C) torque

(D) radial force

29. A newton is a measure of what?

(A) work

(B) energy

(C) acceleration

(D) force

30. A vector has which two components?

(A) magnitude and direction

(B) direction and force

(C) magnitude and speed

(D) speed and force

Looking at the Answers

1. **B.** The definition of *mass* is the amount of matter an object has. Therefore, the best answer is Choice (B).

2. **C.** Choice (A) gives the definition of potential energy; Choice (B) gives the definition of mass; and Choice (D) is the sum total of potential and kinetic energy. So Choice (C) is the best answer.

3. **D.** For this problem, all you have to do is use the equation for potential energy, which looks like this: $E_p = m \times g \times h$. Here are the calculations:

$$E_p = 5 \times 9.81 \times 10 = 491$$

After doing the calculations, you need to decide whether the correct answer is 491 newtons or 491 joules. Because the unit for energy is the joule, the correct answer is 491 joules. The newton is a unit of force.

4. **C.** The first thing to do with this problem is to eliminate the answers that don't fit. The unit for energy is the joule, not the newton, so you can eliminate Choices (B) and (D). Now work with what you have first: mass, gravity, and height. Here's your formula and the calculations:

$$E_p = m \times g \times h$$
$$E_p = 10 \times 9.81 \times 20 = 1962 \text{ J}$$

You know that as the object falls, it loses potential energy and gains kinetic energy. So at three-quarters of the way down, its kinetic energy will be much higher than its potential energy. As a result, of the remaining two answers, only Choice (C) makes sense.

If you want to do the math, determine the total potential energy of the object at a height of 5 meters using the same formula as the preceding one, and then subtract that number from the amount of kinetic energy at 20 meters, like this:

$$E_p = 10 \times 9.81 \times 5 = 490.5 \text{ J}$$
$$1962 - 490.5 = 1471.5 \text{ J}$$

5. **C.** Use the equation for kinetic energy to solve this problem:

$$E_k = \frac{1}{2} m \times v^2$$
$$E_k = m \times g \times h = 15 \times 9.81 \times 15 = 2207.25$$
$$2207 = \frac{1}{2} 15 \times v^2$$
$$v^2 = \frac{2207}{7.5} = 294.3$$
$$v \cong 17$$

6. **B.** First calculate the initial kinetic energy of the ball, like this:

$$E_k = \frac{1}{2} m \times v^2 = \frac{1}{2} 30 \times 100^2$$
$$E_k = 15 \times 10000 = 150000 \text{ J}$$

At the highest point, all that initial kinetic energy has been transferred into potential energy. Therefore, set the energies equal to each other, and then solve for height using the potential energy equation. Look at the calculations:

$$E_p = E_k = 150000 \text{ J}$$
$$E_p = m \times g \times h$$
$$150000 \text{ J} = 30 \times 9.81x = 294.3x$$
$$x = \frac{150000}{294.3} = 509.68$$

7. **A.** Four fundamental forces exist: strong and weak (both nuclear forces), electromagnetic, and gravitational. So the odd man out here is normal force, Choice (A). (*Normal force* is a force that acts perpendicular to the point of plane at which two objects touch.)

8. **B.** *Frictional force* is the force that resists motion, always operating in the opposite direction of motion. The other definitions given are all definitions of different types of forces: Choice (A) is normal force, Choice (C) is buoyant force, and Choice (D) is tension.

9. **C.** To solve this problem, use the formula for calculating normal force on an inclined plane. Here's the formula and calculations:

$$F_n = mg\cos(\text{incline}\angle) = 30 \times 9.81 \times \cos(30) = 294.3 \times 0.866 \cong 255$$

10. **D.** Nonfundamental forces are a consequence of fundamental forces. They're a combination or variant of fundamental forces and make up many of the forces you encounter in the world. Choices (A) and (B) aren't completely wrong, but Choice (D) is the most accurate definition. Choice (C) isn't correct because, although nonfundamental forces may be more complex than fundamental forces in some cases, they most certainly can be explained by known physics. We explain several of them in Chapter 14.

11. **C.** Although Choice (A) may be the most famous of Newton's laws, Choice (C) is the correct answer.

12. **A.** *Centripetal force* is the force that causes an object to follow a curved path and that is always pointing toward the center of the axis of rotation.

13. **D.** Choices (A) and (D) are the two obvious choices, and you can eliminate Choice (A) because energy is part of the question. Work is the amount of energy a force transfers over a distance. Although energy and work have the same units and are similar, work is more specific than energy. If an object is manipulated and returned to its original position, energy can be transferred without work being done. The net work done is zero, but energy still may have been exchanged.

14. **B.** Because the question discounts friction, essentially you're just lifting the box 5 feet. All the ramp does is provide a mechanical advantage. As a result, less force is needed, but it must be applied over a greater distance. First figure out the amount of energy required to lift the box to the top of the ramp. Here's how:

$$E_p = m \times g \times h = 50 \times 9.81 \times 5 = 2452.5 \text{ J}$$

Assuming you recall that E_p equals work, which equals force times distance, the rest is a piece of cake. Check out the calculations:

$$E_p = W = 2452.5 \text{ J}$$
$$W = f \times d$$
$$2452.5 = f \times 20$$
$$f = 122.6 \text{ N}$$

15. **A.** To answer this problem, you need to know the force required to overcome friction and the force required to push the box up the ramp without friction. Then you have to add the two together. To calculate the force to overcome friction, you first need to calculate the normal force, like this:

$$F_n = mg \cos(\text{incline}\angle) = 20 \times 9.81 \times \cos(25) = 196.2 \times 0.91 \cong 178$$

Using the normal force and the coefficient of friction, calculate the frictional force. Here's how:

$$F_f = \mu F_n = 0.13 \times 178 \cong 23 \text{ N}$$

To calculate the force required to push the box up the ramp without friction, first figure out the height the box is being lifted. You do this with a little trigonometry:

$$\sin \theta = \frac{\text{opposite}}{\text{hypotenuse}} = \sin 25° \cong 0.423$$
$$0.423 \times \text{hypotenuse} = \text{opposite} = 0.423 \times 20 \cong 8.45$$

To lift the box 8 feet, you figure it like this:

$$E_p = m \times g \times h = 20 \times 9.81 \times 8.45 \cong 1658 \text{ J}$$

You now have everything you need to calculate the force required to move the box up the ramp without friction. Look at these calculations:

$$E_p = W \cong 1658 \text{ J}$$
$$W = f \times d$$
$$1658 = f \times 20$$
$$f = 83 \text{ N}$$

Now add the two forces to get your answer:

$$F_{\text{tot}} = 23 + 83 = 106 \text{ N}$$

16. **D.** In this question, Choices (A) and (B) are both wrong and more closely resemble an elastic collision. Choice (C) has some of the properties of an inelastic collision in that the objects combine as one, but the objects don't necessarily come to a stop in all cases. Therefore, the correct answer is Choice (D), because it more accurately defines what an inelastic collision is.

17. **C.** In perfectly elastic collisions, each object transfers its energy to the other, so assume the first object starts with zero velocity and the second transfers all its kinetic energy to the first object. So you need to set up an equation to show the conservation of momentum and all the energy from the first object being transferred to the other. Here's what your work should look like:

$$(30 \text{ kg})(10 \text{ m/s}) + (15 \text{ kg})(0 \text{ m/s}) = (30 \text{ kg})(0 \text{ m/s}) + (15 \text{ kg})(v_{2_r})$$

$$v_{2_r} = \frac{(30 \text{ kg})(10 \text{ m/s})}{15 \text{ kg}}$$

$$v_{2_r} = 20 \text{ m/s}$$

18. **B.** *Power* is defined as the rate at which work is done or energy is converted.

19. **A.** To answer this question, use this formula:

$$P = \frac{W}{t}$$

But first you must calculate the amount of work or energy used to lift 30,000 kilograms 200 miles at 9.81m/s²:

$$E_p = m \times g \times h = 30000 \times 9.81 \times 200 = 58860000 \text{ J}$$

Now plug the values into the power formula and do the math:

$$P = \frac{58860000}{30} = 1962000W = 1962 \text{ kW}$$

20. **B.** Boyle's Law relates pressure to volume. Charles's Law, on the other hand, relates pressure to temperature. The Ideal Gas Law relates pressure to temperature and volume and amount of matter and the intrinsic properties of a gas. Newton's Third Law isn't a law that applies only to gases and deals with forces, so it clearly isn't the correct answer choice.

21. **D.** In this situation, pressure doesn't change, so you use Charles's Law (the ratio of volume to temperature) to figure out the answer. Check out the calculations:

$$\frac{V_1}{T_1} = \frac{V_2}{T_2}$$

$$\frac{1}{280} = \frac{x}{320}$$

$$x = \frac{320}{280} = 1.14 \text{ L}$$

22. **C.** By definition, *mechanical advantage* allows more work to be done with less force.

23. **D.** The six simple machines are lever, inclined plane, wedge, wheel and axle, screw, and pulley. The only answer selection listed that isn't one of these is Choice (D), a winch.

24. **A.** Each pulley adds a mechanical advantage of 1. One pulley simply changes the direction of force: $\frac{1}{1}$. Two pulleys mean you pull half as hard: $\frac{1}{2}$. Add another pulley, and you need to pull one-third as hard: $\frac{1}{3}$. So use the equation that relates mechanical advantage to force to find out what force is required to lift the load. Here's the math:

$$\frac{1}{3} \times 600 = 200 \text{ N}$$

25. **A.** All you need to know is how mechanical advantage is calculated. The formula and calculations look like this:

$$MA = \frac{r_{wheel}}{r_{axle}} = \frac{5}{2} = 2.5$$

26. **D.** For this problem, you just need to convert the frequency into angular velocity and change minutes to seconds. Here's how:

$$\omega = \frac{9 \times \pi \times 2}{60} = 0.94 \text{ rad}/\text{s}$$

27. **B.** Force equals mass times acceleration, so

$$F = ma = (45 \text{ kg})(9.81 \text{ m}/\text{s}^2) = 441 \text{ N}$$

28. **C.** *Rotational force* is the force that spins an object around an axis. This type of force is different from *centripetal force,* which is the force always pointed inward toward the axis. *Radial force* is just another name for centripetal force. *Centrifugal force* is the opposite of centripetal force; it's the outward force pointing away from the axis. Another name for rotational force is *torque,* so the correct answer is Choice (C).

29. **D.** A newton (N) is a measure of force. One newton equals 1 kilogram × m/s².

30. **A.** A vector has two components, magnitude and direction. The defining characteristic that separates velocity from speed is the fact that velocity is a vector with both speed and magnitude, while speed has only magnitude.

Chapter 16

Making Sense of Electricity

The world is wired, and the military is no exception. Numerous devices run on electricity, from the lights that illuminate military bases to complex guidance and navigation systems. If you're planning on pursuing a career in the military that involves any sort of aptitude in mechanics or engineering, you need a fundamental understanding of electricity and its practical applications in order to be considered trainable. This chapter helps you develop that aptitude and prove your knowledge and skills on any of the electronics sub-tests you're required to take.

Going with the Flow: Electrical Current

Electrical current is where the rubber meets the road with electricity. Current means flow, and flow is what powers everything electric, from light bulbs to appliances to entire cities. The following sections explain what makes current flow, how various electrical circuits function, the difference between conductors and insulators, what resistance is and what causes it, and much more. These sections form the foundation on which any understanding of electrical principles and concepts is built.

Understanding what makes electricity tick

Electricity is a big force with a small source. The small source consists of subatomic particles called *electrons*. As explained in Chapter 12, every atom contains protons, neutrons, and electrons. The protons and neutrons are stuffed into the atom's nucleus, which carries a positive charge, while the electrons orbit the nucleus like planets around the sun. The electrons move a whole lot faster, don't have any appreciable mass, and don't travel a predictable path.

When atoms of certain types of elements, such as copper, are bunched up together, as they are in a wire, some electrons, called *free electrons,* roam among neighboring atoms. In the absence of a positive or negative charge, these electrons pretty much wander aimlessly.

Apply a negative charge to one end of that wire and a relatively positive charge to the other end, and those electrons tend to move from the negative toward the positive end of the wire, as shown in Figure 16-1. This flow of electrons is *electrical current*.

Figure 16-1:
Applying a
relatively
negative
charge
forces free
electrons to
move pre-
dominantly
in one
direction.

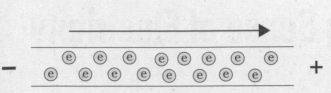

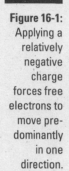

Electrical charge is measured in coulombs (C). A *coulomb* is the equivalent of 6.25×10^{18} electrons. An *ampere* is one coulomb per second. The equation looks like this: $I = \frac{Q}{t}$, where I is amperage, Q is coulombs, and t is time in seconds.

Current problems are fairly straightforward. The questions provide you with two of the three values you need and ask you to calculate the third value.

An ammeter is inserted into a circuit at a certain point and measures 28 coulombs of charge passing through the point over the course of 5 seconds. What is the current?

The following equations show how you arrive at the solution:

$$I = \frac{Q}{t}$$
$$Q = 28 \text{ C}$$
$$t = 5 \text{ s}$$
$$I = \frac{28 \text{ C}}{5 \text{ s}} = 5.6 \text{ A}$$

Recognizing common conductors

Elements in which electrons flow freely are *conductors*. Elements and substances in which electrons do not flow freely, such as rubber, plastic, and wood, are *insulators*. Insulating material covers wires to prevent the undesired flow of electrons from the wire to anything it may otherwise come in contact with, such as your fingers.

Almost all metals are conductive to one degree or another, but certain metals are more conductive than others. The top three conductors are silver, aluminum, and copper, in that order. You don't see much silver wiring because it's so expensive. You don't see much aluminum wiring because aluminum isn't very flexible. Copper wiring, which is less expensive, is more common.

Wire differs not only in composition but also in structure (solid-core versus stranded) and gauge (thickness), as explained in the following sections.

Stranded versus solid-core

Solid-core wire consists of a single strand of wire. It's more rigid than stranded wire and cheaper to manufacture. Because it's cheaper and works fine for carrying current over long distances with few sharp turns, solid core is the wire of choice for electrical infrastructure, such as connecting outlets to an electrical box in a home. *Stranded wire,* though more expensive, is more flexible, making it a better choice for power cords, light fixtures, appliances, speakers, headphones, and so on.

Wire gauges

Gauge represents wire thickness or diameter, which determines the amount of current a wire can safely carry — the larger the gauge, the smaller the diameter of the wire. For stranded wire, gauge represents the total cross-sectional area of the wire; due to space between the strands, a stranded wire is slightly thicker than a solid core wire of the same gauge. Power lines don't use the gauge scale because they're much larger and carry much higher currents.

Naming common insulators

Insulators (also called *dielectrics*) are materials that have an extremely high resistance (the opposite of conductance). Glass, paper, Teflon, and ceramic are good examples of insulators. In each of these three materials, the outer shell of electrons is tightly bonded to the atoms, meaning no free electrons flow through the material. Other good insulators are rubber and plastic, which are two common materials used by electricians for safety when working on energized equipment.

Cross-breeding with semiconductors

A *semiconductor* is a crystallized structure with relatively few *valance* (free) electrons. A semiconductor functions as a cross between a conductor and an insulator. Semiconductors typically act more like conductors at high temperatures and like insulators at lower temperatures.

A process called *doping* is used to create semiconductors. Doping consists of intentionally introducing impurities into an extremely pure substance to give it a certain conductive property. The doping process can produce two different types of semiconductors:

- **p-type:** An *acceptor dopant* produces a hole by removing an electron from the substance. (The *p* stands for positive.)
- **n-type:** A *donor dopant* adds a free electron, which is easily excitable. (The *n* stands for negative.)

A *transistor* is a semiconductor. (See "Investigating a circus of circuits" later in this chapter for more about transistors.)

Tackling volts, amperes, and ohms

Understanding the concepts of voltage, amperage, and resistance, which are measured in volts, amps, and ohms, respectively, is key to doing well on the electronics subtest. You've no doubt encountered the terms *volt* and *amp* — most or all of the electrical outlets in your home are 120 volts, and if you open your electrical box, you may see circuit breakers labeled in amperage, such as 10, 15, or 20. However, you may not fully understand what all this terminology means. The following sections bring you up to speed.

Measuring potential energy in volts

Voltage is the force that drives electrons from Point A to Point B. Consider voltage to be like water pressure in a garden hose. If the water pressure builds up in a garden hose, the volume of water exiting the hose nozzle is greater. The same is true for electricity; if voltage is higher, the volume of flow of electrons is greater. It's actually a relative measure of the difference in charge between two points (terminals). Both terminals can have a negative charge, but as long as one terminal is more negatively charged than the other, a *potential difference* (p. d.) or voltage exists between the terminals. A 9-volt battery, for example, has a potential difference of 9 volts between the positive and negative terminals.

Measuring current in amperes

Current is the measure of electrons through a circuit or point in a circuit. Current is similar to the flow of water in a pipe, only instead of fluid moving through a pipe, the current consists of electrons flowing across a conductor. Electric current is measured in amperes, or amps, with one amp equivalent to one coulomb per second.

Measuring resistance in ohms

Resistance (measured in *ohms*) is anything on a circuit that restricts the flow of electrons. Resistance transforms electrical energy into light, heat, motion, or some other form of energy, such as magnetism. In a light bulb, for example, resistance causes the electrons in the filament to emit light. Various characteristics of an element determine its resistance, including the following:

- ✔ **Material:** The type of material contributes significantly to an element's resistance. Copper and silver have very low resistance, whereas ceramics and glass have very high resistance.

- ✔ **Length:** The longer the wire or resistor, the greater the resistance. Ever wonder why the filament in a light bulb is often coiled? To make it longer and increase its resistance. Although the filament appears to be only a couple inches long, it's actually about 6.5 feet!

- ✔ **Diameter:** The narrower the wire or resistor, the greater the resistance. Light bulb filaments are very narrow, typically 1/100th of an inch.

- ✔ **Temperature:** For almost all materials, as temperature rises, so does resistance. The notable exception here is semiconductors, in which resistance drops when temperature rises.

The ohm is often represented with the Greek letter omega: Ω

Describing the relationship of volts, amps, and ohms with Ohm's Law

Although you're likely to encounter many questions on the exam that test your general understanding of electricity, you're also likely to encounter mathematical problems relating to voltage, amperage, and resistance. To answer such a question, harness the power of Ohm's Law, which states that a current through a conductor between two points is directly proportional to voltage and inversely proportional to resistance.

In mathematical notation, Ohm's Law looks like this:

$$I = \frac{V}{R} \text{ or } V = IR$$

This equation becomes very important in calculating voltage, current, and resistance in circuits. But first, you need a general understanding of the different types of circuits, as explained in the following section.

Investigating a circus of circuits

To do well on the electronics subtest, you need to know how to identify different circuit types and the properties of each type, including complete, open, series, parallel, and short circuits. So you need to be able to make sense of basic wiring diagrams (called *schematics*).

Wiring diagrams are packed with symbols that are about as intuitive as Egyptian hiero-glyphics. Each symbol represents a component of a circuit. You don't need to know every-thing about the components of a circuit, but to make sense of a basic schematic, you should know some basic facts about each component and be able to recognize its symbol. The fol-lowing list names and briefly explains common terminology and components relating to elec-trical circuits (see Table 16-1 for component symbols):

- **Circuit:** A network of electrical components connected by conductors (wires) through which current can flow.

- **Power supply:** The source of electricity, which may be a battery or a power outlet. On the test, the power supply is often labeled "V" for voltage and may include the specific voltage, depending on the problem. Current flows from the negative to the positive terminal.

- **Wire:** That which carries electricity to the other components in the circuit. Lines rep-resent wires or conductors that carry the current.

- **Load:** Any device in a circuit that consumes power — for example, your television set.

- **Switch:** Any device that can break the circuit and stop the flow of current.

- **Ground:** The place in a circuit where the voltage drops to zero, making it a convenient point from which to measure other voltages in the circuit. Circuits in homes are all grounded for safety. If an appliance or piece of equipment becomes faulty, the fault immediately acts as a short, causing a circuit breaker to trip or a fuse to blow. The same is true if you get shocked. You cause a short and trip the circuit breaker. Hopefully, this prevents you from being killed, but don't try this at home.

- **Resistor:** A two-terminal component that reduces the flow of current or causes voltage to drop. On the test, the symbol for resistor represents any device that reduces the flow of current or causes the voltage to drop. This can be a component that's called a resistor or any device that provides resistance, such as a light bulb, toaster, vacuum cleaner, or washing machine.

- **Capacitor:** A passive electrical component that consists of a pair of conductors with an insulator, or dielectric, sandwiched between. Electrons flow to one of the conductors until the conductor is so full of electrons that the voltage can't push even one more electron onto the conductor, at which point current stops flowing. Then, when the volt-age is no longer applied, the capacitor releases the stored electrons in the form of a current. (For a clearer understanding of how capacitors may be used, see "Converting AC to DC and vice versa with rectifiers and inverters," later in this chapter.)

- **Inductor:** A passive electrical component that opposes a change in current. As electric-ity flows through the inductor, it produces a magnetic field that initially induces a cur-rent in the opposite direction. (See "Creating magnetic fields with electricity," later in this chapter, for details.) When the magnetic field is established, it no longer induces current in the wire, allowing current from the source to flow freely. When power from the source is turned off, the magnetic field collapses, inducing a current in the same direction as current from the source.

Table 16-1	Component Symbols
Component	*Symbol*
Ground	
Resistor	
Capacitor	
Inductor	
Diode	anode / cathode — diode symbol; varicap; light emitting; zener
Transistor, p-type (p-n-p)	
Transistor, n-type (n-p-n)	
Power supply, battery	
Power supply, AC voltage source	
Power supply, current source	
Power supply, voltage source	
Wire	
Wires, connected	
Wires, unconnected	
Meter, voltmeter	
Meter, ammeter	
Meter, ohmmeter	
Switch, on/off	
Switch toggle	
Switch, push button, normally open	
Switch, push button, normally closed	
Motor	
Fuse	
Light	
Transformer	

↗ **Diode:** A two-terminal electrical component that conducts electricity in only one direction. Every diode has an *anode* (p for positive), and a *cathode* (n for negative) for controlling the direction in which current flows. One of the most common diodes is the *light-emitting diode* (*LED*), often used as an indicator light in electronic equipment, including computers. LEDs emit energy in the form of photons. Table 16-1 shows the symbol for an LED and three other diodes:

- **Standard:** Allows current to pass in one direction only.

- **Varicap:** Doesn't allow any current to pass. Unlike the other types of diodes, it's more like a capacitor. The difference between it and a capacitor is that its capacitance varies directly with applied voltage.

- **Zener:** Allows current to pass in the direction that the arrow points but also in the opposite direction if the applied voltage is higher than the breakdown, or Zener voltage. This voltage is intrinsic to the diode by its construction.

↗ **Transistor:** A semiconductor that amplifies or switches an electronic signal.

↗ **Fuse:** A device designed to prevent damage to other components in the circuit by self-destructing before excess current can reach sensitive components. A fuse functions as a conductor when current is below its amp limit. When current reaches or exceeds the amp limit, the conductive material melts or burns, stopping the flow of current.

↗ **Transformer:** A device that increases or reduces voltage.

↗ **Transducer:** A device that transfers one type of energy into another; for example, electrical to mechanical or vice versa.

The following sections describe several circuits you're likely to see on the test and tell you how to calculate resistance and conductance. The example questions relating to circuits provide some strategies for answering these types of questions.

Complete (closed) circuit

A *complete (closed) circuit* is one in which electricity can flow freely, as shown in Figure 16-2. The circuit has no breaks (gaps) in it, forming a closed loop.

Figure 16-2: A complete (closed) circuit.

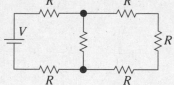

Open circuit

An *open circuit,* like the one shown in Figure 16-3, has a break in the loop, so current can't flow. In this example, the break is an open switch. Flip the switch, and this becomes a complete (closed) circuit.

Figure 16-3: An open circuit.

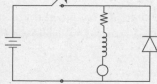

Series circuit

In a *series circuit,* such as the one shown in Figure 16-4, the resistors are all on the same loop. The current must pass through each and every component to complete the circuit. Each R represents a device that provides some resistance, such as a light bulb. Holiday lights are often wired in series; if one bulb burns out, they all go out.

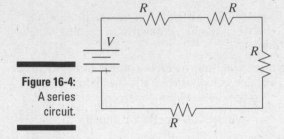

Figure 16-4:
A series
circuit.

 In a series circuit, the same current flows through each component. The electrons have only one path to follow and nothing is gobbling them up, so the same number of electrons flows through each device at the same rate. This property of a series circuit is expressed as follows: $I_1 = I_2 = I_3 = I$.

However, a voltage drop occurs at each resistor equal to the resistance of the component multiplied by the circuit's current. The total voltage is equal to the sum of the voltage at each resistor and is expressed as follows: $V_{\text{tot}} = V_1 + V_2 + V_3$.

Using Ohm's Law of $V = IR$, you can see that the following is also true: $IR_{\text{tot}} = IR_1 + IR_2 + IR_3$, where IR_{tot} represents current times the total resistance in the series. Divide both sides by I, and you find that $R_{\text{tot}} = R_1 + R_2 + R_3$.

R_{tot} may also be written as R_s for Resistance series.

 Now apply what you know about the series circuit to the following voltage question.

What is the voltage drop across R_3?

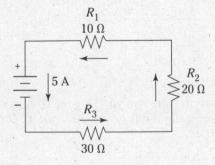

For this problem, you have more information than you need. All you need to do is plug the numbers into the Ohm's Law equation and do the math: $V_3 = IR_3 = (5 \text{ A})(30 \text{ }\Omega) = 150 \text{ V}$.

A slightly more challenging question may ask you to find the voltage or potential difference for the circuit. Because the current (amperage) remains the same, proceed as follows:

$$V = IR_1 + IR_2 + IR_3$$
$$V = (5 \times 10) + (5 \times 20) + (5 \times 30)$$
$$V = 50 + 100 + 150 = 300 \text{ V}$$

Parallel circuit

In a *parallel circuit,* like the one shown in Figure 16-5, the current divides up and flows through all components at the same time. Unlike in a series circuit, if the current is broken at any component, only that component is affected. Current continues to flow through the other components.

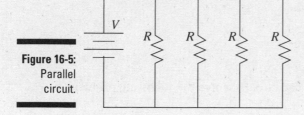

Figure 16-5:
Parallel
circuit.

In a parallel circuit, voltage or potential difference is the same for all of the resistors in parallel and is expressed as follows: $V = V_1 = V_2 = V_3$.

Unlike a series circuit, current is divided and spread out among all of the parallel resistors, so total amperage is equal to the sum of amperage of all resistors and is expressed as $I = I_1 + I_2 + I_3$.

Using Ohm's Law of $I = V/R$, you can then see that the following is also true: $\frac{V}{R_{\text{tot}}} = \frac{V}{R_1} + \frac{V}{R_2} + \frac{V}{R_3}$, where R_{tot} is the total resistance of all three resistors. Multiply both sides by $\frac{1}{V}$, and you get the following equation that shows the relationship between total resistance of a parallel circuit to that of each individual component: $\frac{1}{R_{\text{tot}}} = \frac{1}{R_1} + \frac{1}{R_2} + \frac{1}{R_3} + ... + \frac{1}{R_n}$ or $R_{\text{tot}} = \left[\frac{1}{R_1} + \frac{1}{R_2} + \frac{1}{R_3} + ... + \frac{1}{R_n} \right]^{-1}$.

Series-parallel circuit

A *series-parallel circuit* is a combination of resistors in series and in parallel, as shown in Figure 16-6. These circuits can be a little tricky — at first glance, you may think that R_1, R_3, and R_5 are in series, while R_2 and R_4 are parallel. However, current flows through R_1 and splits, flowing through two parallel components. One parallel component is obviously R_4. The other, not-so-obvious parallel component is comprised of R_2 and R_3. The only component parallel to R_1 is R_5.

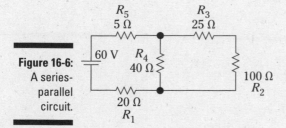

Figure 16-6:
A series-
parallel
circuit.

When calculating resistance for a series-parallel circuit, combine the rules for both. To determine the total resistance for the circuit shown in Figure 16-6, add the resistance for the series components first:

$$R_s = R_1 + R_5$$
$$R_s = 20 + 5 = 25 \ \Omega$$

Next, calculate the resistance for the parallel components:

$$\frac{1}{R_p} = \frac{1}{R_4} + \frac{1}{R_2 + R_3}$$
$$\frac{1}{R_p} = \frac{1}{40} + \frac{1}{125} = \frac{25}{1,000} + \frac{8}{1,000} = \frac{33}{1,000}$$
$$R_p = \frac{1000}{33} = 30.30 \ \Omega$$

Now all that's left is adding R_s and R_p:

$$R_{\text{tot}} = R_s + R_p$$
$$25 + 30.30 = 55.30 \ \Omega$$

Using what you know about serial and parallel circuits, solve the following problem.

What is the current passing through R_{load}?

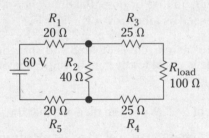

The question gives you the voltage and all the resistance values. Using those values, you can determine the total current in amperes. Here's how:

1. **Determine the total resistance for the resistors in the parallel circuit (R_2, R_3, R_{load}, and R_4).**

$$\frac{1}{R_{\text{parallel}}} = \frac{1}{R_2} + \frac{1}{R_3 + R_{\text{load}} + R_4} = \frac{1}{40 \ \Omega} + \frac{1}{25 \ \Omega + 100 \ \Omega + 25 \ \Omega}$$
$$R_{\text{parallel}} = \frac{1}{40} + \frac{1}{150} = \frac{15}{600} + \frac{4}{600} = \frac{19}{600}$$
$$R_{\text{parallel}} = \frac{600}{19} = 31.6 \ \Omega$$

2. **Add in the resistance for the series resistors.**

$$R_{\text{tot}} = R_1 + R_{\text{parallel}} + R_5$$
$$R_{\text{tot}} = 20 \ \Omega + 31.6 \ \Omega + 20 \ \Omega = 71.6 \ \Omega$$

3. **Using the Ohm's Law equation, determine the current using the voltage and total resistance.**

$$V = IR$$

$$I = \frac{60 \text{ V}}{71.6 \text{ }\Omega} = 0.84 \text{ A}$$

4. **Using the total current and the total resistance for the resistors in the parallel circuit, determine the voltage drop across the parallel circuit.**

$$V_{R_{\text{parallel}}} = IR_{\text{parallel}} = (0.84 \text{ A})(31.6 \text{ }\Omega) = 26.5 \text{ V}$$

5. **Now that you know the voltage and resistance, solve for the current passing through R_{load}, which is represented as I_{load}.**

$$I_{\text{load}} = \frac{V_{R_{\text{parallel}}}}{R_3 + R_{\text{load}} + R_4} = \frac{26.5 \text{ V}}{25 \text{ }\Omega + 100 \text{ }\Omega + 25 \text{ }\Omega} = 0.2 \text{ A}$$

Keep the following key facts in mind:

✔ The current that runs through every resistor in series is the same.

✔ The current that runs through resistors in parallel is inversely proportional to the resistance.

✔ The voltage drop across each resistor in parallel is the same.

Short circuit

A *short circuit* occurs when a circuit is closed with nothing on the circuit to provide any resistance. Electricity flows unrestricted from positive to negative, generating a lot of heat along the way.

Short circuits are bad. Fortunately, they don't last very long. In the best-case scenario, a short circuit trips a circuit breaker before serious damage occurs. In the worst-case scenario, a short circuit causes the wiring to heat up, which results in a fire or melts the wire to break the connection. In the case of a battery, a short circuit quickly discharges the battery and can cause it to explode.

Figure 16-7 shows a circuit with a shorting key. When this key is closed, the current bypasses the load and becomes a short circuit. This means that the current is able to flow with very little or no resistance, essentially resulting in infinite current. When this happens, the current bypasses the light bulb, causing it to no longer be lit. The current literally follows the path of least resistance.

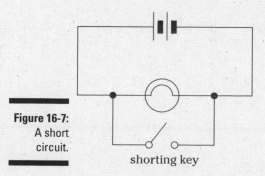

Figure 16-7:
A short
circuit.

shorting key

Calculating resistance

To calculate resistance, you need to know the current and voltage going across the resistor or load. In some cases, this is easy to find or is given to you; in other cases, it's slightly more complex. Here's an example.

Find the resistance in R_2.

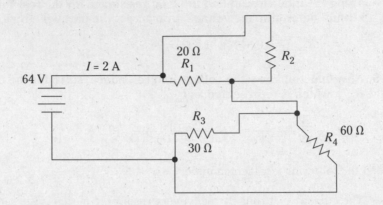

The first order of business is to redraw that goofy diagram so you can tell which resistors are in parallel and in series, like so:

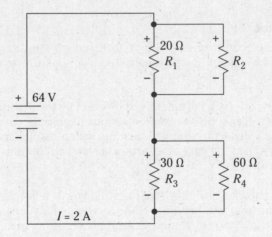

The second diagram shows which resistors are in parallel much more clearly. Now you can proceed to solve the problem.

You know the resistance values for R_3 and R_4, which enables you to determine the total resistance of $R_3 + R_4$ and the voltage drop across R_3 and R_4:

$$\frac{1}{R_{3//4}} = \frac{1}{R_3} + \frac{1}{R_4} = \frac{1}{30\ \Omega} + \frac{1}{60\ \Omega} = \frac{2}{60\ \Omega} + \frac{1}{60\ \Omega} = \frac{1}{20\ \Omega}$$

$$\frac{1}{R_{3//4}} = \frac{1}{20\ \Omega}$$

$$R_{3//4} = 20\ \Omega$$

$$V_{3//4} = IR_{3//4} = (2\ \text{A})(20\ \Omega) = 40\ \text{V}$$

From this, you can easily determine the voltage drop across R_1 and R_2:
$V_{1/2} = V - V_{3/4} = 64\text{ V} - 40\text{ V} = 24\text{ V}$. Using the Ohm's Law equation, the total resistance of $R_1 + R_2$ is then $R_{1/2} = \frac{V_{1/2}}{I} = \frac{24\text{ V}}{2\text{ A}} = 12\ \Omega$.

Knowing the resistance of R_1 and the total resistance of $R_1 + R_2$, you can now determine the resistance of R_2:

$$\frac{1}{R_{1/2}} = \frac{1}{R_1} + \frac{1}{R_2}$$

$$\frac{1}{R_2} = \frac{1}{R_{1/2}} - \frac{1}{R_1}$$

$$\frac{1}{R_2} = \frac{1}{12\ \Omega} - \frac{1}{20\ \Omega} = \frac{5}{60\ \Omega} - \frac{3}{60\ \Omega} = \frac{1}{30\ \Omega}$$

$$\frac{1}{R_2} = \frac{1}{30\ \Omega}$$

$$R_2 = 30\ \Omega$$

Calculating conductance

Conductance (G) is the opposite of resistance. Whereas resistance is a measure of restricted electron movement, conductance is a measure of how easily an electric current travels through a material. Conductance is the inverse of resistance: $G = \frac{1}{R}$. You express conductance in units called siemens (S).

Working with wattage and kilowatts

Chapter 14 explains how to calculate power in watts. Power is expressed as watts in the realm of electricity too, but the concept is a little different. With electricity, power is the rate at which electrical energy is transferred. Mathematically, the following three expressions represent power:

$$P = IV$$

$$P = I^2 R$$

$$P = \frac{V^2}{R}$$

With these handy dandy equations, you're ready to tackle power questions.

An air conditioning unit is rated at 2,400 watts and is powered by a 120 V electrical cord. How much resistance does the unit have?

To calculate resistance, you need to know amperage and voltage. Use one of the power equations to calculate amperage:

$$P = IV$$

$$I = \frac{P}{V} = \frac{2,400\text{ W}}{120\text{ V}} = 20\text{ A}$$

With amperage and volts, you have everything you need to calculate resistance:
$R = \frac{V}{I} = \frac{120}{20} = 6\ \Omega$.

Determining your electric bill

Electric bills are measured in kilowatt hours (kW-h or kWh). One kilowatt hour is the power used to light a 100-watt light bulb for ten hours. The equation for calculating kW-h goes like this: $E = Pt$, where E is energy, P is power in watts, and t is time in hours.

A 120 W light bulb is left on for 24 hours. How much energy is consumed in kW-h?

$$E = Pt$$
$$E = 120\text{ W} \times 24\text{ h} = 2{,}880\text{ W-h}$$
$$2{,}880\text{ W-h} \times \frac{1\text{ kW-h}}{1{,}000\text{ W-h}} = 2.88\text{ kW-h}$$

One kW-h equals 3,600,000 joules, but this isn't something you need to memorize. If the question asks for the answer in joules, it provides the conversion factor. In this case, 2.88 kW-h is $2.88 \times 3{,}600{,}000 = 10{,}368{,}000$ joules.

Differences exposed: Direct versus alternating current

You've heard of AC/DC, and we're not talking about the band here. DC is direct current. It flows in one direction from Point A to Point B. Alternating current (AC), on the other hand, switches direction, constantly moving back and forth. As a result, AC has a frequency, which is the one thing DC doesn't have. If you're near an AC transformer, you may hear it hum; that's the frequency talking, vibrating the materials through which the current flows.

AC features several advantages for power distribution over DC:

✓ It minimizes losses to resistance by transmitting at high voltages.

✓ It's easy to step up or step down voltage for different applications.

✓ It's the type of energy power plants generally produce, so no conversion is required to transport or use it.

Exploring differences in single- and three-phase AC

AC current is *sinusoidal* (wavy). If you graph the flow, it looks like a sound wave rising and falling according to its frequency. In a single-phase system, voltage and current drop to zero twice in the cycle, as shown in Figure 16-8. As you may guess, this fluctuating voltage and current has its drawbacks, the most obvious being that it causes vibration in machinery.

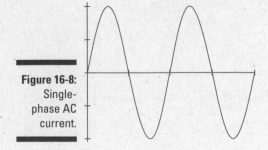

Figure 16-8: Single-phase AC current.

Three-phase AC current solves this problem and offers additional benefits. With three-phase current, each phase is $\frac{1}{3}$ out of sync with the others, so although each phase fluctuates, at no time does the voltage or current drop to zero (see Figure 16-9). Power stays essentially constant throughout the entire cycle. Three-phase AC current offers three important benefits:

✔ It produces little to no vibration.

✔ It requires smaller wires than single-phase current to support the same load; therefore, more power can be supplied to the load with smaller wires.

✔ It has the ability to produce a rotating magnetic field in an electric motor, allowing for simpler motor design. (See "Electric motors" later in this chapter for details.)

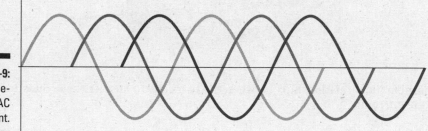

Figure 16-9: Three-phase AC current.

Grasping the fundamentals of transformers

A *transformer* is an AC device that raises or lowers voltage. Using transformers, electricity can be carried along high-voltage lines (in excess of 25,000 V) and then stepped down to a lower voltage (120 V or 240 V) suitable for everyday use.

A basic transformer consists of two coils of wire wound around a common metallic core, as shown in Figure 16-10. In this example, a high-voltage current flows through the outer (primary) coil, creating a strong magnetic field that *induces* a current in the inner (secondary) coil. The relative voltage in the two coils depends on the difference in the number of times each wire is wound around the core. If the secondary coil is wrapped half as many times around the core, its voltage is equal to half the primary coil's voltage. If the secondary coil is wrapped twice as many times around the core, its voltage is equal to twice the voltage of the primary coil. The mathematical relationship looks like this: $\frac{V_s}{V_p} = \frac{N_s}{N_p} = \frac{I_p}{I_s}$, where V_s and V_p are voltage in the secondary and primary windings respectively, N_s and N_p are the number of turns in the secondary and primary windings, and I_p and I_s are amperage in the primary and secondary windings. Because transformers have no mechanical or moving parts, they're about 99 percent efficient, losing a negligible amount of power through resistance in the coils.

A power line connects to a household electric cable through a transformer. The power line has a voltage of 60,000 V with a current of 1 A. The ratio of primary windings to secondary windings is 250:1. What is the current and voltage of the household electric cable?

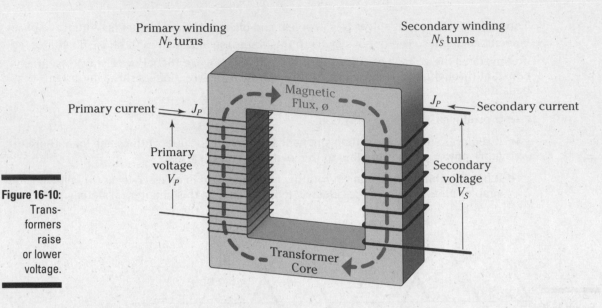

Figure 16-10:
Trans-
formers
raise
or lower
voltage.

Use the mathematical relationships between the two coils to answer these questions. First, calculate the current:

$$\frac{N_s}{N_p} = \frac{I_p}{I_s}$$

$$I_s = I_p \frac{N_p}{N_s} = 1 \text{ A} \left(\frac{250}{1}\right) = 250 \text{ A}$$

To calculate the voltage, take a similar approach:

$$\frac{N_s}{N_p} = \frac{V_s}{V_p}$$

$$V_s = V_p \frac{N_s}{N_p} = 60,000 \text{ V} \left(\frac{1}{250}\right) = 240 \text{ V}$$

Knowing the purpose of filters and how they function

Filters amplify certain signals while attenuating or minimizing others, typically to remove undesirable components from a frequency signal. Filters come in many forms, including *high pass* (accentuating high frequencies) and *low pass* (accentuating low frequencies). The word "pass" refers to the signals that the filter allows to pass through it. Other signals are filtered out. Combining a low pass filter with a high pass filter results in a *band pass filter*, which accentuates a very narrow band of frequencies. This type of filter is very useful in FM radio tuners.

Converting AC to DC and vice versa with rectifiers and inverters

Rectifiers change AC to DC through a series of diodes (D_{1-4}) that redirect the AC current (represented by a wave) to flow in one direction (represented by arrows), as shown in Figure 16-11. Here, the diodes aligned as a bridge produce the output current across the load. Current output from the diodes tends to rise and fall, as shown by the waveform with the dotted line. The capacitor in the circuit charges as the voltage nears its peak and discharges as the voltage drops, making the current steadier. Smoothing filters, not shown in the figure, make the output voltage and current even more uniform.

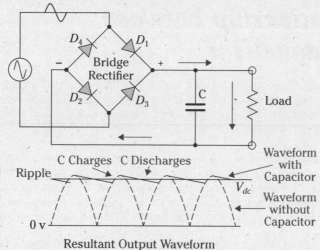

Figure 16-11:
A rectifier converts AC to DC.

Inverters convert DC to AC. They're far more complicated and used to take up much more space than rectifiers until the advent of solid-state electronics.

Tuning in to AM and FM

You probably tune in to AM and FM radio stations in your car without ever giving a second thought to what they really are. For the exam, you should at least know the primary difference between the two:

- ✔ **AM:** Short for *amplitude modulation,* AM transmits audio by varying the amplitude of the radio wave, as shown in Figure 16-12.

- ✔ **FM:** Short for *frequency modulation,* FM transmits audio by varying the frequency of the radio wave, as shown in Figure 16-12.

In both cases, transmitters, receivers, and transceivers (devices that send and receive signals) use different filters to convert media content, such as music, into a signal and then change the signal back into media content.

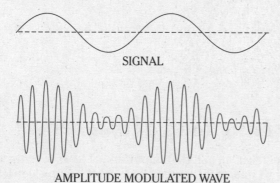

SIGNAL

AMPLITUDE MODULATED WAVE

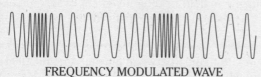

Figure 16-12:
AM versus FM signals.

FREQUENCY MODULATED WAVE

Exploring the Relationship between Electricity and Magnetism

Electricity is nothing without magnetism and vice versa. Magnets are crucial for generating electricity and enabling transformers to raise and lower voltage. Magnets are also essential in all sorts of electrical devices, including motors, ceiling fans, speakers, and many other tools, appliances, and toys.

You don't need to fully grasp the relationship between electricity and magnetism for the test. It can get very involved very fast. However, you do need to know some of the principles of magnetism, how magnets work to generate electricity, the roles magnets play in an electric motor and other common devices, and some of the math that's involved. The following sections assist you in prepping for any questions you may encounter related to electromagnetism.

Magnetism is a force field, a magnetic field that acts on certain materials, including iron. As shown in Figure 16-13, magnets have two poles, typically labeled *N* (north) and *S* (south). The lines of force for each pole are directed away from each pole toward the opposite pole, which is why the north sides of two magnets repel one another while the north and south sides of two magnets attract one another.

What's most interesting and useful regarding magnets is how magnetic forces interact with electrical forces. Magnets in motion around conductors, for example, induce current in the conductors to generate electricity. Electrical current may also create magnetism and be used to convert electrical energy into mechanical energy, as in the case of an electric motor.

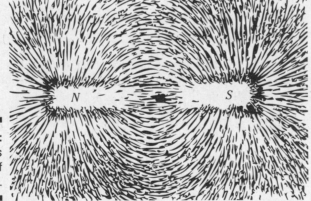

Figure 16-13: A magnet's lines of force.

Brushing up on the basic laws of magnetism

A stationary magnetic field in and of itself isn't all that important, at least in terms of practical applications (and the test). What's important, especially as it relates to electricity, is the movement of a current through the magnetic field or the movement of the magnetic field itself. The relative motion of magnetic fields and conductors is what drives mechanical motion and generates current.

Several laws and equations make the relationships between magnetism and electricity more understandable, the most important of which are four equations known as Maxwell's equations — Gauss's Law, Faraday's Law, Gauss's Law for magnetism, and Ampere's Law with the Maxwell correction. (For the test, simply know that these are the four laws that make up Maxwell's equation. You don't need to know the math behind these laws, which is a little bit complex.) These equations are the basis for why moving a magnet through a coil of wires generates a current and why wrapping a current-carrying wire around a ferrous metal core generates a magnetic field.

The two laws to focus on most are Gauss's Law and Faraday's Law, explained in the following sections.

Gauss's Law

Gauss's Law states that the electric flux (the density of a magnetic field) through a closed surface is proportional to the total charge enclosed. Basically, this means that the amount of flux going into a point is the same as the amount coming out. This law has an equation, but it involves calculus and vectors, both of which are too in-depth for what you need to know. Just know that Gauss's Law deals with explaining flux through points and is one of Maxwell's equations.

Faraday's Law

Faraday's law describes the relationship between electromagnetism and current. It specifically addresses the following:

- ✔ The relationship between the number of current-carrying coils wrapped around a ferrous core and the strength of the magnetic field generated
- ✔ How a moving magnetic field imparts a current on a coil wrapped around a ferrous core

As you proceed through the following sections, Gauss's Law and Faraday's Law begin to make more sense.

Creating magnetic fields with electricity

Whenever current flows through a wire, a magnetic field develops around the wire, as shown in Figure 16-14. If you were to lay a compass on top of the wire, you would see its arrow align with the magnetic field. The magnetic field is perpendicular to the wire and its direction is either clockwise or counterclockwise depending on the direction in which the current flows.

Figure 16-14: The magnetic field surrounding a conductor in which current is flowing.

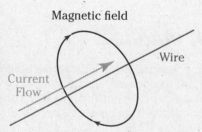

Magnetic field

Wire

Current Flow

To increase the magnetic field, you can coil the wire, as shown in Figure 16-15, forming a *solenoid*. The more coils of wire, the stronger the magnetic field. If the current flowing through the solenoid is a DC current, the magnetic field remains constant. If the current running through the coil is AC, then the field changes direction at the same rate as the frequency of the electric current running through the coil.

Solenoid or inductor? What's the difference?

If you think the description of a solenoid makes it sound a whole lot like an inductor, you're not too far afield. Structurally, the two are the same — they're both coiled conductors. The difference is in how they're used. The primary purpose of an inductor is to oppose changes in current.

Solenoids may be used as inductors, but they have plenty of other uses as well. Electric door locks, for example, are solenoids. A current passes around a moveable metal core to pull it down or push it up, locking or unlocking the doors. Solenoids are also used in relays to flip switches.

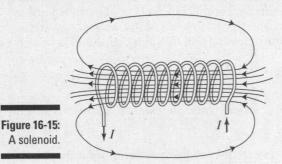

Figure 16-15:
A solenoid.

Wrap the wire around a ferrous metal core, such as iron, and you have a magnet, as shown in Figure 16-16. Because the metal core has a high *magnetic permeability,* it multiplies the strength of the magnetic field, potentially making the magnetic field thousands of times stronger. Magnetic permeability is to magnetic fields as conductivity is to electric current.

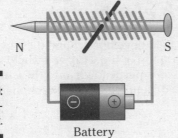

Figure 16-16:
An electro-magnet.

Battery

Generating electricity with magnets

You can make a magnet with electricity, but can you make electricity with a magnet? Yes, and that's exactly the principle that generators use to produce electricity. Pass a conductor through a magnetic field, and the magnetic field deflects the path of free electrons to make them flow in a specific direction through the conductor. This creates a potential difference in the conductor, which results in a flow of current, as shown in Figure 16-17.

The more conductors you pass through the magnetic field and the faster you do it, the more current is generated, which is the idea behind generators. A generator consists of two parts, as shown in Figure 16-18: the *stator* (the stationary part) and the *rotor* (the part that rotates). Either part may function as the *field* or *armature:*

✔ **Field:** Short for magnetic field, it may be formed by a permanent magnet or electromagnet

✔ **Armature:** The part that passes through the magnetic field to produce electricity

Figure 16-17:
Passing a
conductor
through
a mag-
netic field
produces
current
in the
conductor.

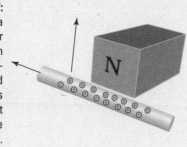

Although either the stator or rotor may function as the armature, the armature is usually on the stator and the magnetic field spins around it. This arrangement facilitates the transfer of current. As the magnetic field rotates relative to the armature, the rotating field causes the wire coils in the armature to generate an oscillating current at the same frequency as the machine rotates.

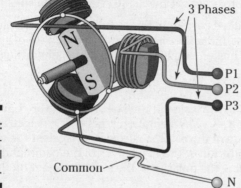

Figure 16-18:
An elec-
trical
generator.

An electrical generator doesn't really generate power; instead, it converts mechanical energy into electrical energy. Something must turn the rotor. Windmills capture the power of wind to turn a rotor. At Hoover Dam, water flow turns the rotors. Most generating plants use coal or nuclear power to boil water and produce steam to turn the rotors. If you have a gas-powered generator, the gas engine turns the rotor. With small generators, you can turn the rotor by hand . . . or foot. What's important to remember is that electric generators convert mechanical energy into electrical energy.

Converting electrical energy to mechanical energy using electric motors

You can convert mechanical energy into electrical energy using a generator, but can you convert electrical energy back into mechanical energy? Yes, of course, and that's the principle behind electric motors. An electric motor uses electricity to produce a strong magnetic field to turn a rotor inside the motor, as shown in Figure 16-19. The motor's casing holds the stator (stationary) part, while the rotor spins freely inside the casing.

Electric motors work differently depending on the type of current, as explained in the following sections.

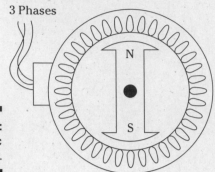

Figure 16-19:
An electric
motor.

3 Phases

AC motors

AC motors use the fluctuating nature of AC current to their advantage. As the current fluctuates, the magnetic field fluctuates, resulting in a rotating magnetic field, which turns the rotor. The magnets on the rotor "chase" the moving magnetic field in the stator. The two most common types of AC motors are synchronous and induction:

- ✔ **Synchronous:** The rotor spins at the same rate as the alternating current passing through the stator. Synchronous motors spin at the same rate, regardless of the load.

- ✔ **Induction:** The rotor follows the induced current in the stator, so the rotor spins at a slightly slower rate than the current. Induction motors change their rate of speed depending on the load, but generate higher torque and require smaller starting currents.

DC motors

In a DC motor, two permanent magnets line the inside of the stator. The rotor contains two electromagnets connected to a *commutator* — a split metal ring that carries electricity to the two electromagnets. A brush on either side of the rotor's axle presses against the commutator to supply electrical current. As the rotor turns, the two halves of the commutator alternate between positive and negative, flipping the polarity of the electromagnet on the rotor.

Take a look at Figure 16-20. The C1 half of the commutator is connected to the negative terminal, while the C2 is connected to the positive terminal. As the rotor turns, the halves switch position, so C1 is positive, and C2 is negative, reversing the current through the coils in the rotor and changing the polarity of the rotor: The end of the rotor labeled S in the figure now becomes N, and N becomes S, so each end of the rotor is almost continuously pushed away from one stationary magnet and drawn toward the other.

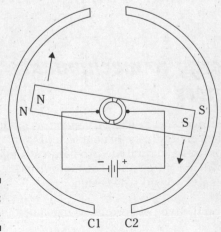

Figure 16-20:
A DC motor.

C1   C2

DC motors come in three main types:

- **Shunt:** Field coils are connected to armature coils in parallel, and the speed of the motor is controlled by the DC circuitry. Shunt motors generally have a constant speed, which can be adjusted.

- **Series:** Field coils are connected to armature coils in a series. The speed of series motors varies with the load.

- **Compound:** Field coils are connected to armature coils in parallel and series. Compound motors operate mostly like shunt motors but usually handle larger loads.

Surveying the World of Modern Electronics

When you have an understanding of electricity, magnetism, and electrical circuitry and components, you're ready to tackle modern electrical devices you may encounter on the test — radios, computers, televisions, and even high definition televisions (HDTVs). The following sections bring you up to speed and explain a few important concepts not yet covered in this chapter.

Radios

Figure 16-21 shows a simplified schematic of a superheterodyne (superhet) radio receiver. The term *superheterodyne* refers to a technique for tuning into radio frequencies. An antenna receives the radio signal and passes it to a radio frequency (RF) amplifier, which amplifies the signal and passes it to the mixer. A local oscillator functions as the tuner, selecting the frequency to tune into. Using a band pass filter, the mixer attenuates (diminishes) all other frequencies and passes the selected frequency to the intermittent frequency (IF) amplifier. The IF amplifier refines the filtered frequency and amplifies it. A demodulator then converts the radio frequency to a form that can be recognized by an output device. The amplifier amplifies the signal and sends it to speakers, headphones, or some other output device.

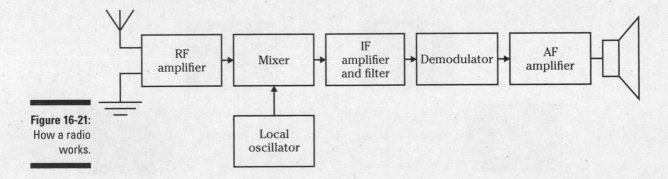

Figure 16-21: How a radio works.

Computers

A computer consists of five essential components, as shown in Figure 16-22. You may encounter questions about these components on the exam. Following is a brief description of each component:

- **Input:** A component that enables you to pass data to the computer for processing. Input devices include keyboards, mice, joysticks, game controls, microphones, digital camcorders, and Webcams.

✔ **Processor:** The computer's brain, also referred to as the central processing unit (CPU). It essentially crunches numbers to process instructions and data.

✔ **Control:** Instructions (software) that tell the processor how to complete specific tasks. The control component consists of four types of software:

 • **Basic input/output system (BIOS):** The startup instructions.

 • **Operating system:** Instructions that enable the various hardware components and devices to communicate with one another. The operating system also handles basic tasks, including file and system management.

 • **Applications:** Programs that perform specific tasks, such as word processors, spreadsheets, graphics programs, and games. Applications run on top of the operating system, using it to communicate with input and output devices.

 • **Algorithms:** Rules for storing and retrieving data so the computer can more easily locate data stored in RAM. (See the following bullet for more on RAM.)

✔ **Memory:** Storage for software and data that make it accessible for the processor to work with. Memory has several layers, including the following:

 • **Read-only memory (ROM):** Long-term memory that stores instructions on computer chips that can be read from but not written to (or not written to very often). ROM is typically used to store the computer's BIOS.

 • **Disk storage:** Long-term memory, sometimes referred to as permanent memory, that stores data on hard disks (magnetic storage) or CDs or DVDs (optical storage).

 • **Random access memory (RAM):** Short-term memory that's available only when the computer is turned on. A computer reads from ROM or a disk and stores the data and instructions in RAM to make them more readily accessible to the processor.

 • **Cache:** A type of RAM that provides quicker access to data and instructions the processor uses most frequently.

 • **Register:** Memory on the processor that gives the processor almost instant access to instructions and data.

✔ **Output:** Anything the computer generates, including whatever appears on screen or in print and the audio that plays through the speakers.

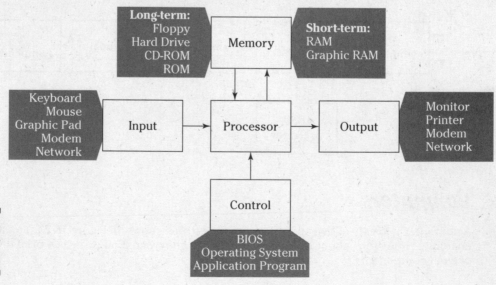

Figure 16-22: Computer components.

Televisions

A television is like a radio with a video component. In fact, the first three modules for both audio and video are similar to those used in a radio. They tune in to a particular frequency, amplify it, and then decode it, as shown in Figure 16-23. After passing through these first three modules, the signal splits into different components — the sound component that acts like the rest of the radio, the video amplifier, and the sync separator.

The *video amplifier* controls the brightness and contrast of the displayed image. The *sync separator* divides the horizontal and vertical sync signals:

- **Horizontal sync signal:** A short pulse that has a distinct start and end pattern, signifying the beginning and end of a line of transmission. Each line makes up a line of display on the television.

- **Vertical sync signal:** A longer pulse that has a distinct start and end pattern denoting when a frame starts and ends.

The two signals work together to produce the frames that comprise the moving picture. In a standard TV set, the cathode ray tube (CRT) variety, an electron gun fires a narrow stream of electrons against the plasma screen, illuminating the dots (pixels) that create the image. The gun travels super fast across the screen (horizontally) and up and down (vertically) to produce a frame. The vertical sync signal triggers the display of all the horizontal sync signals that produce a single frame. It then pulses to produce the next frame. A flyback transformer generates high voltage signals at high frequency, making the electron gun move much faster horizontally than it does vertically.

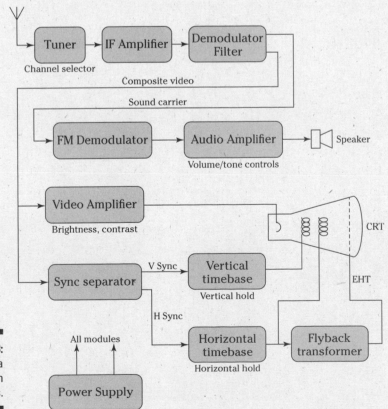

Figure 16-23:
How a television works.

HDTVs

High definition televisions display a higher resolution than their older counterparts. While standard resolution is generally 576i, 576p, 480i, or 480p, high-def televisions have a resolution of 720i, 720p, 1,080i, or 1,080p. The difference in resolution can produce an image up to five times sharper than regular definition television.

The number represents the number of vertical pixels, while the letter represents the type of scan: *i* for *interlaced* or *p* for *progressive*. Interlaced means the picture is transmitted so one field paints all the odd frames and the next field paints all the even frames. The fields are commonly painted at a higher frequency so the interlaced scan has the same frame rate as a progressive scan. With progressive scanning, all the lines of a frame are drawn in sequence and displayed at once. Progressive scanning signals consume twice as much bandwidth as interlaced scanning signals. Advances in digital technology have enabled transmission of high-definition signals with less bandwidth than was previously required through analog transmission and some older methods of digital transmission.

Chapter 17

Testing Your Electronics Knowledge

On the Armed Services Vocational Aptitude Battery (ASVAB) Electronics Information subtest, you have 9 minutes to answer 20 questions. (This chapter provides 25 questions in order to be thorough about the types of questions you might see on the test.) You may be able to answer some of the fact questions in a few seconds, whereas the problems that require math are likely to take much longer.

Prior to taking this practice exam, you may want to consider reading or reviewing Chapter 16 to brush up on basic electronics and some of the more common formulas. Or just take the practice test cold to identify electronics information you need to work on.

ASVAB Electrical Information

This section presents 25 questions that challenge a broad range of electronics knowledge, skills, and reasoning. Questions reflect the depth and level of difficulty you may encounter on the ASVAB Electronics Information subtest. Give yourself about 9 minutes to complete the test. Choose the best answer for each question from the choices provided.

1. What kind of charge do electrons have?

   (A) positive

   (B) negative

   (C) neutral

   (D) magnetic

2. What is the term used to describe the flow of electrons across a conductive material?

   (A) voltage

   (B) power

   (C) current

   (D) resistance

3. What is a coulomb?

   (A) the measure of an electrical charge

   (B) the measure of the amount of electrical charge that flows through a given point

   (C) the measure of the difference in electrical potential

   (D) the measure of the power of an electrical circuit

4. An ammeter is inserted in a circuit and measures the current at that point to be 5 amperes. The measurement was taken for 12 seconds, and the current remained a constant 5 amperes. How many coulombs of charge passed that point over the 12 seconds of measurement?

   (A) 0.42 coulombs

   (B) 2.4 coulombs

   (C) 30 coulombs

   (D) 60 coulombs

5. Which of the following is NOT a good conductor?

   (A) silver

   (B) aluminum

   (C) copper

   (D) glass

6. What is a major advantage of a solid-core wire compared to a wire with a stranded core?

   (A) flexibility

   (B) cost

   (C) size

   (D) reusability

7. Semiconductors are commonly doped with materials called dopants. What kind of dopant adds free electrons to a semiconductive material?

   (A) n-type

   (B) g-type

   (C) s-type

   (D) p-type

8. The amount of resistance of a given material depends on all EXCEPT which one of the following?

   (A) material type

   (B) length

   (C) diameter

   (D) current

9. Which of the following is a symbol for a power supply?

   (A) ⏚

   (B) ⎓WWW⎓

   (C) ⎓ᅵᆈᅵᆄ⎓

   (D) ⎓ᅵᅡ⎓

10. In the circuit shown in the following figure, what would happen to the light if the shorting key shut?

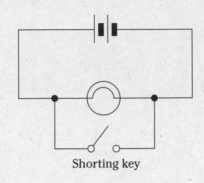

Shorting key

(A) The light would get brighter.

(B) The light would shut off.

(C) The light would turn on.

(D) The light would get dimmer.

11. What does it mean for a circuit to be open?

(A) There is no voltage, but current flow exists.

(B) There is voltage and current flow.

(C) There is voltage but no current flow.

(D) There is no current flow and no voltage.

12. Given the circuit in the following figure, what is the circuit's current?

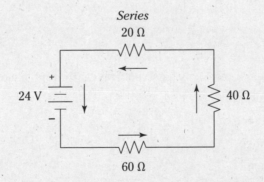

(A) 5 amperes

(B) 0.5 amperes

(C) 0.2 amperes

(D) 2 amperes

13. Given the parallel circuit in the following figure, what is the current through resistor R_1?

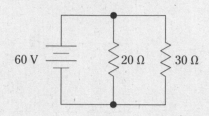

(A) 3 amperes

(B) 2 amperes

(C) 5 amperes

(D) 0.5 amperes

14. Given the circuit in the following figure, what is the resistance of R_2?

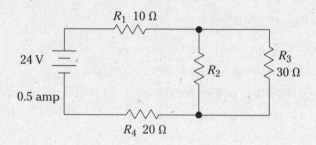

(A) 15 Ω

(B) 25 Ω

(C) 35 Ω

(D) 45 Ω

15. The measure of how easily a current travels through a material is known as

(A) resistance.

(B) conductance.

(C) capacitance.

(D) reluctance.

16. An electric fan is rated as a 480-watt fan. Assuming the power supplied to the fan is 120 volts, how much current is drawn by the fan?

(A) 2 amperes

(B) 4 amperes

(C) 8 amperes

(D) 16 amperes

17. Assuming you leave a 60-watt light on for 48 hours, you run your 4,800-watt washing machine for 2 hours, and you watch a TV that uses 2,000 watts of power for 4 hours, how many total kilowatt-hours of power did you use?

    (A) 20.5 kilowatt-hours

    (B) 17.6 kilowatt-hours

    (C) 12.5 kilowatt-hours

    (D) 10.9 kilowatt-hours

18. Which of the following is an advantage of using AC for power distribution compared to DC?

    (A) Most electronic devices use AC.

    (B) AC causes less interference with magnetic fields and radio waves.

    (C) Being able to transmit at higher voltages minimizes losses to resistance.

    (D) DC is cheaper to produce and transmit.

19. All of the following are advantages for three-phase AC EXCEPT which of the following?

    (A) Smaller wires are required with three-phase AC to support the same load supplied by single-phase AC.

    (B) Little to no vibration is created.

    (C) It's easier to produce a rotating magnetic field in an electric motor, allowing for a simpler design.

    (D) Less complex wiring is required for electrical components.

20. What is the purpose of a transformer?

    (A) to change current from AC to DC

    (B) to raise or lower voltage in an AC circuit

    (C) to change current from DC to AC

    (D) to raise or lower current in a DC device

21. A major power line is connected to a neighborhood transformer. The power line's voltage is 120,000 volts and the neighborhood power lines are 10,000 volts. What is the ratio of windings between the major power line and the neighborhood power lines in the transformer?

    (A) 6:1

    (B) 1:6

    (C) 12:1

    (D) 1:12

22. Tuning your FM radio to a certain frequency is an example of using what type of filter?

    (A) band pass filter

    (B) band reject filter

    (C) high pass filter

    (D) low pass filter

23. Which of the following is NOT one of Maxwell's equations?

    (A) Gauss's Law

    (B) Faraday's Law

    (C) Ampere's Law

    (D) Charles's Law

24. Which of the following is NOT a type of DC motor?

    (A) a shunt motor

    (B) a series motor

    (C) an induction motor

    (D) a compound motor

25. For a high-definition television (HDTV) what does the *p* stand for in 1080p?

    (A) p-type dopant

    (B) picture type

    (C) parted

    (D) progressive

Answers and Explanations

Following are the answers to the preceding questions so you can see how well you did. For more information, you can read the accompanying answer explanations or, for more detailed topic discussions, turn to Chapter 16.

1. **B.** Electrons are negatively charged. Protons hold a positive charge, and neutrons are neutral.

2. **C.** Current is the flow of electrons. Voltage and power refer to pressure, and resistance counters the flow of electrons.

3. **A.** By definition, the coulomb is a measure of electrical charge. If you answered Choice (B), you're confusing coulomb with ampere. If you answered Choice (C) or (D), you really need to read Chapter 16.

4. **D.** Because the ampere measures the coulombs of electricity that pass a certain point per second, use the following equation:

$$I = \frac{C}{t} \Rightarrow 5 \text{ A} = \frac{C}{12 \text{ s}}$$
$$C = (5 \text{ A})(12 \text{ s}) = 60 \text{ C}$$

5. **D.** Silver, aluminum, and copper are all good conductors. Glass is a common insulator because of its high resistance and relative inability to conduct electricity.

6. **B.** Solid-core wire is cheaper because fewer strands are required to manufacture it.

7. **A.** Dopants come in two varieties, n-type and p-type, so you can immediately eliminate Choices (B) and (C). Because the dopant is adding electrons, it's making the material more negative, and *n* stands for negative.

8. **D.** Material type, diameter, and length are all physical characteristics of a material; current isn't. Although a higher current may cause the material to heat up, changing its resistant properties, the temperature causes the change, not the amount of current. Only material characteristics can change a material's conductivity; current can't.

9. **C.** Choice (C) represents a battery, which is a power supply. If you had trouble with this question, take another look at the table of electrical components and their corresponding symbols in Chapter 16.

10. **B.** With the shorting key open, the current has nowhere to go other than through the light, illuminating it. When the shorting key is closed, the current takes the path of least resistance around the light, so the light shuts off. This would trip a breaker, too, but that's not an answer choice.

11. **C.** When a circuit is open, the current flow stops, so eliminate Choices (A) and (B). Voltage remains, but current stops flowing, so Choice (D) isn't correct either.

12. **C.** In this equation, use what you know about series circuits to find the total resistance, and then use Ohm's Law to solve for current:

$$R_{tot} = R_1 + R_2 + R_3 = 20\ \Omega + 40\ \Omega + 60\ \Omega = 120\ \Omega$$

$$V = IR \Rightarrow I = \frac{V}{R} \Rightarrow I_{tot} = \frac{V_{battery}}{R_{tot}} = \frac{24\ V}{120\ \Omega} = 0.2\ A$$

13. **A.** In a parallel circuit, the voltage (potential difference) is the same for all the resistors, so use Ohm's Law:

$$V = IR \Rightarrow I = \frac{V}{R} \Rightarrow I_1 = \frac{V_{tot}}{R_1} = \frac{60\ V}{20\ \Omega} = 3\ A$$

14. **D.** First, determine the total resistance using voltage and amperage:

$$V_S = I_{tot}R_{tot} \Rightarrow R_{tot} = \frac{V_s}{I_{tot}} = \frac{24\ V}{0.5\ A} = 48\ \Omega$$

Using this number, you can easily find the total resistance of the two parallel resistors:

$$48\ \Omega = 10\ \Omega + 20\ \Omega + R_{\frac{2}{3}}$$

$$R_{\frac{2}{3}} = 18\ \Omega$$

Recall that the inverse of the total resistance in parallel resistors is equal to the sum of the inverse resistance of each resistor, so:

$$\frac{1}{18\ \Omega} = \frac{1}{R_2} + \frac{1}{R_3} = \frac{1}{R_2} + \frac{1}{30\ \Omega}$$

$$\frac{1}{R_2} = \frac{1}{18\ \Omega} - \frac{1}{30\ \Omega} = \frac{1}{45\ \Omega} \Rightarrow R_2 = 45\ \Omega$$

15. **B.** Conductors carry current, so it stands to reason that conductance is the measure of how easily current travels through a material. Resistance is the opposite.

16. **B.** Use the equation that relates power to voltage and current:

$$P = IV$$

$$480\ W = (I)(120\ V) \Rightarrow I = \frac{480\ W}{120\ V} = 4\ A$$

17. **A.** To solve this problem, add up the total power used by each load multiplied by the time each load was used. Don't forget to divide by 1,000 to convert watt-hours into kilowatt-hours:

$$E = Pt$$

$$E = (60 \text{ W})(48 \text{ h}) + (4,800 \text{ W})(2 \text{ h}) + (2,000 \text{ W})(4 \text{ h}) = 20,480 \text{ W-h} \left(\frac{1 \text{ kW-h}}{1000 \text{ W-h}} \right) = 20.48 \text{ kW-h}$$

18. **C.** This is one of those answers you either know or don't know, but if you don't know, you can improve your odds by immediately eliminating Choice (D); even if it were true, it would be an advantage of DC over AC. Choice (A) is somewhat subjective, so cross that off your list, too, and choose between Choices (B) and (C).

19. **D.** The wiring of three-phase components is not necessarily simpler, even if some of the machines have simpler designs.

20. **B.** The purpose of a transformer is to raise or lower voltage in an AC circuit. A rectifier or inverter changes current from AC to DC or DC to AC.

21. **C.** The ratio for the transformer is primary (major power line) to secondary (neighborhood power line):

$$\frac{N_p}{N_s} = \frac{V_p}{V_s} = \frac{120,000 \text{ V}}{10,000 \text{ V}} = \frac{12}{1} = 12:1$$

22. **A.** The high pass filter screens out low frequencies and the low pass filter screens out high frequencies, but for an FM tuner, you need both to focus on a very narrow range of frequencies. A band pass filter does both. A band reject filter does the exact opposite by rejecting a narrow range of frequencies.

23. **D.** Maxwell's equations are Gauss's Law, Faraday's Law, Gauss's Law for magnetism, and Ampere's Law with the Maxwell correction. Charles's Law applies to ideal gases.

24. **C.** Induction motors are inherently AC motors. The others are DC.

25. **D.** The *p* in 1080p stands for *progressive;* that is, every line in the scan is displayed on the screen for every frame. This differs from 1080i (the *i* stands for *interlaced*), which first displays all odd lines and then all even lines on the frames.

Part IV
Practice Tests

The 5th Wave   By Rich Tennant

"I always get a good night's sleep the day before a test so I'm relaxed and alert the next morning. Then I grab my pen, eat a banana, and I'm on my way."

In this part . . .

Practice may not ensure perfect scores on your Officer Candidate Tests, but it can help significantly in improving your scores in the following ways:

- ✔ Reveals what you know and don't know so you have a clear idea of your strengths and weaknesses and areas you need to work on.

- ✔ Provides you with a good feel for how quickly you need to work in order to complete each section of the test.

- ✔ Gives you hands-on experience with answering specific types of questions so you know how to approach each question.

- ✔ Challenges you to put your knowledge into practice so you can solve problems and answer questions more quickly and with greater accuracy.

This part features four practice tests: the Air Force Officers Qualifying Test (AFOQT), Aviation Selection Test Battery Officer Aptitude Rating (ASTB OAR), Armed Services Vocational Aptitude Battery General Technical (ASVAB GT), and Armed Services Vocational Aptitude Battery Marine Officer Candidate School (ASVAB Marine OCS).

Chapter 18

AFOQT Academic Aptitude Practice Test

. . . .

*T*his practice AFOQT (Air Force Officer Qualifying Aptitude Test) tests your skills on the Verbal Analogies, Arithmetic Reasoning, Word Knowledge, and Mathematics Knowledge subtests. To make the most of this practice run, mimic the testing conditions you'll encounter on the real test: test in a quiet room, take few breaks (if any), and don't jump from subtest to subtest. Also, use a watch or clock to time yourself. Part of the challenge is completing each section in the allotted time. Mark your answers on the answer sheets provided. When you've completed this practice test, turn to Chapter 19 to check your answers. We provide detailed explanations for all the answers as well as an abbreviated answer key.

Answer Sheet

Use the ovals provided with this practice test to record your answers.

Verbal Analogies

1. Ⓐ Ⓑ Ⓒ Ⓓ Ⓔ	8. Ⓐ Ⓑ Ⓒ Ⓓ Ⓔ	15. Ⓐ Ⓑ Ⓒ Ⓓ Ⓔ	22. Ⓐ Ⓑ Ⓒ Ⓓ Ⓔ
2. Ⓐ Ⓑ Ⓒ Ⓓ Ⓔ	9. Ⓐ Ⓑ Ⓒ Ⓓ Ⓔ	16. Ⓐ Ⓑ Ⓒ Ⓓ Ⓔ	23. Ⓐ Ⓑ Ⓒ Ⓓ Ⓔ
3. Ⓐ Ⓑ Ⓒ Ⓓ Ⓔ	10. Ⓐ Ⓑ Ⓒ Ⓓ Ⓔ	17. Ⓐ Ⓑ Ⓒ Ⓓ Ⓔ	24. Ⓐ Ⓑ Ⓒ Ⓓ Ⓔ
4. Ⓐ Ⓑ Ⓒ Ⓓ Ⓔ	11. Ⓐ Ⓑ Ⓒ Ⓓ Ⓔ	18. Ⓐ Ⓑ Ⓒ Ⓓ Ⓔ	25. Ⓐ Ⓑ Ⓒ Ⓓ Ⓔ
5. Ⓐ Ⓑ Ⓒ Ⓓ Ⓔ	12. Ⓐ Ⓑ Ⓒ Ⓓ Ⓔ	19. Ⓐ Ⓑ Ⓒ Ⓓ Ⓔ	
6. Ⓐ Ⓑ Ⓒ Ⓓ Ⓔ	13. Ⓐ Ⓑ Ⓒ Ⓓ Ⓔ	20. Ⓐ Ⓑ Ⓒ Ⓓ Ⓔ	
7. Ⓐ Ⓑ Ⓒ Ⓓ Ⓔ	14. Ⓐ Ⓑ Ⓒ Ⓓ Ⓔ	21. Ⓐ Ⓑ Ⓒ Ⓓ Ⓔ	

Arithmetic Reasoning

1. Ⓐ Ⓑ Ⓒ Ⓓ	8. Ⓐ Ⓑ Ⓒ Ⓓ	15. Ⓐ Ⓑ Ⓒ Ⓓ	22. Ⓐ Ⓑ Ⓒ Ⓓ
2. Ⓐ Ⓑ Ⓒ Ⓓ	9. Ⓐ Ⓑ Ⓒ Ⓓ	16. Ⓐ Ⓑ Ⓒ Ⓓ	23. Ⓐ Ⓑ Ⓒ Ⓓ
3. Ⓐ Ⓑ Ⓒ Ⓓ	10. Ⓐ Ⓑ Ⓒ Ⓓ	17. Ⓐ Ⓑ Ⓒ Ⓓ	24. Ⓐ Ⓑ Ⓒ Ⓓ
4. Ⓐ Ⓑ Ⓒ Ⓓ	11. Ⓐ Ⓑ Ⓒ Ⓓ	18. Ⓐ Ⓑ Ⓒ Ⓓ	25. Ⓐ Ⓑ Ⓒ Ⓓ
5. Ⓐ Ⓑ Ⓒ Ⓓ	12. Ⓐ Ⓑ Ⓒ Ⓓ	19. Ⓐ Ⓑ Ⓒ Ⓓ	
6. Ⓐ Ⓑ Ⓒ Ⓓ	13. Ⓐ Ⓑ Ⓒ Ⓓ	20. Ⓐ Ⓑ Ⓒ Ⓓ	
7. Ⓐ Ⓑ Ⓒ Ⓓ	14. Ⓐ Ⓑ Ⓒ Ⓓ	21. Ⓐ Ⓑ Ⓒ Ⓓ	

Word Knowledge

1. Ⓐ Ⓑ Ⓒ Ⓓ Ⓔ	8. Ⓐ Ⓑ Ⓒ Ⓓ Ⓔ	15. Ⓐ Ⓑ Ⓒ Ⓓ Ⓔ	22. Ⓐ Ⓑ Ⓒ Ⓓ Ⓔ
2. Ⓐ Ⓑ Ⓒ Ⓓ Ⓔ	9. Ⓐ Ⓑ Ⓒ Ⓓ Ⓔ	16. Ⓐ Ⓑ Ⓒ Ⓓ Ⓔ	23. Ⓐ Ⓑ Ⓒ Ⓓ Ⓔ
3. Ⓐ Ⓑ Ⓒ Ⓓ Ⓔ	10. Ⓐ Ⓑ Ⓒ Ⓓ Ⓔ	17. Ⓐ Ⓑ Ⓒ Ⓓ Ⓔ	24. Ⓐ Ⓑ Ⓒ Ⓓ Ⓔ
4. Ⓐ Ⓑ Ⓒ Ⓓ Ⓔ	11. Ⓐ Ⓑ Ⓒ Ⓓ Ⓔ	18. Ⓐ Ⓑ Ⓒ Ⓓ Ⓔ	25. Ⓐ Ⓑ Ⓒ Ⓓ Ⓔ
5. Ⓐ Ⓑ Ⓒ Ⓓ Ⓔ	12. Ⓐ Ⓑ Ⓒ Ⓓ Ⓔ	19. Ⓐ Ⓑ Ⓒ Ⓓ Ⓔ	
6. Ⓐ Ⓑ Ⓒ Ⓓ Ⓔ	13. Ⓐ Ⓑ Ⓒ Ⓓ Ⓔ	20. Ⓐ Ⓑ Ⓒ Ⓓ Ⓔ	
7. Ⓐ Ⓑ Ⓒ Ⓓ Ⓔ	14. Ⓐ Ⓑ Ⓒ Ⓓ Ⓔ	21. Ⓐ Ⓑ Ⓒ Ⓓ Ⓔ	

Mathematics Knowledge

1. Ⓐ Ⓑ Ⓒ Ⓓ	8. Ⓐ Ⓑ Ⓒ Ⓓ	15. Ⓐ Ⓑ Ⓒ Ⓓ	22. Ⓐ Ⓑ Ⓒ Ⓓ
2. Ⓐ Ⓑ Ⓒ Ⓓ	9. Ⓐ Ⓑ Ⓒ Ⓓ	16. Ⓐ Ⓑ Ⓒ Ⓓ	23. Ⓐ Ⓑ Ⓒ Ⓓ
3. Ⓐ Ⓑ Ⓒ Ⓓ	10. Ⓐ Ⓑ Ⓒ Ⓓ	17. Ⓐ Ⓑ Ⓒ Ⓓ	24. Ⓐ Ⓑ Ⓒ Ⓓ
4. Ⓐ Ⓑ Ⓒ Ⓓ	11. Ⓐ Ⓑ Ⓒ Ⓓ	18. Ⓐ Ⓑ Ⓒ Ⓓ	25. Ⓐ Ⓑ Ⓒ Ⓓ
5. Ⓐ Ⓑ Ⓒ Ⓓ	12. Ⓐ Ⓑ Ⓒ Ⓓ	19. Ⓐ Ⓑ Ⓒ Ⓓ	
6. Ⓐ Ⓑ Ⓒ Ⓓ	13. Ⓐ Ⓑ Ⓒ Ⓓ	20. Ⓐ Ⓑ Ⓒ Ⓓ	
7. Ⓐ Ⓑ Ⓒ Ⓓ	14. Ⓐ Ⓑ Ⓒ Ⓓ	21. Ⓐ Ⓑ Ⓒ Ⓓ	

Verbal Analogies

Time: 8 minutes for 25 questions

Directions: This section of the test measures your ability to reason and see relationships among words. Choose the option from the answer choices provided that best completes the analogy developed at the beginning of each question and shade in the corresponding oval on your answer sheet.

1. HELMET is to HEAD as
   (A) POCKET is to PANTS
   (B) EARRING is to EAR
   (C) GLOVES is to FINGERS
   (D) SCARF is to WINTER
   (E) TISSUE is to NOSE

2. GAUGE is to MEASURE as
   (A) FURNACE is to HEAT
   (B) TWINE is to TWIST
   (C) WOOD is to SPLINTER
   (D) HAMMER is to LEVEL
   (E) SPEEDOMETER is to RACE

3. CRUEL is to COMPASSION as CRAVEN is to
   (A) PEEVISHNESS
   (B) STRENGTH
   (C) DESIRE
   (D) COURAGE
   (E) FAME

4. BLUSH is to EMBARRASSMENT as
   (A) SNEER is to DISDAIN
   (B) TREMBLE is to TEMERITY
   (C) BLANCH is to HEALTH
   (D) FROWN is to CONTENTMENT
   (E) LAUGH is to IRRITATION

5. IMMOBILE is to MOVE as
   (A) ANONYMOUS is to ANNOUNCE
   (B) SILLY is to LAUGH
   (C) REPARABLE is to FIX
   (D) INEDIBLE is to EAT
   (E) STIFF is to BEND

6. SOLACE is to MOURNER as CONGRATULATIONS is to
   (A) LOSER
   (B) JUDGE
   (C) INCUMBENT
   (D) VICTOR
   (E) SPECTATOR

7. NATION is to ALLIANCE as
   (A) TECHNOLOGY is to COMPUTER
   (B) POSTER is to LADDER
   (C) CURRENT is to CHASM
   (D) SCHOOL is to DESK
   (E) STRUT is to WING

8. METEOROLOGY is to WEATHER as
   (A) TELMATOLOGY is to TELEVISION
   (B) PSYSCHOLOGY is to BEHAVIOR
   (C) ETYMOLOGY is to DEFINITIONS
   (D) EMBRYOLOGY is to SENILITY
   (E) SCIENTOLOGY is to SCIENTISTS

9. DECIPHER is to CODE as
   (A) SOLVE is to EQUATION
   (B) LAUNCH is to MISSION
   (C) FINISH is to CONCLUSION
   (D) INTERRUPT is to INTERMISSION
   (E) EXAMINE is to EVIDENCE

Go on to next page

10. SOLITARY is to COMPANIONSHIP as THRIFTY is to
    (A) CHEAPNESS
    (B) MONEY
    (C) PRODIGALITY
    (D) POVERTY
    (E) FRIENDLINESS

11. ARENA is to COMPETITION as
    (A) GUEST is to HOTEL
    (B) ARTWORK is to MUSEUM
    (C) TRAIN is to TRACK
    (D) HOSPITAL is to SURGERY
    (E) BARRACKS is to BASE

12. DECIBEL is to SOUND as
    (A) FOOT is to RULER
    (B) POUND is to SCALE
    (C) MASS is to GRAM
    (D) KILOGRAM is to METRIC
    (E) OUNCE is to WEIGHT

13. HUNGRY is to RAVENOUS as IMPROPER is to
    (A) COLD
    (B) OUTRAGEOUS
    (C) POLITE
    (D) GORGEOUS
    (E) ACTIVE

14. WORD is to VOCABULARY as
    (A) GOOSE is to GANDER
    (B) TRACTOR is to PLOW
    (C) ISLAND is to ARCHIPELAGO
    (D) PARAGRAPH is to SENTENCE
    (E) ELECTRONICS is to MEDIA

15. PURIFY is to IMPERFECTION as
    (A) MAGNIFY is to MINUTAE
    (B) RAREFY is to UBIQUITY
    (C) DETOXIFY is to POISON
    (D) GLORIFY is to FAME
    (E) PERSONIFY is to EPITOME

16. WEAVER is to FABRIC as WRITER is to
    (A) PAPER
    (B) TEXT
    (C) PUNCTUATION
    (D) GRAMMAR
    (E) SYLLABLE

17. SEXTANT is to NAVIGATE as
    (A) ABYSS is to DEEPEN
    (B) SCALPEL is to HEAL
    (C) BAROMETER is to HUMIDIFY
    (D) LUNG is to CIRCULATE
    (E) CAMOUFLAGE is to MIMIC

18. PUNDIT is to EXPERTISE as
    (A) SCHOLAR is to ERUDITION
    (B) JUDGE is to DECISION
    (C) DONOR is to FAIRNESS
    (D) ORATOR is to LOQUACIOUSNESS
    (E) DOLT is to DISCERNMENT

19. DESICCATE is to MOISTURE as SAP is to
    (A) TRICK
    (B) ENERGY
    (C) PORTION
    (D) VECTOR
    (E) ANALYSIS

20. BUFFOON is to FOOLISH as
    (A) SOLDIER is to RECKLESS
    (B) TEACHER is to WISE
    (C) BOOR is to CRASS
    (D) DERELICT is to OPULENT
    (E) NURSE is to PATIENT

21. MOROSE is to JOLLITY as
    (A) BIGOTED is to INTRANSIGENCE
    (B) INFECTED is to ILLNESS
    (C) ARGUMENTATIVE is to EVIDENCE
    (D) ARROGANT is to HUMILITY
    (E) ECSTATIC is to JOY

Go on to next page

22. CHARLATAN is to FRAUD as TRICKSTER is to
    (A) SINCERITY
    (B) ABSTRACTION
    (C) CHICANERY
    (D) ABSOLUTION
    (E) DIDACTICISM

23. CONFLAGRATION is to FIRE as
    (A) OCEAN is to WAVE
    (B) ICE is to GLACIER
    (C) CHANDELIER is to CANDLE
    (D) PLATEAU is to LANDSCAPE
    (E) MANSION is to RESIDENCE

24. AUDACIOUS is to TREPIDATION as
    (A) TACITURN is to GARRULOUSNESS
    (B) REVERENTIAL is to RESPECT
    (C) DANGEROUS is to PERIL
    (D) EVOLVING is to GROWTH
    (E) INSIGNIFICANT is to TRIVIALITY

25. ASSUAGE is to SORROW as DAMPEN is to
    (A) DISILLUSIONMENT
    (B) GRIEF
    (C) PRECIPITATION
    (D) ENTHUSIASM
    (E) ENERVATION

STOP DO NOT TURN THE PAGE UNTIL TOLD TO DO SO.
DO NOT RETURN TO A PREVIOUS TEST.

Arithmetic Reasoning

Time: 29 minutes for 25 questions

Directions: The questions in this section are designed to measure your general mathematical reasoning ability. They are word problems based on essential arithmetic skills. Choose the best answer for each question from the answer choices provided and shade in the corresponding oval on your answer sheet.

1. Frank runs a distance of $5\frac{1}{2}$ miles by running 22 laps around a circular track. How long is one lap of the track?

   (A) 4 miles

   (B) 2.5 miles

   (C) 0.4 miles

   (D) 0.25 miles

2. The local paper sold 400 classified ads at $7.50 each. How much was received from the sale of these ads?

   (A) $30

   (B) $300

   (C) $330

   (D) $3,000

3. Quality control supervisors at a cookie factory inspect a sample of 50 cookies from each batch of 5,000 to determine whether the sandwich cookie was assembled correctly. They find defects in 3 cookies. Based on this, how many cookies from the full batch of cookies should they expect to be defective?

   (A) 300

   (B) 50

   (C) 30

   (D) 15

4. If 48 pounds of popcorn are packed into bags, each holding $\frac{3}{4}$ of a pound, how many bags will be needed?

   (A) 12

   (B) 16

   (C) 36

   (D) 64

5. You buy a suit at a shop that is offering $75 off all suits. After you choose your suit, the $75 is deducted from the price and then 6% sales tax is added to the reduced cost. If your final bill is $343.44, what was the original price of the suit?

   (A) $393.33

   (B) $397.83

   (C) $399.00

   (D) $400.00

6. If the speed of sound is slightly more than 900 feet per second, how fast would you be traveling if you reached Mach 4, or 4 times the speed of sound?

   (A) 225 feet per second

   (B) 360 feet per second

   (C) 3,600 feet per second

   (D) 36,000 feet per second

7. Chris can paint a room in 3 hours. Tom can paint the same room in 2 hours. If they work together, how long will it take them to paint the room?

   (A) 300 minutes

   (B) 72 minutes

   (C) 60 minutes

   (D) 50 minutes

8. In last week's primary election, the incumbent received 15,412 votes and the challenger received 9,962 votes. By how many votes did the incumbent win?

   (A) 545

   (B) 5,450

   (C) 6,550

   (D) 25,374

Go on to next page

9. Three people, working together, can unload a truck in 2 hours. If 12 trucks must be unloaded within 8 hours, how many people should be assigned to the job?

   (A) 2

   (B) 6

   (C) 9

   (D) 12

10. A recipe for 3 dozen cookies calls for 2 eggs. If you have a dozen eggs, how many cookies can you make?

    (A) 18

    (B) 36

    (C) 216

    (D) 432

11. You need to paint the exterior of a house that is 50 feet wide, 120 feet long, and 25 feet high. The house has 2 doors, each 4 feet by 9 feet, and 30 windows, each 4 feet by 5 feet. If a gallon of paint covers 175 square feet, how many gallons will you need?

    (A) 49

    (B) 45

    (C) 44

    (D) 23

12. Bulbs are planted in 3 rows with 8 bulbs in each row. If bulbs sell for 4 for $3, how much will the planting cost?

    (A) $6

    (B) $12

    (C) $18

    (D) $36

13. A potted palm tree in Katarina's apartment just touches the ceiling that is 8 feet high. If the pot in which the tree is planted is 20 inches tall, how tall is the part of the tree that extends above the pot?

    (A) 6 feet 4 inches

    (B) 7 feet 8 inches

    (C) 9 feet 8 inches

    (D) 12 feet

14. The washers at the Laundromat cost $1.50 per wash load, and the dryers give 6 minutes of time for 25 cents. Suzi generally runs one load of colored clothes and one of whites, but she finds that she can put both loads into one dryer if she runs it for at least 45 minutes. If she picks up $10 worth of quarters before heading to the Laundromat, how much will she have left when the laundry is done?

    (A) $5.00

    (B) $6.50

    (C) $6.75

    (D) $8.25

15. During contract negotiations, $\frac{7}{8}$ of the union members voted on a new contract proposal. Of those voting, $\frac{2}{3}$ voted to approve the contract. If the union has 3,600 members, how many voted to approve?

    (A) 1,200

    (B) 1,500

    (C) 2,100

    (D) 2,400

16. A type of brass is composed of 70% copper, 25% zinc, and 5% nickel, by weight. If a sample of this brass weighs 120 pounds, how many pounds of nickel does it contain?

    (A) 5 pounds

    (B) 6 pounds

    (C) 30 pounds

    (D) 60 pounds

17. Mrs. Zhang drives 60 miles at a constant speed. If her trip takes 72 minutes, what is her speed in miles per hour?

    (A) 40

    (B) 50

    (C) 60

    (D) 70

Go on to next page

18. In a recent survey, voters in Hank's town were asked what political party they voted for most often. Six hundred people indicated that they voted Republican. If this represents about three-fifths of the town's voters, how many voters are there in the town?

(A) 200

(B) 360

(C) 1,000

(D) 1,800

19. If a charter airline flies planes that each holds 220 people, how many planes will the airline need for a charter group of 1,100 passengers?

(A) 3

(B) 4

(C) 5

(D) 6

20. Raul loaned his brother $8,000 with the agreement that his brother would repay the loan with interest after 5 years. At the end of 5 years, Raul's brother paid him $9,200. What was the annual interest rate Raul charged his brother?

(A) 1.15%

(B) 3%

(C) 15%

(D) 18.4%

21. If 1 package of frozen lasagna serves 4 people, how many packages will be needed to serve 20 people?

(A) 5

(B) 10

(C) 20

(D) 80

22. If your heart beats 65 times a minute, how many times does it beat in an hour?

(A) 108

(B) 125

(C) 3,900

(D) 23,400

23. A car that sells for $20,000 loses 17% of its value in the first year. What is the value of the car after a year?

(A) $3,000

(B) $3,400

(C) $16,600

(D) $17,000

24. Kijana is considering whether to buy or lease a new car. The car he wants sells for $20,000. He could lease the car by making a first payment of $2,500 and then paying $375 a month after that. After how many months will the cost of leasing exceed the cost of buying the car?

(A) 48

(B) 47

(C) 46

(D) 45

25. What is the cost of carpeting a room that measures 12 feet by 18 feet if carpet costs $15 per square yard?

(A) $3,240

(B) $1,080

(C) $360

(D) $120

STOP DO NOT TURN THE PAGE UNTIL TOLD TO DO SO. DO NOT RETURN TO A PREVIOUS TEST.

Word Knowledge

Time: 5 minutes for 25 questions

Directions: This section of the test measures your knowledge of words and their meanings. For each question, choose the word that is closest in meaning to the capitalized word and shade in the corresponding oval on your answer sheet.

1. CURTAIL
    (A) shorten
    (B) hang
    (C) enliven
    (D) hamper
    (E) reprimand

2. IRATE
    (A) tame
    (B) empathetic
    (C) angry
    (D) thrifty
    (E) generous

3. HEDONISTIC
    (A) dull-witted
    (B) self-aware
    (C) pleasure-seeking
    (D) emotionally-deprived
    (E) ultra-ambitious

4. QUANDARY
    (A) speculation
    (B) captivity
    (C) curiosity
    (D) ecstasy
    (E) predicament

5. STINGY
    (A) pragmatic
    (B) extravagant
    (C) reliable
    (D) frugal
    (E) inhibited

6. PAUCITY
    (A) abundance
    (B) scarcity
    (C) pride
    (D) ignorance
    (E) anxiety

7. TIMOROUS
    (A) belligerent
    (B) weary
    (C) disappointed
    (D) energetic
    (E) fearful

8. VERACITY
    (A) dignity
    (B) truthfulness
    (C) urbanity
    (D) obsession
    (E) pleasure

9. RELEGATE
    (A) demote
    (B) decline
    (C) defend
    (D) defile
    (E) denounce

10. PRUDENT
    (A) disturbed
    (B) extroverted
    (C) cautious
    (D) punctual
    (E) regular

Go on to next page

11. MUNIFICENT
    (A) reserved
    (B) amiable
    (C) malicious
    (D) generous
    (E) gullible

12. FLOUT
    (A) distend
    (B) repel
    (C) blame
    (D) liberate
    (E) defy

13. JOVIAL
    (A) stubborn
    (B) dejected
    (C) sneaky
    (D) cheery
    (E) foolish

14. ELUDE
    (A) romanticize
    (B) predict
    (C) escape
    (D) anticipate
    (E) distort

15. DEARTH
    (A) dexterity
    (B) awkwardness
    (C) lack
    (D) sage
    (E) warmth

16. COERCE
    (A) suppress
    (B) force
    (C) applaud
    (D) value
    (E) define

17. BERATE
    (A) reprimand
    (B) reprise
    (C) reinforce
    (D) reduce
    (E) revise

18. ARDENT
    (A) bitter
    (B) passionate
    (C) insincere
    (D) aimless
    (E) minimal

19. AFFABLE
    (A) solitary
    (B) furtive
    (C) good-natured
    (D) dull
    (E) mean-spirited

20. DIVULGE
    (A) trust
    (B) separate
    (C) withdraw
    (D) reveal
    (E) waste

21. PRISTINE
    (A) tranquil
    (B) pure
    (C) stealthy
    (D) prudish
    (E) dilatory

22. NEOPHYTE
    (A) beginner
    (B) donor
    (C) compromiser
    (D) arbiter
    (E) orator

Go on to next page

23. PERVASIVE
    (A) negligent
    (B) flexible
    (C) elusive
    (D) elementary
    (E) widespread

24. VAPID
    (A) quarrelsome
    (B) gentle
    (C) bland
    (D) strict
    (E) chatty

25. TACITURN
    (A) garrulous
    (B) pious
    (C) baffling
    (D) quiet
    (E) exclusive

STOP DO NOT TURN THE PAGE UNTIL TOLD TO DO SO.
DO NOT RETURN TO A PREVIOUS TEST.

Mathematics Knowledge

Time: 22 minutes for 25 questions

Directions: The questions in this section are designed to measure your understanding of the mathematics you studied in school. They include concepts from arithmetic, algebra, and geometry. Choose the best answer for each question from the choices provided and shade in the corresponding oval on your answer sheet.

1. The area of a rectangle 25 feet wide and 40 feet long is
   (A) 100 ft^2
   (B) 130 ft^2
   (C) $1,000 \text{ ft}^2$
   (D) $1,300 \text{ ft}^2$

2. $3x^2y(4x-5y) =$
   (A) $-3x^2y^2$
   (B) $12x^3y - 15x^2y^2$
   (C) $12x^2y - 15x^2y^2$
   (D) $12x^3y - 15x^2y$

3. The members in the marching band find that if they organize into rows with 5 members in each row, 1 person is left over. If they form rows of 6 people, they still have 1 person left over. Which of these could be the number of band members?
   (A) 131
   (B) 141
   (C) 151
   (D) 161

4. Which of the following numbers is prime?
   (A) 27
   (B) 47
   (C) 57
   (D) 77

5. If $\triangle RST$ and trapezoid $WXYZ$ are cut off the polygon in the following figure, what polygon is left?

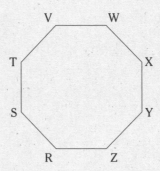

   (A) trapezoid
   (B) rectangle
   (C) pentagon
   (D) hexagon

6. If $2a - 3b = -1$ and $a - b = 2$, then $b =$
   (A) 3
   (B) 5
   (C) 7
   (D) 9

7. Jorge wants to use some of his leftover boards to enclose a triangular section of land as a flower garden. He has chosen boards for two of the sides of the triangle. One is 3 feet long and the other is 5 feet long. He has other boards of different lengths to choose from for the third side. Which length board could NOT make the third side of the triangle?
   (A) 2 feet
   (B) 3 feet
   (C) 5 feet
   (D) 7 feet

Go on to next page

8. $3^r \cdot 2^r \cdot 6^t =$

   (A) 6^{r+t}

   (B) 6^{rt}

   (C) 12^{rt}

   (D) 36^{r+t}

9. A teacher needs to give each of her students 1 sheet each of red and yellow paper for an art project. The red paper comes in packs of 12 sheets but the yellow paper comes in packs of 15 sheets. The teacher buys the minimum number of packs of each paper that will guarantee equal amounts of each color. How many students can complete the project?

   (A) 27

   (B) 30

   (C) 54

   (D) 60

10. If $\frac{1}{2}x - \frac{3}{5} = \frac{1}{3}x + \frac{1}{4}$, then $x =$

    (A) 0.42

    (B) 1.02

    (C) 2.1

    (D) 5.1

11. Alberto saves $12 each week. Dahlia already has saved $270 and each week she spends $15 of that savings. When they both have the same amount in savings, they combine their money. What is the combined amount?

    (A) $120

    (B) $216

    (C) $240

    (D) $432

12. If $x^2 - 7x + 12 = 0$, then $x =$

    (A) $x = -3$ or $x = 4$

    (B) $x = 3$ or $x = -4$

    (C) $x = -3$ or $x = -4$

    (D) $x = 3$ or $x = 4$

13. If the cost of manufacturing storage containers is $580 plus 18 cents per container, what is the cost of manufacturing 5,000 containers?

    (A) $900

    (B) $1,480

    (C) $29,000

    (D) $90,580

14. The simplest form of

    $$3ab^3 - 4ab^2 + 2a^2b^2 - \left(4a^2b + 3ab^2 - ab^3\right)$$

    is which of the following?

    (A) $4ab^3 - 7ab^2 - 2a^2b^2$

    (B) $-ab^3 - ab^2 - 2a^2b^2$

    (C) $4ab^3 - 7ab^2 + 2a^2b^2 - 4a^2b$

    (D) $2ab^3 + ab^2 + 2a^2b^2 - 4a^2b$

15. At the moment that a 35-foot maple tree casts a shadow 7 feet long, how long is the shadow of a 6-foot man in inches?

    (A) 1.2

    (B) 5.83

    (C) 14.4

    (D) 30

16. If $5^{2x-1} = 125$, then $7^{x-3} =$

    (A) $\frac{1}{7}$

    (B) 7

    (C) 49

    (D) -7

17. A worker assembling toy cars must place four wheels on each car body. If the worker has 432 car bodies and 1,584 wheels available, how many complete toy cars can he assemble?

    (A) 396

    (B) 432

    (C) 1,152

    (D) 1,584

Go on to next page

18. The sum of the measures of the angles of a hexagon is
    (A) 180°
    (B) 360°
    (C) 540°
    (D) 720°

19. How many cubic feet of packing foam will fit in a shipping carton 2 feet long, 3 feet wide, and 16 inches high?
    (A) 8
    (B) 9
    (C) 96
    (D) 1,152

20. Find the distance between two points on a graph that are represented by $(6, -3)$ and $(-6, 2)$.
    (A) 5
    (B) 12.04
    (C) 13
    (D) 17

21. If the radius of a circle is doubled, by what percent does the area increase?
    (A) 400%
    (B) 300%
    (C) 200%
    (D) 100%

22. A bag contains balls and blocks in various colors. If $\frac{3}{4}$ of the objects in the bag are balls and $\frac{2}{5}$ of the objects are red, what fraction would you expect to be red balls?
    (A) $\frac{3}{10}$
    (B) $\frac{7}{20}$
    (C) $\frac{8}{15}$
    (D) $\frac{23}{20}$

23. If 8,974 and 4,905 are rounded to the nearest hundred and then added, what is the sum?
    (A) 13,800
    (B) 13,879
    (C) 13,900
    (D) 14,000

24. Temperatures in degrees Celsius can be converted to degrees Fahrenheit with the formula $F = \frac{9}{5}C + 32$. Find the Fahrenheit equivalent of a temperature of 20° Celsius.
    (A) 68° Fahrenheit
    (B) 93.6° Fahrenheit
    (C) 42.4° Fahrenheit
    (D) $-6.\overline{6}°$ Fahrenheit

25. Express the sentence "Six more than three times a number, x, is twenty-seven" as an equation.
    (A) $6 > 3x + 27$
    (B) $3x + 6 = 27$
    (C) $6x + 3 = 27$
    (D) $x = 27 \times 3 + 6$

STOP DO NOT TURN THE PAGE UNTIL TOLD TO DO SO.
DO NOT RETURN TO A PREVIOUS TEST.

Chapter 19

AFOQT Academic Aptitude Practice Test: Answers and Explanations

● ●

After you've tried your hand at the first practice test, you're ready to see how you did. In this chapter, you can find the answers to the practice Air Force Officer Qualifying Test (AFOQT) in Chapter 18. We provide the answers in two different formats: with detailed explanation and in a bare-bones answer key. We suggest you read through the detailed answers for each question to get the most out of your studies, but if you're running low on time and simply need the answers, take a look at the answer key at the end of the chapter. If you're feeling a little fuzzy on any of the questions on this test, check out Parts II and III. We discuss verbal and reading skills in Part II and math and arithmetic in Part III.

Verbal Analogies Answers

1. **C.** A helmet is used to protect the head; gloves protect the fingers. None of the other choices fits the "is used to protect" relationship sentence.

2. **A.** A gauge is used to measure; a furnace is used to heat. None of the other choices fits the "is used to" relationship sentence.

3. **D.** A cruel person lack compassion; a craven person lacks courage. Don't be misled into choosing "strength." A craven person may be strong but cowardly. None of the other choices fits the "lacks" relationship sentence.

4. **A.** A blush is a sign of embarrassment; a sneer is a sign of disdain (scorn). None of the other choices fits the "is a sign of" relationship sentence.

5. **E.** Something immobile is unable to move; something stiff is unable to bend. None of the other choices fits the "is unable to" relationship sentence. Don't be tricked by Choice (D), "inedible is to eat." You can't eat something inedible, but that isn't the relationship sentence. You can't say "something inedible is unable to eat."

6. **D.** Solace is offered to a mourner; congratulations are offered to a victor. None of the other choices fits the "is offered to" relationship sentence.

7. **E.** A nation is part of an alliance; a strut is part of a wing. None of the other choices fits the "is a part of" relationship sentence.

8. **B.** Meteorology is the study of weather; psychology is the study of behavior. Telmatology is the study of swamps; etymology is the study of word origins; embryology is the study of embryos; scientology is a religion created by L. Ron Hubbard.

9. **A.** To decipher is to figure out a code; to solve is to figure out an equation. None of the other choices fits the "to figure out" relationship sentence.

10. **C.** A solitary person lacks companionship; a thrifty person lacks prodigality (wastefulness). Don't be tricked by cheapness, money, and poverty — words often associated with thriftiness. These words don't fit into the "lacks" relationship sentence.

11. **D.** An arena is a location where competition takes place; a hospital is a location where surgery takes place. None of the other choices fits into the "is a location where something takes place" relationship.

12. **E.** A decibel is a unit of sound; an ounce is a unit of weight. None of the other choices (although they're closely related words) fits into the relationship of "is a unit of."

13. **B.** Hungry to an extreme degree is ravenous; improper to an extreme degree is outrageous. None of the other choices means extremely improper.

14. **C.** A word is part of vocabulary; an island is part of an archipelago. None of the other choices fits into the "is part of" relationship sentence.

15. **C.** To purify is to remove imperfection; to detoxify is to remove poison. None of the other choices fits into the "is to remove" relationship sentence.

16. **B.** A weaver makes (or creates) fabric; a writer makes (or creates) text. Some of the other choices may be tempting because they're often associated with writers; however, text is what the writer creates just as fabric is what the weaver creates.

17. **E.** A sextant is used to navigate; camouflage is used to mimic. None of the other choices fits into the "is used to" relationship sentence.

18. **A.** A pundit is someone known to have expertise; a scholar is someone known to have erudition (scholarliness). None of the other choices fits into the "is known to have" relationship sentence.

19. **B.** To desiccate is to remove moisture; to sap is to remove energy. None of the other choices fits into the "is to remove" relationship sentence.

20. **C.** A buffoon is known for being foolish; a boor is known for being crass (ill-mannered). Of course, you must know the vocabulary for this question. A *buffoon* is a clown or a foolish person; a *boor* is a crass, ill-mannered person. None of the other choices fits into the "is known for being" relationship sentence.

21. **D.** Someone morose lacks jollity; someone arrogant lacks humility. *Morose* means gloomy, and *jollity* is cheeriness. None of the other choices fits into the "lacks" relationship sentence.

22. **C.** A charlatan engages in fraud; a trickster engages in chicanery (trickery). Again, you must know the vocabulary to correctly answer this question. A *charlatan* is a quack or fraud; *chicanery* is deceptiveness. None of the other choices fits the "engages in" relationship sentence.

23. **E.** A conflagration is a large fire; a mansion is a large residence. None of the other choices fits the "is a large" relationship sentence.

24. **A.** Someone who's audacious lacks trepidation; someone who's taciturn lacks garrulousness. None of the other choices fits the "lacks" relationship sentence.

25. **D.** To assuage is to lessen someone's sorrow; to dampen is to lessen someone's enthusiasm. *Assuage* means to relieve or ease. None of the other choices fits into the relationship sentence.

Arithmetic Reasoning Answers

1. **D.** $5\frac{1}{2}$ miles divided by 22 laps is $5\frac{1}{2} \div 22 = \frac{11}{2} \cdot \frac{1}{22} = \frac{1}{4} = 0.25$ miles.

2. **D.** Multiply the price of an ad by the number of ads sold: $400 \times \$7.50 = \$3,000$.

3. **A.** If 3 of 50 cookies were defective, the supervisors would expect a similar proportion of the whole batch to be defective. Here's the proportion you would set up: $\frac{3}{50} = \frac{x}{5,000}$. Cross-multiply to get $50x = 15,000$, and then divide each side by 50 to find that $x = 300$.

4. **D.** Divide the amount of popcorn by the size of the bag to find the number of bags needed. $48 \div \frac{3}{4} = \frac{\overset{16}{48}}{1} \times \frac{4}{3} = 64$. Estimation also can eliminate choices for you. If the bags held 1 pound, 48 bags would be needed. If the bags were smaller, more bags would be needed.

5. **C.** If x is the price of the suit, the reduced price is $x - 75$. To find the amount with the tax, change 6% to 0.06, add 1 (100% of the cost), and multiply $1.06(x - 75)$, setting that equal to 343.44. Solve the equation $1.06(x - 75) = 343.44$ to find the value of x. Distribute to remove the parentheses, like so: $1.06x - 79.50 = 343.44$. Add 79.50 to 343.44 to get $1.06x = 422.94$. Divide both sides by 1.06 to get $x = 399$. As you can see, the original price of the suit is $399.

6. **C.** Four times the speed of sound is four times 900 feet per second: $900 \times 4 = 3,600$ feet per second.

7. **B.** In one hour, Chris can paint $\frac{1}{3}$ of the room, and Tom can paint $\frac{1}{2}$ of the room. So working together they can paint $\frac{1}{3} + \frac{1}{2} = \frac{2+3}{6} = \frac{5}{6}$ of the room. To paint the whole room, they need $1 \div \frac{5}{6} = 1 \cdot \frac{6}{5} = 1\frac{1}{5}$ hours, or $1\frac{1}{5} \times 60 = 72$ minutes.

8. **B.** Subtract to find the margin of victory: $15,412 - 9,962 = 5,450$ votes.

9. **C.** If 3 people can unload 1 truck in 2 hours, then 3 people would need 24 hours to unload 12 trucks. If only 8 hours are available, 3 teams of 3 people each are needed. In other words, to get the job done in the required time, you need to assign 9 people.

10. **C.** First, determine how many cookies a batch makes: 3 dozen $\times$ 12 cookies in a dozen = 36 cookies. A dozen eggs $\div$ 2 eggs = 6 batches. 36 cookies per batch $\times$ 6 batches = 216 cookies.

11. **B.** The exterior of the house has two sides that measure 50 feet by 25 feet and two that measure 120 feet by 25 feet. That's a total area of $2 \times 50 \times 25 + 2 \times 120 \times 25 = 2,500 + 6,000 = 8,500$ square feet. You won't paint the windows or the doors, so figure the measurements of the doors and windows and subtract them from the total: $2 \times 4 \times 9 + 30 \times 4 \times 5 = 72 + 600 = 672$ square feet are doors and windows. So you know that $8,500 - 672 = 7,828$ square feet need to be painted. Divide by 175 to find the number of gallons of paint (each gallon covers 175 square feet). Be sure to round up, because you can't buy part of a gallon. $7,828 \div 175 \approx 44.7$, so you need 45 gallons of paint.

12. **C.** 3 rows $\times$ 8 bulbs per row = 24 bulbs. 24 bulbs $\div$ 4 bulbs for $3 = 6 groups. 6 groups $\times$ $3 = $18.

13. **A.** 8 feet − 20 inches = 7 feet 12 inches − 1 foot 8 inches = 6 feet 4 inches.

14. **A.** First, determine how much it costs Suzi to do the wash: 2 washers $\times$ $1.50 = $3. Then figure out how many quarters for the dryer: 45 minutes needed for the dryer $\div$ 6 minutes for each quarter = 7.5 quarters. But, of course, that rounds up to 8. Next, calculate how much 8 quarters is in dollars: $8 \times 0.25 = $2. Now total them up: $3 for the washers + $2 for the dryers = $5 to wash and dry. If Suzi had $10 worth of quarters and spent $5 to do the laundry, she has $5 left.

15. **C.** $\frac{7}{8} \times 3{,}600^{450} = 3{,}150$ of the union members voted. $\frac{2}{3} \times 3{,}150^{1{,}050} = 2{,}100$ voted to approve the contract.

16. **B.** The brass is 5% nickel, so figure what 5% of the 120 pounds is: $0.05 \times 120 = 6$. As you can see, 6 pounds are nickel.

17. **B.** $\frac{^5 \, 60 \text{ miles}}{_6 \, 72 \text{ minutes}} \times \frac{60^{10} \text{ minutes}}{1 \text{ hour}} = 50$ mph. Therefore, Mrs. Zhang traveled 50 miles per hour.

18. **C.** $600 \div \frac{3}{5} = \frac{^{200} \, 600}{1} \times \frac{5}{3} = 1{,}000$. Thus, 1,000 people are in the town.

19. **C.** $\frac{1{,}100}{220} = \frac{110 \div 11}{22 \div 11} = \frac{10}{2} = 5$. So 5 planes are needed.

20. **B.** Raul's brother returned the $8,000 plus $1,200 interest. According to the formula $I = P \times r \times t$, $1{,}200 = 8{,}000 \times r \times 5$ years. Simplify to get $1{,}200 = 40{,}000 \times r$. Divide both sides by 40,000 to find that $r = \frac{1{,}200}{40{,}000} = \frac{3}{100} = 3\%$.

21. **A.** 20 people ÷ 4 people per package = 5 packages.

22. **C.** $\frac{65 \text{ beats}}{1 \text{ minute}} \times \frac{60 \text{ minutes}}{1 \text{ hour}} = \frac{3{,}900 \text{ beats}}{1 \text{ hour}}$.

23. **C.** Start by calculating the part of the value lost in the first year (keeping in mind that 17% = 0.17): $20{,}000 \times 0.17 = 3{,}400$. The value of the car after a year is $20{,}000 - 3{,}400 = 16{,}600$. Alternately, you could consider that if the car loses 17% of its value, it holds 100% – 17% = 83% of its value. You can then figure that 83% of $20,000 is $16,600.

24. **B.** The cost of the lease is $2{,}500 + 375x$, where x is the number of months. Solve $2{,}500 + 375x \ge 20{,}000$ by subtracting 2,500 to get $375x \ge 17{,}500$, and then divide to find $x \ge 46\frac{2}{3}$. The cost of leasing exceeds the cost of buying by the 47th month.

25. **C.** The dimensions of the room are given in feet, but carpeting is sold by the square yard. So, to begin, conversion is necessary. There are 3 feet in a yard, so 12 feet are equal to 4 yards and 18 feet to 6 yards. Multiplying 4 yards by 6 yards gives you 24 square yards. Multiply 24 square yards by $15 per square yard to get $360. Alternately, you could multiply 12 feet by 18 feet and then divide by 9 feet per square yard to get the number of square yards. The problem with this method is that many people forget there are 9 square feet in each square yard.

Word Knowledge Answers

1. **A.** *Curtail* (verb) means to shorten.

2. **C.** *Irate* (adjective) means very angry.

3. **C.** *Hedonistic* (adjective) means pleasure-seeking.

4. **E.** A *quandary* (noun) is a predicament or dilemma.

5. **D.** *Stingy* (adjective) means frugal.

6. **B.** *Paucity* (noun) means a lack or scarcity.

7. **E.** *Timorous* (adjective) means fearful (think "timid").

8. **B.** *Veracity* (noun) means truthfulness (the root *veri* means "truth").

9. **A.** *Relegate* (verb) means to demote or move to a lower position.

10. **C.** *Prudent* (adjective) means cautious or careful.

11. **D.** *Munificent* (adjective) means generous.

12. **E.** *Flout* (verb) means to defy or show contempt for.

13. **D.** *Jovial* (adjective) means jolly or cheery.

14. **C.** *Elude* (verb) means to escape or avoid capture.

15. **C.** *Dearth* (noun) means a scarcity or lack.

16. **B.** *Coerce* (verb) means to convince using force.

17. **A.** *Berate* (verb) means to scold or reprimand.

18. **B.** *Ardent* (adjective) means passionate.

19. **C.** *Affable* (adjective) means good-natured or sociable.

20. **D.** *Divulge* (verb) means to reveal or tell.

21. **B.** *Pristine* (adjective) means pure and untouched.

22. **A.** A *neophyte* (noun) is a beginner.

23. **E.** *Pervasive* (adjective) means widespread or common.

24. **C.** *Vapid* (adjective) means bland or dull.

25. **D.** *Taciturn* (adjective) means quiet or uncommunicative.

Mathematics Knowledge Answers

1. **C.** The area of a rectangle is the product of the length and the width: $A = 25 \times 40 = 1,000$ ft^2.

2. **B.** With the distributive property, you get this answer:

$$3x^2y(4x - 5y)$$
$$= 3x^2y \cdot 4x - 3x^2y \cdot 5y$$
$$= 12x^3y - 15x^2y^2$$

3. **C.** The number of people in the band must be one more than a multiple of five but also one more than a multiple of six. So subtract one from each of the answer choices and consider their divisors. All are multiples of five. A number is divisible by six if it's divisible by both two and three. All the choices are divisible by two, so test for divisibility by three by adding the digits. If the sum of the digits is divisible by three, the number is divisible by three. $1 + 3 + 0 = 4$, $1 + 4 + 0 = 5$, $1 + 5 + 0 = 6$, and $1 + 6 + 0 = 7$. As you can see, only 150 is divisible by five and six, so there are 151 band members.

4. **B.** Both 27 and 57 are divisible by 3, because their digits add to a multiple of 3 ($2 + 7 = 9$ and $5 + 7 = 12$). Because 77 is divisible by 7 and 11, only 47 is prime.

5. **C.** Eliminate $\triangle RST$ and trapezoid *WXYZ* and count the sides of the remaining polygon. A polygon with five sides is a pentagon.

6. **B.** If $2a - 3b = -1$ and $a - b = 2$, then $a = 2 + b$ when you substitute, $2a - 3b = 2(2 + b) - 3b = -1$. Distribute and simplify: $4 + 2b - 3b = 4 - b = -1$. Solve $4 - b = -1$ to find $b = 5$ and $a = 7$.

7. **A.** The third side of a triangle must be less than the sum of the other two sides. All the answer choices fit that criterion. In order for that relationship to hold all the way around the triangle, however, the third side plus 3 feet long must be more than 5 feet. So a board 2 feet long won't do the job.

8. **A.** Here's how to solve:

$$3^r \cdot 2^r \cdot 6^t$$
$$= (3 \cdot 2)^r \cdot 6^t$$
$$= 6^r \cdot 6^t$$
$$= 6^{r+t}$$

9. **D.** You're looking for the least common multiple of 12 and 15. You could look at the prime factorization of each number to determine the least common multiple, but a quick list of multiples probably is faster. Multiples of 12 include 24, 36, 48, 60, 72, and more. Multiples of 15 include 30, 45, and 60. The first multiple on both lists is 60, so that's the number of sheets of each color of paper the teacher will buy.

10. **D.** Multiply $\frac{1}{2}x - \frac{3}{5} = \frac{1}{3}x + \frac{1}{4}$ by the common denominator of all the fractions.

$60\left(\frac{1}{2}x - \frac{3}{5}\right) = 60\left(\frac{1}{3}x + \frac{1}{4}\right)$ becomes $30x - 36 = 20x + 15$. Solve to find that $10x = 51$ and $x = 5.1$.

11. **C.** You can tackle this problem algebraically. Let x be the number of weeks until Alberto and Dahlia have the same amount of money. $12x = 270 - 15x$ means that $27x = 270$ and $x = 10$. They will have the same amount in 10 weeks, and at that time they'll each have $120. If they pool their money, they'll have $240.

12. **D.** Factor $x^2 - 7x + 12 = 0$ to $(x - 3)(x - 4) = 0$ and set each factor equal to zero. $x = 3$ or $x = 4$.

13. **B.** The cost is $580 + $0.18 \times 5,000 = 580 + 900 = $1,480$.

14. **C.** Here's how to simplify the problem:

$$3ab^3 - 4ab^2 + 2a^2b^2 - \left(4a^2b + 3ab^2 - ab^3\right)$$
$$= 3ab^3 - 4ab^2 + 2a^2b^2 - 4a^2b - 3ab^2 + ab^3$$
$$= 3ab^3 + ab^3 - 4ab^2 - 3ab^2 + 2a^2b^2 - 4a^2b$$
$$= 4ab^3 - 7ab^2 + 2a^2b^2 - 4a^2b$$

15. **C.** If a 35-foot maple tree casts a shadow 7 feet long, the length of the shadow is one-fifth the height of the tree. A 6-foot man is 72 inches tall. One-fifth of 72 is 14.4.

16. **A.** Because $125 = 5^3$, $5^{2x-1} = 5^3$, so $2x - 1 = 3$ and $x = 2$. Substitute $x = 2$ into $7^{x-3} = 7^{2-3} = 7^{-1} = \frac{1}{7}$.

17. **A.** The worker certainly can't make more than 432 cars, so you know that Choices (C) and (D) are out. The real question, then, is whether he has an adequate number of wheels to build all 432 cars. He has 1,584 wheels available, which, when divided by four (because each car needs four wheels), gives him 396 sets of wheels. Therefore, he can make 396 cars.

18. **D.** The sum of the measures of the angles of a hexagon is equal to the number of sides, reduced by 2, times 180°. The hexagon has 6 sides, so $(6 - 2) \cdot 180° = 4 \cdot 180° = 720°$.

19. **A.** Be careful to convert the 16 inches to feet before multiplying to find the volume. 16 inches are equivalent to $\frac{16}{12} = 1\frac{1}{3}$ feet. The carton can hold $2 \times 3 \times 1\frac{1}{3} = 2 \times \cancel{3} \times \frac{4}{\cancel{3}} = 8$ ft³.

20. **C.** The distance between $(6, -3)$ and $(-6, 2)$ is

$$\sqrt{(x_2 - x_1)^2 + (y_2 - y_1)^2}$$
$$= \sqrt{(-6 - 6)^2 + (2 - -3)^2}$$
$$= \sqrt{(-12)^2 + (2 + 3)^2}$$
$$= \sqrt{(-12)^2 + (5)^2}$$
$$= \sqrt{144 + 25}$$
$$= \sqrt{169}$$
$$= 13$$

21. **B.** If the radius of a circle is doubled, $A = \pi r^2$ becomes $A = \pi (2r)^2 = 4\pi r^2$. Don't be seduced by the 400%, however. The question is "by what percent does the area increase?" The increase is $4\pi r^2 - \pi r^2 = 3\pi r^2$. The percent increase is $\frac{\text{increase}}{\text{original}} = \frac{3\pi r^2}{\pi r^2} = 300\%$.

22. **A.** You should expect that if $\frac{3}{4}$ of the objects are balls and $\frac{2}{5}$ are red, $\frac{3}{2\cancel{4}} \times \frac{2}{5} = \frac{3}{10}$ will be red balls. Note that you can't be certain that this is the case, however. A bag with 15 balls and 5 blocks could have 5 red blocks and 3 red balls. It contains $\frac{3}{4}$ balls, and $\frac{2}{5}$ of the objects are red, but only $\frac{3}{20}$ are red balls. The expectation, however, would be that the red objects are proportionally spread over blocks and balls, so you expect that $\frac{2}{5}$ of the balls, or $\frac{2}{5}$ of $\frac{3}{4}$ of the objects, are red balls.

23. **C.** Rounded to the nearest hundred, 8,974 becomes 9,000; 4,905 becomes 4,900. Adding these together gives you 13,900.

24. **A.** $F = \frac{9}{5}C + 32 = \frac{9}{\cancel{5}}(\cancel{20})^4 + 32 = 36 + 32 = 68$.

25. **B.** Don't be misled by "more than"; the question asks for an equation, not an inequality. "Six more than" translates to adding six to "three times a number," or $3x$. The verb "is" translates to the equal sign, giving you $3x + 6 = 27$.

Answer Key for AFOQT Academic Aptitude Practice Test

Verbal Analogies

1. C	6. D	11. D	16. B	21. D
2. A	7. E	12. E	17. E	22. C
3. D	8. B	13. B	18. A	23. E
4. A	9. A	14. C	19. B	24. A
5. E	10. C	15. C	20. C	25. D

Arithmetic Reasoning

1. D	6. C	11. B	16. B	21. A
2. D	7. B	12. C	17. B	22. C
3. A	8. B	13. A	18. C	23. C
4. D	9. C	14. A	19. C	24. B
5. C	10. C	15. C	20. B	25. C

Word Knowledge

1. A	6. B	11. D	16. B	21. B
2. C	7. E	12. E	17. A	22. A
3. C	8. B	13. D	18. B	23. E
4. E	9. A	14. C	19. C	24. C
5. D	10. C	15. C	20. D	25. D

Mathematics Knowledge

1. C	6. B	11. C	16. A	21. B
2. B	7. A	12. D	17. A	22. A
3. C	8. A	13. B	18. D	23. C
4. B	9. D	14. C	19. A	24. A
5. C	10. D	15. C	20. C	25. B

Chapter 20

ASTB OAR Practice Test

• •

The U.S. Navy, Marine Corps, and Coast Guard use the Aviation Selection Test Battery Officer Aptitude Rating (ASTB OAR) as a component of the selection process for various pilot training programs and for selection into Officer Candidate School. This practice exam tests your skills on the Math Skills, Reading Skills, and Mechanical Comprehension subtests of the ASTB OAR.

As with the first practice test, you're better off treating this test as if it's the real thing. So, among other things (such as taking the test in a quiet room and without breaks), be sure to use a watch or clock to time yourself. Part of the challenge is completing each section in the allotted time. Mark your answers on the answer sheets provided. When you've completed the practice test, head to Chapter 21 to check your answers. We provide detailed explanations for all the answers as well as an abbreviated answer key.

Answer Sheet

Use the ovals provided with this practice test to record your answers.

Math Skills

1. Ⓐ Ⓑ Ⓒ Ⓓ	8. Ⓐ Ⓑ Ⓒ Ⓓ	15. Ⓐ Ⓑ Ⓒ Ⓓ	22. Ⓐ Ⓑ Ⓒ Ⓓ
2. Ⓐ Ⓑ Ⓒ Ⓓ	9. Ⓐ Ⓑ Ⓒ Ⓓ	16. Ⓐ Ⓑ Ⓒ Ⓓ	23. Ⓐ Ⓑ Ⓒ Ⓓ
3. Ⓐ Ⓑ Ⓒ Ⓓ	10. Ⓐ Ⓑ Ⓒ Ⓓ	17. Ⓐ Ⓑ Ⓒ Ⓓ	24. Ⓐ Ⓑ Ⓒ Ⓓ
4. Ⓐ Ⓑ Ⓒ Ⓓ	11. Ⓐ Ⓑ Ⓒ Ⓓ	18. Ⓐ Ⓑ Ⓒ Ⓓ	25. Ⓐ Ⓑ Ⓒ Ⓓ
5. Ⓐ Ⓑ Ⓒ Ⓓ	12. Ⓐ Ⓑ Ⓒ Ⓓ	19. Ⓐ Ⓑ Ⓒ Ⓓ	
6. Ⓐ Ⓑ Ⓒ Ⓓ	13. Ⓐ Ⓑ Ⓒ Ⓓ	20. Ⓐ Ⓑ Ⓒ Ⓓ	
7. Ⓐ Ⓑ Ⓒ Ⓓ	14. Ⓐ Ⓑ Ⓒ Ⓓ	21. Ⓐ Ⓑ Ⓒ Ⓓ	

Reading Skills

1. Ⓐ Ⓑ Ⓒ Ⓓ	8. Ⓐ Ⓑ Ⓒ Ⓓ	15. Ⓐ Ⓑ Ⓒ Ⓓ	22. Ⓐ Ⓑ Ⓒ Ⓓ
2. Ⓐ Ⓑ Ⓒ Ⓓ	9. Ⓐ Ⓑ Ⓒ Ⓓ	16. Ⓐ Ⓑ Ⓒ Ⓓ	23. Ⓐ Ⓑ Ⓒ Ⓓ
3. Ⓐ Ⓑ Ⓒ Ⓓ	10. Ⓐ Ⓑ Ⓒ Ⓓ	17. Ⓐ Ⓑ Ⓒ Ⓓ	24. Ⓐ Ⓑ Ⓒ Ⓓ
4. Ⓐ Ⓑ Ⓒ Ⓓ	11. Ⓐ Ⓑ Ⓒ Ⓓ	18. Ⓐ Ⓑ Ⓒ Ⓓ	25. Ⓐ Ⓑ Ⓒ Ⓓ
5. Ⓐ Ⓑ Ⓒ Ⓓ	12. Ⓐ Ⓑ Ⓒ Ⓓ	19. Ⓐ Ⓑ Ⓒ Ⓓ	26. Ⓐ Ⓑ Ⓒ Ⓓ
6. Ⓐ Ⓑ Ⓒ Ⓓ	13. Ⓐ Ⓑ Ⓒ Ⓓ	20. Ⓐ Ⓑ Ⓒ Ⓓ	27. Ⓐ Ⓑ Ⓒ Ⓓ
7. Ⓐ Ⓑ Ⓒ Ⓓ	14. Ⓐ Ⓑ Ⓒ Ⓓ	21. Ⓐ Ⓑ Ⓒ Ⓓ	

Mechanical Comprehension

1. Ⓐ Ⓑ Ⓒ Ⓓ	8. Ⓐ Ⓑ Ⓒ Ⓓ	15. Ⓐ Ⓑ Ⓒ Ⓓ	22. Ⓐ Ⓑ Ⓒ Ⓓ
2. Ⓐ Ⓑ Ⓒ Ⓓ	9. Ⓐ Ⓑ Ⓒ Ⓓ	16. Ⓐ Ⓑ Ⓒ Ⓓ	23. Ⓐ Ⓑ Ⓒ Ⓓ
3. Ⓐ Ⓑ Ⓒ Ⓓ	10. Ⓐ Ⓑ Ⓒ Ⓓ	17. Ⓐ Ⓑ Ⓒ Ⓓ	24. Ⓐ Ⓑ Ⓒ Ⓓ
4. Ⓐ Ⓑ Ⓒ Ⓓ	11. Ⓐ Ⓑ Ⓒ Ⓓ	18. Ⓐ Ⓑ Ⓒ Ⓓ	25. Ⓐ Ⓑ Ⓒ Ⓓ
5. Ⓐ Ⓑ Ⓒ Ⓓ	12. Ⓐ Ⓑ Ⓒ Ⓓ	19. Ⓐ Ⓑ Ⓒ Ⓓ	
6. Ⓐ Ⓑ Ⓒ Ⓓ	13. Ⓐ Ⓑ Ⓒ Ⓓ	20. Ⓐ Ⓑ Ⓒ Ⓓ	
7. Ⓐ Ⓑ Ⓒ Ⓓ	14. Ⓐ Ⓑ Ⓒ Ⓓ	21. Ⓐ Ⓑ Ⓒ Ⓓ	

Math Skills

Time: 25 minutes for 25 questions

Directions: The questions in this section are designed to measure your understanding of the mathematics you studied in school. They include concepts from arithmetic, algebra, and geometry. Choose the best answer for each question from the answer choices provided and shade in the corresponding oval on your answer sheet.

1. A case of 12 cans of soda costs $5.40. What is the cost of one can?

   (A) 43.5 cents

   (B) 44 cents

   (C) 45 cents

   (D) 45.5 cents

2. How long will it take to drive 420 miles at 60 miles per hour?

   (A) 8 hours

   (B) 7 hours

   (C) 6 hours

   (D) 5 hours

3. $6\frac{3}{8} \times 5\frac{1}{3} =$

   (A) $30\frac{1}{8}$

   (B) 34

   (C) $3\frac{7}{8}$

   (D) $11\frac{17}{24}$

4. Which of the following statements is true of every equilateral triangle?

   (A) The base and height of the triangle are the same length.

   (B) All three angles have the same measure.

   (C) The triangle contains an obtuse angle.

   (D) The length of the base is an even number.

5. What is the value of y if $y = -3x + 5$ and $x = -4$?

   (A) –2

   (B) –7

   (C) 17

   (D) 7

6. $4.51 \times 10^5 =$

   (A) 4.5100000

   (B) 451

   (C) 451,000

   (D) 225.5

7. Solve for x: $\frac{x}{4} - 7 = -3$.

   (A) 40

   (B) 16

   (C) 1

   (D) 2.5

8. Which of the following is NOT a prime number?

   (A) 31

   (B) 41

   (C) 51

   (D) 61

9. Find the value of $(x+4)\left(\frac{x}{2}\right)^3$ when $x = 6$.

   (A) 54

   (B) 108

   (C) 270

   (D) 1,080

10. $\left(t^5\right)^2 =$

    (A) $7t$

    (B) $10t$

    (C) t^7

    (D) t^{10}

Go on to next page

11. The sum of two consecutive numbers is 69. Find the smaller number.

    (A) 33

    (B) 34

    (C) 35

    (D) 36

12. At a certain time of day, a 3-foot pole casts a 4-foot shadow. At the same time, a flag-pole casts a 36-foot shadow. How tall is the flagpole?

    (A) 27 feet

    (B) 36 feet

    (C) 45 feet

    (D) 48 feet

13. Evaluate $\dfrac{4x-3y}{2x^2+y} - xy^2$ when $x = 2$ and $y = -1$.

    (A) $-\dfrac{3}{7}$

    (B) -5

    (C) $-\dfrac{1}{3}$

    (D) 3

14. Ashton is 30 miles north of Benton and 40 miles west of Columbus. Find the distance from Benton to Columbus.

    (A) 10 miles

    (B) 50 miles

    (C) 70 miles

    (D) 120 miles

15. $\sqrt{12(147)} =$

    (A) 42

    (B) 84

    (C) 98

    (D) 126

16. Which of the following is the square of an odd number?

    (A) 1,296

    (B) 1,369

    (C) 1,444

    (D) 1,764

17. Twice a number reduced by three more than the number results in six. Find the number.

    (A) 9

    (B) 4.5

    (C) 3

    (D) 0

18. The product of −3.2 and 7.9, rounded to the nearest tenth, is

    (A) 25.3

    (B) 25.2

    (C) −25.3

    (D) −25.2

19. $x^2 - 9$ is equivalent to

    (A) $(x-3)^2$

    (B) $(x+3)^2$

    (C) $-(x+3)^2$

    (D) $(x-3)(x+3)$

20. If a 3-x-5-inch photograph is enlarged so that its longer side is 10 inches long, the shorter dimension of the photo will be

    (A) $3\dfrac{1}{3}$ inches

    (B) 6 inches

    (C) 8 inches

    (D) 10 inches

21. If $\dfrac{x-5}{3} = 7$, then $x =$

    (A) 4

    (B) 9

    (C) 26

    (D) 36

22. The area of a right triangle whose legs measure 10 inches and 8 inches is

    (A) 80 square inches

    (B) 40 square inches

    (C) 20 square inches

    (D) 6 square inches

Go on to next page

23. A bag contains 12 marbles. Of those marbles, 3 are red, 5 are blue, and 4 are white. If one marble is chosen at random, what is the probability that it is not white?

    (A) $\frac{1}{4}$

    (B) $\frac{1}{3}$

    (C) $\frac{2}{3}$

    (D) $\frac{3}{4}$

24. If $i = \sqrt{-1}$, then $(3+2i)(4-i)=$

    (A) $12 - 2i$

    (B) $12 - 5i$

    (C) $10 + 5i$

    (D) $14 + 5i$

25. A circle has a diameter of 8 inches. What is the area of a sector of the circle cut off by an angle of 45 degrees?

    (A) π

    (B) 2π

    (C) 4π

    (D) 8π

STOP DO NOT TURN THE PAGE UNTIL TOLD TO DO SO.
DO NOT RETURN TO A PREVIOUS TEST.

Reading Skills

Time: 25 minutes for 27 questions

Directions: Each question in this section consists of a passage you should assume to be true. The passage is followed by four possible answer choices. After you read the passage, select the answer choice that can be inferred only from the passage itself and shade in the corresponding oval on your answer sheet. More than one choice may be both true and reasonable, but only one can be inferred solely from the information in the passage.

1. The sundial is one of the oldest of all scientific instruments. In principle, it's simple: The sun shines on the dial, and the protruding piece casts a shadow along the hour lines marked on the flat plate. Yet, its simplicity is deceptive. The dial must be precisely laid out with respect to the equator in order for the instrument to be accurate in showing the correct hour.

   (A) The sundial is the oldest scientific instrument known to mankind.

   (B) Directional calculations must be made before situating a sundial.

   (C) The sundial is too simple to be an accurate instrument for telling time.

   (D) A sundial can be placed in any direction in a garden.

2. Studies of written numerals in diverse cultures reveal an unexpected cross-cultural convergence: All civilizations employ a similar system of writing the first three numbers. The symbol for the number one is repeated two times for the number two and three times for the number three. Historians are at a loss to explain this mathematical mystery.

   (A) Some cultures represent the number two by using the symbol for five minus three.

   (B) Cross-cultural convergence doesn't exist with regard to numbers four and higher.

   (C) All numerical systems are an outgrowth of one ancient system.

   (D) Some ancient civilizations represented the numbers one, two, and three by drawing one horizontal bar, two horizontal bars, and three horizontal bars, respectively.

3. Electronic readers (e-readers) are no longer the wave of the future; they are the here and now. Marketers anticipated that book lovers would welcome these simple, compact, and affordable gadgets, but the overwhelmingly positive welcome from the general public came as a surprise. Perhaps the convenience of e-readers accounts for their popularity, or maybe it's just the novelty of owning the latest bit of technology. Either way, it appears that print publishers had better take note of the trend to replace an extensive personal library with a single e-reader.

   (A) More people are buying e-readers than are buying traditional print books.

   (B) E-readers are popular because they are relatively inexpensive and technologically complex.

   (C) The mass public embrace of the e-reader was unanticipated by those who first promoted the new technology.

   (D) In the near future, print publishing is going to be obsolete.

Go on to next page

4. Desert plants have physical and behavioral adaptations that help them survive the extreme heat and aridity of their environment. They tend to grow tall and thin to present as small a surface area to the hot rays of the sun as possible. They also have developed special means of storing and preserving water. For example, many are capable of remaining dormant during dry seasons and come to life when water is more abundant.

   (A) Desert plants grow tall and thin to allow water to glide easily to their roots.

   (B) Seasonal adaptation is one method plants use to survive harsh climates.

   (C) The ability to adapt aids vegetation in propagating in intemperate weather conditions.

   (D) The aridity of the desert is hostile to flowering plants.

5. The term "horsepower" was originally coined to describe the output of a steam engine. No unit of measurement existed to denote this new source of energy, so comparing it to a known power, that of draft horses, was helpful. James Watt calculated (somewhat optimistically according to more modern calculations) that a horse could produce 33,000 foot-pounds per minute; this became one unit of mechanical horsepower.

   (A) New technology often creates the need for new terminology.

   (B) The term "horsepower" is a misnomer because steam engines are far more powerful than horses.

   (C) The term "horsepower" was replaced by BTUs when James Watt recalculated the energy output of draft horses.

   (D) Every new invention creates unthought-of repercussions in the world of technology.

6. The Iditarod, a 1,000-mile dog sled race across Alaska from Wasilla to Nome along the Iditarod Trail, began as a way to preserve the tradition of mushing. In Alaska's early years, dog sleds "mushed" their way across terrain inaccessible to any vehicle. The race was conceived by Dorothy G. Page as part of Alaska's Centennial celebration in 1967. Originally a short race of 9 miles, the journey now takes between 9 and 12 grueling days, pushing both man and dogs to the limit of endurance.

   (A) The Iditarod covers between 9 and 12 miles of snow-covered terrain.

   (B) The first winner of the Iditarod was Dorothy G. Page.

   (C) Preserving Alaskan traditions was important to Dorothy G.Page.

   (D) The 1,200-mile dog sled race can be completed in 9 days.

7. Although the Galápagos Islands were accidently discovered by the Bishop of Panama in 1535, they were not annexed by Ecuador until 1832. In 1835 the most famous visitor to the islands, a young naturalist named Charles Darwin, arrived on board the HMS *Beagle*. Observing that several species of birds and tortoises differed from island to island, Darwin conceived his theory of evolution based on the principles of natural selection.

   (A) Charles Darwin was the first naturalist to set foot on the Galápagos Islands.

   (B) Scientific observation provided significant clues that led Darwin to make a major scientific contribution.

   (C) After Ecuador annexed the Galapágos Islands, political development and scientific exploration flourished.

   (D) Scientific observation provided the answers to questions that Darwin had been pondering for years.

Go on to next page

8. The average shopper often is snowed under by the vast selection of goods artfully arrayed in a modern mega-market. While just a decade or two ago store shelves held 20 to 30 varieties of breakfast cereal, today more than 100 choices are available. Shoppers find themselves frozen in place, eyes glazed over as they fall under the spell of rampant consumerism.

   (A) Modern supermarkets have fresher and better food than those of two decades ago.

   (B) Smart consumers, who want to purchase breakfast cereal, should go to a local "mom-and-pop" grocery store.

   (C) Some consumers find themselves intimidated by the overwhelming diversity of products available for purchase.

   (D) To find the best choices in vegetables and fruits, you should shop in modern mega-markets.

9. Human beings are the only mammals that consume chili peppers. Scientists who study human preferences wonder why people choose to eat something that will produce a degree of pain. Several theories have attempted to explain the appeal of the spicy fruits, which range from relatively mild jalapeños to the excruciatingly hot Indian jolokia, one of many sizzling Indian peppers. Although peppers do lower blood pressure and increase salivation, these medicinal benefits don't account for the human willingness to endure the pain.

   (A) Chili peppers from India are among the most incendiary.

   (B) All mammals that consume chili peppers prefer the milder varieties.

   (C) Scientists have known about the medicinal properties of chili peppers for many years.

   (D) All human beings, at one time or another, consume chili peppers.

10. The *Mona Lisa* is arguably the most famous portrait in the world. Critics often try to justify this inexplicable fascination with a painting of a relatively obscure woman. They point to the artist's use of light and shadow, the illusion of depth, and the richness of color. But for most people, it is the Mona Lisa herself, her enigmatic smile, that touches our hearts and remains locked in our collective memories.

    (A) The *Mona Lisa* is the most famous landscape painting in the world.

    (B) The lure of the *Mona Lisa* lies in the subject's mysterious smile.

    (C) No one knows the identity of the woman who posed for the *Mona Lisa*.

    (D) Most people find the artist's technique to be the most appealing aspect of the *Mona Lisa*.

11. Vampire bats have always been depicted as supernatural or frightening, but new scientific evidence points to their being helpful to humans. The saliva from these bats is a powerful anticoagulant. After the bat makes an incision in its victim (usually livestock; rarely humans), the bat's saliva allows the victim's blood to flow freely. This anticoagulant, which is harmless to humans, may someday be a boon to heart patients.

    (A) The bite of a vampire bat usually causes immediate death to the victim.

    (B) Vampires are humans who can transform into bats.

    (C) Bat saliva has been documented as a life-saving medication.

    (D) The saliva of vampire bats has potential medical benefits.

Go on to next page

12. Researchers who study television viewers' attitudes have uncovered an interesting piece of information: Of the total numbers of viewers who claimed to enjoy regularly watching a certain program, only 45 percent designated that program a "high-quality viewing experience." The other 55 percent gave it ratings that ranged from "average" to "poor."

    (A) A majority of television viewers regularly watch programs they consider excellent.

    (B) Those viewers who watch a limited number of television programs single out those they consider worthwhile.

    (C) Many viewers will continue to watch programs they consider average at best and poor at worst.

    (D) Few television viewers will watch programs they consider poorly written.

13. Many young parents consider disposable diapers to be the greatest invention of the 20th century. Before disposables, diapers were made of cloth, and a family had only two options: lots of home laundry or a diaper service that would pick up soiled diapers and drop off fresh ones. Today, even families that try to be totally green and use only environmentally sound products will shy away from more green cloth ones and bend their rules for the convenience of disposable diapers.

    (A) Disposable diapers are all totally green.

    (B) Cloth diapers are more environmentally sound than disposables ones.

    (C) The use of cloth diapers is more economical than the use of disposable ones.

    (D) Disposable diapers are the single most environmentally wasteful product.

14. The human mind is endlessly inventive; witness the technological explosion of the past half century if you have any doubt. And this is how far we've come since 1951 when UNIVAC, the first commercial computer, was installed. UNIVAC took up almost an entire room. Now think about how compact the omnipresent PCs and Macs have become and how prevalent computers and smart boards are in classrooms. And everyone is walking around with hand-held technology: an iPhone, Blackberry, or iPad. You can be sure more amazing ideas are germinating in some future scientist's fertile imagination.

    (A) The first personal computer was invented in 1951.

    (B) All homes in the U.S. have at least one computer in the home.

    (C) Every school has installed computers in the classrooms.

    (D) Many of the technological advances have reduced the size of devices.

15. It is the job of the team leader to decide when and where to hold team meetings. He or she will determine the agenda, the equipment necessary, and the list of attendees. If technology is needed, the team leader will arrange for laptop computers and a large screen for PowerPoint presentations.

    (A) The team leader must make a PowerPoint presentation at all team meetings.

    (B) The team leader has the authority to call a team meeting and to decide the format of the presentation.

    (C) Neither iPads nor personal laptops are permitted at team meetings.

    (D) The use of technology in the form of PowerPoint presentations will enhance the efficiency of team meetings.

Go on to next page

16. Jessica discovered two problems with the new motorbike that she purchased. She noticed a tiny scratch on the fender when she got home from the dealership. She also heard a faint clicking noise whenever she put the bike in gear. Her concern about the clicking noise kept her up half the night. On the other hand, she quickly put the minor scratch out of her mind. She figured it was only one of many that she'd accrue in the years to come.

    (A) The two problems with her new bike kept Jessica up at night.

    (B) Jessica worried more about the scratch on her fender than the clicking noise.

    (C) Jessica was more concerned about the internal working of her bike than its appearance.

    (D) After Jessica got a scratch on her bike, she didn't care about any other physical damage it may endure.

17. Human life faces the same alternatives that confront all other forms of life — of adapting to the conditions under which they must live or becoming extinct. Human beings have an advantage over the sagebrush in that they can move from one city or state or country to another, but after all, that is not much of an advantage. For though they may improve their situations slightly, they will still find that in any civilized country the main elements of their problems are the same.

    (A) The ability to move from place to place confers an advantage of people over plant life, but people can't always solve their problems by moving.

    (B) In most civilized countries, the ability to move from city to city provides a dramatic means to change the course of one's life.

    (C) Those people who choose to remain near their place of birth are often the most satisfied with their lives.

    (D) More people in the U.S. move from city to city than in any other country in the world.

18. Ocean acidification is one of the consequences of the increase in carbon dioxide in the atmosphere. The issue stems from the falling pH (the measure of acidity or alkalinity of water) of the ocean water as it absorbs CO_2. A lower pH makes it difficult for some marine life to survive. On the other hand, recent findings indicate the life cycle of other species benefits from a lower pH.

    (A) The acidification of the ocean is causing problems for all sea life.

    (B) Many marine organisms will die if the pH of ocean water continues to fall.

    (C) The discovery of the benefits of a lower pH has caused shock waves throughout the oceanographic community.

    (D) The determination of the ecological effects of the falling pH of the ocean is inconclusive.

19. Thomas Edison is a quintessentially American inventor. He epitomizes the American hero in that he was a completely self-made, self-taught adventurer who worked diligently on his inventions until he achieved success. The list of his accomplishments is impressive — the electric light, the phonograph, the motion picture camera. We owe much to this brilliant scientist.

    (A) Anyone who wants to be a brilliant inventor like Edison must attend a prestigious college.

    (B) Americans traditionally value hard work and self-improvement.

    (C) To be an astute inventor, one should be self-taught and eager to seek new frontiers.

    (D) No other American has achieved as much as Thomas Edison.

Go on to next page

20. You don't need a whole garden to grow tomatoes; you can plant them in a tub or a pot. Select a container that has adequate drainage before you begin. You can fill it with soil, but synthetic mixes work well, too. Plant the seedlings about 4 inches apart and be sure to water them without drowning them. Like most vegetables, tomatoes like lots of sunlight, so place the container in a sunny spot. Before you know it, you'll be enjoying homegrown salad.

    (A) The first step in planting a tub garden is to select a container that won't allow water to remain stagnant.

    (B) You should use synthetic soil, which is cleaner and healthier for potted plants.

    (C) To ensure proper growth, no more than four seedlings should be planted in a pot.

    (D) The most important element for tomato growth is adequate watering.

21. "Toasted skin" is a new skin condition medical doctors are noticing among laptop computer users who place their computers directly on their laps. The unprotected skin on the thigh presents a mottled appearance from having sustained a mild burn from the heat emitted by the computer. The condition, which is rarely serious, only occurs with prolonged use of the laptop in the same position.

    (A) Prolonged use of a laptop placed directly on the thighs can occasionally cause skin cancer.

    (B) Moving the position of the laptop from the thighs or placing a protective cover on the thighs can prevent "toasted skin."

    (C) Laptop computers are generally more dangerous to use than desktop computers.

    (D) "Toasted skin" is just one more example of people harming their health by being careless with technology.

22. Frederick Douglass's fame as an orator has long been secure. His position as the champion of an oppressed race, and at the same time an example of its possibilities, was as picturesque as it was unique. His life may serve for all time as an incentive to aspiring souls who would fight the battles and win the love of mankind. The average American of today who sees, when his attention is called to it, and deplores, if he be a thoughtful and just man, the deep undertow of race prejudice cannot, except by reading the painful records of the past, conceive of the mental and spiritual darkness to which slavery condemned its victims and, to a lesser extent, their oppressors.

    (A) A study of the past will reveal that slavery claimed as its victims not only the slaves themselves but also their oppressors.

    (B) Frederick Douglass serves as the best example of a man who survived slavery by quietly submitting to oppression.

    (C) The average American is not thoughtful enough to understand the painful history of slavery in America.

    (D) Frederick Douglass is more famous for his skill at oratory than his authorship of his autobiography.

Go on to next page

23. In 1950, the famous Italian American physicist Enrico Fermi was having a lunch discussion with some fellow scientists about the possibility of extraterrestrial life when he asked a simple question: "But, where is everybody?" This seemingly naïve query became the basis for the Fermi Paradox, which states that given all the planets in all the solar systems, it is presumptuous to assume that we are alone. The underlying premise of Fermi's question is the foundation for SETI (Search for Extraterrestrial Intelligence), an exploratory science that searches for life on other planets.

(A) Fermi and his fellow scientists were convinced that life exists on other planets.

(B) SETI has found evidence of some form of life on planets in a neighboring galaxy.

(C) According to the Fermi Paradox, the laws of probability suggest that life in some form exists on other planets.

(D) It is ironic that Fermi was looking for fellow scientists rather than other intelligent life forms when he asked his famous question.

24. Oases, or "islands" of vegetation, dot the vast sea of sand that is the Sahara Desert. These fertile spots are fed by underground springs: Water rises to the surface and is trapped by impermeable surrounding rocks. Oases, which range in size from a small cluster of bushes or date palms to whole cities, provide essential water and shade to travelers who traverse the arid and desolate miles of sand that comprise much of northern Africa.

(A) Most oases consist of a few date palm trees in the middle of the desert.

(B) The water in an oasis springs from underground pipes that are fed by a larger body of water.

(C) Most travelers who traverse the Sahara Desert use camels because they are able to travel many miles without water.

(D) An oasis may be of critical importance to trade and transportation routes.

25. Memories often are unreliable; we tend to rewrite them to highlight our triumphs and minimize our flaws. The mental editing process is not conscious, but it explains the puzzling way different people remember the events of the same day very differently. Relying on memory may be no more accurate than reading historical fiction to understand historical events.

(A) Memories of momentous specific events tend to be more accurate than memories of ordinary days.

(B) Memory is a critical component of most creative projects.

(C) Memories often are influenced by personal involvement in the events being recalled.

(D) Family members often have similar memories of important events in their family's history.

26. Excavation is the primary method archeologists use to recover information. After they're found, archeological deposits must be carefully examined and meticulously recorded. Precise determinations of site boundaries, artifact type and style, and feature functions must be noted and verified. Such practices preserve the all-important contextual record and permit future study.

(A) Preserving the integrity of the deposit site is essential for accurate records.

(B) Permanently dismantling an archeological find is critical to the success of a dig.

(C) Archeologists must be more careful and precise in their work than other scientists.

(D) The artifacts that are carefully collected by archeologists often are modified by the process of collection.

Go on to next page

27. Plagiarism is a serious problem in both high schools and colleges. Easy access to information on the Internet has led many students to substitute the work of others for their own work without citing sources. A guidance counselor in a local high school recently gave all seniors a questionnaire about copying information. The results are similar to those in many other educational institutions across the country: 40 percent of the students who responded admitted that they had plagiarized at some point, and 75 percent indicated that they knew of others who had copied information or had actually purchased prewritten essays on the Internet.

    (A) All high school students have plagiarized at some point in their educational careers.

    (B) Internet sites that sell prewritten essays to students should be banned.

    (C) Plagiarism is a pervasive problem that has been exacerbated by the Internet.

    (D) More high school students have plagiarized than those who admitted to doing so in questionnaires.

STOP DO NOT TURN THE PAGE UNTIL TOLD TO DO SO.
DO NOT RETURN TO A PREVIOUS TEST.

Mechanical Comprehension

Time: 19 minutes for 25 questions

Directions: The questions in this section are designed to measure your knowledge and understanding of mechanics. Choose the best answer for each question from the answer choices provided, and shade in the corresponding oval on your answer sheet.

1. What is a force?

   (A) any influence that imparts an acceleration on a free body

   (B) the amount of matter an object has

   (C) a vector that is the result of one object's influence on another

   (D) the amount of energy stored within an object due to its position in space

2. A projectile with a mass of 5 kilograms is thrown exactly parallel to the ground from a height of 40 meters. The initial velocity of the object is 20 m/s parallel to the ground and 0 m/s in the vertical direction. Assuming the acceleration due to gravity is 9.81 m/s^2, how far would the projectile travel before it strikes the ground?

   (A) 47 meters

   (B) 52 meters

   (C) 55 meters

   (D) 57 meters

3. A cannon pointing straight up shoots a 45 kilogram cannonball. The initial velocity of the cannonball is 125 m/s. Assuming the acceleration due to gravity is 9.81 m/s^2, what is the highest point the cannonball will reach?

   (A) 593 meters

   (B) 796 meters

   (C) 1256 meters

   (D) 1593 meters

4. Which of the following is NOT considered a fundamental force?

   (A) gravitational

   (B) electromagnetic

   (C) centripetal

   (D) nuclear

5. What is normal force?

   (A) force that is perpendicular to the point or plane of contact between two objects

   (B) force that acts in the opposite direction of an applied force and resists motion

   (C) upward acting force in a fluid caused by the pressure of the fluid around an object

   (D) the magnitude of pull exerted by a string, cable, line, or similar object

6. Which of the following best characterizes fundamental forces?

   (A) forces that affect all matter on a subatomic level

   (B) forces that are similar to fundamental forces but are more complex and cannot be explained by known physics

   (C) forces that govern the physical world

   (D) forces that are a consequence or combination of all forces in the known world

7. A 50 kilogram box needs to be lifted 5 meters. If the maximum force to move the box is 100 newtons, how long must the ramp be to push the box up to a position 5 meters above the ground? Assume there are no frictional forces and the acceleration due to gravity is 9.81 m/s^2.

   (A) 22.5 meters

   (B) 23.5 meters

   (C) 24.5 meters

   (D) 25.5 meters

Go on to next page

8. If 124 newtons of force is required to push a 20 kilogram box up a ramp with an incline angle of 30°, what is the coefficient of friction assuming acceleration due to gravity is 9.81 m/s²?

   (A) 0.13

   (B) 0.15

   (C) 0.17

   (D) 0.19

9. In an elastic collision, the objects involved in the collision do what?

   (A) bounce off each other and move in opposite directions

   (B) fragment and move apart in many different directions

   (C) combine and come to a complete stop

   (D) combine and move in the same direction proportional to the direction of force in the system

10. Two objects are about to experience a head-on collision: A 15 kilogram object traveling at 5 m/s right to left and a 30 kilogram object traveling at 10 m/s left to right. Assuming a completely inelastic collision, what is the final velocity of the 15 kilogram object and what direction is it traveling (left or right)?

    (A) 5 m/s to the right

    (B) 5 m/s to the left

    (C) 15 m/s to the right

    (D) 15 m/s to the left

11. What is work?

    (A) total amount of matter an object has

    (B) amount of force required to move an object over a distance

    (C) rate at which energy is converted

    (D) rate at which potential energy is converted to kinetic energy

12. A crane has a 100,000 kilogram capacity. The crane lifts a load at its capacity to a height of 40 meters over the course of 30 seconds. How much power did the crane use for the lift? Assume the acceleration due to gravity is 9.81 m/s² and that the crane lifted the load with a constant velocity.

    (A) 1248 kilowatts

    (B) 1308 kilowatts

    (C) 1842 kilowatts

    (D) 3924 kilowatts

13. If a 2 liter aluminum bottle is filled with helium at 280 Kelvin to 120 kilograms/cm², what pressure will be inside the bottle if the temperature is raised to 320 Kelvin? Assume volume remains the same and no gas escapes from the bottle.

    (A) 137 kilograms/cm²

    (B) 132 kilograms/cm²

    (C) 127 kilograms/cm²

    (D) 117 kilograms/cm²

14. Which of the following is a simple machine?

    (A) pump

    (B) hydraulic lift

    (C) pulley

    (D) winch

15. A pulley system has four pulleys with a total mechanical advantage of 4. The load force is 1200 newtons. What force must be applied to lift the load?

    (A) 200 newtons

    (B) 300 newtons

    (C) 600 newtons

    (D) 1800 newtons

16. An object revolves around the earth with a radial velocity of 628 radians/hr. Assuming the value of π is 3.14, at what frequency does the object circumnavigate the globe?

    (A) 400 revolutions/hr

    (B) 200 revolutions/hr

    (C) 100 revolutions/hr

    (D) 50 revolutions/hr

Go on to next page

17. How much does B weigh?

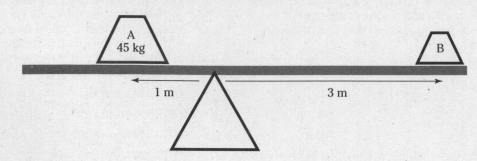

(A) 45 kilograms

(B) 30 kilograms

(C) 27.5 kilograms

(D) 15 kilograms

18. A 5 centimeter cube of material with a mass of 120 grams is placed in a 4 liter bucket of water. Assuming the density of water is 1 gram/cm^3, what happens to the cube?

(A) It floats on top of the water.

(B) It sinks quickly to the bottom.

(C) It floats but is almost completely submerged.

(D) It sinks slowly to the bottom.

19. Newton's Second Law is most commonly written as:

(A) $E = m \times g \times h$

(B) $F_{net} = m \times a$

(C) $e = mc^2$

(D) $W = F \times d$

20. Which of the following is the mechanical advantage of a wheel with a radius of 60 centimeters and an axle with the radius of 15 centimeters?

(A) 2

(B) 3

(C) 4

(D) 5

Go on to next page

21. What weight needs to be applied to the right end of the following lever to lift the weight on the left end?

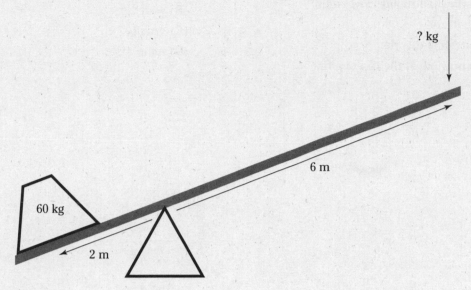

(A) 60 kilograms

(B) 30 kilograms

(C) 20 kilograms

(D) 15 kilograms

22. Which of the following wedges has the greatest mechanical advantage?

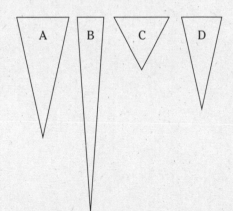

23. A hydraulic system is comprised of two square water columns. One column has a surface area of 3 meters x 3 meters and the other has a surface area of 12 meters x 12 meters. How far do you need to depress the piston in the smaller column to raise the piston in the larger column 2 meters?

(A) 8 meters

(B) 24 meters

(C) 72 meters

(D) 32 meters

Go on to next page

24. Which of the following is NOT an example of pure potential energy?

    (A) a snowball rolling down a hill

    (B) a battery

    (C) a stretched spring

    (D) a snowball at the top of a hill

25. Which of the following is a unit for work?

    (A) horsepower

    (B) watt

    (C) gravity

    (D) joule

STOP DO NOT TURN THE PAGE UNTIL TOLD TO DO SO.
DO NOT RETURN TO A PREVIOUS TEST.

Chapter 21

ASTB OAR Practice Test: Answers and Explanations

*I*f you've come to this chapter, you've likely worked your way through the Aviation Selection Test Battery Officer Aptitude Rating (ASTB OAR) practice test from Chapter 20. So now you're ready to check your answers. We provide the answers in two different formats: with detailed explanation and in a bare-bones answer key. We suggest you read through the detailed answers for each question to get the most out of your studies, but if you're running low on time and simply need the answers, take a look at the answer key at the end of the chapter. If you have trouble with any of the questions on this test, put in some extra time with Parts II and III, where we discuss English, math, and mechanics skills.

Math Skills Answers

1. **C.** $\$5.40 \div 12$ cans = 45 cents per can. Because all the answers are similar, you know the cost is at least 40 cents per can. 40×12 is $\$4.80$, but $\$5.40$ is an additional 60 cents. That 60 cents represents 5 cents per can.

2. **B.** 420 miles at 60 miles per hour =

$$\frac{420 \text{ miles}}{1} \cdot \frac{1 \text{ hour}}{60 \text{ miles}} = \frac{420 \text{ hours}}{60} = 7 \text{ hours}$$

3. **B.** $6\frac{3}{8} \times 5\frac{1}{3} = \frac{48+3}{8} \times \frac{15+1}{3} = \frac{\overset{17}{\cancel{51}}}{\cancel{8}} \times \frac{\overset{2}{\cancel{16}}}{\cancel{3}} = 34$

4. **B.** By definition, an equilateral triangle has three sides of equal length, but every equilateral triangle is also *equiangular*. In other words, all three angles have the same measure. Because each angle measures $60°$, the triangle doesn't contain an obtuse angle. It isn't true that the base and height of the triangle are the same length. The height, measured perpendicular to the base, will be shorter than the sides. Equilateral triangles come in all sizes, so it's not possible that the length of the base is an even number for every equilateral triangle.

5. **C.** $y = -3x + 5 = -3(-4) + 5 = 12 + 5 = 17$

6. **C.** $4.51 \times 10^5 = 4.51 \times 100{,}000 = 451{,}000$. Also remember that 4.51×10^5 means to move the decimal point five places to the right: $4.51 \times 10^5 = 4.\underline{51000} = 451{,}000$.

7. **B.** First add 7 to both sides, and then multiply both sides by 4 to get your answer:

$$\frac{x}{4} - 7 = -3$$
$$\frac{x}{4} = 4$$
$$x = 16$$

8. **C.** *Prime numbers* are numbers that have no factors other than themselves and 1, so you're looking for an answer choice that's divisible by some other number. All the answer choices are odd, so none is divisible by 2. Check for divisibility by 3 by adding the digits; if the sum of the digits is a multiple of 3, the number is divisible by 3. The sum of the digits of 31 is 4 and of 41 is 5. However, the sum of the digits of 51 is 6, so 51 is divisible by 3 and therefore not prime.

9. **C.** $(x+4)\left(\frac{x}{2}\right)^3 = (6+4)\left(\frac{6}{2}\right)^3 = 10(3)^3 = 10(27) = 270$

10. **D.** When a power is raised to a power, the exponents are multiplied: $\left(t^5\right)^2 = t^5 \cdot t^5 = t^{10}$.

11. **B.** Represent the two consecutive numbers as x and $x + 1$. The sum of x and $x + 1$ is $2x + 1$ and that equals 69. Simplify to get your answer:

$$2x + 1 = 69$$
$$2x = 68$$
$$x = 34$$

12. **A.** In each case, the pole and its shadow form the legs of a right triangle with the sun's rays as the hypotenuse. Because the two shadows occur at the same time of day, the angle of the sun is the same, and so the triangles are similar. The proportion $\frac{\text{pole}}{\text{shadow}} = \frac{\text{pole}}{\text{shadow}}$ can be solved to find the height of the flagpole. $\frac{3}{4} = \frac{x}{36}$ can be cross-multiplied to produce the equation $4x = 3 \cdot 36 = 108$. Dividing by 4 shows you that $x = 27$ feet.

13. **A.** Replace x with 2 and y with –1, like this:

$$\frac{4x - 3y}{2x^2 + y} - xy^2 = \frac{4(2) - 3(-1)}{2(2)^2 + (-1)} - (2)(-1)^2$$

Simplify the powers and remove the unnecessary parentheses:

$$\frac{4(2) - 3(-1)}{2(2)^2 + (-1)} - (2)(-1)^2 = \frac{4(2) - 3(-1)}{2(4) - 1} - (2)(1)$$

Next, perform the multiplications:

$$\frac{4(2) - 3(-1)}{2(4) - 1} - (2)(1) = \frac{8 + 3}{8 - 1} - 2$$

Simplify the numerator and denominator of the fraction, change the 2 to a fraction with a denominator of 7 and then subtract to get your answer:

$$\frac{8 + 3}{8 - 1} - 2 = \frac{11}{7} - \frac{14}{7} = -\frac{3}{7}$$

14. **B.** If you sketch the locations described, you'll see that Ashton, Benton, and Columbus are the vertices of a right triangle. Use the Pythagorean theorem to get your answer: $\sqrt{30^2 + 40^2}$ $= \sqrt{900 + 1{,}600} = \sqrt{2{,}500} = 50$. Or note that 30 and 40 are multiples of 3 and 4, so the hypotenuse will be a corresponding multiple of 5. So the distance is 50.

15. **A.** Multiplying 12×147 isn't likely to be helpful. Instead, factor each of the numbers, looking for factors that are perfect squares:

$$\sqrt{12(147)} = \sqrt{4 \cdot 3(147)} = \sqrt{4 \cdot 3(3 \cdot 49)} = \sqrt{4 \cdot 9 \cdot 49} = \sqrt{4}\sqrt{9}\sqrt{49} = 2 \cdot 3 \cdot 7 = 42$$

16. **B.** Odd numbers end in 1, 3, 5, 7, or 9, so their squares will end in the same digits that occur at the end of $1^2, 3^2, 5^2, 7^2,$ and 9^2. Because $1^2 = 1, 3^2 = 9, 5^2 = 25, 7^2 = 49,$ and $9^2 = 81$, you know that the square of an odd number will end in 1, 9, or 5. Only 1,369 could be the square of an odd number.

17. **A.** The sentence "Twice a number reduced by three more than the number results in six" translates to this equation: $2x - (x + 3) = 6$. Remove the parentheses by distributing the negative in front of the parentheses, and then combine like terms. Add three to both sides to get your answer:

$$2x - (x + 3) = 6$$
$$2x - x - 3 = 6$$
$$x - 3 = 6$$
$$x = 9$$

18. **C.** The product is the result of multiplication, and a quick estimate ($-3 \times 8 = -24$) eliminates the two positive answer choices. When you know your answer is negative, you simply need to multiply 3.2 and 7.9 to determine which of the remaining choices is correct. To multiply 3.2 and 7.9, you can think of the problem as $(3 + 0.2)(7 + 0.9)$ and FOIL: $(3 + 0.2)(7 + 0.9) = 21 + 2.7 + 1.4 + 0.18 = 25.28$. Your answer is -25.28, which rounds to -25.3.

19. **D.** Factor the difference of square as the sum and difference of the same two terms: $x^2 - 9 = x^2 - 3^2 = (x - 3)(x + 3)$.

20. **B.** One dimension of the 3-x-5-inch photo is doubled so that the longer side becomes 10 inches. Therefore, the other dimension should be doubled as well, making the shorter dimension $2 \times 3 = 6$ inches.

21. **C.** Multiply both sides by 3, and then add 5 to both sides:

$$\frac{x - 5}{3} = 7$$
$$x - 5 = 21$$
$$x = 26$$

22. **B.** The area of a triangle is $\frac{1}{2}bh$. In a right triangle, the legs can be used as base and height because they're perpendicular. Here's your equation and answer:

$$A = \frac{1}{2}bh = \frac{1}{2}(10)(8) = 40 \text{ square inches}$$

23. **C.** Four of the marbles are white, so eight aren't white:

$$\frac{8}{12} = \frac{2}{3}$$

24. **D.** $(3 + 2i)(4 - i) = 12 - 3i + 8i - 2i^2 = 12 + 5i - 2i^2$ but because $i = \sqrt{-1}$, $i^2 = -1$. Substitute -1 for i^2:

$$12 + 5i - 2i^2 = 12 + 5i - 2(-1) = 12 + 5i + 2 = 14 + 5i$$

25. **B.** The diameter of the circle is 8 inches, so the radius is 4 inches. The area of the whole circle is $\pi r^2 = \pi \cdot 4^2 = 16\pi$. The area of the sector is a fraction of that:

$$\frac{45°}{360°} \times 16\pi = \frac{1}{8} \times 16\pi = 2\pi$$

Reading Skills Answers

1. **B.** Choice (B) is supported by the information that careful directional calculations are necessary before situating a sundial. Choice (A) is inaccurate; the sundial is "*one of the* oldest," not necessarily *the* oldest. Choice (C) is contradicted by the statement "its simplicity is deceptive." Choice (D) also is contradicted by the information in the passage.

2. **D.** Choice (D) is supported by the statement "The symbol for the number one is repeated two times for the number two and three times for the number three." Choice (A) may be true, but it isn't supported by any information in the passage. The passage also doesn't give enough information to support either Choice (B) or Choice (C).

3. **C.** Choice (C) is supported by the statement "the overwhelmingly positive welcome from the general public came as a surprise." Choice (A) is an assumption that can't be supported by the information in the passage. Choice (B) is inaccurate, because the e-readers are technologically simple. Choice (D) may be true, but no evidence in the passage conclusively supports it.

4. **B.** Choice (B) is supported by the statement that some desert plants "are capable of remaining dormant during dry seasons." Choice (A) may be true, but the passage doesn't provide supporting evidence. Choices (C) and (D) cover topics that aren't addressed in the passage.

5. **A.** Choice (A) is correct because it summarizes the main point of the passage — that the invention of the steam engine created the need for new terminology. Choice (B) is a misinterpretation of the passage. No evidence in the passage supports Choice (C). Choice (D) may be true, but the phrase "Every invention" makes it too general to be supported by the passage.

6. **C.** Choice (C) is supported by the information that Ms. Page conceived the race as a means of honoring the tradition of dog sled mushing. Choices (A), (B), and (D) are inaccurate; the race covers 1,000 miles, and Ms. Page never won it.

7. **B.** Choice (B) is supported by the evidence that Darwin's observations of the adaptations in species sparked his theory of evolution. No information in the passage can confirm Choice (A). Choice (C) is incorrect because nothing in the passage addresses political development. Choice (D) is based on the assumption that Darwin had pondered the question for years, but no evidence in the passage supports that assumption.

8. **C.** Choice (C) is the main point of the passage (that shoppers are "snowed under" by the overwhelming choices), so it's the correct answer. Choice (A) is most likely true, but evidence in the passage doesn't support it. Choice (B) expresses an attitude that isn't supported by the passage. Choice (D) may be true, but fruits and vegetables aren't mentioned in the passage.

9. **A.** Only Choice (A) can be supported by information in the passage ("the excruciatingly hot Indian jolokia"). Choice (B) may or may not be true, but it isn't supported by the information in the passage. Choice (C) is probably true, but no information in the passage supports it. Choice (D) is a generalization that can't be proved.

10. **B.** The last sentence of the passage supports the point that most people find the subject's smile intriguing, so Choice (B) is the best answer. Choice (A) is incorrect because the painting is a portrait, not a landscape. Choice (C) isn't supported by any information in the passage (in truth, most experts agree that she is Lisa del Giocondo). Choice (D) is contradicted by the last sentence of the passage.

11. **D.** The passage states that vampire bat saliva "may someday be a boon to heart patients," so Choice (D) is the correct answer. Choice (A) isn't supported by evidence in the passage. Choice (B) is off topic (and rather silly). Choice (C) makes an assumption that isn't supported by the passage.

12. **C.** According to the passage, more than half of TV viewers will watch programs they consider poor to average. Choice (A) is incorrect based on the statistics in the passage. Choice (B) is incorrect because the passage doesn't address viewers who watch a limited number of programs. Choice (D) is contradicted by the statistics in the passage.

13. **B.** The last sentence of the passage implies that cloth diapers are more environmentally sound than disposable ones. Choice (A) is contradicted by the passage. Choice (C) is incorrect because the cost of cloth versus disposable diapers isn't addressed in the passage. Choice (D) is a sweeping generalization that can't be supported by the information in the passage.

14. **D.** Choice (D) can be reasonably inferred because the passage makes a point of how large the UNIVAC was (room-sized) and how small computers have become (compact and hand-held). Choice (A) is incorrect, because no date is given for the first personal computer. (UNIVAC was a commercial computer.) Choices (B) and (C) are both too general and can't be supported by the information in the passage.

15. **B.** Choice (B) is the correct answer because the passage states that deciding the time, place, and format of team meetings is the team leader's job. Choice (A) is incorrect because a PowerPoint presentation is an option, not a requirement. Choice (C) can't be supported by the passage. Choice (D) may be true, but it can't be reasonably inferred from the information in the passage.

16. **C.** Jessica's concern for the noise in her bike's engine was more troubling to her than the scratch, so Choice (C) is the best answer. Choice (A) is wrong because only one problem kept her up all night. Choice (B) is contradicted by the information in the passage. Choice (D) is incorrect because a tiny scratch didn't bother her, but larger damage may be more disturbing to her.

17. **A.** The last sentence of the passage states that human beings "will still find that in any civilized country the main elements of their problems are the same." So the best answer is Choice (A). Choices (B), (C), and (D) all may be true, but they can't be reasonably supported by evidence in the passage.

18. **D.** Because some species benefit from and some are harmed by the falling pH of the ocean, the effects are inconclusive, making Choice (D) the correct answer. Choices (A) and (B) are contradicted by the fact that some organisms benefit from the falling pH. Choice (C) can't be supported by the passage; no information supports "shock waves."

19. **B.** Choice (B) is correct because it's clear from the phrases "quintessentially" and "American hero" that Americans value Edison's work ethic. Choices (A), (C), and (D) are too general in their assumptions to be reasonably inferred from the passage.

20. **A.** The first sentence makes the point that you have to start out with the proper container: a tub that allows water to drain. So Choice (A) is the correct answer. Choice (B) isn't implied by the passage. Choice (C) is incorrect because the passage never states how many plants can fit in a container. Choice (D) may be true, but the passage doesn't rank the relative importance of sunlight and water.

21. **B.** Choice (B) can be reasonably inferred from the passage. Because placing the laptop directly on the unprotected thighs causes the condition, moving it or protecting the skin would likely prevent it. Choice (A) is true, but it can't be inferred from the information in the passage. Choices (C) and (D) are both generalizations that can't be reasonably supported by the evidence in the passage.

22. **A.** Choice (A) is correct because "slavery condemned its victims and, to a lesser extent, their oppressors." Choice (B), which is historically inaccurate, is contradicted by the passage ("His life may serve for all time as an incentive to aspiring souls who would fight the battles"). Choice (C) is a generalization that can't reasonably be supported by the passage. Choice (D) may or may not be true, but it can't be proved by the information in the passage.

23. **C.** Fermi's question was based on the laws of probability; the existence of so many planets in so many solar systems in so many galaxies presents the logical probability of life in some form. So Choice (C) is best. Choice (A) makes too great an assumption by stating that Fermi and his fellow scientists "were convinced." Choice (B) can't be supported by any evidence in the passage. Choice (D) is just silly.

24. **D.** From the sentence that states that oases "provide essential water and shade to travelers who traverse the arid, desolate miles of sand," it can be reasonably inferred that these fertile spots are critical to travelers, making Choice (D) the correct answer. Choice (A) can't be supported because the passage states that oases range in size. No information in the passage suggests that oases are fed by pipes, so Choice (B) is wrong. Choice (C) is true, but it can't by supported by the passage because camels are never mentioned.

25. **C.** The first sentence in the passage states that we "adjust" our memories to make ourselves seem better; this adjustment implies the influence of personal involvement. So Choice (C) is most accurate. Choices (A) and (B) aren't supported by any information in the passage. The passage actually implies the opposite of Choice (D), because each person personally edits his or her memories.

26. **A.** Choice (A) can be reasonably inferred from several pieces of information in the passage ("deposits must be carefully and meticulously recorded," "precise determinations . . . must be noted and verified," and "such practices preserve the all-important contextual record"). "Permanently dismantling" a find would be counter to preserving the context, so Choice (B) is inaccurate. Choice (C) makes a comparison that can't be supported by the evidence in the passage. Choice (D) may be true, but it isn't addressed in the passage.

27. **C.** The passage states that plagiarism is a "serious problem" that has been made worse by the Internet, which makes Choice (C) the correct answer. Choice (A) may be true, but it's too general to be reasonably supported by the passage. Choices (B) and (D) are also probably true, but again, they can't be supported by the passage.

Mechanical Comprehension Answers

1. **A.** The definition of force is any influence that imparts an acceleration on a free body, so the correct answer is Choice (A).

2. **D.** To solve this problem, start by noting the object's characteristics at the beginning and end of its flight. Here are the beginning flight characteristics: 5 kilograms, 40 meters high, 20 m/s velocity. Here are the end flight characteristics: 5 kilograms, 0 meters high, 0 m/s velocity.

   Next, calculate the object's potential energy prior to launch, which is also the object's kinetic energy at its landing point:

   $$E_{k(\text{final})} = E_{p(\text{init})} = (9.81 \text{ m} / \text{s}^2)(40 \text{ m})(5 \text{ kg}) = 1962 \text{ J}$$

   Using the formula for kinetic energy along with what you know about the object's kinetic energy and mass, you can calculate its velocity to determine how fast it falls:

   $$E_k = \frac{1}{2}mv^2 \qquad v^2 = \frac{2E_k}{m} = \frac{2(1962 \text{ J})}{5 \text{ kg}} = 784.8 \text{ m}^2 / \text{s}^2 \qquad v = \sqrt{784.8 \text{ m}^2 / \text{s}^2} = 28 \text{ m} / \text{s}$$

   Because acceleration is the change in velocity over time, you can use the following formula to determine the time the object was in flight:

   $$a = \frac{(v_{fi} - v)}{t}, v_i = 0 \text{ m} / \text{s} \qquad t = \frac{v_f}{a} = \frac{28 \text{ m} / \text{s}}{9.81 \text{ m} / \text{s}^2} = 2.85 \text{ s}$$

   Now all you need to do is multiply the total time the object was in flight by its horizontal velocity:

   $$s = vt = (20 \text{ m} / \text{s})(2.85 \text{ s}) = 57 \text{ m}$$

3. **B.** At its highest point, all the cannonball's initial kinetic energy has been transferred into potential energy. Therefore, you need to set the energies equal to one other and solve for height using the potential energy equation:

$$E_{k_1} = E_{p_2} = \frac{1}{2}mv^2$$

$$E_{k_1} = \frac{1}{2}(45 \text{ kg})(125 \text{ m}/\text{s})^2 = 351562.5 \text{ J}$$

$$351562.5 \text{ J} = mgh = (45 \text{ kg})(9.81 \text{ m}/\text{s}^2)(h)$$

$$h = \frac{351562.5 \text{ J}}{(45 \text{ kg})(9.81 \text{ m}/\text{s}^2)} = 796 \text{ m}$$

4. **C.** The four fundamental forces are strong and weak (both nuclear forces), electromagnetic, and gravitational. Of the choices, the only force that doesn't match that description is Choice (C), centripetal force.

5. **A.** *Normal force* is a force that's perpendicular to the point or plane of contact between two objects. The other definitions are all definitions of different types of forces; Choice (B) is frictional, Choice (C) is buoyant, and Choice (D) is tension.

6. **C.** Fundamental forces are the building blocks of all other forces, so the best answer is Choice (C). Choice (A) isn't completely wrong, because fundamental forces do affect matter at a subatomic level, but Choice (C) is the best choice.

7. **C.** Use the formula $d = \frac{W}{F}$ to solve this problem. The question gives you F (100 newtons), so first you need to figure out how much work is involved. Assuming no friction, W (work) is what's required to lift the box 5 feet. Here are the calculations:

$$W = E_p = mgh = (50 \text{ kg})(9.81 \text{ m}/\text{s}^2)(5 \text{ m}) = 2452.5 \text{ J}$$

Now you have everything you need to solve for distance:

$$d = \frac{2452.5 \text{ J}}{100 \text{ N}} = 24.5 \text{ m}$$

8. **B.** You know the force required to move the box up the ramp with and without friction, so subtract the required force without friction from the total force exerted to find the frictional force, and then solve for the coefficient of friction:

$$F_{up} = mg\sin(\theta) = (20 \text{ kg})(9.81 \text{ m}/\text{s}^2)\sin(30°) = 98.1 \text{ N}$$

$$F_{fr} = F_{tot} - F_{up} = 124 \text{ N} - 98.1 \text{ N} = 25.9 \text{ N}$$

$$F_n = mg\cos(\theta), F_{fr} = \mu F_n \qquad \mu = \frac{F_{fr}}{F_n} = \frac{25.9 \text{ N}}{(20 \text{ kg})(9.81 \text{ m}/\text{s}^2)\cos(30°)} = 0.15$$

9. **A.** In elastic collisions, objects bounce off each other. You can instantly rule out Choices (C) and (D), because objects "combine" in inelastic collisions. You also can rule out Choice (B), because objects don't necessarily fragment in elastic collisions.

10. **A.** Use the equation for inelastic collisions with the understanding that momentum is conserved. Also keep in mind that movement to the left is negative and movement to the right is positive. As a result:

$$m_1v_{1_i} + m_2v_{2_i} = (m_1 + m_2)v_f$$
$$(15 \text{ kg})(-5 \text{ m/s}) + (30 \text{ kg})(10 \text{ m/s}) = (15 \text{ kg} + 30 \text{ kg})(v_f)$$
$$v_f = \frac{225 \text{ kg(m/s)}}{45 \text{ kg}} = 5 \text{ m/s to the right}$$

11. **B.** *Work* is defined as the amount of energy required to move an object over a distance.

12. **B.** Figure out how much work the crane does during the 30-second lift, and then divide that amount by the total number of seconds:

$$P = \frac{W}{t}$$
$$W = Fd = (100,000 \text{ kg})(9.81 \text{ m/s}^2)(40 \text{ m}) = 39,240 \text{ kJ}$$
$$P = \frac{39,240 \text{ kJ}}{30 \text{ s}} = 1308 \text{ kW}$$

13. **A.** When dealing with gases and relating their temperatures to pressures and volumes, you must use Kelvin instead of Celsius. In this situation, volume doesn't change, so consider only temperature and pressure:

$$\frac{P_1}{T_1} = \frac{P_2}{T_2}$$
$$\frac{120 \text{ kg/cm}^2}{280 \text{ K}} = \frac{V_2}{320 \text{ K}}$$
$$V_2 = \frac{(120 \text{ kg/cm}^2)(320 \text{ K})}{280 \text{ K}} = 137 \text{ kg/cm}^2$$

14. **C.** The six simple machines are lever, inclined plane, wedge, wheel and axle, screw, and pulley. The only answer selection listed that is one of these is Choice (C), a pulley.

15. **B.** In this problem, don't think too hard about the math. This problem is a simple one relating load and force applied by the mechanical advantage:

$$MA = \frac{F_{load}}{F_{applied}}$$
$$4 = \frac{1200 \text{ N}}{F_{applied}} \quad F_{applied} = \frac{1200 \text{ N}}{4} = 300 \text{ N}$$

16. **C.** Convert the angular velocity into frequency in revolutions per hour:

$$\omega = 2\pi f \quad f = \frac{\omega}{2\pi} = \frac{628 \text{ rad/hr}}{2(3.14)}$$
$$f = 100 \text{ revolutions/hr}$$

17. **D.** The lever's mechanical advantage is 3, so only 15 kilograms are needed on the right end of the lever to balance the 45 kilograms on the left end.

18. **C.** The cube's volume is $5 \times 5 \times 5 = 125 \ cm^3$, so its density is:

$$\frac{120 \ g}{125 \ cm^3} = 0.96 \ g/cm^3$$

Because the cube is only slightly less dense than water, it floats but is almost entirely submerged.

19. **B.** Newton's Second Law states that the rate of change of an object or its acceleration (a) is directly proportional to the magnitude of a net force ($Fnet$) and indirectly proportional to the object's mass (m). So Choice (B) is the correct answer.

20. **C.** Use the formula for the mechanical advantage of a wheel to solve this problem:

$$MA = \frac{r_{wheel}}{r_{axle}} = \frac{60 \ cm}{15 \ cm} = 4$$

21. **D.** The mechanical advantage is 3 (6 meters ÷ 2 meters), so one-third the weight is needed. One-third of 45 is 15 kilograms.

22. **B.** The equation for determining the mechanical advantage of a wedge goes like this:

$$MA = \frac{S}{W}$$

where S is slope and W is width of the wide end. The wedge with the greatest ratio of slope to width is the one with the greatest mechanical advantage, which in this case is Choice (B).

23. **D.** First, determine the volume of fluid needed to raise the piston in the larger column 2 meters:

$$V = Ah$$
$$V_{load} = (144 \ m^2)(2 \ m)$$
$$V_{load} = 288 \ m^3$$

Now determine how far you need to depress the piston in the smaller column to displace 288 m³ of fluid:

$$288 \ m^3 = (9 \ m^2)(h)$$
$$h = \frac{288 \ m^2}{9 \ m} = 32 \ m$$

24. **A.** A snowball in the process of rolling down a hill has both potential and kinetic energy.

25. **D.** The three common units for work are the newton-meter (N-m), joule (J), and foot-pound (ft-lb).

Answer Key for ASTB OAR Practice Test

Math Skills

1. C	6. C	11. B	16. B	21. C
2. B	7. B	12. A	17. A	22. B
3. B	8. C	13. A	18. C	23. C
4. B	9. C	14. B	19. D	24. D
5. C	10. D	15. A	20. B	25. B

Reading Skills

1. B	7. B	13. B	19. B	25. C
2. D	8. C	14. D	20. A	26. A
3. C	9. A	15. B	21. B	27. C
4. B	10. B	16. C	22. A	
5. A	11. D	17. A	23. C	
6. C	12. C	18. D	24. D	

Mechanical Comprehension

1. A	6. C	11. B	16. C	21. D
2. D	7. C	12. B	17. D	22. B
3. B	8. B	13. A	18. C	23. D
4. C	9. A	14. C	19. B	24. A
5. A	10. A	15. B	20. C	25. D

Chapter 22

ASVAB GT Practice Test

• •

*T*his practice exam tests your skills on the Arithmetic Reasoning, Word Knowledge, and Paragraph Comprehension subtests of the Armed Services Vocational Aptitude Battery General Technical (ASVAB GT) for admission to the Army and other military services. Take out your watch or clock so you can time yourself. Part of the challenge of this exam is completing each section in the allotted time. And be sure to mimic the other testing conditions you're likely to find on test day: a quiet room, few breaks (if any), and not going back and forth between tests. Mark your answers on the answer sheet provided. When you've completed the practice test, check your answers in Chapter 23. There we provide detailed answers with explanation as well a simple answer key if you're in a hurry.

Answer Sheet

Use the ovals provided with this practice test to record your answers.

Arithmetic Reasoning

1. Ⓐ Ⓑ Ⓒ Ⓓ	8. Ⓐ Ⓑ Ⓒ Ⓓ	15. Ⓐ Ⓑ Ⓒ Ⓓ	22. Ⓐ Ⓑ Ⓒ Ⓓ	29. Ⓐ Ⓑ Ⓒ Ⓓ
2. Ⓐ Ⓑ Ⓒ Ⓓ	9. Ⓐ Ⓑ Ⓒ Ⓓ	16. Ⓐ Ⓑ Ⓒ Ⓓ	23. Ⓐ Ⓑ Ⓒ Ⓓ	30. Ⓐ Ⓑ Ⓒ Ⓓ
3. Ⓐ Ⓑ Ⓒ Ⓓ	10. Ⓐ Ⓑ Ⓒ Ⓓ	17. Ⓐ Ⓑ Ⓒ Ⓓ	24. Ⓐ Ⓑ Ⓒ Ⓓ	
4. Ⓐ Ⓑ Ⓒ Ⓓ	11. Ⓐ Ⓑ Ⓒ Ⓓ	18. Ⓐ Ⓑ Ⓒ Ⓓ	25. Ⓐ Ⓑ Ⓒ Ⓓ	
5. Ⓐ Ⓑ Ⓒ Ⓓ	12. Ⓐ Ⓑ Ⓒ Ⓓ	19. Ⓐ Ⓑ Ⓒ Ⓓ	26. Ⓐ Ⓑ Ⓒ Ⓓ	
6. Ⓐ Ⓑ Ⓒ Ⓓ	13. Ⓐ Ⓑ Ⓒ Ⓓ	20. Ⓐ Ⓑ Ⓒ Ⓓ	27. Ⓐ Ⓑ Ⓒ Ⓓ	
7. Ⓐ Ⓑ Ⓒ Ⓓ	14. Ⓐ Ⓑ Ⓒ Ⓓ	21. Ⓐ Ⓑ Ⓒ Ⓓ	28. Ⓐ Ⓑ Ⓒ Ⓓ	

Word Knowledge

1. Ⓐ Ⓑ Ⓒ Ⓓ	8. Ⓐ Ⓑ Ⓒ Ⓓ	15. Ⓐ Ⓑ Ⓒ Ⓓ	22. Ⓐ Ⓑ Ⓒ Ⓓ	29. Ⓐ Ⓑ Ⓒ Ⓓ
2. Ⓐ Ⓑ Ⓒ Ⓓ	9. Ⓐ Ⓑ Ⓒ Ⓓ	16. Ⓐ Ⓑ Ⓒ Ⓓ	23. Ⓐ Ⓑ Ⓒ Ⓓ	30. Ⓐ Ⓑ Ⓒ Ⓓ
3. Ⓐ Ⓑ Ⓒ Ⓓ	10. Ⓐ Ⓑ Ⓒ Ⓓ	17. Ⓐ Ⓑ Ⓒ Ⓓ	24. Ⓐ Ⓑ Ⓒ Ⓓ	31. Ⓐ Ⓑ Ⓒ Ⓓ
4. Ⓐ Ⓑ Ⓒ Ⓓ	11. Ⓐ Ⓑ Ⓒ Ⓓ	18. Ⓐ Ⓑ Ⓒ Ⓓ	25. Ⓐ Ⓑ Ⓒ Ⓓ	32. Ⓐ Ⓑ Ⓒ Ⓓ
5. Ⓐ Ⓑ Ⓒ Ⓓ	12. Ⓐ Ⓑ Ⓒ Ⓓ	19. Ⓐ Ⓑ Ⓒ Ⓓ	26. Ⓐ Ⓑ Ⓒ Ⓓ	33. Ⓐ Ⓑ Ⓒ Ⓓ
6. Ⓐ Ⓑ Ⓒ Ⓓ	13. Ⓐ Ⓑ Ⓒ Ⓓ	20. Ⓐ Ⓑ Ⓒ Ⓓ	27. Ⓐ Ⓑ Ⓒ Ⓓ	34. Ⓐ Ⓑ Ⓒ Ⓓ
7. Ⓐ Ⓑ Ⓒ Ⓓ	14. Ⓐ Ⓑ Ⓒ Ⓓ	21. Ⓐ Ⓑ Ⓒ Ⓓ	28. Ⓐ Ⓑ Ⓒ Ⓓ	35. Ⓐ Ⓑ Ⓒ Ⓓ

Paragraph Comprehension

1. Ⓐ Ⓑ Ⓒ Ⓓ	8. Ⓐ Ⓑ Ⓒ Ⓓ	15. Ⓐ Ⓑ Ⓒ Ⓓ
2. Ⓐ Ⓑ Ⓒ Ⓓ	9. Ⓐ Ⓑ Ⓒ Ⓓ	
3. Ⓐ Ⓑ Ⓒ Ⓓ	10. Ⓐ Ⓑ Ⓒ Ⓓ	
4. Ⓐ Ⓑ Ⓒ Ⓓ	11. Ⓐ Ⓑ Ⓒ Ⓓ	
5. Ⓐ Ⓑ Ⓒ Ⓓ	12. Ⓐ Ⓑ Ⓒ Ⓓ	
6. Ⓐ Ⓑ Ⓒ Ⓓ	13. Ⓐ Ⓑ Ⓒ Ⓓ	
7. Ⓐ Ⓑ Ⓒ Ⓓ	14. Ⓐ Ⓑ Ⓒ Ⓓ	

Arithmetic Reasoning

Time: 36 minutes for 30 questions

Directions: The questions in this section are designed to measure your mathematical reasoning ability. They are word problems based on essential arithmetic skills. Choose the best answer for each question from the answer choices provided and shade in the corresponding oval on your answer sheet.

1. A grocer buys rolls from the local baker for $4 a dozen and sells them for $0.50 per roll. If he sells 8 dozen rolls per day, what is his daily profit?

   (A) $16

   (B) $12

   (C) $8

   (D) $4

2. A lecture hall is designed to seat 250 students. If designers estimate that 12% of the population is left-handed, how many left-handed desks should be installed?

   (A) 12

   (B) 24

   (C) 30

   (D) 37

3. An office staff includes 36 men and 24 women. What percentage of the staff is female?

   (A) 66.7%

   (B) 60%

   (C) 40%

   (D) 24%

4. Jesse and Jane start from the same rest stop on the interstate but drive in opposite directions. If Jesse drives at 55 miles per hour and Jane drives at 60 miles per hour, how far apart will they be after 3 hours?

   (A) 15 miles

   (B) 165 miles

   (C) 180 miles

   (D) 315 miles

5. Thirty percent of what number is 60?

   (A) 18

   (B) 20

   (C) 180

   (D) 200

6. The furlong is a measurement of distance sometimes used in horse racing. A furlong is one-eighth of a mile, and a mile is 5,280 feet. How many feet are in 5 furlongs?

   (A) 8,448

   (B) 3,300

   (C) 1,056

   (D) 660

7. Mr. Singh earns $12.20 an hour for the first 40 hours he works in a week and $1\frac{1}{2}$ times that for any hours beyond 40. What will his salary be in a week when he works 43 hours?

   (A) $488.90

   (B) $542.90

   (C) $786.90

   (D) $668.00

8. If you can walk a mile in 12 minutes, how long will it take you to walk a quarter mile?

   (A) 3 minutes

   (B) 9 minutes

   (C) 15 minutes

   (D) 48 minutes

Go on to next page

9. Jennifer earns $6 per hour plus 2% commission on everything she sells. Last week she worked 40 hours and sold $1,820 of merchandise. How much did she earn for the week?

(A) $36.40

(B) $240.80

(C) $276.40

(D) $364.00

10. Alan chooses a suit that sells for $350, but it is on sale for 20% off. What is the sale price?

(A) $280

(B) $330

(C) $343

(D) $370

11. If you buy a coffee maker for $63.79 and pay with a $100 bill, how much change will you receive?

(A) $47.21

(B) $37.79

(C) $37.21

(D) $36.21

12. Betsy left home at 9:30 a.m. and arrived at her grandmother's home, 153 miles away, at 12:30 p.m. How fast was she driving?

(A) 50 miles per hour

(B) 51 miles per hour

(C) 52 miles per hour

(D) 53 miles per hour

13. Alex's professor assigns him 479 pages of reading for a history course. If he can read 30 pages a day, how long will it take him to complete the assignment?

(A) 14 days

(B) 15 days

(C) 16 days

(D) 17 days

14. A baseball team had 4, 7, 6, and 13 hits in their first four games. How many total hits did they record?

(A) 17

(B) 20

(C) 26

(D) 30

15. If a baseball player had a batting average percentage of 0.290 and he had 300 at-bats, how many hits did he have?

(A) 10

(B) 29

(C) 87

(D) 97

16. Jeff committed to studying for 4 hours for his midterm. If he has been studying for 185 minutes, how many minutes of studying does he have left?

(A) 5

(B) 25

(C) 55

(D) 181

17. A shipment of 500 water bottles is delivered, and 20 are immediately removed and distributed to the office staff. The remaining bottles are equally divided and shipped to three stores. How many bottles does each store receive?

(A) 173

(B) 167

(C) 160

(D) 25

18. Each week, Chime puts one-half of his paycheck aside to pay bills and one-fifth in his savings account. If Chime's weekly paycheck is $550, how much money does he have left after bills and savings?

(A) $165

(B) $275

(C) $385

(D) $440

Go on to next page

19. Magdalena bought several shares of stock in a small company for $350. She held the stock for a year and then sold it for $1,050. What was the percent increase in Magdalena's investment?

    (A) $33\frac{1}{3}$%

    (B) 50%

    (C) 200%

    (D) 300%

20. A class of science students recorded the temperature each morning at 6 a.m. for five consecutive days. The class recorded the following temperatures: 42 degrees, 37 degrees, 35 degrees, 41 degrees, and 45 degrees. What was the average temperature for the five days?

    (A) 33 degrees

    (B) 35 degrees

    (C) 38 degrees

    (D) 40 degrees

21. Your savings account pays 4% interest per year. You deposit $300 in this account and a year later interest is added to your account. You then deposit an additional $200 and leave the account undisturbed for another year. How much interest will be added to your account at the end of the second year?

    (A) $20.48

    (B) $20.00

    (C) $12.00

    (D) $8.00

22. If you pay for a $4.27 purchase with a $10 bill, how much change will you receive?

    (A) $6.27

    (B) $6.73

    (C) $5.27

    (D) $5.73

23. A train travels 432 miles in 6 hours. At that rate, how far will it travel in 11 hours?

    (A) 235 miles

    (B) 792 miles

    (C) 864 miles

    (D) 2,160 miles

24. On a map, 1 inch represents 5 miles. If two cities are 238 miles apart, how far apart do they appear on the map?

    (A) 21 inches

    (B) 47.6 inches

    (C) 238 inches

    (D) 1,190 inches

25. Tony earns $11 an hour plus 2% commission on all the sales he makes. If his total sales during a 40-hour work week were $8,000, how much did he earn?

    (A) $440

    (B) $600

    (C) $1,600

    (D) $2,040

26. A refrigerator originally priced at $800 is on sale for $600. By what percent has the price of the refrigerator been reduced?

    (A) 20%

    (B) 25%

    (C) 60%

    (D) 75%

27. Alina wins a lottery and puts three-eighths of her prize money into her savings account. If she saves $450, how much was the lottery prize?

    (A) $168.75

    (B) $1,200

    (C) $1,350

    (D) $3,600

Go on to next page

28. A car rental company charges $29 per day plus $0.15 per mile. If a car was rented for 3 days and the final bill was $118.50, how far was the car driven?

    (A) 790 miles

    (B) 596 miles

    (C) 210 miles

    (D) 79 miles

29. Paul builds a 3-foot-wide walkway around a rectangular pool that's 25 feet wide and 50 feet long. How many tiles, each 1 foot by 1 foot, does he need for the walkway?

    (A) 234

    (B) 486

    (C) 1,736

    (D) 3,750

30. Jessica and Jennifer live 9 miles apart along the same road. Each leaves her own home at noon and begins walking along the road toward the other's home. If Jessica walks at 3 miles per hour and Jennifer walks at 2.4 miles per hour, at what time will they meet?

    (A) 1:40 p.m.

    (B) 2:15 p.m.

    (C) 3:00 p.m.

    (D) 3:45 p.m.

STOP DO NOT TURN THE PAGE UNTIL TOLD TO DO SO.
DO NOT RETURN TO A PREVIOUS TEST.

Word Knowledge

> **Time:** 11 minutes for 35 questions
>
> **Directions:** The questions in this section are designed to test your vocabulary knowledge. Some of the questions ask you to find the choice closest in meaning to the word in the question. Other questions present you with a sentence that contains the word. In both types of questions select the word or phrase that is nearest in meaning to the underlined word and shade in the corresponding oval on your answer sheet. Those questions that present the word in a sentence may provide context clues that you can use to help you figure out the meaning of the underlined word.

1. <u>Thwart</u> most nearly means

   (A) strengthen

   (B) steal

   (C) prevent

   (D) improve

2. <u>Allay</u> most nearly means

   (A) relieve

   (B) befriend

   (C) combine

   (D) rest

3. <u>Salvo</u> most nearly means

   (A) exploration

   (B) solution

   (C) agreement

   (D) bombardment

4. <u>Scant</u> most nearly means

   (A) inadequate

   (B) numerous

   (C) weary

   (D) lazy

5. <u>Gamely</u> most nearly means

   (A) childishly

   (B) arguably

   (C) willingly

   (D) possibly

6. <u>Tainted</u> most nearly means

   (A) spirited

   (B) painful

   (C) reddish

   (D) contaminated

7. <u>Parsimony</u> most nearly means

   (A) frugality

   (B) infidelity

   (C) believability

   (D) illegibly

8. <u>Desist</u> most nearly means

   (A) wonder

   (B) scatter

   (C) cease

   (D) uphold

9. <u>Deftness</u> most nearly means

   (A) silence

   (B) skill

   (C) ignorance

   (D) nullification

10. <u>Terse</u> most nearly means

    (A) brief

    (B) ineffective

    (C) tense

    (D) energetic

11. <u>Perplexity</u> most nearly means

    (A) complexity

    (B) inflexibility

    (C) confusion

    (D) inaccuracy

Go on to next page

12. <u>Guile</u> most nearly means
    (A) honesty
    (B) accessibility
    (C) measurement
    (D) deviousness

13. <u>Malleable</u> most nearly means
    (A) pliable
    (B) breakable
    (C) foolish
    (D) indirect

14. <u>Prosaic</u> most nearly means
    (A) fine
    (B) ordinary
    (C) fancy
    (D) alarming

15. <u>Obtuse</u> most nearly means
    (A) shy
    (B) large
    (C) dull-witted
    (D) self-reliant

16. <u>Mirth</u> most nearly means
    (A) integrity
    (B) satisfaction
    (C) laughter
    (D) misery

17. <u>Scrupulous</u> most nearly means
    (A) cheerful
    (B) conscientious
    (C) sarcastic
    (D) curious

18. <u>Plethora</u> most nearly means
    (A) excess
    (B) seclusion
    (C) illusion
    (D) dilemma

19. <u>Negligent</u> most nearly means
    (A) righteous
    (B) careless
    (C) weighty
    (D) painful

20. <u>Vindictive</u> most nearly means
    (A) innocent
    (B) alert
    (C) unwilling
    (D) vengeful

21. The captain believed the fine weather to be an <u>auspicious</u> omen.
    (A) golden
    (B) buoyant
    (C) fierce
    (D) favorable

22. Shorter than previous editions, the new handbook eliminated all <u>superfluous</u> material.
    (A) excellent
    (B) incorrect
    (C) unnecessary
    (D) obsolete

23. After the long hike, the soldiers were <u>enervated</u>.
    (A) vibrant
    (B) exhausted
    (C) frightened
    (D) bold

24. The lieutenant believed any sign of weakness would <u>undermine</u> his authority.
    (A) bolster
    (B) identify
    (C) weaken
    (D) endorse

Go on to next page

25. The discussion of politics soon turned <u>acrimonious</u>.
    (A) loud
    (B) bitter
    (C) friendly
    (D) gloomy

26. The judge was revered for her <u>acumen</u>.
    (A) kindness
    (B) generosity
    (C) intelligence
    (D) diligence

27. Further action may be required if both sides of the conflict remain <u>intransigent</u>.
    (A) unyielding
    (B) aggressive
    (C) tenuous
    (D) indecisive

28. The <u>turgid</u> river formed an impassible barrier.
    (A) muddy
    (B) rapid
    (C) swollen
    (D) unstable

29. Sexism in the workplace has been a <u>contentious</u> issue for several decades.
    (A) controversial
    (B) dormant
    (C) pleasant
    (D) overemphasized

30. A gullible man, he was unable to detect <u>subterfuge</u> in others.
    (A) humor
    (B) deception
    (C) ferocity
    (D) extravagance

31. Using <u>specious</u> logic, the attorney attempted to sway the jury.
    (A) long-winded
    (B) quirky
    (C) fallacious
    (D) forceful

32. The sergeant was surprised at the <u>temerity</u> of the new recruits.
    (A) fearfulness
    (B) audacity
    (C) knowledge
    (D) rawness

33. Divided loyalty creates a <u>quandary</u> for those who observe cheating.
    (A) penchant
    (B) pathos
    (C) predicament
    (D) peril

34. The media is often <u>castigated</u> for its role in stoking sensationalism.
    (A) praised
    (B) incarcerated
    (C) precluded
    (D) rebuked

35. The group leader was surprised by the <u>multifarious</u> duties she was required to complete.
    (A) menial
    (B) diverse
    (C) arbitrary
    (D) illogical

STOP DO NOT TURN THE PAGE UNTIL TOLD TO DO SO.
DO NOT RETURN TO A PREVIOUS TEST.

Paragraph Comprehension

Time: 13 minutes for 15 questions

Directions: The section tests your reading comprehension: your ability to read a passage and answer a question based on what is stated or implied in the passage. Carefully read each paragraph and the question that follows. Based on what is stated or implied in the passage, select the best answer for each question from the four choices provided and shade in the corresponding oval on your answer sheet.

When you show up for your appointment to take the ASVAB, make sure you are properly prepared. You should have familiarized yourself with the format of the test before scheduling an appointment. Most importantly, you need to arrive at the venue on time, for latecomers will not be admitted and will have to reschedule their test appointments. All you need to bring with you is a valid picture ID. All necessary writing tools will be supplied at the test site.

1. According to the passage, you must do all of the following on the day of the ASVAB EXCEPT

   (A) bring a valid picture ID.

   (B) bring two sharpened #2 pencils.

   (C) be punctual.

   (D) know what to expect.

Althea Gibson, the first African American woman to win a Grand Slam tennis tournament, was a trailblazing athlete. Although Gibson was born into a poor family in South Carolina, her athletic talent drew the attention of Dr. Walter Johnson, a Virginia physician who became her patron. Honing her impressive natural talent, she went on to win 11 major titles, including the French Open, Wimbledon, and the U.S. Open. Eventually she became New Jersey State Commissioner of Athletics, a post she held for ten years. Gibson is often referred to as "the Jackie Robinson of tennis," because she broke the color barrier in tennis and became the most renowned female athlete of the 1950s.

2. It can be inferred from the passage that Althea Gibson is a trailblazing athlete because

   (A) she won more tournaments than Jackie Robinson.

   (B) she won Wimbledon, the French Open, and the U.S. Open in the same year.

   (C) she was the first African American female athlete to win national and international recognition.

   (D) she became the first female African American baseball player.

Go on to next page

The *Tyrannosaurus rex,* originally believed to have been the most bloodthirsty of all the dinosaurs who roamed the earth 200 million years ago, may have gotten a bad rap. Recent evidence suggests that the *T. rex* may have been a rather slow-moving scavenger rather than a ferocious predator. Indeed, anatomical analyses of recently discovered thigh and forearm bones may spur a revision of the Hollywood portrait of the rapacious flesh-devouring *T. rex.*

3. The new interpretation of recent scientific findings suggests that the popular culture characterization of the *T. rex* is

   (A) undeniably verifiable

   (B) categorically unfounded

   (C) possibly inaccurate

   (D) absolutely true

Mustangs, feral horses that roam free in certain regions of the western United States, are descendants of horses brought to this continent by the Spanish. Since 1971, these herds have been protected by an Act of Congress that identifies them as "living symbols of the historical and pioneer spirit of the West." The current population is estimated at 33,000.

4. Which of the following is the best title for this passage?

   (A) Why Mustangs Roam the West

   (B) Our Legacy from Spain

   (C) Protective Acts of Congress

   (D) Equine Symbols of the Wild West

In the Hebrew Scriptures the chief badge of sanctity conferred on God's angels was wings and the ability to fly. If we come down to the mythology of more recent times, we find our pious ancestors in New England thoroughly convinced that the witches they flogged and hanged were perfectly able to navigate the air on a broomstick — thus antedating the Wrights' experiments with heavier-than-air machines by more than 250 years.

5. It can be inferred from this passage that

   (A) in New England, witches had the ability to fly.

   (B) the human fascination with flight is based on mankind's desire to be holy.

   (C) the Wright brothers based their experiments with aircraft on biblical notions.

   (D) the ability to fly has been associated with powers of both good and evil.

In a vague way the earliest balloonists recognized that power, independent of wind, was necessary to give balloons steerage way and direction. Steam was in its infancy, but the efforts to devise some sort of an engine light enough to be carried into the air were untiring. The suggestion was made that the explosion of small quantities of gun-cotton and the expulsion of the resulting gases might be utilized in some fashion to operate propelling machinery. Though the suggestion was not developed to any useful point, it was of interest as forecasting the fundamental idea of the gas engines of today, which have made aviation possible — that is, the creation of power by a series of explosions within the motor.

6. The writer of this passage would most likely agree that

   (A) the search for a method of powering balloons was fortuitous in the development of aviation history.

   (B) the suggestion to use small explosions to provide power for the balloon was very useful to early balloonists.

   (C) the advent of the steam engine revolutionized balloon engineering.

   (D) inventors of hot air balloons soon gave up the idea of creating an engine that's light enough to be carried aloft.

During the first period of feudalism, that is to say from the middle of the 9th to the middle of the 12th centuries, the inhabitants of castles had little time to devote to the pleasures of private life. They had not only to be continually under arms for the endless quarrels of the King and the great chiefs, but they had also to oppose the Normans on one side and the Saracens on the other, who, being masters of the Spanish peninsula, spread like the rising tide.

7. The author's main purpose in writing this paragraph is to

   (A) explain the priorities in the feudal society.

   (B) argue the merits of feudalism as a way of life.

   (C) detail the importance of privacy in feudal castles.

   (D) propose a new way of examining feudal life.

Go on to next page

During the last quarter of the 18th century and during the first half of the 19th century, France was the chief center for the activities of submarine inventors. However, very few of the many plans put forward in this period were executed. The few exceptions resulted in little else than trial boats, which usually did not live up to the expectations of their inventors or their financial backers and were, therefore, discarded in quick order. In spite of this lack of actual results, this particular period was of considerable importance to the later development of the submarine. Almost every one of the many boats then projected or built contained some innovation, and, in this way, some of the many obstacles were gradually overcome.

8. With which of the following statements would the writer most likely agree?

   (A) Early experiments in France with submergible boats were of no value to later scientists who were eventually successful.

   (B) After submarines became a reality, scientists realized how impractical and ridiculous the early inventions were.

   (C) The financial backers of the early prototypes of the submarine became wealthy when obstacles to success were overcome.

   (D) The creation of the modern submarine owes a debt to those early inventors who refused to be discouraged by failure.

Ancient astronomy may seem very elementary to those of the present day who have been familiar from childhood with the great truths of nature, but, in the infancy of science, the men who made such discoveries must have been sagacious philosophers. The stars had been studied, and some great astronomical discoveries had been made, untold ages before those to which our earliest historical records extend.

9. The writer most likely means the phrase "sagacious philosophers" to refer to

   (A) religious leaders.

   (B) wise astronomers.

   (C) ancient historians.

   (D) scientific inventors.

An apparently new strain of tuberculosis (TB) emerged in South Africa in 2006. In the mainly Zulu community in Kwa-Zulu-Natal province, most of the victims were also infected with HIV. The fatality rate among those infected is highly alarming. Within three weeks after testing positive for TB, 52 of 53 patients died.

10. The passage supports which of the following conclusions about the people in Kwa-Zulu-Natal province?

   (A) Anyone who has contracted TB has also contracted HIV.

   (B) Anyone who has contracted HIV has also contracted TB.

   (C) Most of the patients who have TB also have HIV.

   (D) The combination of TB and HIV is always fatal.

The creation of Napster, the online music sharing Web site, was the brainchild of a Northeastern University college student. He figured out a way to enable people to share MP3 files. They could avoid purchasing music commercially and save hundreds of dollars. While the idea was brilliant, it was also deemed illegal, infringing on the intellectual property rights of music artists. Before Napster was shut down by court order, it had 80 million users, happily downloading the music they loved.

11. Napster was shut down because

   (A) too many people were using it and the system crashed.

   (B) it violated the intellectual property rights of musicians.

   (C) underage users were exposed to inappropriate lyrics.

   (D) the college student who created it never applied for a patent for his creation.

Go on to next page

To adjust the equipment on the soldier, first slip the arms one at a time through the pack suspenders as through the sleeves of a coat; by means of the adjusting buckles on the belt suspenders, raise or lower the belt until it rests well down over the hip bones on the sides and below the pit of the abdomen in front; raise or lower it in the rear until the adjusting strap lies smoothly across the small of the back; by means of the adjusting buckles on the pack suspenders, raise or lower the load on the back until the top of the haversack is on a level with the top of the shoulders, the pack suspenders, from their point of attachment to the haversack to the line of tangency with the shoulder, being horizontal. The latter is absolutely essential to the proper adjustment of the load.

12. According to the passage, what is absolutely essential to the proper adjustment of the soldiers' equipment?

    (A) that the adjusting strap rests smoothly on the small of the back

    (B) that the pack suspenders are horizontal from their attachment to the shoulders

    (C) that the belt lies on the hip bones on the sides and the pit of the abdomen in the front

    (D) that the soldier slips one arm at a time into the suspenders

There could be no doubt as to what the Congress would do on the 15th of June, 1775. Unquestionably George Washington was the fittest man for the post. Twenty years earlier he had seen important service in the war with France. His position and character commanded universal respect. Once Congress adopted unanimously the motion, it only remained to be seen whether Washington would accept. On the next day he came to the sitting with his mind made up. The members, he said, would bear witness to his declaration that he thought himself unfit for the task. Since, however, they called him, he would try to do his duty. He would take the command, but he would accept no pay beyond his expenses.

13. It can be inferred from this passage that

    (A) George Washington was eager to become the first president of the United States.

    (B) no one in the United States was as qualified as George Washington to become the first leader of the new nation.

    (C) the selection of George Washington to become the Chief Executive was a shock to most citizens.

    (D) George Washington did not display the same confidence in his ability as did the other members of Congress.

Go on to next page

No one knows for sure who came up with the idea for the Ryder Cup, an international golf competition between the best American and British professionals, but many have enjoyed the matches. Early in the 1920s, the first matches were played in Gleneagles, Scotland, with the British team trouncing their American opponents. In 1926 Samuel Ryder, a wealthy English seed merchant who was one of the spectators, was moved to commission a trophy to encourage this ongoing tradition of competition. The first Ryder cup was presented to the American team in 1927.

14. Which of the following can be inferred from the passage?

(A) The United States won the first official Ryder Cup.

(B) Great Britain has never won a Ryder Cup on American soil.

(C) Samuel Ryder was an outstanding member of the first British Ryder Cup team.

(D) The Ryder Cup tournament is always held in Scotland.

When purchasing a new television, the first decision the modern consumer faces is LCD or plasma. Unfortunately, there's no quick and easy answer. One difference is the composition of the screen: glass for plasma and plastic for LCDs. So consider the placement (less glare with plastic) and durability (plastic is more easily scratched than glass). As far as the picture itself, plasmas usually have truer color, but LCDs have brighter pictures. Perhaps you should just go with the one that looks the nicest in your home.

15. The writer's purpose in this passage is to

(A) encourage you to purchase a plasma TV.

(B) alert you to the evils of electronic purchases.

(C) assist you in decorating your home in a modern style.

(D) help you resolve an electronics dilemma.

STOP DO NOT TURN THE PAGE UNTIL TOLD TO DO SO.
DO NOT RETURN TO A PREVIOUS TEST.

Chapter 23

ASVAB GT Practice Test: Answers and Explanations

$\bullet \bullet$

After you've spent the time going through the practice Armed Services Vocational Aptitude Battery General Technical (ASVAB GT) test in Chapter 22, check your answers here in this chapter to see how you fared. We provide the answers in two different formats: with detailed explanation and in a bare-bones answer key. We suggest you read through the detailed answers for each question to get the most out of your studies, but if you're running low on time and simply need the answers, take a look at the answer key at the end of the chapter. If this practice test causes you any trouble, flip to Parts II and III for some extra studying. In those parts, we discuss English and math skills.

Arithmetic Reasoning Answers

1. **A.** Eight dozen rolls is $8 \times 12 = 96$ rolls. At $0.50 per roll, the grocer will bring in an income of $48. (Fifty cents is half of a dollar, so think half of 96.) The grocer purchased the rolls for $4 per dozen, or $8 \times 4 = 32$. Income minus cost is $48 - 32 = 16$.

2. **C.** Twelve percent of the 250 desks should be left-handed, so multiply $0.12 \times 250 = 30$. Do the multiplication mentally by thinking 12 for every 100. You have 200 and half of 100, so $12 + 12 + 6 = 30$. Or you can think 10% of 250 is 25, and 2% of 250 is 2×2.5, or 5. So $25 + 5 = 30$.

3. **C.** Twenty-four women out of a total staff of $36 + 24 = 60$ people is $\frac{24}{60} = \frac{4}{10} = 40\%$.

4. **D.** If Jesse and Jane drive in opposite directions at 55 and 60 miles per hour respectively, each hour they move $55 + 60 = 105$ miles farther apart. If they drive this way for 3 hours, they will be $3 \times 105 = 315$ miles apart.

5. **D.** A proportion will solve this problem easily. $\frac{part}{whole} = \frac{\%}{100}$ becomes $\frac{60}{x} = \frac{30}{100}$ when the given information is inserted, and equal fractions suggest $x = 200$. Or consider that 30% of 100 is 30, and you want twice that, so 30% of 200 is 60.

6. **B.** $\frac{1}{8}$ of a mile $= \frac{1}{8} \times 5,280$ feet $= \frac{5,280}{8} = \frac{1,320}{2} = 660$ feet. So each furlong is 660 feet. Multiply by 5 to find that 5 furlongs is 3,300 feet.

7. **B.** If Mr. Singh works 43 hours, he earns $12.20 an hour for the first 40 hours and $1\frac{1}{2} \times \$12.20$ per hour for the additional three hours. So $\$12.20 \times 40 = \$488.00$ and $1\frac{1}{2} \times \$12.20 \times 3 = \frac{3}{2} \times \overset{6.10}{\cancel{12.20}} \times 3 = 9 \times 6.10 = 54.90$. Add $488 + 54.90$ to find that Mr. Singh's total earnings are $542.90.

8. **A.** A quarter of the distance should take a quarter of the time, so if you can walk a mile in 12 minutes, you can walk a quarter mile in $12 \div 4 = 3$ minutes.

9. **C.** Jennifer's base salary was $6 per hour $\times$ 40 hours = $240. Her commission was 2% of $1,820 = $36.40. (Multiply $1,820 by two and move the decimal point two places left.) Add salary plus commission to find Jennifer's total earnings: $240 + $36.40 = $276.40.

10. **A.** Twenty percent off of a $350 purchase is $2 \times 10\%$ of 350, or 2×35. Alan saves $70 on the suit, so $350 - 70 = 280$.

11. **D.** Find $100 – $63.79 mentally by making change. You need $0.01 to make $63.80; $0.20 to make $64; $6 to make $70; and another $30 to make $100. So $0.01 +$0.20 + $6 + $30 = $36.21.

12. **B.** Betsy traveled 153 miles in 3 hours, so 153 ÷ 3 = 51 miles per hour.

13. **C.** 479 pages ÷ 30 pages a day is best estimated as 480 ÷ 30 = 48 ÷ 3 =16 days.

14. **D.** 4 + 7 + 6 + 13 = (4 + 6) + (7 + 13) = 10 + 20 = 30 hits.

15. **C.** Batting average is number of hits divided by number of at-bats, so $\frac{\text{hits}}{\text{at-bats}} = \frac{x}{300} = 0.290$. Multiply 0.290 × 300 = 87 hits.

16. **C.** To figure out how many minutes are in 4 hours, multiply 4 × 60 = 240 minutes. Subtract 240 – 185 = 55 minutes. Another method is to divide 185 ÷ 60 = 3 hours 5 minutes, the amount of time Jeff has already studied. 1 hour – 5 minutes = 55 minutes.

17. **C.** Removing 20 bottles leaves 500 – 20 = 480 to be distributed to the 3 stores. So 480 ÷ 3 = 160 bottles.

18. **A.** Chime earmarks = $\frac{1}{2} + \frac{1}{5} = \frac{5+2}{10} = \frac{7}{10}$, so he has $\frac{3}{10}$ left, and $\frac{3}{10} \times 55\emptyset = 3 \times 55$ $= 3 \times 5 \times 11 = 15 \times 11 = 165$. Or you can work through the money amounts. Half of $550 goes to pay bills, leaving $275. He saves $\frac{1}{5}$ of his salary, or $110. So $275 + $110 = $385, and $550 – $385 = $165.

19. **C.** The increase in the price of the stock was $1,050 – $350 = $700. Percent increase is $\frac{\text{increase}}{\text{original}}$ expressed as a percent, so $\frac{700}{350} = 2$ or 200%.

20. **D.** The average refers to the mean, so add the readings and divide by 5. First add 42 degrees + 37 degrees + 35 degrees + 41 degrees + 45 degrees = 200 degrees. Then find the average temperature by dividing 200 ÷ 5 = 40 degrees. You also can find the average by starting with the middle value (the median) and averaging the pull of the higher and lower values. The median here is 41 degrees. Express the difference between 41 degrees and each of the values as a positive or negative number: 42 degrees is +1, 37 degrees is –4, 35 degrees is –6, 41 degrees is 0, and 45 degrees is +4. Add the positive and negative numbers: +1 + –4 + –6 +0 + 4 = –5. Divide –5 by 5 to get –1, and the mean is one unit lower than the median: 41 – 1 = 40 degrees.

21. **A.** Begin with the original deposit of $300 and add 4% interest, or $12. (Four percent is 4 for each 100, and you have 3 hundreds. So 3 × 4 = 12.) At the end of the first year, the balance is $312. Add the additional $200 to bring the balance to $512. At the end of the second year, interest is calculated as 4% of $512, which is $20.48.

22. **D.** Make change to figure this problem: It takes $0.03 to make $4.30, another $0.70 to make $5, and another $5 to make $10. So $10.00 – $4.27 = $5.73

23. **B.** You can find the speed of the train in miles per hour, and then multiply by 11 hours, or you can solve the problem with proportional thinking. Use short division to divide 432 miles ÷ 6 hours = 72 miles per hour. Multiply that product by 11 hours to get 792 miles. If you want to use a proportion, it's $\frac{432}{6} = \frac{x}{11}$. Multiplying 432 by 11 is more difficult, but remember that you can reduce the fraction $\frac{432}{6} = \frac{72}{1}$ and then $\frac{72}{1} = \frac{x}{11}$. Cross-multiply to get $x = 792$.

24. **B.** If two cities are 238 miles apart, and each 5 miles is represented by 1 inch, divide the distance apart by 5: 238 ÷ 5 = 47.6 inches.

25. **B.** Multiply Tony's salary rate of $11 an hour by the 40 hours he works, which gives you $440. Then calculate his commission: 2% of $8,000, or $2 for every $100 sold, gives him a commission of $160. Add the commission and the salary to find that he earned $160 + $440 = $600.

26. **B.** The refrigerator that originally cost $800 was reduced $200 to sell for $600. The reduction of $200 is $\frac{200}{800} = \frac{1}{4} = 25\%$.

27. **B.** Here's one way to solve this problem: $450 is $\frac{3}{8}$ of her prize money, so divide $450 \div \frac{3}{8} = {}^{150}\cancel{450} \times \frac{8}{\cancel{3}} = \$1,200$. Or you can use mental math: $450 is $\frac{3}{8}$ of her prize money, so $150 is $\frac{1}{8}$ of the prize, and $150 \times 8 = \$800 + \$400 = \$1,200$ is the whole prize.

28. **C.** The charge for 3 days was $3 \times \$29 = \$87$. So $118.50 - \$87 = \$31.50$ was the charge for mileage. Divide $31.50 by $0.15 to get 210 miles.

29. **B.** The area of the pool and walkway combined is $(25 + 6) \times (50 + 6) = 31 \times 56 = 1,736$ square feet. The area of the pool is $25 \times 50 = 1,250$ square feet. To get the area of the walkway, subtract $1,736 - 1,250 = 486$ square feet. Each tile covers 1 square foot, so you need 486 tiles.

30. **A.** Walking toward one another, Jessica and Jennifer cover $3 + 2.4 = 5.4$ miles per hour. To find the time that elapses before they meet, divide the distance of 9 miles by 5.4 miles per hour: $9 \div 5.4 = 1.\overline{6}$ hours, or 1 hour and 40 minutes after noon. So they'll meet at 1:40 p.m.

Word Knowledge Answers

1. **C.** *Thwart* (verb) means to prevent something from occurring.

2. **A.** *Allay* (verb) means to relieve or calm.

3. **D.** *Salvo* (noun) means a simultaneous discharge of weapons or bombardment.

4. **A.** *Scant* (adjective) means meager or inadequate.

5. **C.** *Gamely* (adverb) means in a willing or plucky manner.

6. **D.** *Tainted* (adjective) means contaminated or impure.

7. **A.** *Parsimony* (noun) means stinginess or frugality.

8. **C.** *Desist* (verb) means to stop or cease.

9. **B.** *Deftness* (noun) means skill or dexterity.

10. **A.** *Terse* (adjective) means brief.

11. **C.** *Perplexity* (noun) means confusion.

12. **D.** *Guile* (noun) means deviousness or slyness.

13. **A.** *Malleable* (adjective) means able to be shaped or pliable.

14. **B.** *Prosaic* (adjective) means ordinary or commonplace (even dull).

15. **C.** *Obtuse* (adjective) means dull-witted or stubborn.

16. **C.** *Mirth* (noun) means laughter or gaiety.

17. **B.** *Scrupulous* (adjective) means honest or conscientious.

18. **A.** *Plethora* (noun) means abundance or excess.

19. **B.** *Negligent* (adjective) means careless or neglectful.

20. **D.** *Vindictive* (adjective) means seeking revenge or vengeful.

21. **D.** *Auspicious* (adjective) means fortunate or favorable.

22. **C.** *Superfluous* (adjective) means unnecessary.

23. **B.** *Enervated* (adjective from the verb *to enervate*) means exhausted or weakened.

24. **C.** *Undermine* (verb) means to weaken.

25. **B.** *Acrimonious* (adjective) means bitter.

26. **C.** *Acumen* (noun) means keen insight or intelligence.

27. **A.** *Intransigent* (adjective) means stubbornly unyielding.

28. **C.** *Turgid* (adjective) means swollen.

29. **A.** *Contentious* (adjective) means controversial or argumentative.

30. **B.** *Subterfuge* (noun) means trick or deception.

31. **C.** *Specious* (adjective) means false or fallacious.

32. **B.** *Temerity* (noun) means boldness or audacity.

33. **C.** *Quandary* (noun) means a dilemma or predicament.

34. **D.** *Castigated* (verb) means scolded or rebuked.

35. **B.** *Multifarious* (adjective) means varied (the root *multi* means many).

Paragraph Comprehension Answers

1. **B.** You don't need two sharpened #2 pencils for admission to the ASVAB. This question is a detail question. To find the answer, scan the passage until you find the list of things required for entrance into the test. The last sentence states that "writing tools will be supplied at the test," so Choice (B) is the correct answer.

2. **C.** Trailblazing implies breaking through obstacles and creating new inroads. Althea Gibson trailblazed when she became the first African American female athlete to win national and international recognition. Choices (A) and (D) are inaccurate statements, and you can't know whether Choice (B) is true based on the information in the passage. So Choice (C) is the best answer.

3. **C.** Based on the new findings, the representation of the *T. Rex* as a bloodthirsty predator is most likely inaccurate. Of course, scientists don't have absolute factual evidence, so that eliminates Choices (A), (B), and (D).

4. **D.** An appropriate title should reflect the main idea of the passage. The passage makes a point of identifying mustangs as "living symbols of the . . . West." Choice (D) repeats this point (*equine* means horse). Choice (A) isn't answered by the passage, and Choices (B) and (C) are too general.

5. **D.** The only inference that can be supported by the passage is Choice (D). Choice (A) is merely superstition (although many believed in witches at the time). Choice (B) begins correctly with the human fascination with flight, but then it becomes inaccurate by linking that fascination with man's desire to be holy. Choice (C) also is inaccurate: The Wright brothers didn't base their experiments on biblical notions.

6. **A.** The last sentence, "Though the suggestion . . . was of interest as forecasting the fundamental idea of the gas engines of today, which have made aviation possible," implies that the search for power for balloons led to important aviation advances. Thus, it was *fortuitous* (happening by lucky chance). As a result, Choice (A) is the correct answer. The information in the passage contradicts Choice (B), and Choice (C) is incorrect because the steam engine isn't mentioned in the passage. Choice (D) isn't covered by the information in the passage either.

7. **A.** Choice (A) is the only inference that can be made from the passage. The author points out that war with neighboring rulers took priority over private concerns in feudal times. Choice (C) contradicts the author's main point, and Choice (B) is far too general. Choice (D) is off-topic. The author doesn't propose a new way to look at feudal life. He describes the main concern for those in the castle: protection from enemies.

8. **D.** The last sentence indicates that each new invention added some innovation that was built upon until submarines became a reality, making Choice (D) the best answer. Choice (A) is contradicted by this point, and no information in the passage supports Choice (B) or (C).

9. **B.** The phrase "sagacious philosophers" most likely refers to astronomers who were astute and perceptive enough to make discoveries in ancient times. No evidence in the passage supports religious leaders, historians, or inventors.

10. **C.** The only conclusion that can be supported by the passage is that "most of the victims [of TB] were also infected with HIV." Only Choice (C) supports this conclusion. Choices (A) and (B) are too comprehensive and can't be supported by the evidence. Choice (D) is contradicted by the statistics in the passage.

11. **B.** According to the passage, Napster was shut down for "infringing on the intellectual property rights of music artists," so Choice (B) is correct. Choice (A) is inaccurate; in fact, Napster never crashed. Choices (C) and (D) aren't addressed in the passage.

12. **B.** The passage covers many steps in the process of adjusting equipment, but the last sentence states that the "latter" (referring to the last step mentioned) is essential. This step, which is reflected in Choice (B), is keeping the suspenders horizontal across the shoulders. All the other choices are steps in the process, but they aren't designated "absolutely essential."

13. **D.** According to the passage, Washington "thought himself unfit for the task." This line contradicts Choice (A). The passage doesn't contain enough information to support Choice (B). Choice (C) is contradicted by the information that "Unquestionably, George Washington was the fittest man for the post." So Choice (D) is the best answer.

14. **A.** It can be inferred from the passage that the United States won the first Ryder Cup, because the U.S. team won in 1927, the first year the Cup was officially presented. The passage doesn't address Choice (B), and it is, in fact, untrue. Choices (C) and (D) are false based on the information in the passage. (In case you're wondering, the British team became Team Europe in 1979).

15. **D.** The writer's purpose is to help you decide what kind of TV is best for you. Because "there's no quick and easy answer," it's a *dilemma* (a difficult predicament). Choice (A) is one-sided and not supported by the writer. Choices (B) and (C) are off-topic, leaving Choice (D) as the best answer.

Answer Key for ASVAB GT (General Technical) Practice Test

Arithmetic Reasoning

1. A	7. B	13. C	19. C	25. B
2. C	8. A	14. D	20. D	26. B
3. C	9. C	15. C	21. A	27. B
4. D	10. A	16. C	22. D	28. C
5. D	11. D	17. C	23. B	29. B
6. B	12. B	18. A	24. B	30. A

Word Knowledge

1. C	8. C	15. C	22. C	29. A
2. A	9. B	16. C	23. B	30. B
3. D	10. A	17. B	24. C	31. C
4. A	11. C	18. A	25. B	32. B
5. C	12. D	19. B	26. C	33. C
6. D	13. A	20. D	27. A	34. D
7. A	14. B	21. D	28. C	35. B

Paragraph Comprehension

1. B	4. D	7. A	10. C	13. D
2. C	5. D	8. D	11. B	14. A
3. C	6. A	9. B	12. B	15. D

Chapter 24

ASVAB Marine OCS Composite Practice Test

• •

*T*his practice exam tests your skills on the General Science, Arithmetic Reasoning, Mathematics Knowledge, and Electronic Comprehension subtests of the Armed Services Vocational Aptitude Battery Marine Officer Candidate School Composite (ASVAB Marine OCS). When sitting down to take this test, be sure to recreate the testing conditions you'll face during the true test. For example, use a watch or clock to time yourself. Part of the challenge is completing each section in the allotted time. And be sure to take the test all at once and without many breaks. Mark your answers on the answer sheet provided. When you've completed the practice test, check your answers in Chapter 25. There we provide detailed answers with explanation as well a simple answer key if you're in a hurry.

Answer Sheet

Use the ovals provided with this practice test to record your answers.

General Science

1. Ⓐ Ⓑ Ⓒ Ⓓ   8. Ⓐ Ⓑ Ⓒ Ⓓ   15. Ⓐ Ⓑ Ⓒ Ⓓ   22. Ⓐ Ⓑ Ⓒ Ⓓ
2. Ⓐ Ⓑ Ⓒ Ⓓ   9. Ⓐ Ⓑ Ⓒ Ⓓ   16. Ⓐ Ⓑ Ⓒ Ⓓ   23. Ⓐ Ⓑ Ⓒ Ⓓ
3. Ⓐ Ⓑ Ⓒ Ⓓ   10. Ⓐ Ⓑ Ⓒ Ⓓ   17. Ⓐ Ⓑ Ⓒ Ⓓ   24. Ⓐ Ⓑ Ⓒ Ⓓ
4. Ⓐ Ⓑ Ⓒ Ⓓ   11. Ⓐ Ⓑ Ⓒ Ⓓ   18. Ⓐ Ⓑ Ⓒ Ⓓ   25. Ⓐ Ⓑ Ⓒ Ⓓ
5. Ⓐ Ⓑ Ⓒ Ⓓ   12. Ⓐ Ⓑ Ⓒ Ⓓ   19. Ⓐ Ⓑ Ⓒ Ⓓ
6. Ⓐ Ⓑ Ⓒ Ⓓ   13. Ⓐ Ⓑ Ⓒ Ⓓ   20. Ⓐ Ⓑ Ⓒ Ⓓ
7. Ⓐ Ⓑ Ⓒ Ⓓ   14. Ⓐ Ⓑ Ⓒ Ⓓ   21. Ⓐ Ⓑ Ⓒ Ⓓ

Arithmetic Reasoning

1. Ⓐ Ⓑ Ⓒ Ⓓ   8. Ⓐ Ⓑ Ⓒ Ⓓ   15. Ⓐ Ⓑ Ⓒ Ⓓ   22. Ⓐ Ⓑ Ⓒ Ⓓ   29. Ⓐ Ⓑ Ⓒ Ⓓ
2. Ⓐ Ⓑ Ⓒ Ⓓ   9. Ⓐ Ⓑ Ⓒ Ⓓ   16. Ⓐ Ⓑ Ⓒ Ⓓ   23. Ⓐ Ⓑ Ⓒ Ⓓ   30. Ⓐ Ⓑ Ⓒ Ⓓ
3. Ⓐ Ⓑ Ⓒ Ⓓ   10. Ⓐ Ⓑ Ⓒ Ⓓ   17. Ⓐ Ⓑ Ⓒ Ⓓ   24. Ⓐ Ⓑ Ⓒ Ⓓ
4. Ⓐ Ⓑ Ⓒ Ⓓ   11. Ⓐ Ⓑ Ⓒ Ⓓ   18. Ⓐ Ⓑ Ⓒ Ⓓ   25. Ⓐ Ⓑ Ⓒ Ⓓ
5. Ⓐ Ⓑ Ⓒ Ⓓ   12. Ⓐ Ⓑ Ⓒ Ⓓ   19. Ⓐ Ⓑ Ⓒ Ⓓ   26. Ⓐ Ⓑ Ⓒ Ⓓ
6. Ⓐ Ⓑ Ⓒ Ⓓ   13. Ⓐ Ⓑ Ⓒ Ⓓ   20. Ⓐ Ⓑ Ⓒ Ⓓ   27. Ⓐ Ⓑ Ⓒ Ⓓ
7. Ⓐ Ⓑ Ⓒ Ⓓ   14. Ⓐ Ⓑ Ⓒ Ⓓ   21. Ⓐ Ⓑ Ⓒ Ⓓ   28. Ⓐ Ⓑ Ⓒ Ⓓ

Mathematics Knowledge

1. Ⓐ Ⓑ Ⓒ Ⓓ   8. Ⓐ Ⓑ Ⓒ Ⓓ   15. Ⓐ Ⓑ Ⓒ Ⓓ   22. Ⓐ Ⓑ Ⓒ Ⓓ
2. Ⓐ Ⓑ Ⓒ Ⓓ   9. Ⓐ Ⓑ Ⓒ Ⓓ   16. Ⓐ Ⓑ Ⓒ Ⓓ   23. Ⓐ Ⓑ Ⓒ Ⓓ
3. Ⓐ Ⓑ Ⓒ Ⓓ   10. Ⓐ Ⓑ Ⓒ Ⓓ   17. Ⓐ Ⓑ Ⓒ Ⓓ   24. Ⓐ Ⓑ Ⓒ Ⓓ
4. Ⓐ Ⓑ Ⓒ Ⓓ   11. Ⓐ Ⓑ Ⓒ Ⓓ   18. Ⓐ Ⓑ Ⓒ Ⓓ   25. Ⓐ Ⓑ Ⓒ Ⓓ
5. Ⓐ Ⓑ Ⓒ Ⓓ   12. Ⓐ Ⓑ Ⓒ Ⓓ   19. Ⓐ Ⓑ Ⓒ Ⓓ
6. Ⓐ Ⓑ Ⓒ Ⓓ   13. Ⓐ Ⓑ Ⓒ Ⓓ   20. Ⓐ Ⓑ Ⓒ Ⓓ
7. Ⓐ Ⓑ Ⓒ Ⓓ   14. Ⓐ Ⓑ Ⓒ Ⓓ   21. Ⓐ Ⓑ Ⓒ Ⓓ

Electronics Information

1. Ⓐ Ⓑ Ⓒ Ⓓ   8. Ⓐ Ⓑ Ⓒ Ⓓ   15. Ⓐ Ⓑ Ⓒ Ⓓ
2. Ⓐ Ⓑ Ⓒ Ⓓ   9. Ⓐ Ⓑ Ⓒ Ⓓ   16. Ⓐ Ⓑ Ⓒ Ⓓ
3. Ⓐ Ⓑ Ⓒ Ⓓ   10. Ⓐ Ⓑ Ⓒ Ⓓ   17. Ⓐ Ⓑ Ⓒ Ⓓ
4. Ⓐ Ⓑ Ⓒ Ⓓ   11. Ⓐ Ⓑ Ⓒ Ⓓ   18. Ⓐ Ⓑ Ⓒ Ⓓ
5. Ⓐ Ⓑ Ⓒ Ⓓ   12. Ⓐ Ⓑ Ⓒ Ⓓ   19. Ⓐ Ⓑ Ⓒ Ⓓ
6. Ⓐ Ⓑ Ⓒ Ⓓ   13. Ⓐ Ⓑ Ⓒ Ⓓ   20. Ⓐ Ⓑ Ⓒ Ⓓ
7. Ⓐ Ⓑ Ⓒ Ⓓ   14. Ⓐ Ⓑ Ⓒ Ⓓ

General Science

Time: 11 minutes for 25 questions

Directions: The questions in this section are designed to measure your general science knowledge. Choose the best answer for each question from the answer choices provided and shade in the corresponding oval on your answer sheet.

1. What area of science is defined as the study of animals?

   (A) botany

   (B) zoology

   (C) anatomy

   (D) genetics

2. What subdivision of life contains several related families?

   (A) species

   (B) class

   (C) order

   (D) genus

3. Which of the following is a defining characteristic of a living organism?

   (A) consumption

   (B) homeostasis

   (C) sleep

   (D) motion

4. Which cell organelle is responsible for respiration and regulates the cell's metabolism?

   (A) vacuole

   (B) Golgi body

   (C) nucleus

   (D) mitochondrion

5. What is a lysosome?

   (A) a cube-shaped structure that contains enzymes to help break down cell waste and prepare it for excretion

   (B) a part of a cell that contains DNA and controls cell reproduction

   (C) a part of a cell that modifies, sorts, and packages complex molecules

   (D) a protein layer that surrounds a cell, controlling what enters and exits and protecting the cell from the outside environment

6. Which of the following would NOT be considered a significant source of protein?

   (A) lamb

   (B) pasta

   (C) chicken

   (D) steak

7. 104 degrees Fahrenheit is _____ degrees Celsius.

   (A) 26

   (B) 38

   (C) 40

   (D) 58

8. Your thyroid is a part of what system in your body?

   (A) respiratory

   (B) circulatory

   (C) nervous

   (D) lymphatic

Go on to next page

9. A substance is considered to be a base if its pH level is what?

   (A) greater than 7

   (B) less than 7

   (C) 7

   (D) between 6 and 8

10. How many protons does the atom $^{18}_{8}O$ have?

    (A) 18

    (B) 8

    (C) 10

    (D) 26

11. About how long does it take the earth to make one full rotation about its axis?

    (A) 25 hours

    (B) 364 days

    (C) 365 days

    (D) 24 hours

12. What type of rock is formed by applying large amounts of heat and pressure deep under the earth's surface?

    (A) sedimentary

    (B) metamorphic

    (C) marble

    (D) igneous

13. All the following are continents EXCEPT

    (A) Greenland.

    (B) Australia.

    (C) Asia.

    (D) Europe.

14. Which of the following is NOT an atmospheric layer?

    (A) stratosphere

    (B) thermosphere

    (C) mesosphere

    (D) cumulosphere

15. Which of the following planets is nearest the sun?

    (A) Neptune

    (B) Venus

    (C) Uranus

    (D) Jupiter

16. A pound is approximately how many grams?

    (A) 254 grams

    (B) 1 kilograms

    (C) 2 kilograms

    (D) 454 grams

17. A quarter-mile track is 440 yards. How many meters is it?

    (A) 1,600 meters

    (B) 0.4 kilometers

    (C) 460 meters

    (D) 880 meters

18. Which of the following is NOT an example of an endothermic process?

    (A) activating an ice pack

    (B) melting ice cubes

    (C) boiling water

    (D) burning a candle

19. Water forming on the outside of a glass of ice water is an example of which of the following?

    (A) condensation

    (B) precipitation

    (C) evaporation

    (D) convection

20. Which of the following components of the circulatory system carries blood away from the heart?

    (A) capillaries

    (B) veins

    (C) arteries

    (D) ventricles

21. Yeast belongs to which of the following kingdoms?

    (A) fungi

    (B) protista

    (C) planta

    (D) monera

Go on to next page

22. Which of the following gases is most plentiful in earth's atmosphere?

    (A) hydrogen

    (B) oxygen

    (C) nitrogen

    (D) carbon dioxide

23. In a lunar eclipse, which of the following is NOT true?

    (A) The earth blocks the rays of the sun.

    (B) The moon casts a shadow on the earth.

    (C) Part or all the sun's rays are blocked from reaching the moon.

    (D) The earth is positioned between the sun and the moon.

24. Atoms of the same element that have different numbers of neutrons are referred to as

    (A) ions.

    (B) compounds.

    (C) isotopes.

    (D) molecules.

25. Which of the following steps is NOT part of the scientific method?

    (A) Formulate a hypothesis.

    (B) Mix the chemicals.

    (C) Perform research.

    (D) Record the results.

STOP DO NOT TURN THE PAGE UNTIL TOLD TO DO SO. DO NOT RETURN TO A PREVIOUS TEST.

Arithmetic Reasoning

Time: 36 minutes for 30 questions

Directions: The questions in this section are designed to measure your general mathematical reasoning ability. They are word problems based on essential arithmetic skills. Choose the best answer for each question from the answer choices provided and shade in the corresponding oval on your answer sheet.

1. A recipe calls for $4\frac{2}{3}$ cups of flour. If you have $3\frac{1}{2}$ cups, how much more flour do you need?

    (A) $1\frac{1}{2}$

    (B) $1\frac{1}{3}$

    (C) $1\frac{1}{6}$

    (D) $\frac{1}{6}$

2. If you earn $12.30 per hour, how much will you earn by working a 40-hour week?

    (A) $307.50

    (B) $375.00

    (C) $482.00

    (D) $492.00

3. Hector's uncle gave him a baseball card collection from the 1950s. Half the cards were from the Brooklyn Dodgers and one-fourth were from the New York Giants. The rest were evenly divided among the Philadelphia Athletics, the St. Louis Browns, and the Washington Senators. If the collection included 15 cards from the Browns, how many Dodgers cards did Hector's uncle give him?

    (A) 15

    (B) 45

    (C) 60

    (D) 90

4. A DVD player was marked at 40% off the list price. With a coupon for a special sale, you could receive an additional 10% off the marked price. If the original list price of the DVD player before any markdowns was $150, what would you actually pay?

    (A) $54

    (B) $75

    (C) $81

    (D) $90

5. Glendally finds a $40 sweater on sale for 15% off, but she must pay 5% sales tax. If she hands the cashier $50, how much change will she receive?

    (A) $18.00

    (B) $16.00

    (C) $14.30

    (D) $2.00

6. The City Council bylaws require that 60% of the residents vote in favor of a proposal before it can become part of the city's constitution. An initiative to repeal the sales tax did not pass in the last election. If the city has 4,000 residents, what is the minimum number that could have voted against the proposal?

    (A) 1,333

    (B) 1,601

    (C) 2,401

    (D) 2,666

Go on to next page

7. Five workers were observed packing boxes. Two of them could pack four boxes in a minute. One could pack five boxes per minute, and the others could pack three boxes each minute. What is the average number of boxes packed per person per minute?

   (A) 4

   (B) 3.8

   (C) 3.2

   (D) 2.4

8. If 360 students can be transported in eight school buses, how many students can be transported on three buses?

   (A) 45

   (B) 135

   (C) 960

   (D) 1,080

9. Women make up two-thirds of the workforce at a particular company. If 67 men make up the company workforce, how many people does the company employ?

   (A) 201

   (B) 100

   (C) 45

   (D) 33

10. Jamal bought a CD for $9 and a DVD for $23. If he hands the cashier two $20 bills, how much change will he receive?

    (A) $4

    (B) $6

    (C) $8

    (D) $17

11. A refrigerator sells for $520 but the customer must pay 6% sales tax and a $50 delivery and installation fee. What is the total cost of the refrigerator?

    (A) $81.20

    (B) $601.20

    (C) $604.20

    (D) $882.00

12. If you invest $8,000 at 4% simple interest per year, how much will your investment be worth after 5 years?

    (A) $8,320

    (B) $9,600

    (C) $11,200

    (D) $41,600

13. Charles determined that his ideal workout schedule includes aerobics and weight training in a ratio of 3:5. If Charles can devote two hours per day to working out, how many minutes should he spend on weight training?

    (A) 15

    (B) 24

    (C) 45

    (D) 75

14. A recipe calls for $\frac{1}{2}$ cup shortening, 1 cup brown sugar, 2 eggs, $\frac{1}{3}$ cup milk, and $2\frac{3}{4}$ cups of oatmeal. If the recipe is recalculated to use a dozen eggs, how much oatmeal will be needed?

    (A) $16\frac{1}{2}$ cups

    (B) $12\frac{3}{4}$ cups

    (C) 6 cups

    (D) 3 cups

15. In a certain town, the ratio of Democrats to Republicans is 5:4. If 18,000 people live in the town, how many are Democrats?

    (A) 4,500

    (B) 2,000

    (C) 5,000

    (D) 10,000

16. Josh ran 4 miles on Monday, 5 miles on Tuesday, and 6 miles on Wednesday. If he wants to run 26 miles a week, how much farther must he run this week?

    (A) 11 miles

    (B) 15 miles

    (C) 20 miles

    (D) 21 miles

Go on to next page

17. Olivia painted $8\frac{1}{2}$ feet of fence, and Omar painted $6\frac{2}{3}$ feet of fence. How many feet of fence did they paint in all?

(A) $14\frac{1}{6}$

(B) $14\frac{1}{3}$

(C) $14\frac{1}{2}$

(D) $15\frac{1}{6}$

18. The distance from the sun to the earth is 1 astronomical unit (AU); from earth to Jupiter is 4.2 AU; and from Jupiter to Uranus is 13.94 AU. How far is Uranus from the sun?

(A) 19.14 AU

(B) 18.96 AU

(C) 15.36 AU

(D) 14.37 AU

19. If Jake can run at an average speed of $11\frac{1}{3}$ kilometers per hour, how far can he run in $\frac{3}{4}$ hour?

(A) $15\frac{1}{9}$ kilometers

(B) $11\frac{1}{3}$ kilometers

(C) $10\frac{7}{12}$ kilometers

(D) $8\frac{1}{2}$ kilometers

20. A project requires 1,480 hours of work and must be completed in a week. Each worker who can be assigned to the project works 40 hours a week. How many workers must be assigned to complete the project in one week?

(A) 37

(B) 18

(C) 8

(D) 6

21. The area of a triangle is half the product of the base and the height. Find the height of a triangle with an area of $66\frac{2}{3}$ square inches, if the base measures $12\frac{1}{2}$ inches.

(A) $5\frac{1}{3}$ inches

(B) $5\frac{5}{6}$ inches

(C) $10\frac{2}{3}$ inches

(D) $21\frac{1}{3}$ inches

22. The yards gained by a running back totaled 238.5. If he carried the football 18 times, what was his average gain per carry?

(A) 13.5

(B) 13.45

(C) 13.25

(D) 13.2

23. At 8 a.m. seven cars sat in the parking lot. If 13 more cars entered over the next hour and 3 left, how many cars sat in the lot at 9 a.m.?

(A) 4

(B) 6

(C) 10

(D) 17

24. Yesterday the rain gauge recorded $\frac{5}{8}$ inch of rain, and today it recorded another $1\frac{1}{4}$ inches. What was the average rainfall, in inches, over the two days?

(A) $\frac{7}{8}$

(B) $\frac{15}{16}$

(C) $1\frac{3}{8}$

(D) $1\frac{7}{8}$

Go on to next page

25. Mrs. Williamson bought four items on her shopping list that cost $40.49, $11.98, $29.99, and $22.20. If she had a coupon giving her 15% off her total bill, how much did she pay?

    (A) $15.70

    (B) $88.96

    (C) $89.66

    (D) $99.43

26. The distance from the pitcher's mound to home plate in major league baseball is 60.5 feet. Nolan Ryan once threw a fastball that traveled 147.9 feet per second. How long, to the nearest hundredth of a second, did it take that ball to travel from the pitcher's mound to home plate?

    (A) 0.40 seconds

    (B) 0.41 seconds

    (C) 0.45 seconds

    (D) 0.49 seconds

27. The sales tax on the purchase of a flat-screen television is $35.88. If the local tax rate is 0.06, what was the price of the television?

    (A) $215.28

    (B) $598.00

    (C) $1,672.00

    (D) $2,152.80

28. Kurt has $903.44 in his savings account. If he withdraws $112.93 each month to pay his student loan, how many payments can he make?

    (A) 4

    (B) 6

    (C) 8

    (D) 10

29. If 1,260 people need to be transported on buses, each of which can hold 45 people, how many buses are needed?

    (A) 26

    (B) 28

    (C) 30

    (D) 32

30. The speed of light is approximately 2.99 million meters per second. How far does light travel in 1.5 seconds?

    (A) 4.515 million meters

    (B) 4.485 million meters

    (C) 3.991 million meters

    (D) 3.495 million meters

STOP DO NOT TURN THE PAGE UNTIL TOLD TO DO SO. DO NOT RETURN TO A PREVIOUS TEST.

Mathematics Knowledge

Time: 24 minutes for 25 questions

Directions: The questions in this section are designed to measure your understanding of the mathematics you studied in school. They include concepts from arithmetic, algebra, and geometry. Choose the best answer for each question from the answer choices provided and shade in the corresponding oval on your answer sheet.

1. All of the following are true EXCEPT
   (A) $0.038 < 0.308$
   (B) $0.0308 < 0.308$
   (C) $0.0038 < 0.0308$
   (D) $0.3008 < 0.0308$

2. When rounded to the nearest hundredth, 4739.9374 is equal to
   (A) 4700
   (B) 4739.9
   (C) 4739.93
   (D) 4739.94

3. Which of the following is equal to 3^4?
   (A) 12
   (B) 27
   (C) 64
   (D) 81

4. $4(30-18)-4\times30-18$
   (A) –90
   (B) 0
   (C) –96
   (D) 528

5. The train makes the 40-mile trip from Alphatown to Betaville in 37 minutes. John can drive on the road parallel to the train tracks at 50 miles per hour. How much longer will it take to drive?
   (A) 3 minutes
   (B) 10 minutes
   (C) 11 minutes
   (D) 13 minutes

6. Find the value of $\dfrac{a+b^2}{a^2-b}$ if $a=8$ and $b=3$
   (A) $\dfrac{121}{61}$
   (B) $\dfrac{14}{61}$
   (C) $\dfrac{3}{8}$
   (D) $\dfrac{17}{61}$

7. $(x+y)^2$ is equivalent to all the following EXCEPT
   (A) x^2+y^2
   (B) $x^2+2xy+y^2$
   (C) $x^2+xy+yx+y^2$
   (D) $(x+y)(x+y)$

8. One liter of a 50% saline solution is mixed with 1 liter of pure water. What is the concentration of the resulting solution?
   (A) 25%
   (B) 33%
   (C) 50%
   (D) 75%

9. If $2x-7=17$ then $x=$
   (A) 5
   (B) 10
   (C) 12
   (D) 15.5

10. $\dfrac{x^2-5x+6}{x-2}$
    (A) $\dfrac{x^2+1}{-2}$
    (B) $x-3$
    (C) $-4x-3$
    (D) $x^2-\dfrac{1}{2}$

Go on to next page

11. Find the area of a square that's 12 feet on a side.

    (A) 24 square feet

    (B) 48 square feet

    (C) 96 square feet

    (D) 144 square feet

12. Find the circumference of a circle with a radius of 3 yards.

    (A) 6π yards

    (B) 9π yards

    (C) 18π yards

    (D) 81π yards

13. Which of the following statements is NOT true?

    (A) The square of a positive number is positive.

    (B) The square of a negative number is positive.

    (C) The square of zero is zero.

    (D) The square of a number is always larger than the number.

14. Jennifer's average for the first three tests of the term is 86%. Her final exam will count as two tests. What must she score on the final exam to average 90% for the term?

    (A) 92

    (B) 94

    (C) 96

    (D) 98

15. George drives from Baltimore to Charlotte, a distance of 420 miles. The next day, he drives from Charlotte to Norfolk, a distance of 310 miles. On the third day, he drives from Norfolk to Baltimore. If the total trip was 960 miles, how far is Baltimore from Norfolk?

    (A) 230 miles

    (B) 540 miles

    (C) 650 miles

    (D) 730 miles

16. A box contains 12 socks; 6 of those socks are black and 6 are brown. If 2 socks are chosen at random, what is the probability that they are not the same color?

    (A) $\frac{1}{6}$

    (B) $\frac{1}{2}$

    (C) $\frac{6}{11}$

    (D) $\frac{7}{11}$

17. Ten job candidates were asked to take an aptitude test. The following are their recorded test scores. Find the ratio of the mean to the median score.

    | 86 | 78 | 94 | 82 | 94 |
    | 71 | 64 | 89 | 75 | 82 |

    (A) $\frac{163}{164}$

    (B) $\frac{163}{165}$

    (C) $\frac{164}{165}$

    (D) $\frac{164}{163}$

18. Find the area of trapezoid *ABCD* if the mid-segment measures 18 centimeters and the height is 6 centimeters.

    (A) 24 cm^2

    (B) 27 cm^2

    (C) 54 cm^2

    (D) 108 cm^2

19. The length of a rectangle is 2 more than 3 times its width. If the perimeter of the rectangle is 60 centimeters, what is the area?

    (A) 659.75 cm^2

    (B) 420 cm^2

    (C) 210 cm^2

    (D) 161 cm^2

20. Find the sum of the interior angles of an octagon.

    (A) 540 degrees

    (B) 720 degrees

    (C) 900 degrees

    (D) 1080 degrees

Go on to next page

21. If $\triangle ARM \sim \triangle LEG$, $RM = 9$ inches, $EG = 21$ inches, and the area of $\triangle LEG$ is 98 in^2, find the area of $\triangle ARM$.

    (A) 9 in^2

    (B) 18 in^2

    (C) 49 in^2

    (D) 98 in^2

22. Simplify $-17 + -25 - 31 + 48 \times -2 \div -8$

    (A) 1

    (B) -52

    (C) 61

    (D) -61

23. Simplify $= \dfrac{15x^2y^3z}{5xyz^2}$

    (A) $3x^2y^3z^2$

    (B) $10xy^2z$

    (C) $\dfrac{10xy^2}{z}$

    (D) $\dfrac{3xy^2}{z}$

24. Solve the following inequality: $-7 < 2b - 11 < 5$

    (A) $-9 < b < 3$

    (B) $-9 < b < 8$

    (C) $2 < b < 8$

    (D) $2 < x < 3$

25. If $3x - y = 11$ and $x + y = 5$, find x and y.

    (A) $x = 1.5$, $y = 3.5$

    (B) $x = 3$, $y = 2$

    (C) $x = 8$, $y = -3$

    (D) $x = 4$, $y = 1$

STOP DO NOT TURN THE PAGE UNTIL TOLD TO DO SO. DO NOT RETURN TO A PREVIOUS TEST.

Electronics Information

Time: 9 minutes for 20 questions

Directions: The questions in this section are designed to measure your knowledge and understanding of electronics. Choose the best answer for each question from the answer choices provided and shade in the corresponding oval on your answer sheet.

1. The flow of electrons is referred to as what?

    (A) electric potential

    (B) current

    (C) power

    (D) resistance

2. What is the unit for electric potential?

    (A) volt

    (B) watt

    (C) ohm

    (D) ampere

3. What is an insulator?

    (A) material that allows current to pass with relative ease

    (B) material that somewhat resists current flow converting energy into heat

    (C) material that has an extremely high electrical resistance, preventing electrical current from passing through it

    (D) material that stores electric charge and releases its charge when grounded

4. An ammeter is inserted in a circuit and measures the current at that point to be 15 milliamperes (mA). The measurement was taken for 30 seconds and the current remained a constant 15 milliamperes. How many coulombs of charge went past that point over the 30 seconds of measurement?

    (A) 450 coulombs

    (B) 45 coulombs

    (C) 4.5 coulombs

    (D) 0.45 coulombs

5. Which of the following is a good insulator?

    (A) silver

    (B) glass

    (C) aluminum

    (D) copper

6. What is a major advantage of a stranded core wire compared to a solid core wire?

    (A) ability to reuse

    (B) cost

    (C) ability to flex

    (D) size

7. Which kind of dopant adds "holes" to a semiconductive material?

    (A) n-type

    (B) g-type

    (C) s-type

    (D) p-type

8. The amount of resistance of a given material depends on all the following EXCEPT _____.

    (A) current

    (B) material type

    (C) diameter

    (D) length

9. Which of the following is a symbol for a capacitor?

Go on to next page

10. In the following circuit, what happens to the light if the switch is shut?

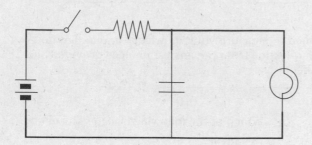

(A) The light would flash.

(B) The light would shut off.

(C) The light would turn on.

(D) The light would get dimmer.

11. In the following parallel circuit, what is the current through resistor R_2?

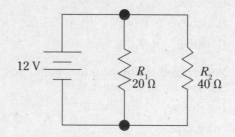

(A) 900 milliamperes

(B) 600 milliamperes

(C) 400 milliamperes

(D) 300 milliamperes

12. Given the following circuit, what is the resistance of resistor R_3?

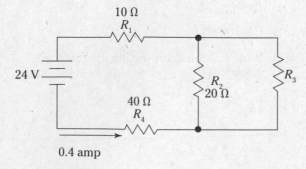

(A) 10 Ω

(B) 15 Ω

(C) 20 Ω

(D) 25 Ω

13. An electric fan is rated as a 240 watt fan. Assuming the power supplied to the fan is 120 volts, how much current does the fan draw?

(A) 2 amperes

(B) 4 amperes

(C) 8 amperes

(D) 16 amperes

14. Assume you leave a 90 watt light on for 50 hours; you run your washing machine for 2 hours, which uses 4800 watts of power; and you watch TV for 4 hours, which uses 1200 watts of power. How many total kilowatt-hours of power did you use?

(A) 20.5 kilowatt-hours

(B) 18.9 kilowatt-hours

(C) 17.6 kilowatt-hours

(D) 10.9 kilowatt-hours

15. For a high-definition television, what does the *i* stand for in 1080i?

(A) interlaced

(B) integral

(C) integrated

(D) intersect

16. To measure electrical current, you would use which of the following meters?

(A) ohmmeter

(B) voltmeter

(C) wattmeter

(D) ammeter

17. A wire with a wire gauge of 10 has which of the following qualities compared to a wire with a gauge of 23?

(A) thinner

(B) thicker

(C) fewer strands

(D) more flexible

Go on to next page

18. Given a transformer with a primary-to-secondary windings ratio of 20:1, as shown here, what is the voltage across R_{load}?

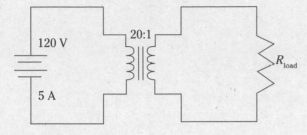

   (A) 60 volts

   (B) 6 volts

   (C) 2400 volts

   (D) 240 volts

19. If you align a compass so that north and south are along a current-carrying wire, in which direction will the compass arrow point?

   (A) north/south

   (B) east/west

   (C) perpendicular to the wire

   (D) parallel to the wire

20. Which of the following devices does NOT transform mechanical energy into electrical energy?

   (A) transformer

   (B) motor

   (C) generator

   (D) magnet

STOP DO NOT TURN THE PAGE UNTIL TOLD TO DO SO.
DO NOT RETURN TO A PREVIOUS TEST.

Chapter 25

ASVAB Marine OCS Composite Practice Test: Answers and Explanations

• •

After you've completed the practice Armed Services Vocational Aptitude Battery Marine Officer Candidate School Composite (ASVAB Marine OCS) test in Chapter 24, use this chapter to evaluate how well you did. You can check your answers with the detailed explanations or with the bare-bones answer key. We suggest you read through the detailed answers for each question to get the most out of your studies, but if you're running low on time and simply need the answers, take a look at the answer key at the end of the chapter. If you discover that you need some extra help on these questions, head to Part III, where we discuss math, science, arithmetic, mechanics, and electronics more in depth.

General Science Answers

1. **B.** The correct answer is Choice (B), because *zoology* literally means "study of animals." *Botany* deals with plants, *anatomy* focuses on the structure of living things, and *genetics* is the study of heredity.

2. **C.** In order from broadest category to most specific are kingdom, phylum, class, order, family, genus, and species. Therefore, order contains one or more families as subcategories.

3. **B.** All living things have the following characteristics in common: homeostasis, organization, metabolism, growth, adaptation, response to stimuli, and reproduction. The only answer choice that matches one of these characteristics is homeostasis. Although consumption, sleep, and motion are all things that living organisms can do, they aren't defining characteristics of life.

4. **D.** Unfortunately, all the answer choices for this question are cell organelles, so you can't eliminate any of them right off the bat. You either know this one or you don't. The mitochondrion regulates a cell's metabolism and performs the function of respiration. Other organelles may assist with the respiration process, but the mitochondrion actually performs this function. *Vacuoles* are plant organelles that help break down cell waste and prepare the waste for excretion. The *Golgi body* sorts and packages complex molecules, and the *nucleus* is the part of the cell that stores DNA and is responsible for cell reproduction.

5. **A.** All the answer choices are accurate descriptions of cell parts, but only one describes the lysosome. The *lysosome* is a cube-shaped structure that contains enzymes to help break down cell waste and prepare it for excretion. If this question tripped you up, you probably need to take a trip to Chapter 12 and review the cell parts.

6. **B.** *P* is for protein and pasta, but that's about the only similarity these two words have in common. The primary source of protein is meat, including lamb, chicken, and steak. The only item on this particular menu that doesn't fit the bill is pasta. Pasta is a good source of carbohydrates but not protein.

7. **C.** To solve this problem, you need to use the equation for converting Celsius into Fahrenheit:

$$°C = \frac{5}{9}(°F - 32°)$$

$$°C = \frac{5}{9}(°104 - 32°) = \frac{5}{9}(72°F) = 40°F$$

8. **D.** The thyroid is the most prominent organ in the lymphatic (immune) system. If you had difficulties with this question or are a little fuzzy on human anatomy, take a look at Chapter 12.

9. **A.** When you're looking at pH, think of lucky number 7. A pH that's above 7 signals a base, and one that's below 7 indicates an acid.

10. **B.** In atomic notation, the top number is the atomic mass; the bottom number is the atomic number, which represents the number of protons. If this question had asked for the number of neutrons, you would subtract the atomic number (8) from the atomic mass (18) to get 10 neutrons.

11. **D.** If you picked Choice (C), you probably confused "rotation" with "revolution." *Rotation* refers to spinning, like a top, and the earth takes about 24 hours to rotate once around its axis. A *revolution* is one trip around the sun, which takes about 365 days. If you picked Choice (A) or (B), we can't begin to guess what you were thinking.

12. **B.** *Metamorphic rock* forms under intense pressure and heat. *Igneous rock* is formed with heat but without the pressure, and *sedimentary rock* is formed from deposits of organic and inorganic materials. *Marble* is a type of metamorphic rock.

13. **A.** Earth's seven continents are Africa, Antarctica, Asia, Australia, Europe, North America, and South America. The landmass listed in the answer choices that isn't one of these continents is Greenland. Greenland is the largest island in the world, but it's not considered a continent.

14. **D.** This question is a little tricky because cumulous clouds are a type of cloud that exists in the troposphere, which is part of the atmosphere. The layers of the atmosphere are troposphere, stratosphere, mesosphere, thermosphere, and exosphere. Cumulosphere isn't a layer of the atmosphere, so it is the correct answer.

15. **B.** The planets in order from closest to farthest from the sun are Mercury, Venus, Earth, Mars, Jupiter, Saturn, Uranus, and Neptune. Of the planets listed in the answer choices, Venus is nearest the sun. It isn't the closest planet to the sun, but Mercury isn't a choice here.

16. **D.** A pound is approximately 454 grams, or little less than half a kilogram. If you chose Choice (C), you probably got mixed up and thought a kilogram was about half a pound.

17. **B.** A yard is a little shorter than a meter, so the meter equivalent will be a number less than 440. Knowing this information, you can easily answer this question through a process of elimination. Choices (A), (C), and (D) are all more than 440, leaving only Choice (B). So 0.4 kilometers is 400 meters.

18. **D.** *Endothermic* refers to a process that requires and absorbs heat. *Exothermic* processes are the opposite; they give off heat. The only process in the list of answer choices that gives off more heat than it requires is burning a candle.

19. **A.** The water in warm, moist air *condenses* on the glass. *Precipitation* refers to water falling from the sky. *Evaporation* is the process of a liquid converting to its gaseous state. *Convection* is the movement of air.

20. **C.** Arteries carry blood away from the heart. Veins carry deoxygenated blood back to the heart.

21. **A.** Yeast is a type of fungus.

22. **C.** Although hydrogen, oxygen, and carbon dioxide get all the press, nitrogen is actually the most plentiful gas, accounting for a whopping 78% of earth's atmospheric composition.

23. **B.** In a lunar eclipse, the earth passes between the sun and the moon, partially or totally blocking the sun's rays from reaching the moon. In a solar eclipse, the moon casts a shadow on the earth.

24. **C.** By definition, *isotopes* are atoms of the same element that have different numbers of neutrons. *Compounds* and *molecules* consist of two or more elements, so you can rule out Choices (B) and (D). An *ion* is an atom that has gained or lost an electron, giving it a positive or negative charge.

25. **B.** The scientific method is an approach for different types of experiments. Not all experiments require the mixing of chemicals, so Choice (B) is the correct answer.

Arithmetic Reasoning Answers

1. **C.** Subtract to get the number of cups of flour needed: $4\frac{2}{3} - 3\frac{1}{2} = 4\frac{4}{6} - 3\frac{3}{6} = 1\frac{1}{6}$.

2. **D.** Multiply $12.30 per hour times 40 hours to get $492.00.

3. **D.** Half of the cards were from the Brooklyn Dodgers, and one-fourth were from the New York Giants: $\frac{1}{2} + \frac{1}{4} = \frac{3}{4}$. The rest — which would be $\frac{1}{4}$ — were evenly divided among three teams. Because $\frac{1}{4} \div 3 = \frac{1}{4} \times \frac{1}{3} = \frac{1}{12}$, one-twelfth of the cards — or 15 cards — were from the Browns. If 15 is one-twelfth of the collection, you know that the collection contains $15 \times 12 = 180$ cards. Half of the collection was from the Dodgers, and half of 180 is 90.

4. **C.** The original price of the DVD player is $150, and 40% of that amount is $60. After the 40% discount, the price is $90. An additional 10% off the $90 price takes an additional $9 off, making the price $81.

5. **C.** Because 15% of $40 is $6, Glendally will pay $34 plus tax. Add 5% of $34, or $1.70, to the $34 to find out what she'll pay: $34 + $1.70 = $35.70. So if she hands the cashier $50, she'll receive $50 – $35.70 = $14.30 change.

6. **B.** If the city has 4,000 residents and the bylaws require 60% of them to pass a proposal, the proposal needs 2,400 votes to pass. If the proposal didn't pass, it didn't receive 2,400 votes. So you know that it received at most 2,399 votes. As a result, the proposal had $4,000 - 2,399 = 1,601$ votes against it.

7. **B.** Add to find the number of boxes packed by the workers in one minute: $4 + 4 + 5 + 3 + 3 = 19$ boxes. Then divide to figure out the boxes per person per minute average: $19 \div 5 = 3.8$.

8. **B.** If 360 students can be transported in eight school buses, you know that $360 \div 8 = 45$ students are on each bus. So three buses will hold $3 \times 45 = 135$ students.

9. **A.** If women make up $\frac{2}{3}$ of the workforce, men make up $\frac{1}{3}$. So 3×67 men = 201 employees.

10. **C.** Jamal's purchase totals $9 + $23 = $32. If he hands the cashier two $20 bills, he'll receive $40 – 32 = $8 change.

11. **B.** The sales tax is $520 \times 0.06 = $31.20, so add $520 + 31.20 + 50 = $601.20.

12. **B.** To find the interest earned, multiply $8,000 \times 4\% \times 5$ years: $8,000 \times 0.04 \times 5 = 320 \times 5 = $1,600 interest. Add this amount to the original investment and the value is $8,000 + 1,600 = $9,600.

13. **D.** Three minutes of aerobics for every 5 minutes of weight training means that he's spending 5 out of every 8 minutes, or $\frac{5}{8}$ of his time, weight training. Two hours is 120 minutes, so he should spend $\frac{5}{1\cancel{8}} \times \cancel{120}^{15} = 75$ minutes on weight training.

14. **A.** To change from 2 eggs to 12, multiply everything in the recipe by 6. The original recipe calls for $2\frac{3}{4}$ cups of oatmeal, so you would need $6 \times 2\frac{3}{4} = {}^{3}\cancel{6} \times \frac{11}{\cancel{4}_2} = \frac{33}{2} = 16\frac{1}{2}$ cups of oatmeal.

15. **D.** If the town has 5 Democrats for every 4 Republicans, it has 5 Democrats out of every 9 residents. If $\frac{5}{9}$ of the town's 18,000 residents are Democrats, the town has 10,000 Democrats.

16. **A.** Add the miles run over the three days: $4 + 5 + 6 = 15$ miles. Then subtract that total from the desired 26 miles: $26 - 15 = 11$ miles.

17. **D.** When adding mixed numbers, add the whole number parts, and then add the fractions: $8\frac{1}{2} + 6\frac{2}{3} = 8 + 6 + \frac{1}{2} + \frac{2}{3}$. You can use the bowtie on the fractions: $14 + \frac{1 \cdot 3 + 2 \cdot 2}{2 \cdot 3} = 14\frac{3 + 4}{6} = 14\frac{7}{6}$. (See Chapter 10 for more on the bowtie shortcut.) You end up with an improper fraction, so you have to convert it to a mixed number and add the whole number part of that mixed number to the whole number you already have to get your answer: $14\frac{7}{6} = 14 + 1\frac{1}{6} = 15\frac{1}{6}$ feet of fence.

18. **A.** Simply add the distances together to get your answer: $13.94 + 4.20 + 1 = 19.14$ AU. Align the decimal points and add a zero to 4.2 if that helps you. You can save the 1 AU from the sun to earth to add on at the end, but don't forget about it.

19. **D.** Jake's speed of $11\frac{1}{3}$ kilometers per hour times the time of $\frac{3}{4}$ hour gives the distance: $11\frac{1}{3} \times \frac{3}{4} = \frac{{}^{17}\cancel{34}}{3} \times \frac{3}{\cancel{4}_2} = \frac{17}{2} = 8\frac{1}{2}$ kilometers.

20. **A.** 1,480 hours ÷ 40 hours per week can become $148 \div 4 = 37$ workers required to complete the project in a week.

21. **C.** The area of a triangle is half the product of the base, and the height and the area is $66\frac{2}{3}$. So base times height is $2 \times 66\frac{2}{3} = 132\frac{4}{3} = 133\frac{1}{3}$. Divide that product by the base of $12\frac{1}{2}$, and you have $133\frac{1}{3} \div 12\frac{1}{2} = \frac{400}{3} \div \frac{25}{2} = \frac{{}^{16}\cancel{400}}{3} \times \frac{2}{\cancel{25}} = \frac{32}{3} = 10\frac{2}{3}$ inches.

22. **C.** You're dividing by a whole number, so the decimal point stays put. Estimate (200 ÷ 20), and you'd expect an answer a bit more than ten. All the answer choices are 13 and a fraction, so you need to work out the fraction: $13 \times 18 = 234$, so $238.5 \div 18 = 13$ with a remainder of 4.5. Because 4.5 is a quarter of 18, $238.5 \div 18 = 13.25$. (If you didn't get to a zero remainder after a couple of decimal places, you'd want to round your answer.)

23. **D.** The hour starts with 7 cars, and then 13 are added and 3 subtracted. So your calculations look like this: $7 + 13 = 20$ and $20 - 3 = 17$.

24. **B.** To find the average, add the readings and divide by the number of readings. In this case, it's easier to change $1\frac{1}{4}$ to an improper fraction. $\frac{5}{8} + 1\frac{1}{4} = \frac{5}{8} + \frac{5}{4} = \frac{5}{8} + \frac{10}{8} = \frac{15}{8}$, so the total rainfall is $\frac{15}{8}$ inches. Don't rush to change that amount to a mixed number, because you still need to divide by two: $\frac{15}{8} \div 2 = \frac{15}{8} \times \frac{1}{2} = \frac{15}{16}$ inch average rainfall.

25. **B.** The original bill is \$40.49 + \$11.98 + \$29.99 + \$22.20 = \$104.66. Because she gets 15% off, she will pay 100% − 15% = 85% of that total. So she pays 0.85 × \$104.66 = \$88.96.

26. **B.** There's no way around this problem except serious division. You have a distance (60.5 feet) and a speed (147.9 feet per second), and you're looking for a time. Distance divided by speed gives you time. You were asked for your answer to be to the nearest hundredth of a second, so you know you have to carry the division out for three decimal places and then round to the nearest hundredth. The division shown here gives you 0.409, which rounds to 0.41 seconds:

$$
\begin{array}{r}
0.409 \\
147.9\overline{)60.5.000} \\
\underline{5916} \\
1340 \\
\underline{0} \\
13400 \\
\underline{13311} \\
89
\end{array}
$$

27. **B.** You know that $0.06x$ = \$35.88, so divide 35.88 by 0.06. Move the decimal point over two places for each number, and this problem becomes 3588 ÷ 6. 3588 ÷ 6 = 598, so the television cost \$598.

28. **C.** A quick estimate (900 ÷ 100) tells you the answer can't be more than nine, so eliminate Choice (D). Technically, you move the decimal point two places in each number and divide, but because you know the answer is going to be a whole number, it's probably faster to try answers by multiplying. Multiply 8 × \$112.93, and you get \$903.44.

29. **B.** Think about 1,260 ÷ 45 as $\dfrac{1{,}260}{9\times 5} = \dfrac{\overset{252}{\cancel{1{,}260}}}{9\times \cancel{5}} = \dfrac{252}{9} = 28$. So 28 buses are needed.

30. **B.** Estimate the answer as this: 3 million meters per second × 1.5 seconds = 4.5 million meters. This estimate suggests that the last two answer choices are too small. You rounded 2.99 up by 0.01, so adjust back down: 2.99 × 1.5 = (3 × 1.5) − (0.01 × 1.5) = 4.5 − 0.015 = 4.485 million meters.

Mathematics Knowledge Answers

1. **D.** To compare these inequalities easily, place each pair of numbers one under another, with the decimal points aligned, and add zeros if the numbers don't have the same number of digits. After you do that, you can ignore the decimal points and leading zeros and simply compare the numbers as though they were whole numbers. As you can see in the following list, the upper number is smaller in each case except the last, so Choice (D) is the correct answer:

0.038	0.0308	0.0038	0.3008
0.308	0.3080	0.0308	0.0308

2. **D.** To round to the nearest hundredth (the second place to the right of the decimal point), look to the thousandth place (the third place to the right). In 4739.9374, the thousandth place contains a 7, so round the hundredths digit up and drop the remaining places, like this: 4739.9374 ≈ 4739.94.

3. **D.** The exponent 4 tells you to use 3 as a factor four times: $3^4 = 3 \cdot 3 \cdot 3 \cdot 3 = 9 \cdot 9 = 81$

4. **A.** To solve this problem, deal with what's in the parentheses first, and then multiply. Do the subtraction last. Here's what your calculations look like:
$$4(30-18)-4\times30-18=4(12)-4\times30-18=48-120-18=-90.$$

5. **C.** Driving 40 miles at 50 miles per hour takes 40 miles $\div \dfrac{50 \text{ miles}}{\text{hour}} = \dfrac{4}{5}$ hour, and $\dfrac{4}{5}$ of an hour is $\dfrac{4}{\cancel{5}}\times\cancel{60}^{12}=48$ minutes. So the drive takes John $48-37=11$ minutes longer.

6. **D.** If $a=8$ and $b=3$, $\dfrac{a+b^2}{a^2-b}=\dfrac{8+3^2}{8^2-3}=\dfrac{8+9}{64-3}=\dfrac{17}{61}$.

7. **A.** $(x+y)^2=(x+y)(x+y)=x^2+xy+xy+y^2=x^2+2xy+y^2$.

8. **A.** The 50% saline solution contains half a liter of salt and half a liter of water. When it's mixed with one liter of pure water, the result is half a liter of salt with one and a half liters of water. The two liters of the new solution are each 25% salt.

9. **C.** If $2x-7=17$, adding 7 to both sides tells you that $2x=24$, and then dividing by 2 gives you $x=12$.

10. **B.** Factor the numerator before trying to cancel: $\dfrac{x^2-5x+6}{x-2}=\dfrac{(x-2)(x-3)}{x-2}=x-3$.

11. **D.** The area of a square is the length of a side, squared, so $12^2=144$ square feet.

12. **A.** The circumference of a circle is the product of π and the diameter, or $2\times\pi\times$ the radius. The radius is 3 yards, so the circumference is $2\times\pi\times3=6\pi$ yards.

13. **D.** It's true that the square of a positive number is positive and that the square of a negative number is also positive, because when two numbers with the same sign are multiplied, the result is positive. Zero squared is zero, but it isn't true that the square of a number is always larger than the number. For any number less than zero or larger than one, the square is larger than the original number. However, for zero and one, the square is equal to the number, and for fractions between zero and one, the square is smaller than the number. For example, $\left(\dfrac{1}{2}\right)^2=\dfrac{1}{4}$.

14. **C.** If Jennifer's average on the three tests is 86%, her total score is $86\times3=258$. Because the exam counts as two tests, her final grade is the equivalent of averaging five tests. To average 90% on five tests, she would need a total of $5\times90=450$ points, which means she needs $450-258=192$ additional points. Divide 192 by 2 to find the grade she needs on the exam: $192\div2=96$.

15. **A.** The trip from Baltimore to Charlotte plus Charlotte to Norfolk is 420 miles + 310 miles = 730 miles. Because the total trip is 960 miles, the distance from Norfolk to Baltimore is $960-730=230$ miles.

16. **C.** The probability that a black sock is the first sock chosen is $\dfrac{6}{12}=\dfrac{1}{2}$. Because 6 brown socks are left among the remaining 11 socks, the probability that the second sock is brown will be $\dfrac{6}{11}$. So the probability of drawing black and then brown is $\dfrac{1}{2}\cdot\dfrac{6}{11}=\dfrac{3}{11}$. But the probability of drawing brown and then black also is $\dfrac{3}{11}$. As a result, the probability of getting two different colors is $\dfrac{3}{11}+\dfrac{3}{11}=\dfrac{6}{11}$.

17. **A.** The mean of the 10 scores is the total divided by 10. The total of $86+78+94+82+94+71+64+89+75+82=813$. The mean is $815\div10$, or 81.5. To find the median, arrange the numbers in order from least to greatest — 64, 71, 75, 78, 82, 82, 86, 89, 94, 94 — and then average the two middle values. Because the middle numbers are both 82, their average is also 82. The ratio of the mean to the median is $\dfrac{81.5}{82}\cdot\dfrac{2}{2}=\dfrac{163}{164}$.

18. **D.** The area of a trapezoid is half the height times the sum of the bases. The length of the midsegment is equal to half the sum of the bases. So the area is equal to the length of the midsegment times the height, or $18\times6=108$ cm^2.

19. **D.** If the length of a rectangle is 2 more than 3 times its width, the length can be expressed as $2 + 3w$. The perimeter is $2l + 2w$ or $2(2 + 3w) + 2w = 60$ centimeters, so $4 + 6w + 2w = 60$. Simplifying, $4 + 8w = 60$ and $8w = 56$ tells you that $w = 7$. Substituting back, you can find that $l = 2 + 3 \cdot 7 = 23$. Because the length and width of the rectangle are 23 and 7, the area is $23 \times 7 = 161$ cm^2.

20. **D.** The sum of the interior angles of an octagon is $(8 - 2) \cdot 180° = 1080°$.

21. **B.** If the triangles are similar in a ratio of 9:21 = 3:7, the ratio of the areas is $3^2:7^2 = 9:49$. Set up the proportion $\frac{A}{98} = \frac{9}{49}$ and solve to find that $A = 18$.

22. **D.** No parentheses and no exponents appear, so move left to right looking for multiplication and division: $-17 + -25 - 31 + (48 \times -2) \div -8 = -17 + -25 - 31 + (-96 \div -8) = -17 + -25 - 31 + 12$. Then add and subtract, moving from left to right: $(-17 + -25) - 31 + 12 = (-42 - 31) + 12 = -73 + 12 = -61$.

23. **D.** $\frac{15x^2y^3z}{5xyz^2} = \frac{15}{5} \cdot \frac{x^2}{x} \cdot \frac{y^3}{y} \cdot \frac{z}{z^2} = 3 \cdot x \cdot y^2 \cdot \frac{1}{z} = \frac{3xy^2}{z}$.

24. **C.** Rewrite the compound inequality as two inequalities: $-7 < 2b - 11$ and $2b - 11 < 5$. Solve each inequality separately. If $-7 < 2b - 11$, add 11 to get $4 < 2b$ and divide by 2 to get $2 < b$. If $2b - 11 < 5$, adding 11 gives you $2b < 16$ and dividing by 2 leaves $b < 8$. The solution is $2 < b < 8$.

25. **D.** Add the equations to eliminate y, and you have the equation $4x = 16$. So $x = 4$. Substituting 4 for x in the second equation tells you that $4 + y = 5$ and $y = 1$.

Electronics Information Answers

1. **B.** The flow of electrons is also known as *current*. *Electric potential* is voltage, *electric power* is the measure of the rate at which electric energy is transferred, and *electric resistance* is the measure of the extent to which a material resists the flow of electric current.

2. **A.** Electric potential is pressure, which is measured in volts. Watts measure power, ohms measure resistance, and amperes measure current.

3. **C.** An *insulator* is the opposite of a conductor — it prevents the flow of current. Choice (A) describes a conductor, Choice (B) describes a semiconductor (though not very precisely), and Choice (D) doesn't even refer to current.

4. **D.** This problem deals with the rate of the flow of current. Because it states the time and current (in amps) and asks for the number of coulombs, use the following equation from Chapter 14:

$$I = \frac{Q}{t}$$

where I is current in amps, Q is charge in coulombs, and t is time in seconds. So plug in the numbers and do the math:

$$15 \text{ mA} = \frac{Q}{30 \text{ s}}$$
$$Q = (15 \text{ mA})(30 \text{ s}) = (450 \text{ mC})$$

Because you're working in milliamps, you need to divide by 1000 to get the answer in amps:

$$\left(\frac{1 \text{ C}}{1000 \text{ } m\text{C}}\right) = 0.45 \text{ C}$$

5. **B.** Glass is a common insulator because of its high resistance and relative inability to conduct electricity. The other three answer choices are the top three conductors — the opposite of insulators.

6. **C.** Stranded core wire is flexible, making it a better choice for power cords, headsets, speaker wires, and similar applications. Solid core wire is actually cheaper, allowing you to rule out Choice (B). The remaining answers, Choices (A) and (D), depend on the application.

7. **D.** This question has only two possible answers, because only two dopants exist: p-type and n-type. As a result, you can immediately eliminate Choices (B) and (C). Recall the difference between a hole and an electron to eliminate the final choice. Electrons add negative charge, so they're n-type dopants. Holes add positive charge, so they're p-type dopants.

8. **A.** Resistance is an intrinsic property of a material, so look for the only choice that isn't related to the material itself. The last three choices all relate to material properties — type, diameter, and length. Current isn't a quality of the material. Although a higher current may cause the material to heat up, changing its resistant properties, the temperature, not the material, causes the change.

9. **D.** A *capacitor* is a passive electrical component that consists of a pair of conductors with an insulator, called the *dielectric,* sandwiched between them. The symbol for a capacitor uses a gap to represent the insulator, which prevents the flow of current. Choice (C) shows a power supply, Choice (B) is a resistor, and Choice (A) is ground.

10. **A.** This question may be a little tricky to figure out at first, but remember what a capacitor does and then think about how its job may affect a circuit. A capacitor stores charge as current is passed into it. As it stores charge, the resistance of the capacitor increases, eventually to infinity unless the current is so strong that it breaks down the dielectric within the capacitor. Assuming that breakdown doesn't happen, eventually the current stops going to the capacitor. In this case, when the switch shuts, the capacitor stores charge more easily than the charge can pass through the light bulb. So the light remains off until the capacitor is charged. When the capacitor is charged, the light illuminates as current passes and the capacitor discharges because current is no longer flowing to it. After the capacitor discharges, it becomes the least resistant flow path again, so the current flows to the capacitor and the light turns off. This cycle repeats until the switch is open or the power source stops providing power. Remember, capacitors don't allow current to pass through them; they actually just realign their charge so that all negative charge is on one side of the dielectric and all positive charge is on the other side. This realignment gives the illusion that current is flowing through the capacitor, but really it's only flowing down a dead-end path.

11. **D.** In a parallel circuit, the voltage drop across both components is the same (12 volts), and the currents across each component combine to give the total current of the circuit. So to find the component current of R_2, use Ohm's Law:

$$V = IR \Rightarrow I = \frac{V}{R} \Rightarrow I = \frac{V_S}{R_2} = \frac{12 \text{ V}}{40 \text{ } \Omega} = 0.3 \text{A} = 300 \text{ mA}$$

12. **C.** This problem presents resistors in series and parallel. You're given the total current, the voltage of the circuit, and the values of all the resistors except R_3. Use what you know about resistors in series and parallel and Ohm's Law to find R_3. Start by determining total resistance using voltage and amperage:

$$V_S = I_{tot} R_{tot} \Rightarrow R_{tot} = \frac{V_S}{I_{tot}} = \frac{24 \text{ V}}{0.4 \text{ A}} = 60 \text{ } \Omega$$

Using this number, you can find the total resistance of the two parallel resistors (R_2 and R_3):

$$R_{tot} = R_1 + R_4 + R_{2/3}$$
$$\frac{1}{R_{2/3}} = \frac{1}{R_2} + \frac{1}{R_3}$$
$$60\ \Omega = 10\ \Omega + 40\ \Omega + R_{2/3}$$
$$R_{2/3} = 10\ \Omega$$

Recall that the inverse of the total resistance in parallel resistors is equal to the sum of the inverse resistance of each resistor, so

$$\frac{1}{10\ \Omega} = \frac{1}{R_3} + \frac{1}{20\ \Omega}$$
$$\frac{1}{R_3} = \frac{1}{10\ \Omega} - \frac{1}{20\ \Omega} = \frac{1}{20\ \Omega} \Rightarrow R_3 = 20\ \Omega$$

13. **A.** For this problem, remember the different equations for calculating power. You want to use the equation that relates power to voltage and current:

$$P = IV$$
$$240\ \text{W} = (I)(120\ \text{V}) \Rightarrow I = \frac{240\ \text{W}}{120\ \text{V}} = 2\ \text{A}$$

14. **B.** For this problem, just add up the total power used by each load multiplied by the time each load was used for. Don't forget to divide by 1000 to convert watts per hour into kilowatts per hour:

$$E = Pt$$
$$E = (90\ \text{W})(50\ \text{h}) + (4800\ \text{W})(2\ \text{h}) + (1200\ \text{W})(4\ \text{h}) = 18,900\ \text{W} - \text{h}\left(\frac{1\ \text{kW} - \text{h}}{1000\ \text{W} - \text{h}}\right) = 18.9\ \text{kW} - \text{h}$$

15. **A.** The *i* in 1080i stands for *interlaced*. Interlaced scan displays all odd lines and then all even lines on the frames. This is different from 1080p (*p* for *progressive*). Progressive scan means every line in the scan is displayed on the screen for every frame.

16. **D.** Current is measured in amps, so you would use an *ammeter* to measure it. An *ohmmeter* measures resistance, a *voltmeter* measures voltage, and a *wattmeter* measures electrical power.

17. **B.** The higher the wire gauge number, the thinner the wire.

18. **B.** The source voltage is 120 volts, and with a 20:1 windings ratio, this transformer steps down the voltage to 1/20th of its original level. 1/20th of 120 is 6.

19. **C.** When a compass is near a current-carrying wire, the magnetic field generated by the wire wields more influence than the earth's magnetic field. As a result, north, south, east, and west are no longer applicable. So you can rule out Choice (A) and Choice (B). The lines of force of the magnetic field are perpendicular to the wire, so the arrow will be perpendicular to the wire as well.

20. **D.** A generator converts the motion of the rotor (mechanical energy) into electrical energy. A transformer increases or decreases voltage and current. A motor converts electrical into mechanical energy. Magnets are used in generators, but alone, they don't convert electrical into mechanical energy or vice versa.

Answer Key for ASVAB Marine OCS Composite Practice Test

General Science

1. B	6. B	11. D	16. D	21. A
2. C	7. C	12. B	17. B	22. C
3. B	8. D	13. A	18. D	23. B
4. D	9. A	14. D	19. A	24. C
5. A	10. B	15. B	20. C	25. B

Arithmetic Reasoning

1. C	7. B	13. D	19. D	25. B
2. D	8. B	14. A	20. A	26. B
3. D	9. A	15. D	21. C	27. B
4. C	10. C	16. A	22. C	28. C
5. C	11. B	17. D	23. D	29. B
6. B	12. B	18. A	24. B	30. B

Mathematics Knowledge

1. D	6. D	11. D	16. C	21. B
2. D	7. A	12. A	17. A	22. D
3. D	8. A	13. D	18. D	23. D
4. A	9. C	14. C	19. D	24. C
5. C	10. B	15. A	20. D	25. D

Electronics Information

1. B	5. B	9. D	13. A	17. B
2. A	6. C	10. A	14. B	18. B
3. C	7. D	11. D	15. A	19. C
4. D	8. A	12. C	16. D	20. D

Part V
The Part of Tens

In this part . . .

No *For Dummies* book would be complete without a Part of Tens. In this book, the Part of Tens features two chapters: "Ten Ways to Optimize Your Study Time" and "Ten Strategies for Tackling Multiple-Choice Questions."

We chose these two chapters because your success on the tests hinges on two things: how well prepared you are going into the test and how effectively you answer the questions during the test. Combine your knowledge and skills with effective test-taking strategies, and you significantly improve your chances of achieving high scores across the board.

Chapter 26

Ten Strategies for Tackling Multiple-Choice Questions

In This Chapter

▶ Discovering how to be successful with multiple-choice questions

▶ Improving your test-taking strategies

Most people prefer multiple-choice questions to the alternatives — fill-in-the-blank or matching questions. You have two to five choices, so you know one of them must be correct. If you know the answer, simply choose it from the available options. If you don't know the answer, eliminate as many wrong answers as possible, and then take your best guess.

Regardless of which approach you follow, you can significantly improve your odds of answering correctly by employing the strategies revealed in this chapter.

Follow Directions

At the beginning of every test section is a description of the section along with directions on how to answer the questions. Even though reading the directions consumes valuable time, this is time well spent. The introductory paragraph provides key information, including how much time you have to complete the section, the number of questions, the skills that the questions are testing, and perhaps other clues such as what to look for in a question — for example, underlined words.

Following directions seems like a no-brainer, especially when you're in the military or planning to pursue a military career, but you'd be surprised at how many examinees skip the instructions and head directly to the questions. As a result, they have no idea how much time they have per question, and they start out with only a vague notion of what the questions in the section are all about.

Key In on the Goal

Every question has a goal, stated or implied, that often comes at the end of the question. Your first step in answering any question is to read the question from beginning to end and identify the goal — what the question is asking. The goal may be to identify a word with a similar or opposite meaning, infer meaning from details embedded in a passage, calculate the area of a parallelogram, or figure out how much power a 60-watt light bulb uses in a normal eight-hour day, but your first step remains the same — identify the goal. As a military leader, you'll be called on frequently to solve problems. To do that successfully, identifying the problem — and the goal — is absolutely imperative.

Don't look at the answer choices until you know what the question is asking. Two questions may be nearly identical, differing only in goal. For example, a question may supply you with the initial value of an investment and the annual rate of return and ask you to calculate the total earnings or the total value of the investment at the end of the year — two very different answers, both of which are sure to appear in the answer choices.

Pace Yourself

From the information provided in the subtest's directions, you can come up with a general idea of how much time you have per question. Calculate the amount of time you have per quarter (each 25 percent of the questions) and use that as a guide to pace yourself. You may need more time answering some questions and less time answering others, so don't try to allocate a fixed amount of time per question; estimating your quarterly time requirements usually is a better approach.

Rushing through the questions and failing to confirm your answers can be just as bad as, if not worse than, running out of time.

Answer the Question Yourself, First

Answer choices often are designed to tempt you to make the wrong choice, as explained later in this chapter. One of the best ways to avoid that trap is to come up with your own answer first. This approach is especially useful when working math problems, but it's also helpful in approaching word power and reading questions.

Before looking at the answer choices, envision in your own mind what the correct answer looks like. For example, if the question is something like "Choose the word most closest in meaning to the word *pragmatic*," first consider what you think the word means. Then make sure the answer you choose matches your definition.

Resist Question Obsession

Be persistent in answering questions, but not overly so. Be prepared to cut your losses and move on to the next question. If you're taking a paper and pencil (P&P) test, jot down the question number and come back to it later if you have extra time. If you're taking a computerized version of the test, select your best guess and move on.

Persistence is to be applauded . . . most of the time, anyway. On the Officer Candidate Tests (OCT), however, persistence can get you into trouble. If you're bound and determined to answer each and every question correctly without guessing, you may get mired in a problem that consumes an inordinate amount of your allotted time. If you spend all your time answering Question 5 of a 20-question section, you're sunk.

Master the Process of Elimination

If you don't know an answer, all is not lost. Using the process of elimination, you may be able to eliminate all but the correct answer or at least eliminate one or two incorrect choices to improve your odds of answering correctly.

On math problems, use your skills at estimating in tandem with the process of elimination to answer questions more quickly. You may be able to save time by calculating a quick figure and then using that estimate to eliminate all but the closest answer choice.

Confirm before Answering (Sometimes)

If you have sufficient time, confirm what you think is the correct answer before making your final choice. Using the process of elimination, consider all the answer choices and then rule out the wrong ones to verify that what you think is the correct answer really is.

 You don't always need to confirm your answer. If you do the math and arrive at an answer that matches one of the answer choices, for example, verifying your answer doesn't make much sense and can waste valuable time. Save confirmation for when you're not quite sure.

Avoid Common Traps

Multiple-choice tests aren't very challenging if the answer choices consist of one reasonable answer and four other choices that are totally bizarre. The test creators know this, so they include at least one or two incorrect answer choices that most people would consider reasonably correct. They also may include a few very tempting choices specifically intended to trip you. Don't fall for it. Following is a list of common traps:

- **Including common (but wrong) answers:** The test designers know the most common wrong answers people choose and the mistakes they often make. You can be sure that commonly wrong answers will appear in the list of choices. Avoiding this trap isn't easy. You need to be careful both in reading the question and following the process for arriving at the correct answer.

- **Making false associations:** Certain words in the question may resonate with words in the answer, such as "bright" and "happy" or "dark" and "gloomy." These words may tempt you to choose an option even if it has nothing to do with the question. To avoid this trap, read and fully understand the question before looking at the answer choices.

- **Using your knowledge against you:** Reading questions are notorious for using your outside knowledge against you. To avoid this trap, rely solely on the information in the reading passage to answer questions about it. In other words, pretend you're starting with a blank slate — you know only what the passage tells you.

- **Altering the question's meaning:** Questions often contain words or phrases that alter the question's meaning. Following are some examples:

  - Choose the option that *best* describes. . . .

  - Which word is *closest* in meaning to. . . .

  - Which word is *most nearly* the *opposite of*. . . .

  - . . . is *always* the case. . . .

  - . . . is *never* true. . . .

  - Choose the option that *doesn't*. . . .

  Phrase traps are designed to derail your train of thought. The best way to avoid these traps is to be aware of them and look for key words that change the overall meaning of the question.

Guess, If Necessary

Your score is a factor of the number of questions you answer correctly. You suffer no penalty for answering questions incorrectly, so it behooves you to guess after exhausting all other possibilities. Blind guessing is okay, but it probably won't help your score much. If you must guess, try to eliminate answer choices to improve your odds.

Review Answers as the Test and Time Allow

If you're taking the P&P version of the test, and you complete a section with time to spare, go back and review your answers. First, make sure you haven't made the somewhat common mistake of getting your answer sheet and questions out of sync; for example, marking an answer for Question 13 when you meant to mark the answer for Question 12. This error can throw all your answers from that point on out of whack and really damage your score.

Next, make sure you haven't marked two answers for the same question or skipped a question. Finally, check and reconfirm any answers you weren't quite sure of.

Don't change an answer unless you have a good reason. Most of the time when examinees change answers, they change a correct answer to an incorrect one. If you do need to change an answer on a P&P version of the test, erase your first selection completely to ensure that the scoring machine doesn't mistake it for your choice.

Chapter 27

Ten Ways to Optimize Your Study Time

In This Chapter

▶ Making the most of your study time

▶ Applying tactics to improve your study habits

*T*he quality of your study time is as important as — or perhaps even more important than — the quantity. But what exactly does *quality study time* mean? For most people, it means studying without any distractions for 30 to 60 minutes at a time, but it's actually much more than that. Quality study time means having a reasonable study routine in place, knowing your weak areas and focusing on those first, using the learning style that's most effective for you, studying actively, practicing to retain knowledge and hone your skills, and more.

In this chapter, we reveal ten tactics for getting more out of your study-time investment.

Know Your Optimum Learning Styles

Different individuals often have different learning styles. Whereas one person may be able to absorb knowledge in a lecture hall, another may have to read everything word for word, and someone else may need to actually get in there and do something with the information in order to retain it. For many people, a combination of learning styles is most effective in reinforcing knowledge and skills. What are your optimum learning styles? The following list can help you answer that question:

- ✔ **Visual** learners do best with books, pictures, diagrams, illustrations, maps, and videos. For them, seeing is not only believing but also understanding.

- ✔ **Auditory** learners often learn most effectively by listening to lectures, participating in class discussions, listening to books on tape, or having someone sit down with them and explain difficult concepts.

- ✔ **Tactile or experiential** learners are hands-on folks. They learn best by experiencing something for themselves.

- ✔ **Logical** learners often develop an understanding of unknown material by relating it somehow to what they already know.

- ✔ **Social or group** learners tend to learn more effectively by talking with others — fellow classmates, tutors, or teachers. Being able to talk through certain concepts helps them understand and retain the information.

- ✔ **Solitary** learners tend to learn most effectively on their own by wrestling with problems until they've solved them or pondering concepts before fully grasping them.

A solitary learning style isn't always the most efficient. When you hit a wall, sometimes you can get around it much faster with someone else's help. Don't be reluctant to reach out for assistance. You often can find answers on the Internet or by asking a friend who's more knowledgeable in a given area.

After identifying your optimum learning styles, try to match these learning styles to appropriate resources. Visual learners, for example, may want to look for visual guides to specific subjects or head to YouTube.com or other Web sites that feature training videos. Auditory learners may do best with books on tape or by teaming up with a study partner. Tactile learners may want to take more notes and work on more problems to reinforce skills and knowledge. Find out what works best for you, and then incorporate it into your study regimen.

Focus on the Most Difficult Subjects First

The subjects you enjoy most usually are the easiest and the most tempting. Avoid the temptation and spend more time studying the subjects you find most difficult — and may not like at all. If a decathlon athlete, for example, knows that he can throw the javelin farther than anyone else in the world, but he can't even make the cut in the high jump, he doesn't waste practice time and effort on throwing the javelin. He focuses more effort on the high jump. Why study what you already know?

Commit to a Study Routine

Set aside a time every day for studying. It doesn't need to be the same time every day, but it does need to be a time you block out specifically for studying for the Officer Candidate Tests (OCT), and it must be at least 30 minutes. How much time and the number of days per week you spend may vary depending on how prepared you already are and the number of days available before the test, but make sure you get enough quality study time in before test day to ensure success.

Unless you make a commitment to study, you won't do it — at least not regularly. Studying only when you feel like it doesn't work. Most people have no trouble talking themselves out of doing something on any given day. You may be too tired one day, too busy the next, or too hungry when you get home from work. And something is always on TV or your DVR that you simply can't miss.

Take a break. If you feel overwhelmed by all the information you're taking in, perhaps your brain needs a breather. Take a ten-minute break to let everything soak in.

Study When You Feel Your Best

When planning your study schedule, make study time a priority and set aside a time during the day when you typically feel your best and are most alert. Usually choosing a study time earlier in the day is best. Waiting until the end of the day, when you're worn out from work, school, or other demands of life usually is a mistake. Fatigue makes for very inefficient study and retention.

If you just don't have time to study until right before you go to sleep, consider waking up 60 to 90 minutes earlier and studying right after you take your shower or eat breakfast. You may find that you need to hit the sack a little earlier than normal, but you'll find that your well-rested brain is more receptive to learning.

Keep Study Time Well Focused

Choose a place to study that's free from distractions. Turn off the TV, stereo, iPod, iPhone, and anything else that may interrupt your study time. No talking, no texting, no Facebook. If you live in a home or apartment with others, let them know that you need a block of uninterrupted study time and, if necessary, banish them from your study space.

Thirty minutes of well-focused study is better than spending two hours sort of studying while watching TV. By keeping study time separate from everything else, you'll soon discover that you get more out of your study time and enjoy everything else that much more.

Study Actively

Even if you're a solitary visual learner, sitting back and absorbing information is rarely enough. You may "get it" by reading about it, but you'll probably forget it soon thereafter if you don't do something else to retain it. When reading a chapter or studying, remain active and alert:

- ✔ Look for clues as to what's most important — chapter titles, headings, and subheadings; bold, italic, or underlined words or phrases; pictures, captions, and charts; and bullet points (especially at the beginning or end of the chapter). Highlight important information and key concepts.

- ✔ Take notes. Whatever you're reading or studying, jot down notes in your own words. This serves two purposes. First, it challenges you to fully understand what you've read to the point at which you can put it in your own words. Second, it reinforces what you've learned by having you repeat it.

- ✔ Be curious and ask questions, especially if you feel you're just not getting it. Put into words what you don't understand, preferably in the form of specific questions, and then reread in an attempt to find the answers.

- ✔ Work through any sample questions, problems, or review exercises.

- ✔ Write a summary (one or two paragraphs) of what you've read or learned as another way to reinforce the knowledge and skills.

- ✔ Regularly review subjects you've studied until you feel you've mastered them. Spending a few minutes every day reviewing difficult material you've already covered can help it become second nature. Consider making flashcards and using them to review, when appropriate.

Practice Taking Tests

Regardless of your learning style, the OCT tests your tactile ability by making you answer questions and solve problems. Don't wait until you're done studying a topic to test yourself on it. Alternate your study with practice questions and problems. Practice not only reinforces what you've learned but also exposes areas where you need to focus more effort.

Team Up with a Study Partner

Teaming up with a study partner usually is a good idea, even if you lean toward being a solitary learner. Study partners can hold each other accountable for sticking with the study routine, help one another set study goals, and provide another opportunity to reinforce learning through discussions of subject matter. And if you hit a wall and can't seem to grasp a concept, your study partner may be able to explain it in a way that makes it crystal clear. This works both ways: By teaching or explaining a concept to your study partner, you reinforce your own learning and understanding.

A bad study partner can be worse than none at all. Choose someone who's serious and committed to success. Otherwise, he may just drag you down.

Expand Your Resources

This book and books like it are only one type of resource for helping you score higher on the OCT. Don't limit yourself to these study guides. While we and others do our best to prepare you for the test, we can't possibly cover every question you'll encounter. This book is a starting point. Branch out to other books, including textbooks, especially in subject areas in which you need the most help. If you're having trouble with basic geometry, for example, you may want to add a high-school geometry book to your resource collection.

Make What You Learn a Part of Your Life

You may not have many opportunities during the day that challenge your ability to solve quadratic equations, explain the fundamentals of photosynthesis, or list the components of an atom. However, you may have plenty of opportunities to read challenging material and extract the key facts, work new words into your conversations, and calculate sales tax and percentages. Continue to exercise your brain and put what you learn into practice. Make learning and using what you learn a part of your everyday life.

Index

• B •

• T •

• U •

• V •

• W •

Apple & Macs

iPad For Dummies
978-0-470-58027-1

iPhone For Dummies,
4th Edition
978-0-470-87870-5

MacBook For Dummies, 3rd
Edition
978-0-470-76918-8

Mac OS X Snow Leopard For
Dummies
978-0-470-43543-4

Business

Bookkeeping For Dummies
978-0-7645-9848-7

Job Interviews
For Dummies,
3rd Edition
978-0-470-17748-8

Resumes For Dummies,
5th Edition
978-0-470-08037-5

Starting an
Online Business
For Dummies,
6th Edition
978-0-470-60210-2

Stock Investing
For Dummies,
3rd Edition
978-0-470-40114-9

Successful
Time Management
For Dummies
978-0-470-29034-7

Computer Hardware

BlackBerry
For Dummies,
4th Edition
978-0-470-60700-8

Computers For Seniors
For Dummies,
2nd Edition
978-0-470-53483-0

PCs For Dummies,
Windows
7 Edition
978-0-470-46542-4

Laptops For Dummies,
4th Edition
978-0-470-57829-2

Cooking & Entertaining

Cooking Basics
For Dummies,
3rd Edition
978-0-7645-7206-7

Wine For Dummies,
4th Edition
978-0-470-04579-4

Diet & Nutrition

Dieting For Dummies,
2nd Edition
978-0-7645-4149-0

Nutrition For Dummies,
4th Edition
978-0-471-79868-2

Weight Training
For Dummies,
3rd Edition
978-0-471-76845-6

Digital Photography

Digital SLR Cameras &
Photography For Dummies,
3rd Edition
978-0-470-46606-3

Photoshop Elements 8
For Dummies
978-0-470-52967-6

Gardening

Gardening Basics
For Dummies
978-0-470-03749-2

Organic Gardening
For Dummies,
2nd Edition
978-0-470-43067-5

Green/Sustainable

Raising Chickens
For Dummies
978-0-470-46544-8

Green Cleaning
For Dummies
978-0-470-39106-8

Health

Diabetes For Dummies,
3rd Edition
978-0-470-27086-8

Food Allergies
For Dummies
978-0-470-09584-3

Living Gluten-Free
For Dummies,
2nd Edition
978-0-470-58589-4

Hobbies/General

Chess For Dummies,
2nd Edition
978-0-7645-8404-6

Drawing
Cartoons & Comics
For Dummies
978-0-470-42683-8

Knitting For Dummies,
2nd Edition
978-0-470-28747-7

Organizing
For Dummies
978-0-7645-5300-4

Su Doku For Dummies
978-0-470-01892-7

Home Improvement

Home Maintenance
For Dummies,
2nd Edition
978-0-470-43063-7

Home Theater
For Dummies,
3rd Edition
978-0-470-41189-6

Living the
Country Lifestyle
All-in-One
For Dummies
978-0-470-43061-3

Solar Power Your Home
For Dummies,
2nd Edition
978-0-470-59678-4

Internet

Blogging For Dummies,
3rd Edition
978-0-470-61996-4

eBay For Dummies,
6th Edition
978-0-470-49741-8

Facebook For Dummies,
3rd Edition
978-0-470-87804-0

Web Marketing
For Dummies,
2nd Edition
978-0-470-37181-7

WordPress
For Dummies,
3rd Edition
978-0-470-59274-8

Language & Foreign Language

French For Dummies
978-0-7645-5193-2

Italian Phrases
For Dummies
978-0-7645-7203-6

Spanish For Dummies,
2nd Edition
978-0-470-87855-2

Spanish
For Dummies,
Audio Set
978-0-470-09585-0

Math & Science

Algebra I
For Dummies,
2nd Edition
978-0-470-55964-2

Biology For Dummies,
2nd Edition
978-0-470-59875-7

Calculus For Dummies
978-0-7645-2498-1

Chemistry For Dummies
978-0-7645-5430-8

Microsoft Office

Excel 2010 For Dummies
978-0-470-48953-6

Office 2010 All-in-One
For Dummies
978-0-470-49748-7

Office 2010 For Dummies,
Book + DVD Bundle
978-0-470-62698-6

Word 2010 For Dummies
978-0-470-48772-3

Music

Guitar For Dummies,
2nd Edition
978-0-7645-9904-0

iPod & iTunes For
Dummies, 8th Edition
978-0-470-87871-2

Piano Exercises
For Dummies
978-0-470-38765-8

Parenting & Education

Parenting For Dummies,
2nd Edition
978-0-7645-5418-6

Type 1 Diabetes
For Dummies
978-0-470-17811-9

Pets

Cats For Dummies,
2nd Edition
978-0-7645-5275-5

Dog Training For Dummies,
3rd Edition
978-0-470-60029-0

Puppies For Dummies,
2nd Edition
978-0-470-03717-1

Religion & Inspiration

The Bible For Dummies
978-0-7645-5296-0

Catholicism For Dummies
978-0-7645-5391-2

Women in the Bible
For Dummies
978-0-7645-8475-6

Self-Help & Relationship

Anger Management
For Dummies
978-0-470-03715-7

Overcoming Anxiety
For Dummies,
2nd Edition
978-0-470-57441-6

Sports

Baseball
For Dummies,
3rd Edition
978-0-7645-7537-2

Basketball
For Dummies,
2nd Edition
978-0-7645-5248-9

Golf For Dummies,
3rd Edition
978-0-471-76871-5

Web Development

Web Design
All-in-One
For Dummies
978-0-470-41796-6

Web Sites
Do-It-Yourself
For Dummies,
2nd Edition
978-0-470-56520-9

Windows 7

Windows 7
For Dummies
978-0-470-49743-2

Windows 7
For Dummies,
Book + DVD Bundle
978-0-470-52398-8

Windows 7 All-in-One
For Dummies
978-0-470-48763-1

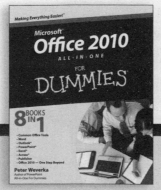

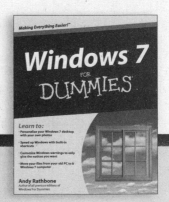

Available wherever books are sold. For more information or to order direct: U.S. customers visit www.dummies.com or call 1-877-762-2974.
U.K. customers visit www.wileyeurope.com or call (0) 1243 843291. Canadian customers visit www.wiley.ca or call 1-800-567-4797.

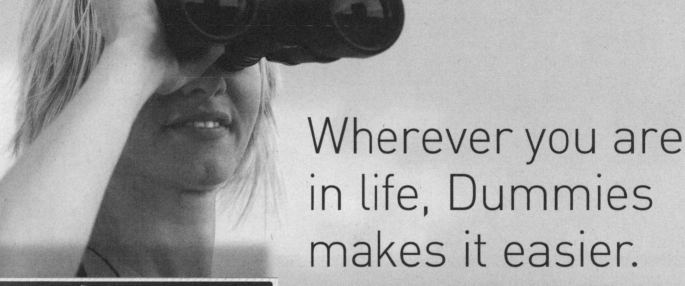

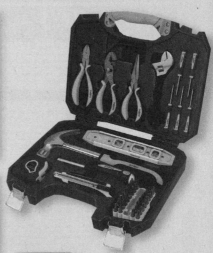